CHURCHILL'S ANCHOR

CHURCHILL'S ANCHOR

THE BIOGRAPHY OF ADMIRAL OF THE FLEET
SIR DUDLEY POUND
OM, GCB, GCVO

ROBIN BRODHURST

Pen & Sword
MARITIME

First published in 2000 by Leo Cooper
Reprinted in this format in 2015 by
PEN & SWORD MARITIME
An imprint of
Pen & Sword Books Ltd
47 Church Street
Barnsley, South Yorkshire
S70 2AS

Copyright © Robin Broadhurst 2000, 2015

ISBN 978 1 47384 183 3

Printed and bound in England
By CPI Group (UK) Ltd, Croydon, CR0 4YY

Pen & Sword Books Ltd incorporates the Imprints of Aviation, Atlas,
Family History, Fiction, Maritime, Military, Discovery, Politics, History,
Archaeology, Select, Wharncliffe Local History, Wharncliffe True Crime,
Military Classics, Wharncliffe Transport, Leo Cooper, The Praetorian Press,
Remember When, Seaforth Publishing and Frontline Publishing

For a complete list of Pen & Sword titles please contact
PEN & SWORD BOOKS LIMITED
47 Church Street, Barnsley, South Yorkshire, S70 2AS, England
E-mail: enquiries@pen-and-sword.co.uk
Website: www.pen-and-sword.co.uk

DEDICATION
CTB
1954–1972

CONTENTS

INTRODUCTION

In the course of writing this biography I have incurred countless debts. Principal amongst these is one to the Pound family. All three of Dudley Pound's children have been remarkably helpful: the late George Pound, Martin Pound and the late Barbara Duff. All three answered endless questions and were generous to a fault in their hospitality. Barbara's husband, Dan Duff, too, answered many questions about his father-in-law, to whom he had been Flag Lieutenant in the Mediterranean. William Nesbitt, the editor of the quarterly Pound Family Newsletter, was indefatigable in producing the results of his research into the American ancestors on Dudley Pound's mother's side, as well as the English roots back as far as the 16th century, at the last count. The family was kind enough to ask me to a family reunion held at the Cabinet War Rooms, which allowed me to draw my own family tree and put faces to names. I hope that they feel I have done justice to their distinguished forebear.

I was fortunate to be awarded a Winston Churchill Fellowship for 1998, which allowed me to travel to the USA and carry out research in both Washington and Newport, which I would not have been able to do otherwise. The Trust is an unsung marvel, and I am enormously grateful to the Director General, Sir Henry Beverley.

Many institutions hold relevant manuscript collections, and I have tried to avail myself of all that is useful. There is no collection of Pound papers. Admirals Cunningham and Blake destroyed the majority of his papers after his death, much to the fury of subsequent historians. What is left is scattered across a large number of centres. Principal amongst these is the Public Record Office at Kew, and I am grateful, as is everybody who researches there, to the hard working and patient staff of the Reading Rooms. Churchill College, Cambridge, holds an unrivalled collection of papers of naval officers, as well as the notes and writings of a number

ix

of biographies, projected and finished. I am grateful to the Master, Fellows and Scholars of the College, and to Dr Piers Brendan, the Keeper of the Archives at the Churchill Archives Centre, and his various predecessors, for allowing me to work there. I am grateful to the Librarian of the National Maritime Museum for the help given while working there, and to the Manuscripts Division of the British Library. The Imperial War Museum holds a limited number of naval papers, and I am very grateful to Rod Suddaby, the Keeper of the Archives at the Museum, for his help and encouragement.

In the USA I received enormous help and hospitality wherever I went. In Washington I must first thank Bernard Cavalcante at the Operational Archives Branch in the Naval Historical Centre for helping me so much while, at the same time, coping with a declassification visit. Secondly Michael J. Klein of the Manuscript Reference Division of the Library of Congress and thirdly, Barry Zerby and Rick Rayburn at National Archives II at College Park. The National Archives are a challenging place to find one's way round, and both of these two were remarkably helpful to a visiting Limey. At the Naval War College, Newport, Rhode Island, the Librarian, Evelyn M. Cherpak, gave me great assistance. I also received help and guidance from the office of the Defence Attache at the British Embassy. Throughout my time in the USA the mere mention of the Churchill Fellowship opened doors, which might well otherwise have remained closed.

I received great help and guidance from a large number of people. Chief amongst those must be a number of officers and individuals who served with Dudley Pound. The late Captain John Litchfield was kind enough to give me a copy of his projected biography of Dudley Pound, and I have shamelessly used it for much of the evidence of their time together in the Mediterranean. The late Vice Admiral Sir Ronald Brockman was extremely kind in answering many questions. Captains Geoffrey Stanning, John Henley and A. R. Bishop all helped, enlightened and encouraged me. Joan Bright Astley encouraged me with her memories and her enthusiasm. Others have helped in one way or another: Admiral Sir Michael Layard, Vice Admirals Michael Gretton and Sir John Webster with their encouragement and help. The latter read much of the book and corrected me on many naval terms that I had got wrong. James Levy gave me the chance to read his unfinished PhD thesis on Admiral Forbes and the Home Fleet. Eric Grove and Jock Gardner gave their enthusiastic encouragement at various moments. John Lee, Chris McCarthy, Gary Sheffield and other members of the British Commission of Military History have continually exhorted me to finish the book. Ned Willmott first introduced me to naval history when I was a cadet at RMA Sandhurst, and took me to Greenwich to listen to Stephen Roskill. Captain James Goldrick of the Royal Australian Navy was kind enough to turn over to me his initial research papers, which he put together when he was working on Pound. I must also thank three people who have kept me going when the light at the end of the tunnel seemed a very long way off: Field Marshal Lord Bramall, Professor Brian Bond of King's College, London, and Michael Simpson of Swansea University. All have been helpful in the extreme, and only I know quite how much I owe to all three.

There are four groups of people without whose special support I would never have finished this book: firstly, Leo Cooper, Henry Wilson and my editor Tom Hartman. They rescued the book when it may well have disappeared, and Tom in particular corrected many gross errors in my English. Secondly, my colleagues at Ampleforth and Pangbourne Colleges have had to suffer my continual witterings about 'my admiral' for more years than I care to remember. They have been remarkably tolerant, and I thank them for their support and encouragement. Thirdly, my pupils who have always evinced an interest, partly I suspect because they knew that with luck I would go off on a long red herring. They would be surprised to learn quite how helpful they have been. Finally, my family, who have always helped and supported me: my father, who proofread the entire book, and particularly improved my grammar, my mother and sister who always said the right things, my three step-children who have been quite remarkably tolerant, despite always asking how 'Douglas' Pound was, but above all my wife, Pea, who has literally kept me sane, cooked, cleaned and generally coped while my mind has been at sea or in the Admiralty, and has provided the inspiration without which this book could not have been written. Despite all of this help I alone am responsible for the mistakes and errors contained.

Robin Brodhurst.

Stanford Dingley.

Summer 2000.

ACKNOWLEDGEMENTS

For permission to quote I am very grateful to a number of people.

Crown copyright is reproduced with the permission of the Controller of Her Majesty's Stationery Office.

Parliamentary copyright material from Hansard is reproduced with the permission of the Controller of Her Majesty's Stationery Office on behalf of Parliament.

Bloomsbury Publishing Plc for extracts from *Downing Street: The War Years*, by J. Martin.

Brassey's for extracts from *The Chiefs*, by Bill Jackson and Dwin Bramall, and *From Churchill's Secret Circle to the BBC*, by Charles Richardson.

Curtis Brown Ltd., London, on behalf of the Estate of Sir Winston Churchill, copyright Winston Churchill, for extracts from *The World Crisis, The Gathering Storm, Finest Hour, The Grand Alliance, The Hinge of Fate, Closing the Ring*, all by Winston Churchill and published by Cassell.

HarperCollins, for extracts from *Churchill and Roosevelt: The Complete Correspondence*, Edited by Warren Kimball, *Naval Policy Between the Wars*, Volumes 1 and 2, *Churchill and the Admirals, Hankey: Man of Secrets*, and *HMS Warspite*, all by S. W. Roskill.

Constable Publishers for extracts from *Fisher and Cunningham* by Richard Ollard, and *The Ironside Diaries*, edited by R. McLeod and R. Kelly.

David Higham Associates for extracts from *Engage The Enemy More Closely*, by Correlli Barnett, published by Hodder and Stoughton, and *The Supreme Command*, by Lord Hankey, published by Allen and Unwin.

Hodder and Stoughton for extracts from *The Fringes of Power*, by Jock Colville, and *The Right of the Line* by John Terraine.

Dr William Gooddy and the National Maritime Museum for extracts from *Starving Sailors*.

Martin Stephen for extracts from his book *The Fighting Admirals*, published by Leo Cooper.

Little, Brown and Company for extracts from *The Battle of the Atlantic, 1939–1943*, by Samuel Eliot Morison.

The Naval Records Society for permission to quote from a number of their volumes: *The Somerville Papers*, edited by Michael Simpson, *The Keyes Papers*, edited by Paul Halpern, and *The Battle of the Atlantic and Signals Intelligence*, edited by David Syrett.

Oxford University Press for extracts from *From the Dreadnought to Scapa Flow* Vol III, *From the Dardanelles to Oran, Operation Menace, Old Friends, New Enemies*, all by A.J. Marder, *Mines, Minelayers and Minelaying*, by JS Cowie.

Routledge for extracts from *Fraser of North Cape*, by Richard Humble, and *End of the Affair*, by Eleanor Gates.

Sutton Publishing for extracts from *Invergordon Scapegoat* by Alan Coles.

Orion Publishing Group for extracts from *Men of War*, edited by Stephen Howarth, and from *The Churchillians*, by Jock Colville. Both were published by Weidenfeld and Nicolson.

Times Newspapers Limited for three extracts from *The Times*.

Mary Tute for extracts from *The Deadly Stroke*, by Warren Tute, published by Collins.

Lady Mary Pawle for extracts from *The War and Colonel Warden*, by Gerald Pawle, published by Harrap.

Lt Col Martin Pound for extracts from the papers of his father, the late Admiral of the Fleet Sir Dudley Pound.

John Somerville for extracts from the papers of his father, the late Admiral of the Fleet Sir James Somerville.

Nicholas Roskill for extracts from the papers of his father, the late Captain Stephen Roskill.

Peggy Melville for extracts from the papers of her husband, the late Lt Col A.D. Melville.

Joan Macdonald and Mary Davey for extracts from the papers of their father, the late Admiral of the Fleet Sir Algernon Willis.

William Ehrman for extracts from the papers of his grandfather, the late Vice Admiral Sir Geoffrey Blake.

Lady Beatrix Evison for extracts from the papers of her father, the late Lord Alexander of Hillsborough.

Mark Litchfield for extracts from the papers of his father, the late Captain

John Litchfield, and particularly his manuscript biography of Pound.

Lord Chatfield for extracts from the papers of his father, the late Admiral of the Fleet Lord Chatfield.

Lord Keyes for extracts from the papers of his father, the late Admiral of the Fleet Lord Keyes, and for quotations from his book *The Naval Memoirs of Lord Keyes, 1916–18*, published by Thornton Butterworth, 1935.

IN AMERICA:

Columbia University for extracts from their interview with Admiral Alan G. Kirk.

The Operational Archives Branch, Naval Historical Centre, Washington Naval Yard, for extracts from the papers of Admiral Harold Stark.

The Naval War College, Rhode Island, for permission to quote from the B. Mitchell Simpson papers.

It has not been possible to trace the copyright holders of the following works despite extensive research. If the owners of these copyrights care to get in touch with the publishers then any subsequent edition will make all due reference.

The Godfrey Naval Memoirs and papers, Churchill College, Cambridge.
The Edwards Papers, Churchill College, Cambridge.
C. Aspinall-Oglander *Roger Keyes*. Hogarth Press, 1951.
W.S. Chalmers *Max Horton and Western Approaches*. Hodder & Stoughton, 1954.
T. Robertson *The Channel Dash*. Evans Bros, 1958.
D. McLachlan *Room 39*. Weidenfeld and Nicolson, 1968.
The Isle of Wight Mercury.
Great Britain and the Empire (Malta newspaper).

All photographs are from the Pound family albums except the following: 19, 24, 25, 27, 28, 29, 30 and 31 which are reproduced by courtesy of the Imperial War Museum.

1

DEATH OF A SAILOR

The QUADRANT meeting between Churchill and Roosevelt and their staffs was held at Quebec between 17 and 24 August 1943. At the end of the conference the British Chiefs of Staff were due to go fishing. All four, General Sir Alan Brooke, Air Chief Marshal Sir Peter Portal, Vice Admiral Lord Louis Mountbatten, and Admiral of the Fleet Sir Dudley Pound, were keen fishermen, and had long been looking forward to the chance to fish in some of the lakes to the north of Quebec. They had already had one day's fishing before the conference on 12 August. After the war Brooke commented:

> This was the first day on which we noticed signs of failing on the part of Dudley Pound. On the way out he had lost his balance and nearly fallen into a small ravine, only just caught in time by Dickie Mountbatten. On the way back we had great difficulty in getting him back to the car. He seemed completely exhausted.[1]

On the 25th Dudley Pound declined to go fishing, saying 'he did not feel well enough to accompany them'. He took to his bed and the Admiralty Surgeon, Commander Miller, flew over from London, discovering that Pound had had a stroke on the last day of the conference. Pound wrote to his eldest son, George, serving on a destroyer in the Mediterranean Fleet, on the 26th:

> Good hunting, Old Man, I hope that the gun will go off soon.

It was to be the last letter that George was to receive from his father. Brooke and Portal left Quebec to fly back to London on the 28th and said goodbye to Pound. Brooke recorded after the war:

1

Little did I realise on saying goodbye to old Dudley Pound that I should never see him again. He was sitting up in an armchair with his feet up and looking far from well. It was shortly after this that he had his first stroke [Brooke was mistaken] on arrival at Washington. He travelled back a sick man, was met by an ambulance on arrival at London, and died shortly afterwards. A very gallant man who literally went on working until he dropped. . . . He was a grand colleague to work with, and now that I realise how sick a man he was lately I withdraw any unkind criticism I may have made in my diary concerning his slowness and lack of drive.[2]

Summoning up his will-power, Pound travelled to Washington where Churchill and Roosevelt were still conferring. On 7 September he attended a meeting of the U.S. Joint Chiefs of Staff with Churchill, Dill and Ismay, and late that evening met the Prime Minister and President again. Both political leaders were convinced that he was very ill. The next morning Churchill recorded:

Pound came to see me in my big bed-sitting room and said abruptly, "Prime Minister I have come to resign. I have had a stroke and my right side is largely paralysed. I thought it would pass off, but it gets worse every day and I am no longer fit for duty." I at once accepted the First Sea Lord's resignation, and expressed my profound sympathy for his breakdown in health. I told him that he was relieved at that moment from all responsibility, and urged him to rest for a few days and then to come home with me in the *Renown*. He was complete master of himself, and his whole manner instinct with dignity.[3]

Pound returned to Britain on *Renown*, remaining in his bed all the way and attended constantly by Commander Miller. When *Renown* arrived at Greenock one of those meeting Churchill, with the task of presenting him with a batch of the daily papers, was Commander David Joel, who had served with Pound on *Colossus* at Jutland. With Commander Miller he helped Pound ashore.

It was an infinitely sad occasion, as, heavily supporting him, we got him into his Drawing Room Car in the special VIP train waiting at the Prince's Pier Station for the Prime Minister and his party to return to London. I was alone with Pound in that small Drawing

2

Room Car for at least 20 minutes while the luggage was being loaded. I suddenly realised that though his mind was broken on current affairs he seemed perfectly lucid in speaking of the old Grand Fleet days. Somehow he took it for granted that I should be there. . . . The intervening years were forgotten.[4]

On arrival in London he rallied and was able to meet the Board of Admiralty. There he confirmed his resignation, which he drafted with his oldest surviving naval friend, Vice Admiral Geoffrey Blake, and his secretary Ronald Brockman. They were both amazed to find that he could hardly write, and that they had to guide his hand when he wrote his signature. To look at he was perfectly normal, but the fact was that he had become semi-paralysed. He was taken to the Royal Masonic Hospital where very few people were allowed to see him.

Throughout early September Pound was continually receiving letters, congratulating him on the award of the O.M. (He had declined a peerage on his resignation.) They ranged from Admiral of the Fleet Lord Chatfield: "You have earned it by long, arduous and immensely responsible work, not only during this war, but throughout your service life," to ordinary seamen who had served with him in earlier times, such as his Action Stations Messenger on *Colossus* in 1916, and another who had served as a rating on *Repulse* in 1921–22. They also included one from the son of Lord Fisher, one of the first naval officers to recognize the promise of the young Pound, and under whom he had worked at the Admiralty in 1915.

During September Pound grew steadily weaker and weaker. His formal retirement from the post of First Sea Lord was announced at the beginning of October and occasioned another flood of letters. The faithful Brockman and Blake, one of whom visited him almost every day, read these to him. They ranged from politicians on both sides of the House of Commons such as Eden and Attlee, members of the Board of Admiralty and the Chiefs of Staff committee, to retired sailors who had served with him before 1914. Four deserve special mention. One is a brief note from Vice Admiral Wilfrid Tomkinson wishing him well and hoping that "the day may come when we again stand together at the bottom of Apple Cake and endeavour to shop some of those old cock pheasants". This, according to a note attached to it by George Pound, was particularly pleasing to his father, as they had fallen out after the Invergordon Mutiny.

3

Secondly, Mountbatten, on the eve of his departure to become Supreme Allied Commander in South East Asia, wrote:

> May I take this opportunity of thanking you from the bottom of my heart for your truly amazing kindness, consideration and help during my time as CCO? I shall never forget the way that an Admiral of the Fleet treated a very young Captain and made him welcome on the COS Committee. The whole Navy owes you a debt of gratitude, but none more than your very loyal and devoted Dickie Mountbatten.

The third is from Air Marshal Sir John Slessor, then the AOC-in-C Coastal Command, but previously a member of the Joint Planning Staff, who, after commiserating, wrote:

> I personally have been in a special position to know what a tremendous burden you have borne over the last 4 years; it has been a privilege and an education to have been associated with you for so long as a planner in the bad old days, and this year under your command in Coastal.

This has fixed to it a reply from Brockman who tells Slessor that the doctors are "not optimistic about his recovery". Finally the Chief of the Air Staff, Air Chief Marshal Sir Peter Portal, wrote saying how sad it was not to be able to address him as First Sea Lord. He went on to say:

> I can't tell you how much I shall miss you from our meetings, or how much I admired, during our three years together the helpfulness, frankness, patience and good humour which you invariably brought to bear on our problems. Besides, I shall never forget your personal kindness to me or your constant appreciation of the work done by the Air Force for the Navy.

All of these letters[5], and there are many from total strangers, show the regard he was held in both by those at the top and those at the bottom.

Geoffrey Blake arranged for the insignia of the Order of Merit to be presented to Pound by the King's Secretary. Although Pound could hardly speak, he communicated, as did both his sons, that he would like to see Churchill, in effect to say goodbye. Blake agreed to try to arrange this, knowing how difficult it might be 'as the PM is extraordinarily sensitive to any such occasion'. With a little persuasion Blake managed to get him to agree.

> The next day, on the way to Chequers, he called in and gave Dudley, I assume, a good deal of pleasure a few days before he died. The PM was, as I knew he would be, greatly affected, and came out of his sick room weeping. They were great friends.[6]

Pound, by that stage was unable to speak, but as Commander Thompson recalled, "He recognised the Prime Minister, and grasped his hand."[7] Jock Colville, one of Churchill's private secretaries, records that Pound was not able to see visitors in hospital, and there is no doubt that he sank fast, despite having, as both his sons remember, periods of lucidity. Brockman dealt with the correspondence and his replies varied from the simple formal acknowledgement to less formal ones explaining that Pound could not receive visitors. Certain people were allowed in to see him and say farewell. Colville records:

> Brendan Bracken, who was no less fond of him than Churchill, called to see him and found A.V. Alexander [The First Lord of the Admiralty] already at his bedside. Alexander told the dying man that without him he would have had difficulty in achieving all that he had. According to Brendan, Pound turned his face to the wall and made no reply.[8]

Tact and modesty were not always among Alexander's qualities.

Pound eventually died on Trafalgar Day 1943 and Churchill decreed that it should be a full-dress funeral in Westminster Abbey, and it certainly had all the trappings of a state funeral. Since the whole of the War Cabinet and the Chiefs of Staff were attending, as well as many notables, and the first warnings of the V weapons were coming through, the Admiralty asked the Air Ministry to provide fighter cover over central London for the service. The coffin had lain overnight in the Admiralty and the procession moved from Horse Guards Parade into Whitehall and then through Parliament Square to Westminster Abbey. The arrangements for the funeral were very detailed, and, as Admiral Stark wrote to Admiral King in Washington, "The big square [Horse Guards Parade] outside the Admiralty was lined with officers and men, and the line of march [via Whitehall] was literally jammed with people."[9] The pallbearers were a highly impressive body of senior officers:

Admiral Sir William Goodenough	Admiral Sir Sydney Fremantle
Admiral of the Fleet Sir Charles Forbes	Admiral Sir Charles Little
Admiral of the Fleet Lord Chatfield	Admiral of the Fleet the Earl of Cork and Orrery
Admiral of the Fleet Lord Keyes	Admiral of the Fleet Sir Reginald Tyrwhitt
Air Chief Marshal Sir Charles Portal	Admiral Harold R. Stark USN
Admiral of the Fleet Sir Andrew Cunningham	General Sir Alan Brooke

Churchill took part in the procession, following behind the Duke of Gloucester, representing the King. Sir Paul Sinker, serving at the Admiralty as Head of War Registry had had much to do with the organization of the funeral, and had a strong recollection of 'waiting for a long time on the parade for two huge figures who arrived late: the Russian representatives'.[10]

The BBC declared that the most moving part of the service was the singing of Parry's setting of 'Crossing the Bar'. One observer, Lt Colonel A.D. Melville, a TA officer at the War Office, recorded in his diary:

> As I walked back [from lunch] a vast crowd had collected around the Abbey and down Whitehall for the First Sea Lord's funeral. The funeral procession was nearly a quarter of a mile long, with two bands, an impressive sight in the gloom and fog as it turned out of Horse Guards into Whitehall. Brookie was one of the pallbearers, so was CAS [Portal] and the rest were senior admirals . . . The PM walked alone in top hat (almost the only one), a striking figure stumping the slow march.[11]

That evening Admiral Stark broadcast on the BBC Home Service and paid his own tribute to Pound:

> A great naval officer has lived here for the past five years working day and night, quietly, effectively, undaunted and determined. He has faced naval problems perhaps more difficult and complex than any First Sea Lord before him ever faced. By clear and straight thinking,

6

and by tireless devotion to duty he successfully met the multitude of tasks which confronted him. Truly it may be said of Admiral [of the Fleet] Sir Dudley Pound he typified Nelson's comment 'Duty is the great business of an office. All private considerations must give way to it, however painful it is.'[12]

The body was cremated at Golders Green and, along with the ashes of Lady Pound, rested on board HMS *Victory* at Portsmouth overnight.

The next day, 26 October 1943, the ashes were taken on board HMS *Glasgow*, commanded by Captain (later Vice Admiral Sir) Edward Evans-Lombe. She went to sea in total silence, without a word of command being uttered, and in the Solent their ashes were scattered by his successor as First Sea Lord, Sir Andrew Cunningham.

Who, however, was this man? His name rarely, if ever, features in the popular histories of the war. He did not have the personal appeal of a Beatty, nor had he commanded at a successful battle as both Jellicoe or Cunningham had done. Yet for over four years this was the man who had held the reins of power in the Admiralty and had been responsible for the supreme direction of the Battle of the Atlantic, possibly the most crucial battle in which Britain was involved through the whole of the Second World War.

2

EARLY LIFE

It is an unlikely thought, but the two men who most closely controlled Britain's naval destinies in World War II both had American connections. Churchill's close American links are well known. Indeed, in 1941 he was to tell the U.S. Congress, "If my father had been American, and my mother British, instead of the other way round, I might have got here on my own . . ." Less well known are the American forbears of Dudley Pound.

On his father's side the Pounds were an old family with a respectable country-gentleman pedigree. They claimed to have come over with the Conqueror and several had been High Sheriff of Hampshire. Dudley Pound's father, Alfred John Pound, had been a King's Scholar at Eton and read Law and History at Exeter College, Oxford, before being called to the Bar in 1871. He served for 12 months as a stipendiary magistrate in British Guiana in 1875 and returned via North America. He took little further part in public life except for standing as a Tory candidate at West Ham in December 1885, when he was beaten by a Radical. He was a countryman by inclinations, and it has been speculated that it was his young American wife who pushed him into this political episode.

Elizabeth Pickman Rogers met Alfred Pound when he was on his American journey. She belonged to a distinguished American family. Bessie, as she was known to her family, came from original New England colonial stock on both sides. On her father's side the Rogers family first arrived in Ipswich, Massachusetts, 16 years after the *Mayflower*, in 1636. The family, after providing the 5th President of Harvard in 1682, became linked to the shipowning Pickman family. Dudley's grandfather married, as his second wife, Elizabeth Pickman, and the marriage brought him very useful commercial connections. With his two elder brothers he founded the firm of N.L. Rogers and Brothers of Salem. They traded with the East Indies, Zanzibar and the South Pacific. By the 1830s they were established as leading members of the Salem mercantile community. The other side of Bessie's family, the Pickmans, went back almost as far. They arrived in New England in 1639 and were all seafarers based at Salem. In the American War of Independence, one of the family, William Pickman, was made Naval Officer of the Port of Salem in 1779[1]. It was his grand-daughter, Elizabeth Leavitt Pickman, who married Richard Saltonstall Rogers. Dudley Pound's mother was thus the product of the union of two families who were among the leading members of the Salem mercantile aristocracy. It is quite likely that the family wealth stemmed from the slave trade, but it is difficult to prove. However, it is unlikely that they would have become quite so prosperous without being involved in the triangular trade. The Marine Society of Salem, founded at the turn of the eighteenth century, was originally limited to "persons who have actually navigated the seas beyond the Cape of Good Hope or Cape Horn", and both the Rogers and Pickman families were members. In 1942 they made Dudley Pound an honorary member in recognition of both his forbears and of his naval position.

If it is possible to see in Winston Churchill a trace of his buccaneering Jerome ancestry in his character, so is it possible to see in Dudley Pound more than a trace of his hardy New England maternal forbears. Their resolution and seagoing abilities had prospered in a competitive and demanding society, driving them to the top. If Dudley Pound was in most ways a most unAmerican half-American, it is still possible to see those traits of hard work, devotion to duty and earnest competition driving him to the top of his profession.

Bessie Rogers was a strong-willed woman of eccentric habits, who was reputed to rule the Pound family roost. As a girl she had developed a habit of "collecting things", other people's things. Her father had decreed that she should always be accompanied when she went shopping. Her accompanist's job was to return or to pay for those items "borrowed". She was extravagant, and there was little left of her share of the Rogers inheritance when she died in 1913. Dudley Pound certainly owed much of his character to his masterful mother, but he did not inherit any financial benefit. Throughout his life he was wholly dependent upon his naval pay. Bessie was not an easy woman to live with and the marriage proved incompatible. There was a parting of the ways after the children had grown up and Dudley rarely spoke of his mother. His own wife, who rarely disguised her feelings, was often heard to complain of "that Rogers woman".

Dudley Pound was born on 29 August 1877 at Wraxall, the family home near Ventnor on the Isle of Wight. After his parents' separation he grew up at his father's house near Buckfastleigh in Devon, where his father encouraged his interests in country pursuits. Here began his lifelong passion for shooting which was to dominate his life outside the Navy. He also rode and fished, and became a knowledgeable ornithologist. Pound told his Naval secretary when he was First Sea Lord that he had toyed with the idea of a military career in the cavalry, but that the sight of a cutter, in the charge of a midshipman, coming alongside a jetty at Stokes Bay, decided him on a career in the Royal Navy. There had also been a tempting offer from an American uncle of a place in Pierpont Morgan's bank in New York[2].

After a term at a crammer he passed the naval entrance examination top of the order of merit out of fifty-eight candidates. He obtained 1846 marks out of a possible 2000, 169 more than the second candidate[3], and joined the Naval Cadet harbour training ship H.M.S. *Britannia* at Dartmouth on 15 January 1891. He was to remain on the active list of the Royal Navy until his death 52 years later, having moved from Cadet to Admiral of the Fleet.

★

The Naval Cadets who joined *Britannia* in January 1891 were all selected boys, the majority coming from private schools. Until the end of the Second World War they were nearly all scions of the officer class, sons of naval families or the professions, few of them wealthy, who would have gone to public schools if they had not entered the Royal Navy. The transition from preparatory school to public school is often a painful one, and it was a similar transition to *Britannia* at the age of 13. The Admiralty was aware that it was no place for weaker souls and was prepared to say so. In a frankly informative guide published in 1914, Entry and Training of Naval Cadets, it probably understated it.

> The boy of sensitive, poetic spirit, the ruminating philosopher, the scholar whose whole heart is in his books, are types that have a real use in the world, but their proper place is not in the Navy[4].

Britannia was a floating hulk, and remained the Navy's cradle for officer-training until 1905. She was a 3-decker of 6,200 tons, built in

1860, and one of the last of the "wooden walls". Nelson and his men would have felt thoroughly at home on board. Moored fore and aft in the River Dart with her guns and all her top hamper removed, except for one mast, *Britannia* looked like a giant houseboat. She was connected to a second hull, *Hindustan*, to provide accommodation for 260 Cadets, and attendant instructors, officers, and ratings. Life was certainly spartan, with a minimum of unoccupied time, and a total lack of privacy. Discipline was strict and taut, rather than inhumane. The unofficial and largely uncontrolled penalties exacted by senior Cadets upon juniors were harsher and more severe than the official punishments. Bullying was probably no more rife in *Britannia* than in any public school in the 1890s. It existed, and became the matter of public speculation when it was raised in a parliamentary debate and a leader in *The Times* on 30 September 1891.

The majority of *Britannia* Cadets were happy enough and soon learned to take life in their stride, and it may be assumed that Cadet Pound did. There were certainly compensations. While brothers and cousins were learning Latin and Greek at public school, they were "mucking about in boats" and learning their trade. Food was perfectly adequate, and their neighbouring Devon villages provided opportunities for cream teas on Sunday afternoons. Prowess in games was less sought after than in later years. Dudley Pound was able to go out shooting and recorded in his Game Book:

26 7 92 My first day's shooting at Dartmouth. 1 Rabbit[5].

The old *Britannia* system of training Naval Cadets, which changed little until 1939, may fairly be criticized for its narrow and unimaginative content, for the suppression of individuality and the discouragement of originality, for its excessive inculcation of veneration for senior rank, which produced a sense of inferiority in the presence of more gold braid, and for its emphasis on unthinking blind obedience. The cadets were strained physically, but not mentally, and it may be said that education, as opposed to professional training, ended for many at 13. Yet it must also be said that the system was geared for transforming 13 year old schoolboys into embryo naval officers with an elementary knowledge of their job sufficient to enable them to take their place on a sea-going ship. In that the system bred the regular naval officers of the First World War, and most of the Admirals of the Second, it cannot be said to have failed. The products were highly professional and dedicated to the Royal Navy in a way that cannot be found in other professions.

Dudley Pound exemplified the qualities of the pre-1914 Royal Navy and also some of the limitations that a narrow, professional training in his formative years had imposed. The Royal Navy of his time was an intensely professional sea service, with a pride and loyalty which the Army did not feel towards its service outside the regimental system. Largely removed from the main stream of contemporary life ashore, and thus inward looking, the pre-1914 Royal Navy thought of little but a second Trafalgar, and hardly at all about the wider issues of defence. Although their natural abilities might vary, men are creatures of their time and experience. The high qualities which made naval officers "the finest body of men in the world" according to Lord Esher in 1903 were not necessarily enough when it came to running a war at the top in concert with politicians, the other services and international allies. In studying Dudley Pound it is not possible to separate him from the naval world in which he grew up from the age of 13, and outside of which he had few interests.

In his passing out examinations in December 1892 Pound obtained First Class Certificates in Seamanship, Mathematics and External Subjects. He later obtained Firsts in all of his Sub-Lieutenant's courses except gunnery. Out of a maximum possible 2000 marks at *Britannia* he obtained 1819 and was top by eighteen marks. The third on the examination list obtained 1706 and the fourth 1673. By comparison Andrew Cunningham, five years later, gained only two Firsts. Chatfield, four years earlier, had obtained only a Second because of an inability to master French, and Keyes had emerged near the bottom of his term. Winston Churchill, five years senior to Pound, was still struggling to pass the Sandhurst entrance examination when Pound went to sea.

*

Pound joined his first seagoing ship, *Royal Sovereign*, a battleship, on New Year's Day 1893. The gunroom that he joined provided little comfort, and no privacy. Midshipmen held a curious place in a ship: they were, as Churchill remarked of that worthy MP, Mr Bossom, "neither one thing nor the other". They held a halfway station, not holding a commission and being still under training, but having it drummed into them that they were young officers and gentlemen. Seasoned petty officers and seamen

12

readily accepted orders from these 16 year olds, saluted them and called them "Sir". The latter, if they were sensible, lent on the experience and advice of their subordinate elders. Pound came to view the time as a midshipman as a key stage in a naval officer's training, when he had a chance to learn not only the craft of a seaman, but the art of handling and leading men. Many years later Pound, recalling his own time as a midshipman, referred to this, when as Second Sea Lord, he took the salute at Dartmouth in 1934:

> From the day you go to sea you have to accept responsibility. You may find yourself, within a few hours of going to sea, in a picket boat in bad weather. Do not be afraid to ask the coxswain's advice. If you do not think that advice is right, then do not take it. Act on your own responsibility, for you are the one responsible[6].

Royal Sovereign was a modern battleship, completed only eight months before Pound joined her. After the series of grotesque experimental hybrids and floating forts of extraordinary appearances which had marked the transition from sail to steam and from wood to iron, the *Royal Sovereign* class looked like real ships again. These were the first really modern battleships; indeed it was after Pound joined her that a British battleship made sail for the last time. The Victorian Navy was thus in a flux of change and reform. The Pax Britannica still prevailed and, though there was a growing competition from France and Russia, the more serious challenge from Germany had not yet materialized.

Pound spent three and a half years as a midshipman. After an uneventful year in *Royal Sovereign*, flagship of the Channel Squadron, he joined the first class cruiser *Undaunted*, which was commissioned for foreign service and sailed for the China station in May 1894. This was an appointment which would have delighted any midshipman, and was likely to be far more exciting than service on a flagship. The Royal Navy had been involved in two wars in China in the previous fifty years, and another, the Boxer Rebellion, was only six years away. The Sino-Japanese war was about to break out and did so at about the time that *Undaunted* was at Nagasaki.

Pound's journal records little other than that which a large number of midshipmens' journals record: the state of the weather, the ship's course and speed, and her position at midday. He watched the Japanese army landing at Talienwhan Bay in March 1894, but little else of interest was recorded. After a year on station he was posted back to England to *Calypso*

13

in the Training Squadron. He took passage in the cruiser *Leander*, a full-rigged ship with auxiliary steam propulsion. This was his first experience of cruising under sail, and the voyage home can have been little different from Nelson's time. The Training Squadron was a similar experience and was the last home of sail in the Royal Navy. It was based in home waters, ranging from Spanish ports, Gibraltar and the Canary Islands, to Scandinavia and Iceland, depending on the seasons of the year.

Dudley Pound did not keep a diary and his midshipman's journal is, on the whole, uninteresting. However, from 1892 to 1938 he kept a meticulous record of his rural activities. Whether as a midshipman or an Admiral he was never too tired to enter his day's sport. During his three years and eight months as a midshipman, including periods of leave, he recorded 112 days' shooting and fishing, sometimes a full day, more often a half-day, or an early morning, or evening expedition before or after work. In June 1893, for example, he recorded that he had "arrived back on board dog tired 2 a.m. (from fishing); my morning watch: not properly roused and went to sleep again; result a week's watch and watch". The Game Book is thus more than simply a record of what he caught or shot. They reveal a man who from his youth neglected no detail in planning or analysing, and who pursued his objectives with great persistence and determination.

Pound's time as a midshipman concluded with his seamanship examination on his nineteenth birthday in August 1896. He gained a First Class certificate, and thus shipped his first stripe as an acting Sub-Lieutenant before leaving for his Sub-Lieutenant's course.

*

Pound's career up to the rank of Captain followed a strictly conventional course, distinguished by early promotion and a steadily growing reputation in a succession of good appointments. As a torpedo specialist he was at the forefront of the technical progress which transformed the old Victorian Navy into the Grand Fleet of 1914. He did not benefit from the short cuts available to such as Beatty and Keyes of active service and connections. He owed nothing to private means or influence, everything to hard work and professional competence.

The course on which Pound embarked in August 1896 comprised a general refresher course at Greenwich and specialized courses at

14

Portsmouth. During the year ashore he spent almost every day of his leave, and most weekends, shooting or fishing, according to season, nearly always accompanied by his father when he was at home in the West Country. He collected a First at Greenwich and another in the Torpedo course at Portsmouth. However, he broke his record with a Second in Gunnery, possibly due to an interruption to the Gunnery course when he went afloat for the Diamond Jubilee Review in 1897.

He was posted in October 1897 to the TBD *Opossum*, a three-funnelled vessel with a turtle deck and a top speed of 27 knots. It was the only destroyer in which he served, and it was an important posting as it brought him into contact for the first time with Roger Keyes, the Lieutenant in command. This chance association between the two future Admirals of the Fleet was the beginning of a periodic professional partnership. Keyes was soon to make a name for himself in the Boxer Rebellion in 1900, and they did not serve long together in *Opossum*.

In January 1898 Pound was appointed as Sub-Lieutenant to the battleship *Magnificent*, Flagship of the Second in Command of the Channel Squadron, and there on his 21st birthday he was promoted Lieutenant, well ahead of most of his term as a result of the seniority he had gained in examinations. As a young watchkeeper Pound had attracted the attention of his admiral, Rear Admiral John Fellowes, who took him on as Flag Lieutenant in October. The duties of Flag Lieutenant were more than purely social, although these were still important. There was no signals officer, and so Pound became responsible for the squadron's communications, and for translating the admiral's tactical instructions into flag signals. Pound obviously did this well and Fellowes reported on him that he conducted himself "with the greatest zeal and ability in his important signals duties and entirely to my satisfaction. He is a most promising officer.[7]" Fellowes had a predeliction for putting officers under arrest. On one occasion Pound was put under arrest and released no less than twelve times while the ship was proceeding from the Hamoaze to Plymouth Sound, a distance of less than three miles![8] Admiral Fellowes also had a passion for quadrilles on bicycles. He had in fact written a book on the subject. One of Pound's tasks was to train up the midshipmen to carry out this bizarre exercise. It was one of his few failures.

Pound was anxious to specialize in torpedoes, and although reform was not yet happening at the Admiralty, Fisher was already making himself heard in the Mediterranean, and Percy Scott was also making noises about

15

gunnery practice. Opportunities for progressive specialists were promising. In the autumn of 1899 Pound was selected for the Long Torpedo Course at HMS *Vernon*, at the early age of 22. The torpedo branch was responsible for all electrics, including the experimental development of wireless telegraphy in ships, as well as for torpedoes, mining and diving. Pound would thus be in the vanguard of applied scientific progress. The course lasted from September 1899 to the end of 1901, and he emerged with his customary First. As a newly qualified Torpedo Officer (and he was entered on the Navy List as Lt(T)) Pound was appointed to the cruiser *Grafton*, flagship of the Pacific Squadron. She was an old ship, more suited to showing the flag than fighting a battle. The Pacific station covered the west coasts of both North and South America, from Alaska to Cape Horn. *Grafton*'s captain was Henry Keppel who was an example of the sailor-courtier officer. He had served on the Royal Yacht and was a friend of the royal family, but he was a fine sea officer. He remained a friend to Pound in later life, and his own career did not finish until 1935. He even outlived Pound.

The *Grafton* commission was the longest of any in Pound's career. He remained on station for three years. It was chiefly memorable for the sport he enjoyed. He fished and shot in Canada, California, Mexico, Chile, Tierra del Fuego and Alaska. He had a week's expedition in the Rockies. Motor cars were unknown and he usually walked, but also used ponies, bicycle and canoes, as well as *Grafton*'s skiff. These three years were the only quiet post ever enjoyed by Dudley Pound. Afterwards he was to serve exclusively in the main fleets or in Whitehall, never far from the centre of affairs, usually at it.

No sooner was he home from the Pacific backwater than he was wanted for the new battleship *King Edward VII*, flagship designate of the Atlantic Fleet. This was an excellent appointment and a sign that he had not been forgotten. Pound was happy to sacrifice most of his foreign service leave and joined his new ship on 5 January 1905. *King Edward VII* was one of the first ships to have any considerable amount of electrical gear and, as Torpedo Lieutenant, Pound was responsible for it, performing the difficult task excellently.

Pound was fortunate to be Torpedo Officer in *King Edward VII* as his new Admiral was Sir William May, one of the brightest stars of the Edwardian Navy and a most likeable senior officer. 'Handsome Willie May', also known as 'Christmas May' for claiming Christmas Island for

Britain, went on to be Second Sea Lord and Commander in Chief of the Home Fleet before running foul of Fisher and not being appointed First Sea Lord in 1911. However, in 1905 he was still firmly in Fisher's good books and his recommendation of Pound counted strongly. There was another important contact for Pound on board. This was the Gunnery Officer, William Wordsworth Fisher, whose career was to match and touch Pound's frequently. As Gunnery and Torpedo officers (G and T) their job was to work closely, and this they did, forming a close professional relationship which endured until WW's death 32 years later when both were Commanders in Chief. Fisher was promoted after their first year together, and Pound was appointed to succeed him as No. 1 (the senior Lieutenant, the rank of Lieutenant Commander had not yet been introduced) with less than eight years seniority as a Lieutenant.

As "First and T" of a fleet flagship Pound was well placed for early promotion to Commander, but he could hardly expect it at his seniority when his two years in *King Edward VII* ended. His captain, Arthur Leveson, later to command the Second Division of the Second Battle Squadron at Jutland, said of Pound "Very zealous and of very good judgement. Very high professional qualification, and in every way to my entire satisfaction"[9]. A month later Pound went to the old battleship *Queen*, the flagship of the Mediterranean Fleet. Here began his long association with the Mediterranean Fleet. His Commander-in-Chief was Sir Charles Drury, and his Captain Ernest Troubridge. His promotion was now assured as soon as he had a little more seniority. However, disappointingly, he left Malta after two years in *Queen* in November 1908 without a Commander's brass hat; instead he had happily acquired a wife.

Dudley Pound and Betty Whitehead, the daughter of Dr John Livesey Whitehead of Ventnor, were married in Malta on 14 October 1908, a few weeks before his relief and return to England. The engagement took place when Betty was staying with friends in Malta, although they had known each other at home on the Isle of Wight. The families had been acquainted since Pound's grandfather had moved his school from Malton in North Yorkshire to Appledurcombe. The wedding was a traditional one with Dudley and his fellow officers in full dress uniform, an arch of swords, and his torpedomen to draw the carriage from the cathedral. Betty was given away by the Commander-in-Chief himself. She was to prove the ideal naval wife, devoted to her husband's career and their children, always ready to make a new home and move at a moment's notice. The newly married couple went to Gozo for their honeymoon, taken there in the Commander-in-Chief's despatch vessel.

The new couple returned to England to Pound's first appointment at the Admiralty. They found a house a few miles outside London, at Walton-on-Thames, where in due course their family grew up, two sons and a daughter. Pound took a gun in a shoot near Betty's home on the Isle of Wight. On 30 June 1909 he was promoted Commander, achieved his brass hat, and was now one of the youngest Commanders in the Royal Navy. There had been earlier promotions for war service, Beatty and Keyes for example, but few if any in peacetime. Promotion below Commander is by seniority; to Commander and Captain it is by selection, after attaining a certain seniority.

Pound's arrival at the Admiralty in 1909 was the beginning of a regular cycle of alternating appointments at sea and in the Admiralty which was to mark the rest of his life. His two years in the Ordnance Department were quiet and need not detain us long, except to note two things. Firstly, this was his only experience in a material branch. Secondly, he came into contact with two crucial influences. The Controller of the Navy, under whom the Ordnance Department directly came, was Rear Admiral Sir John Jellicoe, and the First Sea Lord was Admiral Sir Jackie Fisher. Neither of them was to forget the young Commander Pound. Five years later Fisher, back in his second spell as First Sea Lord, selected Pound as his additional Naval Assistant, and when, after Fisher's fall, Pound was available for service with the Grand Fleet Jellicoe readily agreed to his appointment to a battleship, even though he had less than one year's seniority as a Captain and had never commanded a ship before.

It was during Pound's time at the Admiralty that the infamous *Dreadnought* hoax took place. Some young men in London decided to tweak the nose of the Royal Navy and succeeded in tricking their way onto *Dreadnought*, the Flagship of the Home Fleet, as eastern potentates, where they were received with due ceremony and shown round the ship by the Flag Commander, William Fisher. When the hoax was publicized in London society, and eventually in the newspapers, Fisher decided that he must wipe out the insult to the Royal Navy. Together with Pound he tracked down all of the instigators, and in a series of raids they gave them each a dozen strokes with a cane in such varied places as Hampstead Heath, Pound's office in the Admiralty and a mews. The honour of the Royal Navy was avenged!

18

Pound was too junior to have had any influence upon the reforms which Fisher was imposing so strongly upon the Royal Navy. In the light of what we know of him it is safe to say that, while he probably approved of the reforms, he probably disapproved of the way they were carried out. While he could be ruthless as a senior officer in disposing of other senior officers if he thought them not up to the mark, he never permitted dirty linen to be washed in public. Still less would he allow his personal opinions of brother officers to become known. Fisher's methods were inimical to him, but he probably appreciated that without those methods there would not have been either the reforms or the man. It is instructive to compare Fisher's very public feuds with other naval officers, to the Dudley North affair of 1940 (examined in Chapter 10) which only really became public property in the 1950s, long after Pound's death.

He returned to sea in May 1911 as Commander (i.e. Executive Officer and Second in Command) of the battleship *Superb* in the First Battle Squadron in the Home Fleet. In the era of the big ship a Commander's seatime was spent either commanding a small ship or as second in command of battleships or cruisers. Whereas commanding one's own ship, large or small, has always been the greatest attraction which the Royal Navy has to offer, the job of the executive officer of a large ship was probably the more testing. The Commander was responsible to the Captain for just about everything that happened on board, with the exception of the technical departments: for discipline, welfare and morale, for the ship's cleanliness, smartness and efficiency, and for her overall efficiency as a fighting unit. Most wise Captains left the show to their Commanders, if they had confidence in him, insisting on knowing what was going on, but leaving the detail alone.

Still on the right side of 34 when he joined *Superb*, younger than many of his departmental heads, Pound put everything he had into the job. It is the Commander's job to create from the 1000 or so individuals in the community of a major ship a single focused aim, animated by a common spirit and organized as a fighting unit. On his leadership, personality and human understanding and judgement the ship's character and contentment largely depend. *Superb* excelled in every field. In the pre-1914 fleet coaling was the biggest evolution of all, and *Superb* established a record which was never equalled by embarking (by purely manual labour) 1,300 tons of coal in four hours. In general drill exercises where the Admiral could introduce surprise evolutions ranging from "Let go bower anchor, and weigh by hand" to "Send two fried eggs to flagship", *Superb* was usually the first ship to break the pennant signifying completion of the evolution. The fleet pulling regatta was the greatest sporting event of the year and *Superb* was runner up in 1911, a few months after commissioning, and winner in 1912. In the 1912 gunlayers' tests *Superb* came first in the whole Royal Navy, a success which caused Pound the rare distinction of a formal expression of Their Lordships' appreciation[10].

Throughout the commission Pound kept a record of every competition which *Superb* entered, along with every coaling she undertook, which was seen as a competitive activity in the Royal Navy of the time. The book, in the possession of the Pound family, has a detailed description of every possible shipboard manoeuvre, hand-drawn by Pound himself, and then records of every coaling, regatta, race or other competitive event of the commission. He was to keep a similar record when he was again Executive Officer of *St Vincent*.

From the start of the commission Pound showed himself to be a man of authority who knew his job, and he soon had the opportunity to demo strate his courage as well. On 30 June 1911, a few days after the Coronation Review at Spithead, two seamen were overcome with foul air in the ship's potato hold. A seaman who went to their help was also overcome. Pound, appearing on the scene, had himself at once lowered into the hold with two volunteers, one of whom also passed out. Pound and the other survivor managed to get ropes round the three unconscious men and send them up before they too collapsed. Three of the men concerned died and Pound was awarded the Royal Humane Society's Medal, with its plain blue ribbon worn on the right breast[11]. What the episode says about the Royal Navy's catering arrangements is a different matter.

It was a notable commission and Pound established a reputation as the outstanding Commander in the Home Fleet. His Captain, Ernest Gaunt, was not in his class professionally, and Pound was recognized as the mainspring of *Superb*. Gaunt reported on Pound in his annual report that he had acted "with complete sobriety and to my entire satisfaction. Combines very good organising powers with great executive ability and is thoroughly recommended for early promotion"[12]. Pound always looked back on the *Superb* commission with special satisfaction, and there were frequent letters from "old shipmates on the Super B". It was there that he and G.F.B. Edward-Collins, the navigator, were shipmates for the first time, and this was the start of one of his closest friendships, and of a long

20

professional association. Edward-Collins joined Pound in many later appointments and undoubtedly owed much to Pound's patronage. Another fellow officer was the Gunnery Officer Charles Forbes, later the Commander-in-Chief of the Home Fleet when Pound was in the Mediterranean and then First Sea Lord.

Pound was thus 35 when he came ashore from *Superb* with an established reputation as an executive officer and as a torpedo officer. Outside his two years in the Naval Ordnance Department he had had no naval staff experience. This was not surprising in a navy where the Naval Staff consisted of little more than the Naval Intelligence Division, and few admirals considered they needed a staff to help them in their job. Against the opposition of most senior officers the First Lord, Winston Churchill, had just succeeded in setting up the first Royal Naval Staff College at the Naval War College, Portsmouth, in 1912. On leaving *Superb* Pound was appointed to the War College directing staff.

He was only there for a short time and we have no knowledge of whether he liked it or not. The only episode of note was the birth of his first son, George, on 12 April 1913. In the spring of 1914, after only a year at the War College, the opportunity came for him to go to sea again. W.W. Fisher, by then Captain of the battleship *St Vincent*, asked him to come and serve under him as Commander. It was unusual to serve two terms as the Executive Officer of a battleship, and Pound was advised by the Commandant of the Naval College, Rear Admiral Sir Alexander Bethell, to decline. Pound was determined to go, however, and the outbreak of war in August 1914 found him at sea with the Grand Fleet.

3

WAR SERVICE

Dudley Pound's eight months in *St Vincent* were relatively uneventful. The Grand Fleet's expectations of a second Trafalgar were disappointed and, though Beatty's battle cruisers were in action at Heligoland Bight and Dogger Bank, the Grand Fleet's vigil in northern waters brought no encounter with the High Seas Fleet until May 1916. Despite this, Pound's horizons clearly extended further than his own ship. Both he and W.W. Fisher had excellent brains, among the best in the Grand Fleet, and together they directed their thoughts and ideas to ways and means of taking the naval war into enemy waters. One of these was a plan to destroy the Heligoland dockyard and draw out heavy ships from the German bases and engage them with a part of the Grand Fleet. This was killed by Burney, the Second in Command, Grand Fleet, and a further idea from Fisher and Pound, a month later, was only knocked down by Jellicoe himself.[1]

During his time as Executive Officer in *St Vincent* Pound, most unusually for him, kept a diary. This volume, now at the Imperial War Museum, started as similar to the book he had kept in *Superb*, in that one end of it contains diagrams of every possible shipboard manoeuvre. The other end, instead of holding the records of coalings and regattas, as the previous one had done, is a diary, starting on Sunday 26 July 1914, which records "Walking with Dreyer. Orders to proceed to Portland." Much of the diary is simply taken up with factual detail, thus:

30 July: Preparing for war. Fuzing lyddite. Proceeding to Scapa.
31 July: 6:30 pm Anchored at Scapa.

However, there is also a certain amount of comment as well, such as:

4 August: About 3 am received a signal to prepare for sea and raise steam, and later the astounding news of the supersession of Sir

22

George Callaghan, and the appointment of Sir John Jellicoe in his place was received. What a position for Admiral Callaghan, but if it is best for the country then of course personal considerations must be put on one side, but it does seem a pity and unusual when a man commanding in peacetime is not to be allowed to do so in war.

There are considerable indications of quite advanced thinking in the diary. The R.N.A.S. had not yet been founded and the R.F.C. was only minuscule, and yet on 6 August Pound was writing about finding the German fleet:

What we really want for searching the Norwegian coast is an aeroplane-carrying ship with half a dozen seaplanes.

Similarly, a recurrent theme is the need for aeroplanes to help in the hunt for U-boats, not so much to help in their destruction, but in their location so as to enable destroyers to sink them. On 10 August he recorded:

Personally I believe that if we used a combination of aeroplanes and TBD's we shall render the vicinity of Scapa absolutely untenable for submarines, even if we don't manage to destroy them . . . An organised method of searching for and destroying submarines should be practised in peacetime.

He was also alive to the necessity for aircraft to spot for battleships. He took part in long-range squadron firing by divisions on 10 December at a range of 13,000 yards. Most of their shots were short and he wrote:

We ought to have aircraft to spot for these very long ranges at the commencement of an action. They might be a very great help and certainly will do no harm. There ought to be aeroplanes for giving spotting corrections and others for scouting to report on the number of ships and formations, and whether they are accompanied by torpedo craft, and on which wing they are stationed. They should be able to report the presence of submarines and see whether mines are being dropped. They will be of little value unless practised with the fleet.

By the middle of August Pound was aware of the whole strategy of the remainder of the naval war and the consequent problem of bringing the inferior High Seas Fleet to battle. They were, after all, unlikely to fight a superior fleet. His diary entry for 16 August reflects this, as well as the scare that many people in Britain felt about the possibility of a German descent on the East Coast.

It seems to me that there are two things which may induce their Battle Fleet to come out in the near future; one is a possible attempt to intercept the Expeditionary Force being sent across. This might be attempted in two ways. One would be for them to send over a raiding party of 10,000 men backed up by the High Seas Fleet to prevent it being interfered with, except by our Grand Fleet. This raid would not be sent with any idea of doing any harm itself, but in the hope that the landing of a force in England would so influence public opinion and create such a scare that the government would feel unable to let the BEF go. Or they might attempt to hang up the Expeditionary Force by making an attempt on the transports. This however would appear to be more the work of submarines than their Battle Fleet.

The second thing which might bring them out is the fact that in a short time they are credited with having 3 battleships and 1 battle-cruiser, which are now completing, ready for sea and they may hope to have these ships in the fighting line before we can get the *Benbow*, *Delhi* and *Tiger*. Whether these new German ships would be of much use is quite another question because one knows that even with our long-service personnel, a newly commissioned ship is of doubtful value, whilst with their short-service personnel it would probably require much longer to make them anything like effective.

It will I am sure be the same now as a hundred years ago. The Fleet waiting outside will have a far higher morale than the Fleet waiting inside. However, the net result of the whole thing is that it is very dull work waiting for them to come out.

Personalities in the Royal Navy are mentioned. Thus on 18 September: "R. Backhouse promoted to Captain. If anyone deserves it he certainly does." There was also naval gossip, witness his views on the resignation of Prince Louis of Battenberg on 30 October:

Just heard the news that Prince Louis has resigned from the Board of Admiralty and that Fisher is to take his place. Apparently the papers have been full of innuendo about him on account of his German birth, but no one in the service has his doubts about PL's [sic] loyalty.

However, personally I am a great believer in JF [sic] and think he will wage a more aggressive war, which is what we want. . . . It will be interesting to see what the effect of the new regime will be.

Pound was also exercising his mind on strategy. Working 24 hours a day with W.W. Fisher was obviously stimulating to his mind and, like almost all naval officers, he had no doubts about what would happen when the Grand Fleet met the High Seas Fleet. The problem was in enticing them out and obtaining news of their departure from their bases.

> The question of how we are to know the High Seas Fleet comes out seems a problem. If we have arranged for agents in Denmark we ought to get information if they pass through the Sounds or the Belt, and as it is roughly 500 miles from here this should give us ample warning.
>
> It would therefore seem desirable to block the Heligoland Bight exit with mines and submarines so as to force them to come out via the Baltic. The only alternative seems to be having submarines with long distance W/T laying off Heligoland with fast linking ships.

He recorded the defeat at Coronel, with caustic comments about the Admiralty reinforcing Craddock's squadron of light cruisers with the old slow battleship *Canopus*:

> Received the bad news of the loss of *Good Hope* and probably *Monmouth*. . . . Another unfortunate affair as it looks as if there has been some bungling. The Admiralty say in their report that there was no report of the *Canopus* being engaged, though she had been sent out there to reinforce Admiral Craddock's squadron. Just fancy a squadron of cruisers which was trying to catch enemy commerce raiders going about with the *Canopus*. It was a kind of sop to public opinion as much as to say WE (the Admiralty) did our bit, but something went wrong.

He also drew lessons from the sinking of *Aboukir*, *Hogue* and *Crecy* in September.

> It brings home to one more and more that if you wish to operate in the North Sea we must do it by means of strong forces sweeping rapidly, and suitably screened by destroyers. . . . We have yet to learn that War and Humanity, even to your own people, cannot go hand in hand.

25

For the first three weeks of November 1914 Pound and the crew of *St Vincent* were heavily engaged in constructing an anti-submarine net at Scapa Flow in order to protect the anchorage. Having spent ten days building it and then more erecting it, it was destroyed by a gale on the night of 11–12 November, and then reconstructed by 19 November. He was suitably caustic about the Grand Fleet having to do this.

> A point which has been very forcibly driven home to me is that sections of submarine obstruction suitable for protecting bases should be ready in the dockyards and ships [should be] especially detailed at the outbreak of war to take them to any required destination and lay them out. The Battle Fleet should not have to do this.

The lesson was not properly learnt, and 1939 was to see an exact repetition of this, culminating in the tragic loss of *Royal Oak*.

He was also happy to redesign the staff structure of the Commander-in-Chief Grand Fleet, with definite divisions of the staff into three groups, Strategy (under a Rear Admiral), Tactics, and Stores and Personnel (both under a Captain). His comments on the reasons for this make compelling reading, given what we know of him later, both as a Commander-in-Chief and as First Sea Lord:

> We have always been inclined to understaff our Admirals because we never think a man has enough to do unless he is snowed under with work. This is a huge mistake because unless a man has a certain amount of leisure he cannot be thinking out new things and no progress will be made.

Finally, he received the news of his promotion to Captain on 1 January 1915. The diary finishes there and sadly does not record his move to the Admiralty. It is a fascinating document,[2] giving as it does an insight into the thinking of Pound, showing advanced ideas for the time. His views on naval aviation are far in advance of what were considered normal for the time and fit in well with his views on the use of air power when he became Commander-in-Chief in the Mediterranean.

He was actually promoted Captain on 31 December 1914. His was not the most select position on the list (bottom, i.e. the most junior Commander involved) but six places above it. Nevertheless it was very promising. After his young promotion to Commander, his advance to Captain was equally young, just 37. The war was less than five months

26

old, and, if Kitchener was right, it was going to be a long one. Gratified as he must have been by his promotion, there was a price to pay for it. As a Captain he could not remain as an Executive Officer and thus had to leave *St Vincent*. The whole of his training had prepared him for war, and the whole of the Royal Navy was waiting for *Der Tag*. His hopes, therefore, of being at a twentieth century Trafalgar appeared to be dashed by his posting to the Admiralty. His luck, however, did not desert him.

He was translated straight from the daily routine of a Commander's life in the Grand Fleet to become an additional Naval Assistant to the First Sea Lord, Admiral of the Fleet Lord Fisher. The old man, now 74, had been recalled from frustrating retirement by Churchill to replace Prince Louis of Battenberg, hounded from office by a press campaign levelled at his German birth. Although he had served in the Admiralty during Fisher's first term as First Sea Lord, Pound had had no personal contact with him. However, Fisher was not the man to accept an assistant without the highest credentials and Pound's selection for this important job was an indication that his reputation was high. Whether he was to be envied was a different matter.

Fisher's recall can now be seen as one of those dramatic and impulsive actions to which Churchill was always prone, sometimes with disastrous results, sometimes with advantage. In this case it was the former. Churchill commented:

> He left me with the impression of a terrific engine of mental and physical power burning and throbbing in that aged frame.[3]

His confidence that Fisher's energies were unabated and his judgement unimpaired was neither shared by Pound nor borne out by events. Pound left no account, sadly, of his time as Naval Assistant to the First Sea Lord, but later he confided to Captain Lichfield that Fisher had been

> a very old man, and really only put in about two hours work a day at the Admiralty, and spent the rest of the day at his own leisure.[4]

Pound was being a little unkind here, since Fisher started work around 5:00 a.m., long before his staff, and would frequently retreat to Westminster Abbey to think things out. Nonetheless, Pound's memories conflict sharply with the impression given by Churchill of "an almost unsleeping watch throughout the day and night"[5] which he shared with Fisher. The latter called it "the port and starboard lights", referring to the red ink of the First Lord and the green ink of the First Sea Lord.

Perhaps there was never any real chance of the young politician (Churchill was under 40 when he brought Fisher back) and the old salt working together. They were both such strong individualists, both under the enormous strain of war. The older was tired, suspicious, prickly and vindictive; while the younger was filled with enthusiasm, vitality, imagination and self-confidence. By January 1915, when Pound arrived, the relationship was already under strain over Churchill's insistence on reinforcing the initial failure at the Dardanelles and Fisher's inarticulate resistance to risking further naval losses. The drama, of course, led to the downfall of both Churchill and Fisher, and threatened even the government itself.

The final row, culminating in Fisher's disappearance from his office on 15 May and Asquith's command to him to return "in the King's name" until relieved must have strained Pound's loyalties to the limit. Fisher's subsequent ultimatum to the Prime Minister demanding absolute powers over all naval matters suggests that the old man must have gone out of his mind. There is no evidence that Fisher kept in touch with Pound either when he retired to the home of the Duchess of Hamilton or when re-employed as the Chairman of the Board of Invention and Research.

The real tragedy of 1915 was not that of Fisher, nor really of Churchill. It was a tragedy for the Admiralty as a whole. After the resignation of Battenberg Churchill never had an up to date professional at his elbow to guide him and curb the exuberance of his excesses. It was not until 24 years later that Churchill found that relationship, and it cannot be co-incidental that Pound had been at the epicentre of the earthquake that had engulfed both Churchill and Fisher in 1915. Pound saw only too clearly how not to handle a First Lord who had ideas. It is not too fanciful to say that Churchill also saw how to handle a First Sea Lord properly.

It would be an exaggeration to say that Pound's job as Naval Assistant to Fisher was merely that of a "gofor", but in essence that is what it was. Typical of his job was a memorandum from Fisher on 22 March 1915, asking him to consider these problems:

I.   Suppose (as was certainly imminent the other day) that von Pohl comes out with his entire force and suppose as also true that 500,000 German troops are available in Schleswig and Holstein and the vicinity of Hamburg for extraneous use and that ample number of transports are kept instantly ready. What raiding objects could von Pohl attain say at Harwich and the Thames, on the also certainty that Sir John Jellicoe cannot get south in under 36 hours, as he would have to make a very wide detour to avoid mines, and indeed anyhow von Pohl could lay mines behind him anywhere involving delay on Jellicoe's part to use minesweepers in front of his fleet?

II.   Is it possible a part of von Pohl's fleet getting to the Dardanelles and Constantinople uncaught by Jellicoe through the Straits of Dover and coaling in Spanish ports?

III.   Who is to say what portion of Jellicoe's fleet would be adequate to deal with this German portion and leave the right superiority of English ships behind to deal with German fleet left behind?

IV.   What have we in the south to deal with any sort of German raid effectively before the 24 hours at least before Beatty arrives?[6]

Sadly, we have no sort of reply from Pound.

It was not long before Pound escaped from the Admiralty jungle of intrigue and vendettas. He stayed on only a few months with the new First Sea Lord, the clever but colourless Sir Henry Jackson. Churchill's successor was Arthur Balfour, equally no energizer. Lord Hankey summed up the difference well

In place of two men of driving power, initiative and resource, but occasionally lacking judgement, there were now in charge two men of philosophic temperament and first rate judgement, but less dynamic than their predecessors.[7]

Pound left the Admiralty after only four months, and on 17 May 1915 he was appointed to command the battleship *Colossus* in the Grand Fleet, as Flag Captain to Rear Admiral Ernest Gaunt, his former captain when Commander of the *Superb*.

Pound's frame of mind as he travelled north to Scapa Flow to take command is not difficult to guess. The command of a battleship was the ambition of every naval officer. He had achieved it two years after promotion to Captain, and *Der Tag* had not yet arrived. The Grand Fleet and the High Seas Fleet were yet to meet. As in the Second World War there were great differences between the views of those afloat and those at the Admiralty. Where he had left doubts, uncertainties and frustrations in

Whitehall, in the Grand Fleet there were high and buoyant spirits. The Grand Fleet was the mightiest fighting machine Britain had ever sent to sea, and was only rivalled by the U.S. 7th Fleet in the Pacific in 1944–45. At its full operational strength it consisted of twenty-nine battleships (five more nearly ready), nine battle cruisers, thirty-four cruisers and some eighty destroyers. All these ships had been completed in the last seven years. Ready in support, if necessary, were another nine older battleships and the Harwich force of destroyers. The Grand Fleet under Jellicoe was based at Scapa Flow; the battle cruisers under Beatty were normally at Rosyth. Some ships were usually away being refitted, and (as in May 1916) a squadron of battle cruisers was often at Scapa Flow exercising, in exchange for a squadron of fast battleships at Rosyth. Scapa Flow itself must have been one of the most depressing places in the world when the Grand Fleet arrived there in 1914. By 1915, when the shape of the war had become a little clearer, more thought was put into making it hospitable. A Fleet canteen was built on Flotta and football pitches were laid out. A golf course, on which Jellicoe played regularly, was constructed, each green being the responsibility of an individual ship. Pound, not surprisingly, spent most of his spare time either fishing or shooting, usually taking one of his officers with him. One of his regular companions was Reggie Portal, brother of his future colleague on the Chiefs of Staff Committee in the Second World War.

HMS *Colossus* was Pound's first command. He could well have been nervous when he first took her to sea, and probably was. However, handling a big ship was never a problem to him, nor later when commanding squadrons or fleets. Where in his previous experience as Commander he had been responsible for discipline etc., he was now responsible for everything. If things go well the Captain takes the credit, if they go badly he takes the blame, no matter who made the mistake. 1,000 men and 20,000 tons answered to his every command.

War, whether on sea or on land, is composed of long periods of boredom punctuated by moments of intense excitement. This was notably true for the Grand Fleet. For the first twenty months of the war the Battle Squadrons of the Grand Fleet saw no action. Time and again they put to sea to meet reported sorties of the High Seas Fleet, only to be frustrated by the latter's withdrawal. Apart from sweeps and exercises Jellicoe's ships lay to their anchors in their northern lair, bored, but always ready for *Der Tag*. To their south at Rosyth "the glamour boys" of Beatty's battle

30

cruisers had more action. They had met their German counterparts at both Heligoland and Dogger Bank, but had not yet been thoroughly tested.

When the Grand Fleet was ordered to sea late in the afternoon of 30 May 1916 there was little reason for them to expect anything special. Pound had been in command for over a year and was thoroughly rehearsed in Grand Fleet Battle Orders and all the necessary manoeuvres. The Admiralty had warned Jellicoe that the High Seas Fleet was likely to emerge the next day and at 5:40 p.m. he was ordered to concentrate the fleet at sea "ready for eventualities". The sailing of such a vast armada of over 150 ships was a highly complicated manoeuvre and took time. Nevertheless by 10:30 they were all clear of the Flow.

By noon on 31 May the Grand Fleet was nearing a prearranged meeting with Beatty's squadrons from the Forth. The morning had been calm with reasonable visibility. The twenty-four battleships were ranged in six columns, each in line ahead, disposed abeam, similar to the teeth of a comb. Pound's *Colossus* led the 5th Division, one away from the starboard wing column. Each column was about half a mile apart, and from his bridge Pound could have seen sixteen battleships to port, four to starboard and three astern. So far there was little difference to any other North Sea sweep. The hands were at cruising stations and those off watch went to dinner at noon. Pound, naturally, remained on his bridge watching his ship's stationkeeping and waiting.

At 2:20 Beatty's screening cruisers, 50 miles to the south of the Grand Fleet, reported enemy cruisers in sight. At 2:35 the battle fleet was ordered to raise steam for full speed and at 2:55, when Beatty sighted the enemy battle cruisers, speed was increased to 20 knots and the Grand Fleet cleared for action. It was not until 4:47 that Beatty could signal to Jellicoe that he had sighted the enemy battle fleet and that he was attempting to lure them to the north onto the guns of the Grand Fleet. The two fleets were closing at a combined speed of 45 knots, the Grand Fleet aware of the High Seas Fleet's approach; the High Seas Fleet ignorant of the Grand Fleet's presence. It was at that moment that Jellicoe made his two signals: to the Admiralty "Fleet Action imminent", and to the Grand Fleet "Enemy's battle fleet is coming north". The supreme moment of the war at sea was at hand.

It is not necessary here to retell the story of Jutland. The best modern account is that by Professor Marder[8]. Suffice it to say that between the wars it was re-fought more times than even Trafalgar at every Naval Academy in the world. Jutland was the only occasion when Pound actually fought in action, and it was, therefore, an important, if brief, moment for him.

Jellicoe believed that Beatty was delivering the High Seas Fleet straight onto him from ahead. However, due to considerable disparity in the dead reckoning of both the Grand Fleet and the battle cruisers, action was forced onto Jellicoe far earlier than he anticipated, as the High Seas Fleet was in fact on the Grand Fleet's starboard bow as well as much closer than was thought. The first the Grand Fleet knew of this was when the battle cruisers were spotted by the Grand Fleet at shortly after 6:00. This was a potentially disastrous situation, as the High Seas Fleet might at any moment emerge from the haze and concentrate overwhelming gunfire on the two starboard columns, led by *Marlborough* and Pound's *Colossus*. The thunder of gunfire increased as Beatty took his depleted squadrons across the face of the Grand Fleet, further reducing the visibility. At 6:11, three minutes before the situation was clear enough for Jellicoe to start his deployment, shells began to fall not far short of *Colossus* from an as yet unseen enemy. The first shell, a large yellow projectile, was observed in the air ricocheting over Pound's bridge.

Jellicoe's deployment of the Grand Fleet was masterly. Marder commented, "His decision was fateful in affecting the lives and destinies of countless millions of the world's inhabitants. It was surely the peak moment of the influence of sea power upon history."[9] Churchill, too, was correct in saying that Jellicoe was "the only man who could lose the war in an afternoon". Where Churchill was less correct was in claiming Jellicoe would have been better placed if he had deployed on his centre wing instead of his port wing. Once started, the deployment of all thirty-four capital ships (including Beatty's) was irrevocable. The manoeuvre was as ably carried out as if on peacetime exercises and, when finished, the Grand Fleet was spread out in a sickle-shaped arc across the line of the High Seas Fleet. The German T was perfectly crossed. It was the Grand Fleet's grandest moment and, after all their vain sorties and disappointments, the High Seas Fleet was at last under their guns.

The result, of course, was not what was expected, or hoped for. Twice Scheer, the Commander-in-Chief of the High Seas Fleet, reversed his course when faced with the appalling prospect of annihilation, and Jellicoe, too, sensibly turned away from torpedo attack. Fundamentally the battle turned on the inability of the superior fleet to hold the inferior fleet to action when the latter didn't wish to fight. Jellicoe, once darkness arrived, had little option but to place himself where he expected the High Seas Fleet to be at dawn, given all the information available to him. He had every reason to doubt the information being fed to him from the Admiralty and instead backed the judgement of his own eyes.

Pound, meanwhile, in *Colossus* had been sharply engaged in the two main encounters. At 6:17, while deploying, *Colossus* and other ships in her squadron, towards the end of the battle line, sighted and engaged enemy battleships of the *Kaiser* class at a range of 10,000 yards and achieved a number of hits. During this first encounter the cruiser *Defence*, the bold but foolhardy Arbuthnot's flagship, was observed sinking between the two fleets and, during the intermittent exchanges following the High Seas Fleet's first turn away, *Colossus* opened effective fire on both the cruiser *Weisbaden* and the destroyer *V48*, both of which were sunk.

45 minutes after the first engagement, which had only lasted for about 10 minutes before the enemy was lost to sight, Pound's squadron again sighted the leading German squadrons and opened fire again. Yet again Scheer was caught by surprise as he had expected to slip around the rear of the Grand Fleet. Yet again his T was crossed. The engagement became general as most ships of the Grand Fleet sighted and opened fire on individual enemy ships. In this exchange the High Seas Fleet received thirty-seven hits and the Grand Fleet only two.[10] Both of these were on *Colossus*, which received some damage and nine casualties. One 11 inch shell struck the superstructure abaft the forward funnel and ignited some secondary armament ammunition. The other struck near the first, but did not explode. A third shell burst a few yards short of the ship abreast the bridge, showering the compass platform with splinters and taking an arm off the bridge range taker who was standing next to Pound.

Commander David Joel, Rear Admiral Gaunt's flag lieutenant, has given a personal account of events on the bridge of *Colossus*:

> Early in the proceedings my Admiral told me to make a signal to our Division, "Remember Belgium and the Glorious First of June". I respectfully pointed out that there was as heavy a volume of signalling as could be managed, that no one liked Belgium very much, nor were they very clear about the Glorious First of June, but the Admiral insisted. The Admiral then retired with me to the Conning Tower

[an armoured citadel below the open bridge] leaving Captain Pound . . . on the bridge.

In the Conning Tower we could, through the voice pipes, hear all that was going on on the bridge. I remember whilst we were being straddled and as a result of our being hit when the four-inch anti-torpedo armament ammunition went up all around us that Dudley Pound seemed even more imperturbable than usual. Our shooting was magnificent, and there was no doubt that *Colossus* was on the target.

Meanwhile Captain Pound's handling of the ship was concerned not unsuccessfully with avoiding torpedoes. It is alleged that over twenty torpedoes passed through our line of battle. As the distance between ships is two ships' length the odds are that one in every three torpedoes scores a hit. Actually only one ship, *Marlborough* was hit, and there can be no better tribute to the seamanship of our captain.[11]

Gaunt's retirement into the armoured conning tower, leaving Pound on the open bridge, contrasted with Jellicoe's action in ordering his Flag Captain, Dreyer, to go to the conning tower when fire was about to be opened, while he himself remained on the bridge.

The third encounter was Pound's last, and the High Seas Fleet was not seen again by *Colossus*. During the night there were brushes between light forces, but the cold light of dawn revealed a calm sea with no sign of the enemy. By 4:00 a.m. the Grand Fleet had to accept the evidence of its own eyes that the High Seas Fleet had escaped. The two fleets did not meet again until 21 November 1918 when the High Seas Fleet steamed into the Forth to its internment.

The Grand Fleet returned to Scapa Flow during the afternoon of Friday 2 May, having been at sea for less than 72 hours. After coaling ship they were ready for sea by 9:45 p.m. Less than three months later, on 19 August, the High Seas Fleet emerged again to bombard the north-east coast towns. Alerted by the Admiralty to this, Jellicoe had the Grand Fleet positioned almost to perfection and had signalled "Prepare for immediate action. High Seas Fleet may be sighted at any moment." However, Scheer, who was again, as at Jutland, unaware of the presence of the Grand Fleet, turned away to investigate an inferior British force misleadingly reported by a Zeppelin. It was the last occasion while Pound was in *Colossus* that he had any prospect of action.

After Jutland the Grand Fleet got down to some serious heart-searching and navel examination. The action had revealed serious deficiencies in material. British ships were obviously vulnerable to plunging fire, whereas the German ships could withstand heavy punishment. British shells were inferior compared to German ones. Both of these were so obvious that even Beatty, when he succeeded Jellicoe as Commander-in-Chief of the Grand Fleet later in 1916, made it clear to the Admiralty that he was not anxious to force an action under any but favourable conditions until the deficiencies could be rectified, as indeed they were by 1917.

There had also been human failings, not least in the signalling of the battle cruisers, and in Beatty's handling of his fast battleship squadron. There was also a marked lack of initiative by subordinate flag officers and captains. For the latter, Jellicoe's Grand Fleet Battle Orders must take considerable blame in stifling responses to action. Committees were set up to examine almost every aspect of the battle, and Pound's good technical mind was engaged in one which looked at the development of W/T control of gunfire. In this he was assisted by his own gunnery officer, Lieutenant Commander M. Hawes. They established an effective system, which was adopted by the Grand Fleet.

On 23 June 1917 Gaunt was relieved by the recently promoted Rear Admiral Roger Keyes. Thus Pound and Keyes came together again 20 years after they had first served together in the little *Opossum*. Keyes wrote in his autobiography

> Captain Pound and the gunnery officer, Lieut. Commander Hawes, were very live wires, and the Division had worked up an excellent organisation for divisional fire control, which we frequently practised both in harbour and at sea.[12]

Pound's time in the Grand Fleet was now drawing to a close. On 15 July 1917 he left *Colossus*. Keyes wrote to his wife the previous day

> I got back [after a walk ashore with Beatty] just in time to bathe and dress before my farewell dinner to Pound, who left during the night to take up an appointment at the Admiralty. He is very sad, and I felt so sorry for him, as he will probably not go to sea again during the War, that as a great treat I let him handle the Division on the 11th, when we spent three hours in the Flow.[13]

★

The emphasis after Jutland shifted from surface battles to subsurface. The Germans moved to the U-boat offensive and the Royal Navy was forced to respond to this. It was the catastrophic shipping losses that forced Jellicoe's move to the Admiralty as First Sea Lord in November 1916, and he very soon moved some of the best brains from the Grand Fleet to the Admiralty. These included W.W. Fisher from *St Vincent* who in March 1917 became Director of the Anti-Submarine Division of the Naval Staff, and in July 1917 Pound was appointed to head the new Planning Section of the Operations Division. Despite the personal devotion Jellicoe inspired, his twelve months as First Sea Lord were not happy ones. He was a tired man after twenty-eight months of unremitting strain and responsibility, and he was not fit, nor was he allowed any leave before taking over. This partly explains his reluctance over allowing the formation of a planning staff, and he later dragged his feet over the introduction of convoys. His increasing pessimism did not appeal to Lloyd George and his statement to the War Policy Committee on 20 June 1917 that it might be impossible to carry on the war in 1918 did little to restore any confidence in him. His firmest supporter, the First Lord, Carson, was promoted to the House of Lords in July and Jellicoe never got on well with his successor, Geddes.

Pound arrived at the Admiralty to take over the Planning Section just before Geddes assumed office. He was thus a close observer for a second time of friction between First Lord and First Sea Lord, although in this case far less publicly than that between Fisher and Churchill. Instead there was a complete lack of confidence and a mutual incompatibility between Jellicoe and Geddes. Instead of the spectacular resignation of Fisher with ultimata flying in all directions, Jellicoe was summarily dismissed on Christmas Eve 1917, while lying sick in bed. Having lost the confidence of both the Prime Minister and First Lord, a change was almost certainly correct; what caused enormous affront to many naval officers was that it was done so ungraciously. The Royal Navy was still "a gentleman's profession" and, whatever might be thought of Jellicoe's performance as First Sea Lord, or his fitness for duty, he was regarded as among the greatest living naval officers. Brother senior officers, and we can include Pound as one of these, were outraged by his treatment.

Jellicoe was succeeded by his Deputy First Sea Lord, Rosy Wemyss,

36

who had been appointed for just such an eventuality. He was not, nor would he have claimed to be, in Jellicoe's class as a professional seaman. However, he had other attributes to make him a better choice as First Sea Lord. He had a good, clear and resilient mind, and plenty of common sense. He had great tact and an ability to get on with people of all sorts, not least politicians. His cheerful personality and optimism were just what was needed. Almost immediately the Admiralty became a happier place in which to work.

Pound, although sad to leave *Colossus* and the Grand Fleet, was happy to have a more settled home life. Their second son, Martin, had been born in 1916, and George, now three, enjoyed being in London, and in particular sailing a large model of the King's yacht, *Britannia*, made for his father by his coxswain in *Colossus*.

Pound established the Planning Section of the Operations Division on 16 July 1917. It had extremely limited functions, which specifically excluded the initiation of plans. Jellicoe had been opposed not just to the establishment of a Planning Section, but once this had been forced upon him, to this being allowed to think ahead on its own. In a letter to the First Lord on 9 June 1917 Jellicoe wrote:

> The proper officers for this duty are the senior officers of the War Staff, including myself, the D.C.N.S. and the Director of Operations. Obviously our experience fits us better for this purpose than the experience of more junior officers.[14]

Pound was only allowed two other officers, which with his inclination to do everything himself may well have been sufficient, given their limited brief.

Both Jellicoe and Beatty were highly suspicious of any "wild schemes" for a more offensive naval strategy in the North Sea. Jellicoe saw the Planning Section as a useful method of resisting that uninformed pressure, usually from Westminster and Fleet Street, and the Planning Section's initial purpose was to reject unsound projects and criticisms of Admiralty policy, instead of being used as a think tank. For example, in an article in the *Sunday Pictorial* on 24 June 1917 Churchill had proposed a method of "digging the High Seas Fleet out of its bases like rats". Pound was directed to report on the feasibility and implications of such an operation.

He reported in a minute headed 'Remarks on Mr. Churchill's Proposals' dated August 1917. Churchill had proposed capturing the islands of Borkum, Sylt and Heligoland and holding a base off the German and Dutch coasts. Pound stated that the Naval Staff examined the problem in depth and did not dismiss it out of hand; however, they considered it an unsound and hazardous diversion of naval effort in 1917.

> The foregoing remarks are not intended to show that Mr Churchill's general idea of an offensive in the Heligoland Bight should be vetoed. If anything his proposals do not go far enough.
>
> Should the present measures against the submarines fail we shall be faced with the alternative of dealing with the menace at its root or concluding a peace other than we desire.
>
> In view of what we may have to face in the early part of next year it seems incumbent on us to prepare for operations in the Heligoland Bight with the object of sealing the ports. The organisation of an efficient inshore fighting force under British leadership should not prove an impossible task, and until we have brought the combined naval resources of the Allies to bear at the decisive point we cannot be said to have done all that is possible to ensure victory.[15]

The interest in Pound's paper lies not so much in his admirable and constructive appreciation as in the manner in which he argued the Naval Staff's case against Churchill's proposals, which he was aware would almost certainly be read by Churchill. Although he had been a close observer of Churchill in 1915 as Naval Assistant to the First Sea Lord, this was his first confrontation with Churchill on paper of which we are aware. He had, however, hoisted in the absolute necessity of not saying a direct "No". An objective professional appreciation, in which the advantages were accepted, but the implications were fully explained, was far more likely to be accepted. Churchill was essentially a fair man and usually ready to accept a professional opinion provided that it was not defeatist. These were Pound's tactics in 1917 and they were to be those he was to use in 1939–43.

In meeting Churchill's proposal half way Pound was in fact some considerable way ahead of both Jellicoe and Beatty, who both rejected it out of hand. Pound's conclusion was thus something along these lines:

> O.K., it's not impossible, but the risks and the implications must be understood and weighed against the advantages; we may be forced to try something like this eventually if it looks like being the only

alternative to losing the war, so let's be ready. But the real snag in such a project would be the drain on the fleet which, if we captured the places, holding them would create.[16]

Pound's well-argued case won the day and the project was dropped, if not forgotten. The methodology was to remain with Pound and was to be frequently used in the next war.

In the autumn of 1917 the Naval Staff was further expanded by separating the Planning Section from the Operations Division and creating a separate Plans Division. Pound, who as head of the Planning Section can truthfully be called the Father of Plans, became Assistant Director of the new Division. His co-Assistant Director, who looked after the logistics of planning, was Captain Cyril Fuller, whom Pound was to succeed as Second Sea Lord in 1932. The new Director of Plans was Rear Admiral Roger Keyes, whom Jellicoe was very reluctant to accept. However, Keyes was appointed and gave up his division of the Grand Fleet. Keyes and Pound thus came together for the third time and the combination worked well with Keyes' enthusiasm being channelled by Pound's superior brain and professional judgement.

Keyes turned his attention to the problem of stopping German submarines getting through the Dover Straits. Keyes and Pound believed, against the evidence supplied by Bacon, the Vice Admiral, Dover, that submarines were getting through. The way to stop them, they believed, was to lay a deep minefield and to force the submarines into it by the use of nets and surface patrolling, both by day and by night, with the aid of flares and searchlights. Bacon fundamentally disagreed and told Pound so when he went to Dover to put forward their plan on 27 October 1917. This division of belief ended with the dismissal of Bacon and was the immediate cause of Jellicoe's dismissal as First Sea Lord. When Wemyss succeeded Jellicoe on 27 December he summoned Keyes the next day and said to him, "Well Roger, you have talked a hell of a lot about what ought to be done in the Dover area. Now you must go down there and do it all yourself."[17]

Keyes' move also resulted in another move for Pound. From Assistant Director of Plans he was promoted to become Director of the Operations Division (Home), usually abbreviated to DOD(H), where he found among his staff Commander G.F.B. Edward-Collins. Pound and Keyes worked closely together, despite their separation, on the Zeebrugge project. Pound looked after the Admiralty end of the operation and he was certainly an important factor in the planning. It was he who developed the idea of the smoke to blind the German gunners, which was one of the keys to the success of the operation.

As successively head of the Planning Section, Assistant Director of Plans, and DOD(H), Pound was a key member of the Naval Staff from 1917 to the end of the war. Almost to the very end there seemed every indication that the war would continue well into 1919 and it was not until late September that events began to move rapidly towards a German collapse. This may explain why Pound took a whole fortnight off in September 1918, spending a memorable holiday with Betty shooting and fishing in the remote Highlands as a guest of the Duke of Sutherland, then serving as a Commander R.N.R. on his staff. Early in October it became clear that naval terms for an armistice would soon be required and Pound and the Director of Plans, the newly promoted Fuller, were the Naval Staff Directors most concerned. Pound was closely concerned with preparations for the last great operation of the naval war, the surrender and internment of the High Seas Fleet.

Pound was also involved in the question of the disposal of the German ships. This argument lasted for seven months. The French wanted a share based on the ingenious reasoning that it should be measured by the ships that they had been unable to build during the war. The Americans did not want anybody to have the German ships at all. The British argued that they should be distributed in relation to ships lost, which would have given the Royal Navy the lion's share. Madden, Commander-in-Chief of the newly constituted Atlantic Fleet, had support from the Board of Admiralty in this last position. Ultimately it was the Germans themselves who decided the issue by scuttling their ships at Scapa Flow on 21 June 1919.

Pound left the Admiralty in the summer of 1919 and was, as was normal, placed on half pay to await another appointment. He had a distinguished war record, and had gained invaluable experience, both at sea and at the Admiralty. His services were recognized by the award of a C.B., a very rare distinction for a young Captain as well as the American D.S.M., the French Legion of Honour and the Japanese Order of the Rising Sun. He was not yet 42 and was already a Captain of four and a half year's standing. His own sun was steadily rising.

4

COMMAND AND PLANNING

The defeat of Germany in 1918 saw a definite change come over British naval policy. Prior to this the Royal Navy had known exactly what its challenge was, and had been geared to the maximum expansion possible up to the limit of what the country could afford and the shipyards could build. Nobody had any doubts about the Royal Navy's vital role and needs. However, the coming of peace made such convictions unfashionable. Gone were the days, only ten years before, of "We want eight and we won't wait". Indeed governments were set on economy and retrenchment. It was Churchill who, as usual, summed it up neatly. "The levers must be pulled. Full Speed Astern." For all those officers who had held important appointments during the war and were now trying to adjust to new requirements it was a time of dramatic change as the Royal Navy tried to keep adequate naval forces to fulfil their continuing worldwide commitments.

On paper those commitments were negligible, as there was nobody to challenge the Royal Navy. She had gone to war in 1914 because, among other reasons, she had received a naval challenge from Germany. That challenge had been defeated and the proof of that defeat could, and can still, be seen on the seabed at Scapa Flow. None of Germany's allies had been significant naval powers. France had been bled white. Russia had never been a naval power, and anyway was convulsed in civil war. Italy was seething internally. War against the U.S.A. was unthinkable. There was, thus, no naval challenge to the Royal Navy. The Great War had been "the war to end all wars" and at the conclusion all the victorious powers had agreed upon the setting up of the League of Nations to settle any difficulties between countries; warfare was expected to be a thing of the past. The British Empire was at its greatest extent after the Paris peace conference. It included more than a quarter of the world's inhabited earth and was the greatest imperial power the world had ever known. This was the public picture that encouraged political and public euphoria in 1919.

Reality, as always, was a little different. Economically, Britain was weaker than she had ever been since the industrial revolution. Worse than that was the massive debt owed to the U.S.A. for war materials supplied during the war, when the U.S.A. was feathering its own nest. There was little inclination in Washington to write off this debt. The account was sent in for settlement, not just without discount, but with interest charged. Britain owed the U.S.A. somewhere in the region of $900 million, while she was owed about $2000 million by her European allies. The former debt was demanded, while the latter was largely written off.

The performance of the U.S.A. in 1916–21 still beggars belief. It very soon became apparent that the U.S.A., having profited vastly from the war, called their troops home, disowned the League and rejected all foreign entanglements, except financial ones in her favour, now intended to exploit her postwar economic strength in terms of sea power. Still smarting from the interference from which American shipping had suffered when the Royal Navy had exercised belligerent rights during the early years of the war, the U.S.A. determined never again to suffer from naval inferiority. The huge naval building programme of 1916, which comprised six battleships and six battle-cruisers, would have given the U.S.A. an overwhelming superiority in modern capital ships. Although war between the U.S.A. and Britain was unthinkable, what was not was that a situation might again arise when a neutral U.S.A. might wish to enforce the cherished American principle of the freedom of the seas against belligerents, of which Britain might well be one. Added to this was the outright hostility to Britain of many American naval officers, which was almost taught to them at their naval academies.

However, the Board of Admiralty realized that for the Royal Navy to contemplate a naval armaments race, least of all against the U.S.A., which it could never afford or win, would be disastrous for the British economy. Despite this, the Admiralty realized that it had to retain the security of imperial sea communications. The postwar Admiralty, under Beatty from 1920 to 1927, viewed the long term future course of international relations with considerably less confidence than most politicians, and did not share the public optimism that there would be no more war, nor that, if there was a war, the League would take care of it. Nor did they believe that the day of the battleship was over, as the newly created R.A.F. tried to claim. They did accept that there was a limit to what the country could afford. Their immediate decision was that the two-power standard must go overboard.

In the immediate aftermath of the war, however, British naval expenditure was ruthlessly cut and work on ships already laid down, unless they were nearing completion, was stopped. However, by 1921 the Admiralty was warning that the war-worn and aging ships were in need of replacement. It was accepted that a new capital ship building programme was essential and the 1921 estimates included provision for four 48,000 ton 16-inch gunned battleships. Even the Americans understood the foolhardiness of a naval race, and therefore in the autumn of 1921 they convened the Washington Naval Conference for the five leading naval powers, Britain, U.S.A., Japan, Italy and France, in order to try to reach some mutual agreements on limitations on naval armaments. The negotiations were extremely complicated, and can be followed, if desired, in S.W. Roskill's *British Naval Policy Between The Wars Volume I*. Basically, the problem was to resolve the relative values of displacement, armament, overseas commitment and the age of existing ships. Agreement was eventually reached, not entirely unsatisfactorily from the British point of view. Cruiser strength remained unresolved until the London Naval Conference of 1930. The limitations imposed upon cruisers and destroyers bore no relation to the Royal Navy's absolute requirement for trade protection.

One other outcome of the Washington Naval Conference was the abrogation of the Anglo-Japanese alliance, originally signed in 1905. It has been said, not altogether unfairly, that we exchanged an ally for an isolationist rival. It was not that long before Japan became our leading rival and prospective opponent, without any form of guarantee that the U.S.A. would help us. However, in the long run a continuation of the Anglo-Japanese alliance would have been unlikely to have halted Japan's aggressive expansion in the 1930s, nor her desire to throw in her lot with Germany and Italy. The natural result of the abrogation of the Japanese alliance was the commitment to send a battlefleet to the Far East, capable of taking on a Japanese fleet in the event of a direct threat to British imperial interests. This commitment, and the necessity of a naval base at Singapore, obsessed naval planning between the wars and became a First Sea Lord's nightmare when the storm clouds gathered over Europe, culminating in the disaster to Force Z off the Malayan coast in December 1941.

Another constraint on British defence policy was the infamous Ten Year Rule. The origins of this were quite sensible. When the services asked the government in 1919 for what they should prepare, they were told:

> It should be assumed, for framing revised Estimates, that the British Empire will not be engaged in any great war during the next ten years, and that no Expeditionary Force is required for this purpose.[1]

At that time this must have appeared entirely logical. After all, the Great War was "the war to end all wars" and there was now a League of Nations to stop all future wars, so there was no need to prepare for war in the foreseeable future. It was also part of the drive for economic savings that major cuts could be made in defence spending. A major twist to the Ten Year Rule was given to it in 1928 by Winston Churchill, the Chancellor of the Exchequer from 1925 to 1929. He insisted that the Ten Year Rule should begin afresh every day, unless notice was given to the Chiefs of Staff. It is said that the Secretary to the Cabinet, Sir Maurice Hankey, would wake up each morning and say, "Oh no! The Ten Year Rule starts again today!" It remained in force until 1932, three years before the confrontation with Italy, seven years before the outbreak of war. However, the Ten Year Rule allowed the Treasury to block every claim for money made by all three of the armed forces. For all of them the 1920s and 1930s were truly the "locust years".

Besides these international and national issues there was a third issue which tended to dominate the thinking of the Naval Staff between the wars. That was the relationship with the newly formed R.A.F. In particular this was fought over the body and soul of naval aviation. When the R.A.F. was founded, not altogether inappropriately on 1 April 1918, it took over both the R.F.C. and R.N.A.S. To put it simply, the Royal Navy wanted the R.N.A.S. back, and this dispute, sometimes bitter and never rationally resolved, stirred service loyalties and emotions. More importantly, it diverted effort in both Admiralty and Air Ministry from more important work. The R.A.F. realized long before the Royal Navy that the issue would be decided not on rational service arguments, but on emotional arguments that would appeal to politicians. The admirals disdained to lobby the politicians, unlike the air marshals who saw that exaggerated claims in the right places gained more than a sober appreciation of the Navy's case. The end result was unsatisfactory in almost every respect. It left the Royal Navy weak in the air and with its air arm under divided control. The lead which both the American and Japanese Navies, masters of their own aviation, thus gained, was never to be lost. British maritime thought between the wars, instead of exploiting naval aviation, remained riveted to the battleship. It was to be roundly abused both at Taranto, at its own hand, and off the Malayan coast at the hands of the Japanese.

For the Royal Navy, and Naval Staff in particular, the 1920s and early 1930s were thus years of difficulty and uncertainty: of battling with the Treasury for funds to modernize the battle fleet, and to replace out of date ships: of rivalry with the Air Ministry for the control of naval aviation: of treaty limitations and disarmament, and of defence policy governed by the Ten Year Rule. The size of the Naval Staff itself became an issue for economy. It was reduced from a wartime strength of 336 in November 1918, to 160 in 1919, 118 in 1920, 87 in 1921 and ultimately to 64 in 1922. It was during these locust years that Dudley Pound held Admiralty office, alternating with sea appointments, successively Director of Plans, Chief of Staff to the Mediterranean Fleet, Assistant Chief of Naval Staff, Flag Officer Commanding the Battle Cruiser Squadron and Second Sea Lord. He was thus one of the significant influences in naval policy-making in this period.

*

For those at sea the postwar years were relatively carefree, provided they had escaped the Geddes Axe. Few thought there was a possibility of another major war in their lifetime. With luck they might be involved in a local skirmish in China or the Middle East, bringing distinction and possibly promotion, but their principal tasks were regattas, sporting competitions, showing the flag, social functions and routine weapon training, culminating in the annual replays of the Battle of Jutland in the Combined Fleet Exercises. Not all senior officers insisted on the highest standards of training or efficiency in their commands, and those, like Pound, who did, and drove their ships and fleets hard, often did so at the expense of personal popularity. However, the Royal Navy owed them much when war did come.

The main peacetime strength of the Royal Navy was divided between

45

the Atlantic Fleet, based at home ports, and the Mediterranean Fleet, based at Malta. For some years the two fleets possessed a combined strength of fifteen battleships and three battle cruisers, give or take one or two undergoing long refits. However, these numbers were misleading. Only one of these ships, *Hood*, was of post-Jutland design, and not until the two *Nelson* class battleships came along were any postwar. They were a fine and impressive display of British naval might, unless and until they had to fight modern ships. Further afield, the traditional peacetime foreign naval stations were reconstituted in China, the East Indies, the West Indies, North and South America, and the Cape, where cruiser squadrons and sloops showed the flag and upheld British interests in agreeable yachting conditions. There were other British stations as well. British gunboats operated on the Rhine, on the Danube and even on the Caspian Sea. The white ensign was the visible expression of the far-flung British Empire.

These wide-ranging foreign stations, together with the home ports commands, provided no less than six commands afloat, and three ashore for Commanders-in-Chief. There was the prospect of plenty of sea time for Captains, and twenty-one commands afloat for Flag Officers (of whom there were ninety-two on the active list in 1923). Life at sea was fun and the Royal Navy was master of its own affairs, free of allies and multi-national commands. From time to time there were crises, such as Chanak in 1922, Shanghai in 1927, or natural disasters like the Yokohama earthquake in 1923, or a revolution in South America or Greece. At all of these H.M. ships carried out their traditional humanitarian and protective role. In general, life afloat was pretty even, less likely to be distracted by war than by admirals.

*

For much of 1919 Pound was on half-pay, the occupational hazard of all officers in the armed forces between wars, for whom there were rarely enough jobs. Their third child, a daughter, Barbara, was born this year. They spent it living on the Isle of Wight, near Bessie's parents, and it was coloured by typical family episodes: George dropping a stone on his brother Martin's head from a first floor window and knocking him out, and, much more dangerously, Pound turning on the water geyser, but forgetting to turn on the water. The resulting explosion propelled the

46

geyser through the wall, but mercifully Pound was unscathed.

He returned to sea again in the summer of 1920 in his first postwar appointment, as Captain of the battle cruiser *Repulse*. It was thoroughly in keeping with his character that he wished to prepare himself for this appointment and he therefore spent a busman's holiday in *Hood*, flagship of the Battle Cruiser Squadron, as the guest of his old friends Roger Keyes, commanding the squadron, and Wilfred Tomkinson, the Flag Captain. *Repulse* was a most attractive ship, with fine lines, and was a good command. She and her sister ship *Renown* were roomy and comfortable, with lines of scuttles the length of the ship on the two lower decks, which made them unusually light and airy. Both ships were used in the 1920s to convey the Prince of Wales and his brother, the Duke of York, in a series of royal tours around the Empire, and to Japan and South America, for which service they were ideally suited. Pound missed these cruises, as well as the C.V.O. which was customarily conferred on the Captain, as *Renown* was away while he was in *Repulse*, and he had left the ship before *Repulse* was used in 1925. However, he would probably have regarded such service as a yachting cruise and would have much preferred to command a ship with the fleet.

The commission was uneventful, except for one brief and unusual experience in April 1921 when the normal fleet routine was interrupted by the miners' strike. There were fears of serious disorder and riots, and Pound commanded the Naval Battalion from Chatham and the Nore, which was to be sent to London in case of difficulties. On 10 April Pound took fifty-two officers and 1049 seamen by special train to Victoria station where they were met by the band of the Irish Guards and a horse for Pound. They marched to Kensington Gardens where they lived under canvas. They were in London for ten days, during which time they were inspected by Beatty, the First Sea Lord, and Lord Cavan, commanding all troops in London. Pound organized sports and route marches, including a regatta on the Serpentine.

The Battle Cruiser Squadron brought Pound and Keyes together for the fourth time and their relationship prospered. However, Keyes' posting was only until the spring of 1921, when he departed to the Admiralty as D.C.N.S., and the redoubtable Rear Admiral Walter Cowan replaced him. Like Keyes he was a great rider, although a hunter rather than a polo player. He had a fiery temper and could be a difficult man to serve. He was a martinet and his subordinates' faces had to fit. He had had disciplinary problems on previous ships, involving no less than three mutinies, and *Hood* was not always a happy flagship. Perhaps the tension with his Flag Captain, Geoffrey Mackworth, the successor to Tomkinson, drew Cowan closer to Pound. At any rate, Cowan wrote warmly to Pound, when the latter left the Battle Cruiser Squadron in March 1922:

My dear Pound,

You have just gone and I feel I have not expressed myself in the least how I feel, but in the year we have served together I have had infinite value, support and comfort from you, and though I feel it has never been apparent I have realised and been grateful beyond words to you for your big-minded loyalty and staunchness to me in all matters and under all conditions, and I know so well that my methods and criticisms are often disagreeable and so I value your generous mindedness (which has been unfailing) the more. It's no good my covering a lot of paper but this I say with the utmost sincerity that should war come again and they entrusted me with another command afloat I should move Heaven and earth to get you at my back. Goodbye and again my very grateful thanks.

Yours ever,

Walter Cowan.[2]

Pound certainly was prepared to stand up for his officers against any interference. Vice Admiral Sir Ian Campbell recalls an incident when he was serving on *Repulse*. There was a custom in the Royal Navy that if a ship falls out of station the Admiral would signal "Indicate the name of the officer of the watch", who, under the Captain, was responsible for accurate station-keeping. It was a salutary form of rebuke, but Pound would have none of it. When Cowan addressed this signal to *Repulse*, Pound (who was in his sea cabin) made the reply "Captain A.D.P.R. Pound is Captain of this ship." This must have earned him the respect of all his watch keepers and no doubt kept Cowan quiet. There are frequent accounts of his style of captaincy and his junior officers were clearly devoted to him. Among his watch-keeping Lieutenants was Lord Mountbatten. His father, the Marquess of Milford Haven, the former First Sea Lord, was staying on board, as a guest of Pound's, shortly before he died, and evidently approved of all that he saw.

Pound received extremely good confidential reports from both Keyes and Cowan. Keyes wrote on 31 March 1921, before leaving to become DCNS at the Admiralty:

Although I have not seen much of Capt. P. in the B.C.S., he served as my Flag Capt. in *Colossus* for a short time, was my Asst. when I was D.of P., and I had a good deal to do with him when he was D.O.D. during the last year of the war. He possesses a strong character, an even temper and powerful physique. Keeps himself v. fit. A strong oar, v.g. at games, a keen sportsman. His services as D.O.D. in 1918 are well known at the Admty. In my opinion, his most valuable quality is an extraordinary gift of imagination and clear thinking, and he can put forward his ideas logically and convincingly. He certainly originated the Northern Barrage, the Dover flare patrol over the minefield and persuaded me that an attack on Zeebrugge was a feasible option if an efficient smokescreen could be produced, and he helped enormously to get it produced – for none existed at the time. Capt. P. will always have a happy efficient ship, and he is a good seaman. But he is a v. brilliant staff officer, and if properly made use of, will, *I am convinced,* be of the greatest value to the Service. Specially recomd.

This was endorsed by Admiral Madden, the Commander-in-Chief Atlantic Fleet, with the comment, "A v. able offr. who shd. be kept fully emplyed for the benefit of the Service." Fifteen months later Cowan wrote a similarly laudatory report on Pound.

An offr. of exceptional ability with high qualities of resource and quick and correct instinct for war strategy and tactics. I consider him to be an ideal C.O.S. to a high comd. As Capt. of a ship I have found his only weak point to be a failure to exact from the personnel the highest standard of discipline and efficiency which it is necessary to insist on, now that our numerical strength in ships and men has been so much reduced, and he is inclined to repose undue trust and confidence in offrs. before requiring sufficient proof of their fitness for this. His loyalty and staunchness of backing to me could not have been exceeded.[3]

Neither of these reports could have been much better and there can be no doubts that by this time his performance was under close scrutiny by those in a position to ensure he had a successful and important career.

★

On leaving *Repulse* at the end of 1923 Pound returned to the Admiralty as Director of the Plans Division of the Naval Staff, usually referred to as D. of P. This was one of the most important and responsible of appointments for a senior Captain. Pound, with his previous experience as head of the Planning Section, A.D.of P. and D.O.D.(H) during the war, his recent sea-going experience in *Repulse* and his acceptance of hard work and devotion to duty, was ideal for the job. He joined a Naval Staff headed by Beatty as First Sea Lord and Chief of Naval Staff, and with his immediate superiors, Roger Keyes, again, as D.C.N.S., and Cyril Fuller as A.C.N.S., both of whom were former D.of P.s. It was a very strong team and his position there indicated that Beatty had full confidence in him.

The D. of P. had a wide range of responsibilities. Indeed, it can be claimed that he had a finger in most of the Admiralty pies: strategic planning and the disposition of fleets across the world, new construction programmes, naval base and dockyard requirements, the Naval Estimates, the naval aspects of foreign and defence policy formation. All of these would have flowed across his desk, and on up to the desk of the D.C.N.S. and then the First Sea Lord. To aid him in all of these tasks he had a Captain as Deputy, three Commanders, one of whom he lost in the 1922 economies, one Royal Marine Major, and five civilian staff. In 1923 the three RN officers were an impressive collection: Captain G.H. D'Oyly Lyon, and Commanders J.H. Godfrey and H.H. Harwood, the latter two of whom became Admirals during the war.

Throughout his time as D. of P. Pound's chief problem was to maintain an adequate fleet in order to match British commitments, while also replacing ageing ships. The Admiralty's principal opponent on the latter front was the Treasury, particularly when Churchill was Chancellor of the Exchequer. On the international scene Pound became involved in the vexed question of Turkey. Greece had decided in 1921, somewhat incautiously, to invade Turkey from the area around Smyrna, which the Treaty of Sevres had awarded her in 1919. This had resulted in a catastrophic defeat in Anatolia and, as a result, disaster at Smyrna. The nationalist Turkish army had then advanced on the neutral zone which embraced both the Dardanelles and the Bosphorus, and which was defended by a British force backed by the Mediterranean Fleet. Much of the Atlantic Fleet was despatched to support the former and an inter-

50

national conference was convened as Lausanne in 1922 to renegotiate the original treaty. Pound was one of the team which went to these negotiations under the Foreign Secretary, Lord Curzon. This was Pound's first experience of national policy making.

In 1924 Pound was again attached to the staff of a British delegation to an international conference, this time that led by Lord Parmoor to the League of Nations meeting at Geneva to discuss the Protocol for the Pacific Settlement of International Disputes. The Admiralty was worried by the naval implications of what had been proposed, and Pound was sent out. The First Lord, Lord Chelmsford, wrote to Parmoor on 26 September 1924:

> We have been much exercised at the Admiralty over the Protocol and certain implications that may be involved in it, and so, with the consent of the Prime Minister [MacDonald] I am sending out Capt. Pound, the Director of Plans, who may discuss with you our difficulties and fears. He is the man in the Admiralty who has the subject at his finger ends, and you may take it that he has our complete confidence and authority. I hope you will understand that he is coming out as an Expert Adviser to help you with your most difficult and responsible task, and that our only wish is to assist.[4]

It was during Pound's time as D. of P. that the Anglo-Japanese Alliance of 1902 was formally terminated. As a result of this Pound urged the building of the Singapore Naval Base. He opposed the view of the Commander-in-Chief, China, and of the War Office, that this should be co-located with the commercial port and insisted that it should be separate, and built on the northern shore, on the Johore Straits. This minute, of 17 December 1923, was approved by the Committee of Imperial Defence.[5]

In 1923 an Imperial Conference was held in London and Pound proposed an Imperial Naval Staff, which would direct peacetime naval planning and direct operations in time of war. This was politically unacceptable and would, anyway, probably not have worked in practice, but it does demonstrate that as early as 1923 Pound was being forced to think in global terms and that the issues which confronted him in 1939 were not new to him.

Throughout this period Pound worked hard and played hard. There can be little doubt about the former. He was an inveterate worker all his life, and being amongst the instigators of national policy would have been a very real challenge. During this period the family lived in London (61 Linden Gardens) and Pound took what exercise he could grab. He shot regularly at weekends in the season and had a gun in a syndicate at Ditton Park, the Admiralty Compass Observatory, near Langley. He also shot with Wilfred Tomkinson on occasion at Brandon in Suffolk.

5

STAFFWORK

In the spring of 1925 Pound was appointed as Chief of Staff to Roger Keyes, the new Commander-in-Chief of the Mediterranean Fleet. In the same way that Director of Plans was one of the best appointments for a Captain in the Admiralty, so the two best appointments afloat for a Captain who had commanded his own battleship was as Chief of Staff in the two main fleets. The post carried the rank of Commodore until the holder was promoted to Rear Admiral. Pound was also appointed ADC to the King, which was a sinecure bestowed on most senior Captains until it was relinquished on promotion.

The only criticism of the appointment came from Jellicoe, who wrote to Admiral Dreyer after meeting Chatfield in April 1925:

> I see that Pound goes to the Mediterranean. Chatfield evidently has a high opinion of Pound. Personally I don't quite share that opinion, but of course I don't know much about his work now.[1]

This is a strange comment given Jellicoe's backing of Pound in the Grand Fleet and then selecting him for his Naval Staff in 1917. However, it can possibly be explained by assuming that Jellicoe thought Pound had now become a Beatty man. Jellicoe was never a great admirer of Keyes either, and so this comment may possibly symbolize the way in which the Navy of the 1920s tended to divide into Jellicoe and Beatty factions.

This was the sixth time that Pound and Keyes had served together and this time the partnership was closer than ever. The two were very different characters: both had offensive spirits, but few other similarities. Keyes had made his name as a national hero, both in the Boxer Rebellion, achieving promotion to Commander at 28, and then in the Great War at Zeebrugge in 1918. Pound, on the other hand, had followed the conventional career path. Keyes rode straight and fearlessly, and often unthinkingly, at any obstacle; Pound was more calculating. Administration and detail bored Keyes; it absorbed Pound. Keyes was ambitious and made the fleet his shop window; Pound never personalized his style. Despite these opposites, the two were friends and the partnership ought to have worked. The combination of Keyes' enthusiasm and Pound's efficiency should have produced an ideal blend. Indeed, a successful tenure of this, Britain's premier fleet, ought to have been the prelude to Keyes succeeding Beatty as First Sea Lord. However, in the words of S.W. Roskill, "Keyes' command of the Mediterranean Fleet was not a success".[2]

Keyes had two passions which he indulged while he was Commander-in-Chief. They were parties and polo. These, rather than the training of his fleet, came to dominate his life. As a result Pound ran the day to day life of the fleet. To an extent this was the correct job of the Chief of Staff and Pound revelled in it. Keyes did not make himself popular in his Fleet with the emphasis on polo, which, in the words of Roskill, "he regarded as almost a *sine qua non* for the leader in a fighting service"[3]. There was a strong feeling within the fleet that favouritism was shown to those who played polo. This may not have been true but, correct or incorrect, there can be no doubt that the feeling existed. Nor was Keyes really interested in any tactical developments. Admiral Sir William James considered that his time as Commander-in-Chief "was not successful"[4].

There was pressure to economize on fuel consumption and ammunition expenditure. Bad weather was frequently used as an excuse to cancel sea training. Exercises, anyway, were pretty basic, such as shooting at targets towed at 6 knots, and straightforward, standardized night encounters. Between 1919 and 1939, and this, of course, includes Pound's time in the Mediterranean, there was not a single exercise in the protection of a slow mercantile convoy against submarine or air attack; instead the fleets prepared to refight the battle of Jutland.

Certainly the Mediterranean Fleet was ready for a shake-up when Keyes and Pound arrived in April of 1925. It was Great Britain's main fleet, and was the choice command in the Royal Navy. It was an imposing fleet whose average strength was: two Battle squadrons (eight battleships); two cruiser squadrons (eight–ten cruisers); one or two aircraft carriers; four destroyer flotillas (thirty-two destroyers and four leaders); and a submarine flotilla. Pound certainly electrified the fleet by the way that he not only organized the training and day-to-day administration of the Fleet, but also by the way in which he took an interest in the wellbeing of every ship's company. He also found time for sport, cheerful parties and for educating officers in his own beliefs. Vice Admiral Eric Longley-Cook recalled his time as Chief of Staff. Pound "used to tell young officers about the awful lack of initiative at Jutland and insist that the fleet must be trained on new lines".[5]

Vice Admiral Sir Charles Norris agrees with this and commented that the economy drive from home made things very difficult.

> Pound was ingenious at designing exercises to the last detail so that the best possible use was made of restricted fuel supplies. Battle cruisers were kept down to 11 knots, and he took tremendous risks in exercises leaving the officers and men dead tired. . . . He was respected by most, but not by the weaker brethren.
>
> It was typical of Pound that although filling this extremely hard-worked and responsible appointment he still found time to produce his book 'Shooting in the Mediterranean', which contained the most detailed and useful information on all forms of sport to be had on the station. It is also typical of him that he restricted publication of the book to the officers of the fleet.
>
> On top of all this Pound and his wife threw themselves heart and soul into the sport and entertainment offered by the Malta season.[6]

Pound here fitted in well with his Commander-in-Chief, for Keyes was a splendid host at Admiralty House in Valletta, as well as on his flagship. During a cruise to the French Riviera there were seldom less than thirty-four to lunch or dinner in the Commander-in-Chief's cabin. However, all Keyes' entertaining did not contribute to the morale or happiness of the Fleet. Entertainment tended to become competitive and ships as well as individuals vied with one another to give the best parties. Pound could not afford to compete with Keyes and, living at Floriana, he did not try. Nevertheless he managed to get quite badly into debt.

★

By 1926–27 Keyes was much preoccupied with his future prospects. He had set his heart on becoming First Sea Lord and had been encouraged in this by Beatty. However, two factors acted against him. The first was the farcical *Royal Oak* affair, in which Keyes had a Rear-Admiral and the Captain and executive Officer of *Royal Oak* court-martialled for subverting discipline.[7] This occurred after Pound had left the Mediterranean Fleet and resulted in considerable adverse publicity for the Royal Navy in general, and, possibly unfairly, for Keyes in particular. Secondly was the decision to appoint Admiral Sir Charles Madden to succeed Beatty in 1927. Madden had been Chief of Staff to Jellicoe in the Grand Fleet and it was hoped that his appointment would bring to an end the faction fighting that existed in the Royal Navy between the supporters of Jellicoe and Beatty. Keyes believed that he would succeed Madden, for he was still relatively young, and meanwhile he went to become Commander-in-Chief, Portsmouth. In all of these manoeuvrings Pound played a part. Keyes told Churchill in 1940:

> I made one great mistake 14 years ago, when commanding the Mediterranean Fleet, by following the advice of my Chief of Staff – Pound – and urging Beatty (who intended to hold his office until I was ready to succeed him as First Sea Lord) to let Madden in for his last two years of active service, as Pound maintained that this would put an end to the so-called Beatty–Jellicoe controversy in the Navy.[8]

Whether Keyes did hold this against Pound is uncertain. If he did do so, it was unjust, for Pound was not responsible for Keyes failing to become First Sea Lord. The choice was made by the First Lord, A.V. Alexander, and the First Sea Lord, Madden, in 1930. A combination of Keyes' obsession with polo, the *Royal Oak* affair and the belief by a number of senior admirals that Keyes was deficient intellectually were important, but more so was the probable view of the Labour government that Keyes would not have been politically amenable. They were determined on further disarmament; Keyes would have opposed them. His appointment, in the words of Roskill, "would have resulted in a conflagration".[9]

For some time after Pound's move to the Admiralty as ACNS he wrote to Keyes on a regular basis, keeping the latter informed on the latest state of play in what might be called the First Sea Lord stakes. Thus, shortly after returning to England on 27 April 1926 he wrote:

> As regards Lord Beatty leaving, I believe it is definitely settled that Sir Charles Madden will relieve him. Both Admiral Field and Admiral Dreyer told me that it was settled and I know that the former thinks that it will take place somewhere about July or August because he said that he thought the change would interfere with his summer

56

leave and I would be required to be here to help put Sir Charles into the saddle.

Also Dreyer turned over to me that Sir C.M. wanted various textbooks sent to him. This latter evidence appears to be pretty conclusive that he will not refuse. Both Admiral Dreyer and Field of course told me how entirely 'private' this was.[10]

He also kept Keyes informed on all sorts of general issues and, in particular, with the negotiations at Geneva with which he was involved. All of this was written with the expectation that Keyes would succeed Madden after two years as First Sea Lord.

In fact Pound could have had little influence, not only in the selection of Madden, but also in the selection of Field to succeed Madden in 1930. He was the junior member of the Board of Admiralty as ACNS. However, in a letter to Keyes on 4 March 1930 he does indicate that he would have supported Keyes, even though by then he was commanding the Battle Cruiser Squadron.

We have just heard the news that Admiral Field is to go as First Sea Lord and I am most desperately grieved. It is most unfair to you and a grave mistake from the point of view of the Navy and the Empire. I can only suppose that the Govt. (sic) want someone who will agree to all their reductions, etc. It is the one time we want someone strong who will stick up for them. However I don't suppose Field's constitution will stand it for more than a year, and your chance will surely come yet. Lately there have been consistent rumours that you were going and I was hoping that all was well, and now comes this bombshell. I am sure they will all regret it when they come to their senses.

I suppose that Madden must have played a large part in it and it is the irony of fate that you should have done as much to put him where he is.[11]

Keyes appears still to have had faith in Pound, writing in May 1930 in reply to Pound's congratulations on his promotion to Admiral of the Fleet:

You are a faithful friend and 'believer'. It is very nice to be 'believed in'! Anyhow whether from within or without the Admiralty I mean to fight the navy's battles as long as I live.[12]

He wrote to "My dear Dudley", and signed himself "Yours ever".

Pound had a good staff with which to work in the Mediterranean Fleet. He had tried to get Commander John Godfrey to come as Staff Officer (Operations), but the latter was due to attend the Staff College at Greenwich and explained how important it would be to follow that with an appointment as executive officer of a battleship.[13] Remembering his own time on *Superb*, Pound agreed and instead offered the post to Commander Tom Phillips, who thereby linked himself to Pound for the first time. Godfrey himself said, "Pound as Chief of Staff was unable to mitigate the badness of the Roger Keyes' regime. Keyes was run by Pound."[14] This was a little harsh. Keyes set his own tone. Pound saw to it that the fleet was efficient and well-trained. There were certainly many who thought he overorganized things, in particular his detailed orders and instructions which left little room for initiative. The worst criticism of him came from Admiral Sir William James, who wrote to Godfrey in October 1945:

> I never served with Pound except when he was C.O.S. to Keyes in the Med., and though Keyes was in great measure responsible for the none-too-happy atmosphere it was Pound and Phillips with their storekeeper minds, who quenched all the spark in the fleet. Everything was scheduled, even a snipe shoot in a Greek swamp went into a book because ships were told to report full details of all sport when cruising independently. . . . There was always something missing in their makeup, and they always reminded me of the old storekeeping warrant officer.[15]

Although this addiction to detail was commonly noted, he cannot really be blamed for it in this particular job. It was, after all, his duty as Chief of Staff to look after details, particularly with a Commander-in-Chief like Keyes who patently did not bother about them. James, by 1945, was hardly an objective observer since he had been passed over in the late 1930s. A more accurate assessment comes from Rear-Admiral Royer Dick:

> Dudley Pound as Chief of Staff drove the Mediterranean Fleet very hard. The tension resulting from this showed itself in the *Royal Oak* affair. He had entirely a tactical mind; not interested in broad ideas

or strategy. . . . . I marveled at the energy of Pound, dancing till early in the morning, shooting and working.[16]

This is supported by both Admiral of the Fleet Lord Fraser and Admiral Sir Neville Syfret, who served as successive Fleet Gunnery Officers.[17]

The differences between Pound and Keyes were very noticeable. A Commander-in-Chief must give personal leadership to his command, as well as tone and style. The job of the Chief of Staff is to interpret the wishes of the Commander-in-Chief and to see to the running of the fleet. Keyes was a better fighting admiral than a peacetime admiral. Like Pound he was devoutly patriotic and devoted to the Royal Navy, but, reading his correspondence and studying his time in command, one forms the suspicion that he was overmindful of himself. Neither Keyes nor Pound was perfect, but where Pound's imperfections were balanced by a good brain, total professionalism, devotion to duty and selflessness, Keyes was not a clever man, and vain.

Pound was promoted Rear Admiral on 1 March 1926 at the age of 48 and was relieved as Chief of Staff by Wilfred Tomkinson in December of the same year. He left behind a notable staff: Tom Phillips (S.O.O.), George Creasy (number 2 to Phillips), Fraser (F.G.O), and Mountbatten (Asst. Fleet Wireless Officer), all of whom were future admirals to be associated with him in the Second World War. Pound spent a month shooting in Salonika before returning to England, a fitting finish to his time in the Mediterranean, during which he had recorded nearly 100 days' shooting.

★

In April 1927 Pound relieved Rear Admiral Freddie Dreyer as ACNS and so became the junior member of the Board of Admiralty. The Sea Lords were Beatty as First Sea Lord and Chief of Naval Staff, Brand as Second Sea Lord and Chief of Naval Personnel, Chatfield as Third Sea Lord and Controller, Field as DCNS and W.W. Fisher as Fourth Sea Lord.

Pound took with him as his secretary Paymaster Commander J.R. Hemsted, whom he had got to know in Malta. The role of Secretary is more than that of paper sorter. If the relationship works, an Admiral and his secretary may stay together for the rest of the Admiral's career. The secretary is messmate, confidant, companion and sometimes interpreter between his Admiral and the command, as well as adviser on personal matters. Hemsted was to remain with Pound until his premature death in 1936. Pound took the decision to choose Hemsted seriously, as can be seen from his letter of invitation. Hemsted could have had no illusions about what was expected of him and there was an easy let out for him if he wanted it. It is a rare example of the Pound style, and is thus worth quoting in full. The letter was drafted in Pound's own hand and he added a postscript: "I have marked the letter secret, but you will of course consult Mrs Hemsted."

H.M.S. WARSPITE,
Secret
30 August 1926.

Dear Hemsted,

I have been told by the First Sea Lord that I am to relieve Admiral Dreyer as ACNS in January and I write to ask you whether you would care to come as my Secretary, under certain conditions which I will now put before you.

(A) I suppose I may reasonably expect to get a command after 2 years as ACNS and I should naturally not wish to change Secretaries. If you came with me therefore it would have to be on the understanding that if I wished you to do so you would come on with me.

(B) When things are hectic you must be prepared to work late and the fact that you have arranged to go to the theatre will not influence me in the least in your case any more than it would in my own.

(C) If you come as my Secretary in a seagoing job you must be prepared to run the mess for me.

(D) You must be prepared to do a certain amount of private secretarial work as only in this way can I get time to attend to the questions which I must deal with personally.

You must not mind my putting things to you in this manner because you must remember that I do not know you well. Had I known you well it would have been unnecessary for me to put these conditions to you. Anyway it is much better to have things clearly defined before we start.

As regards your qualifications as a Secretary I am entirely content to take Paymr. Captain Russell's opinion.

The present idea is that I shall leave the Mediterranean on 24 November and shall probably join the Admiralty to take over on 27 December and take on finally as ACNS on 11 January.

Time is short and I should like a reply from you as early as possible giving me information as to whether you care to come and also the date on which your relief should arrive at Malta in order to allow you to get your foreign service leave and be ready to join the Admiralty on 1 January.

By the time I get your reply I hope to have more definite information as to when you would be required to join. It may be found expedient for Admiral Dreyer's Secretary to remain on with me for a month say. I will write and find out about this.

Please go to Major McCausland [the SO(I) Malta] and ask him from me to send your reply by W/T. The telegram should take the following form.

If you accept: From Intelligence Officer to C.O.S. 'Your letter received. Certainly . . .' and then give date on which your relief should arrive in Malta.

If you cannot accept: From Intelligence Officer to C.O.S. 'Your letter received. Impossible.'

I would like you to know that the reason I am not taking Ashton on, even supposing he wished to come which I do not know, is that I'm a bit deaf and he speaks so lowly that I am forced to ask him to repeat nearly every word he says. This is the sole reason as his work has been perfect and I like him very much, but the combination of his voice and my ears did not lead to either comfort or efficiency.

I have marked this letter 'Secret' because it is better to have these things settled before all the world, and particularly the Malta world, begins talking about them.

You will have to explain matters to McCausland but in doing so ask him to keep it to himself.

I remember that you said you might be going with Admiral Harper and should you be in any way committed to him and consider it necessary to consult him I would ask that you should do so by telegram otherwise it will not be possible to get things fixed up. My information which is later than when I spoke to you on the subject is that in the near future he is likely to get a dockyard but not a seagoing command. [Rear-Admiral Harper did not get a dockyard, but retired in September 1929.]

In conclusion I would say that if you decide to link your fortunes with mine and come with me it will give me great pleasure and it will also give my wife great pleasure as she likes both you and Mrs. Hemsted so much.

You should receive this in time to send a letter in reply by *Danae* and can then mention any other points regarding your leave and relief but please also send a wire.

Yours sincerely,

DUDLEY POUND.[18]

★

The Board of Admiralty was one of the most entrenched and powerful institutions in Whitehall. It was not only an administrative department, but also a supply department, as well as designing and providing ships and equipment. The naval side of the Admiralty was constantly refreshed by the experience of officers from sea, while continuity was provided by the permanent civil service secretariat, none more powerful than the distinguished Permanent Secretary, Sir Oswyn Murray, who held office for nearly twenty years between the wars. Unlike the other two service ministries, the Admiralty was also an operational centre able to give orders to senior officers afloat when necessary.

The Board that Pound joined was one of the most powerful between the wars. W.C. Bridgeman, the First Lord, was a respected Tory politician of the old school who had taken office in 1924 and was trusted and liked by his naval and political colleagues. Beatty had been First Sea Lord since 1919 and was, in the words of his biographer, "the last naval hero". He could hold his own in debate with all politicians and dominated the Board. Brand, as Second Sea Lord was both a sailor of distinction and a courtier, combining the best qualities of both. Chatfield, the Third Sea Lord, had the best brain of the entire Board. He was also very close to Beatty, having been his Flag Captain throughout the war in both Battle Cruiser Force and Grand Fleet. Pound's greatest companion was the fourth Sea Lord, W.W. Fisher, his erstwhile captain in *St Vincent* and probably his closest naval friend. The DCNS was Field, who shared the superintendence with

62

Pound of the Naval Staff. He suffered indifferent health and had, on occasions, to hand his work over to Pound.

Three months after Pound's arrival Beatty retired and was replaced, as we have already seen, by Admiral Sir Charles Madden. Although Madden was universally respected in the Navy, he did not have Beatty's charisma, nor was he really well known outside the Navy. He could not match Beatty's standing in Whitehall. This was unfortunate, as it was a period of acute financial stringency, when the Naval Estimates were severely cut and a heavyweight in Cabinet and committee was needed to put the Royal Naval case. The cruiser battle with the Americans was at its height. Madden stated to the Cabinet that the Navy needed a minimum of seventy, and then agreed, against the advice of the Naval Staff, including Pound, to fifty. It was felt by critics that a stronger line ought to have been taken and that this reduction in trade-protection cruisers would not have been accepted by the Bridgeman-Beatty Board. Indeed Roskill goes further, saying:

From Beatty's retirement in 1927 until Admiral Chatfield became First Sea Lord in 1933 the Board of Admiralty became collectively one of the weakest ever to sit in the splendid Board Room which had witnessed so much of Britain's maritime history.[19]

Madden's choice of Field as his successor may well have been taken to keep Keyes out, but it was unfortunate, and a year after that came Invergordon (see Chapter 6), for which the Board of Admiralty bore much responsibility.

It is necessary here to explain the difference between DCNS and ACNS. To put it at its most simple the DCNS was in charge of all strategic matters, including Operations, Plans and Intelligence. The ACNS was in charge of tactical matters and training, including fleet exercises, tactical use of weapons, staff requirements for material, and air matters. Both DCNS and ACNS were responsible to the First Sea Lord for their respective divisions of the Naval Staff.

★

Almost immediately after he had taken over as ACNS Pound was plunged into the acrimonious, and eventually abortive, Geneva Conference on naval armaments, which assembled in June 1927. The British Empire

63

delegation consisted of the First Lord, Bridgeman, Lord Cecil, the Chancellor of the Duchy of Lancaster and a leading advocate of the League of Nations, and Admiral Field, DCNS, as naval adviser. The conference rapidly reached deadlock on the cruiser issue, and when in July Field fell ill Pound was deputed to replace him. Throughout the conference Pound kept Keyes informed:

> The underlying motive is the fact that unless something is done to reduce the estimates they will automatically in a few years reach a total which it does not seem within the bounds of possibility that we should be able to screw out of any Govt. [sic][20]

The conference failed on the cruiser issue between Britain and America. The Americans, to put it simply, did not, or would not, understand the difference between the strategic requirements of Britain with her world-wide Imperial possessions and her dependence on overseas trade, and the USA with their limited overseas commitments. As Pound wrote to Keyes:

> I won't weary you with details of all the various phases the conference went through. We could never get the Americans to say why they wanted their cruisers, but it is quite obvious what is at the back of their minds.
>
> (a) They want "Freedom of the Seas" by which they mean that when they are neutral no one shall interfere with their ships.
>
> (b) To force us to agree to the "Freedom of the Seas" they want "parity".
>
> (c) They want to achieve "parity" *on the cheap*, i.e. force us by treaty to come back to their level instead of having to build up to our level.[21]

The Geneva Conference also saw Pound attending Cabinet meetings where he was generally unimpressed by the politicians, particularly Churchill.

Some criticism of the Board at this period has been made in that they underestimated the threat of submarines and overestimated the threat of surface raiders to British commerce. However, Germany was not yet building submarines, and Beatty, Chatfield, Backhouse, Fisher and other forward looking members of the Board were equally as strong protagonists of the battleship as Pound. Indeed, along with all four of those mentioned, Pound had been an expert witness to the Bonar Law

Committee on the future of the capital ship in 1920. Much of their time was taken up with the obsession, at least until 1935, with the possibility of the next war being against Japan and the potential requirement to despatch a battle fleet to the Far East. It was not until the mid-1930s that Germany and Italy started to become equally dangerous potential enemies.

★

Pound was closely involved with naval air policy and the development of the Fleet Air Arm, in which he had already been closely involved as Director of Plans. There were very few senior officers who had had any experience of flying and Pound was not one of them. There were many who decried the importance of aircraft carriers in naval warfare. Pound, although battleship-minded, like most of his contemporaries, was a strong advocate of naval aviation and of the expansion of the Fleet Air Arm. However, this was a period of strong economies and the Royal Navy had other priorities. Pound showed that the Americans had a substantial superiority in naval aircraft in 1928 and would have a 50% lead by 1934. In fact his figures were too low. The Americans, despite being inferior in carrier tonnage in the 1920s, forged ahead of the Royal Navy as their senior officers became increasingly air-minded. The US Navy had the distinct advantage of not having an independent air force; the Royal Navy was paying the price of the Trenchard legacy.

In both 1928 and 1929 the desire of the Royal Navy to expand and re-equip the Fleet Air Arm was hampered by economies. In 1928 Pound pushed for the expansion, saying, "It is particularly important to learn the effect of aircraft on fleet tactics and naval warfare generally".[22] In the 1929–30 estimates the government had approved the inclusion of a new aircraft carrier. Pound re-examined the need and recommended that the new ship could safely be deferred until 1932–33. It is easy to accuse him of complacency, but the sheer pressure on all three services to economize is difficult to exaggerate and, despite some anxiety in the Far East, the international sky was relatively clear. If it is easy to blame the Admiralty it is easier still to blame the government whose desire for economies forced all three services to cut in some important areas in order to provide for essential needs in others.

It was while Pound was ACNS that he and Beatty started their skiing

65

trips to the Alps. Every year they took over a hotel in Switzerland or Austria, and took with them a party of about fifty young naval officers and their families. They went to such places as Andermatt, Leukerbad and Obergurgl. Foreign holidays were not then as common as they are today. The trips were organized through Thomas Cook and used hotels which were opening for the first time in the winter. There were, of course, no ski tows, and so it was a case of walking uphill for much of the day carrying skis, and then skiing down during the late afternoon. Throughout this period Betty was the perfect naval wife, happy to make a new home, organizing social events, but equally happy to spend a quiet evening at home with the family.

6

BATTLE CRUISERS AND SECOND SEA LORD

Towards the end of 1928 Pound was offered the command of the Battle
Cruiser Squadron, which also involved being second in command of the
Atlantic Fleet. The prospect excited him, particularly as his Commander-
in-Chief in the Atlantic Fleet would be Chatfield, who expressed his own
pleasure in a note dated 26 December 1928:

> My dear Pound,
>
> I am delighted to hear you have been offered the Battle Cruisers and
> I offer you my heartiest congratulations. You have thoroughly earned
> the distinction both by experience and ability and I congratulate
> myself, even more, that I am lucky enough to have you with me. We
> shall be able to continue our Admiralty combination and cooperation
> at sea for I hope the good of the service. Nothing could have given
> more pleasure. Every good wish to you and our combined good
> wishes to your wife also.
>
> Yours ever,
>
> Ernle Chatfield.[1]

Pound's appointment was widely approved. Field, now Commander-in-
Chief in the Mediterranean, told Pound that he was delighted, confirming
his already high opinion, possibly higher than Pound's of him, and W.W.
Fisher was pleased at his friend's promotion. He actually left the
Admiralty in April 1929, handing over for the second time to Wilfred
Tomkinson, and sped on his way by a warm note from the First Lord,
Bridgeman. What meant more to him even than that was a letter from
Fisher:

27 April 1929

My dear Dudley,

I miss you very much. I find myself gravitating towards your room about 1.25 to see if you are lunching at the Club.

I miss that handsome car under the windows. My wife and I don't like the thought that you two have left London, and the Board as a whole is most seriously weakened. I know we have all felt that your counsels were sound, strong and based on real consideration and knowledge. You have kept us all straight over new construction and devised a means of keeping future Boards straight. This and the consolidation of the Fleet Air Arm would alone be sufficient monument to your term of office but there are hundreds of others . . .

Yours ever,

OC (Feeling very deserted)[2]

Fisher always signed his letters to Pound "OC". It stood for Old Champion, his familiar name to a small band of naval friends.

＊

Pound hoisted his flag as Rear Admiral commanding the Battle Cruiser Squadron (usually known as ACQ, the abbreviated signal address) in May 1929. He followed Dreyer, as he had done as ACNS, and the squadron welcomed the change. Dreyer, although he had an impressive presence, could be very intolerant of those whose faces didn't fit. Pound, however, didn't bring a relaxation. Rear Admiral Everett, who was Pound's Flag Lieutenant, remembers him as

a man with terrific energetic vitality and loyalty to the Service, who drove himself to the utmost limits for what he believed was good and expected the same from his juniors. A very friendly man who instilled enthusiasm into all. He enjoyed everything, whether it was on the bridge handling ships, service work, social events or sports. His desire was to build up a family of officers and men bristling with energy and enthusiasm both in Service and non-Service matters.[3]

Since it was his first command afloat as an Admiral, Pound had the opportunity to show his qualities. There was nothing of self-glorification in his performance, as he regarded it just as much as training for himself as he did for his squadron, and he analysed his own actions just as much as those of his captains. He quietly stamped his own personality and standards on his squadron. At sea he was particularly keen on tactical exercises and ship handling. He encouraged his captains to give their junior officers experience in handling their great ships. In harbour he put great emphasis on correct ceremonial. He regularly inspected the squadron from his barge on Sunday forenoon, the Flag Lieutenant taking notes, favourable and critical, which were then signalled to the ships. In his own appearance he was always immaculate.

He was, as usual, able to enjoy his favourite pastimes of shooting and fishing. He had his own clay pigeon trap for practice on board and organized and ran a Staff shoot at Cromarty in 1929 and at Balnagown on the north side of Cromarty Firth in 1930, training sailors as beaters under his coxswain. Admiral Everett comments:

> During the two years he had friends (General Hickman and Commander Wilson) who lived in Helmsdale and invited me and a number of officers to shoot and fish. The routine on one of these visits was generally that we left the ship at Cromarty about 3 or 4:00 am on a Friday, picked up Mrs Pound at Invergordon (who had already had a 30 minute drive) breakfasted with one or other of his hosts, shot all day, followed by fishing in the evening, supper, a game of billiards, and to bed well after midnight, followed by a day's shooting with his other host and another evening fishing. . . . At about 10 or 11:00 pm he departed, arriving on board in the early hours of Sunday morning, yet up in time to go round his squadron in the barge before divisions at 9:30 am. Gibraltar always saw him shooting in the Spanish marshes, infested with leeches![4]

He didn't neglect the officers on board his flagship, taking them on his shooting expeditions and involving them in other sports. Admiral Sir Peter Gretton remembers serving as a midshipman in *Renown* and playing squash with Pound:

> He played a good game from the middle of the court, with his elbows out! He was good to the gunroom, and used to give big breakfasts at sea to which he invited midshipmen. He was not at all aloof or overbearing.

At Funchal I and Dan Duff [later Pound's Flag Lieutenant] found ourselves caught ashore after being at the casino. We saw the admiral's barge at the jetty waiting. Pound waved an arm towards the forepeak, and we clambered on. When we reached the ship he went up the gangway, and we waited half an hour and went up the jacobs ladder and over the boom.[5]

He was able to entertain in return on his flagship some two thousand guests during his command. He liked to meet his officers and their wives socially, and he had a record kept of everyone he served with. This was his 'Shipmate book', and was kept up to date by a newly promoted Paymaster Lieutenant (later Captain) Millett.

One of my jobs was to keep the book up to date. When he carried out an inspection I had to go through the book with the list of officers in the ship being inspected, and let him know what old shipmates he might expect to meet. He could then greet them in the appropriate manner.[6]

He carried on this tradition throughout the remainder of his service, as did other flag officers, such as Mountbatten.

For the whole of his time as ACQ the family lived in a large house, Shiplake, in the village of Buckland Monachorum, about 5 miles to the north of Plymouth. It was a perfect place to bring up children and also allowed Pound to shoot in the evenings in the surrounding countryside, while also being within easy reach of his squadron.

During most of the period of his command the squadron consisted of only three ships, but as second-in-command of the Atlantic Fleet other ships were frequently put under his command. *Hood*, which was usually ACQ's flagship, was undergoing a long refit; instead Pound flew his flag in *Renown*, housed in the quarters which had been used by the Prince of Wales during his world tour. The other two ships were *Repulse*, his old ship, and *Tiger*. His staff included James Hemsted as secretary and Toby Everett as Flag Lieutenant, and later included Fred Edward-Collins as Flag Captain, when he took over from Captain Talbot in December 1930. Edward-Collins had served with Pound before the war as navigator in *Superb*, and twice at the Admiralty, in the Operations Division at the end of the war, and then as Assistant Director of Plans when Pound was ACNS. He was to continue the acquaintance throughout the thirties, both at the Admiralty and in the Mediterranean Fleet. Thus the Admiral's cuddy was full of personal friends and Pound frequently said that his time as ACQ was the happiest of his life. He was in his prime, still in his early fifties, with the finest seagoing command for a Rear Admiral in the Royal Navy, and he enjoyed the personal confidence and friendship of his Commander-in-Chief, Chatfield, the rising star of the Navy.

The Battle Cruiser Squadron had a pretty stereotyped programme. Pound had taken command in May 1929 shortly before the annual Combined Fleet manoeuvres. May and June were spent in Scotland (Invergordon, Scapa Flow and Rosyth) and the rest of the summer was based on the home ports such as Portsmouth, Falmouth and Devonport. In the autumn it was back to Scotland, Invergordon in September, Rosyth in October, before the winter months in home ports again, Portsmouth and Devonport. New Year saw the Combined Fleet exercises based on Gibraltar, working in both the Atlantic and the Mediterranean. Variations in ports visited in the summer months were linked to the "show the flag" mentality operating at the time, and in the summer of 1930 the squadron visited Welsh resorts such as Milford Haven, Bangor and Aberystwyth.

One of the aspects of command that Pound concentrated on was trying to upgrade the performance of his captains. All the captains in his Squadron went on to flag rank, although only Dudley North made it as far as Admiral, and his relationship with Pound ended in great acrimony. An example of the great trouble that he took to help his captains is shown in a letter which shows quite specifically how he set out to help one of them. There can be few admirals who would write quite so frankly and yet so helpfully to a very senior captain with whom he was in daily contact. Happily Captain Chilton was promoted to flag rank in February 1932, becoming Rear Admiral, Yangtze.

My dear [Chilton],

I am going to take a somewhat unusual course in writing to you as I am now going to do, and I would ask you to believe that it is not easy. As you are well aware I shall have to send in a report about you when you leave the squadron and my only excuse for saying what I am about to do is that when I do send in that report I wish it to be entirely favourable. If I had to send in the report at the present time it would be in accordance with the attached paper. From A to B it will be the same whenever I send it in.

71

What I want is to be able to substitute something quite different for B to C. It is only fair to tell you why I should at the present time say that you lack driving power.

When the torpedo was lost off Helmsdale I felt that you discontinued the search before it was reasonably permissible to do so.

When Colonel . . . tried to make out that it was impossible to carry out the scheme [an amphibious exercise] properly I felt that it was you . . . who should have insisted that some way must be found, instead of agreeing with him.

Then again I do feel that if you had been prepared to override the opinions of your officers the targets could have been towed perfectly well the other night.

Coming out of Portland Harbour the other day I am sure that you felt that . . . [the Navigator] was handling the ship in a feeble manner, yet you let him go on doing it.

You may say that all these are small things but you must remember that I only have the opportunity of judging by small things. Having come to the opinion I have I had two courses open to me: (a) To say nothing to you and send in a report . . . in accordance with A to C, or (b) To tell you what I thought.

If I felt that (b) was useless I should not be writing to you, but I do not. I am convinced that you have the driving power but as I have said you subordinate it to the desire not to hurt the feelings of your subordinates. I am writing to you rather than talking to you because frankly I want to avoid an interview I should hate. If you think I have been unfair to you, come and tell me so, otherwise let us agree to forget that I have ever written this letter.

Yours,

Dudley Pound.

The reports A to C were as follows, but the draft from C has not been found.

A.   Captain [Chilton] is an officer of undoubted ability, high sense of duty and great charm of manner. *Repulse* is in good order and the tone is admirable. Captain [Chilton's] loyalty to both his superiors and juniors is beyond question and the honour of the Navy will always be in safe keeping in his hands.

B.   He is a very good organiser but when it comes to carrying out an operation I have on occasions noticed that he is lacking in leadership and driving power, and is content to accept something less than the best. I attribute this defect to a natural disinclination to hurt the feelings of his subordinates.[7]

C.

Three reports were written on Pound as ACQ, by Keyes, Chatfield and Hodges. All of them are worth quoting in full as they emphasize how highly regarded he was in the upper echelons of the Royal Navy. Keyes wrote in March 1930.

> I first came across R/A Pound in 6/17 when I hoisted my flag in *Colossus*, which ship he commanded. I was immensely struck by his high professional ability, his grip of affairs & his unbounded energy. A leader who demands a high standard of service & invariably gets it. He was my principal asst. when I became D.of P. in 10/17, and was subsequently D.O.D. when I was the V/A at Dover; in both capacities his work came under my personal notice. Again, later, he was D. of P. when I was D.C.N.S., in 1922/25, & my c.o.s. in the Medn. (1925/6). I have an unbounded admiration for this offr. As a staff offr., a leader & a sea offr. Possessed of excellent judgement, he is a wise counsellor. I consider that he shd. be, and I believe that he will be, 1 S.L. before his career comes to an end.[8]

Chatfield, writing two months later, made similar points:

> Has commanded the Battle Cruiser Squadron with the highest zeal and ability and has been an exceptional and outstanding R/A. Very loyal, energetic and determined. He is an enthusiast in his work and a remarkable organiser. He works his squadron hard, but is equally keen to look after their welfare. I consider he is marked out for high comd. afloat, both by his tactical skill, his technical knowledge and his personality. He is equally qualified for Admiralty administration.

Hodges, who commanded the Atlantic Fleet after Chatfield, wrote:

> V/A Pound has commanded the B.C.S. with conspicuous success. He is very progressive in all his ideas and in his training and handling of the Squadron is invariably working for the advancement of the Service in all departments. His energy is unbounded and though he

works all those under him harder than most Flag Officers he is popular with everyone and much looked up to. He is certainly marked out for High Command and can be confidently depended upon in any position in which he may be placed for his technical knowledge is as good as his tactical skill and both are of a high order.

Pound was not solely concerned with the affairs of his own squadron. He kept in touch with Roger Keyes once the latter had moved to Portsmouth as Commander-in-Chief there, and he was still involved in planning for him to become First Sea Lord. Thus in October 1929 he wrote from *Renown* that he had been visited by the Naval Secretary to the First Lord, Rear Admiral (later Admiral Sir) George Chetwode, responsible for advising the First Lord on senior appointments. Pound's standing is shown in the way:

Chetwode asked me to make out a plan for filling out all the higher appointments for the next five years or so. This I did after burning the midnight oil last night and posted it off to him today. The gist of it was:

(a)   Field to remain as C-in-C Med. until his 3 years are up in 1931.

(b)   You to relieve Madden in April 1930 and be 1 SL for 2 years, then being relieved by Field.

(c)   Chatfield 1 SL in April 1934 or 1935.

(d)   Chatfield as DCNS in April 1930 until April 1932 and then C-in-C Med until 1934.

I only suggested 2 years for you as 1 SL as I am sure the thing to do is to make it as easy as possible for the Fieldites to give way and this would only give Field one year's unemployment between C-in-C Med and 1 SL. Once you are in the saddle Field may very likely never get there at all. The important thing is to get you into the saddle.[9]

More important were his exchanges with Chatfield, after the latter went to the Mediterranean from the Atlantic in 1930, and with W.W. Fisher who was at the Admiralty as DCNS.

With Chatfield he exchanged views on future naval construction, fleet work and tactics, and even on gunnery matters. With Fisher he was more concerned with the problems of cruisers, which had again become the subject of harsh bargaining with the Americans. Chatfield's letters at first

74

began "My dear Pound", but by 1930 this had changed to "My dear Dudley" and ended "Yours ever, Ernle Chatfield". Among other issues they discussed the need for training in night action, which they both believed the battle fleet must be prepared to fight, unlike Jellicoe's Grand Fleet. The training in night fighting for the Mediterranean Fleet was pushed by Chatfield, Fisher and finally Pound, and culminated in the crushing victory over the Italians at Matapan under Cunningham.

Fisher's last letter to Pound before finishing as DCNS and joining Chatfield as 2 i/c of the Mediterranean Fleet ended:

> I have now turned over to FCD[reyer] and I am collecting my thoughts and foods and chattels for the Mediterranean, cooks, stewards, motor car, house, wine, pickles, whisky and so on, in fact living in a new world. . . . My last days as DCNS were very stimulated by reading accounts of your activities. By George you did wake things up. 12 pence in the shilling, and 24 hours in the Pound with a vengeance. Your stocks are doing all right old chap.[10]

In December 1930 Chatfield wrote to him, in reply to a letter from Pound:

> My hearty congratulations on taking the B.C.'s into Portland in the dark. I am delighted. That sort of thing makes the Navy think and remember and when one thinks of FCD and Weymouth Bay it is even better! It was very bold of you, a proper boldness that gives you a glow of satisfaction and immense self-confidence for the future. An inspiration like that is better training in 10 minutes for the Captains than 10 years in command. I am anxious as to your future and have written to Chetwode about you. I understand you may have to go to Greenwich for a bit until you can relieve Fisher out here, as you must.[11]

These two letters show how highly regarded he was by the two dominant thinkers in the Royal Navy between the wars. The reference to taking the battle cruisers into Portland harbour in the dark shows Pound's confidence in handling large ships. He was to perform a similar feat in 1937 taking the Mediterranean Fleet through the Needles Channel in fog when taking them to Spithead for the Coronation Review.

As an example of the sort of training and exercise that Pound carried out with his squadron it is possible to refer to the memories of Rear Admiral Sir Charles Norris, who in 1929 was Flotilla Navigation Officer in the 5th Destroyer Flotilla. On one occasion Pound and his squadron with the 5th Destroyer Flotilla were ordered to harass and damage the Atlantic Fleet as it emerged from Cromarty Firth, without getting heavily engaged.

Pound's solution was smoke – gallons of it! We embarked hundreds of extra smoke floats. Our force sailed late on the previous night, and before dawn ACQ ordered all of us to fill the Moray Firth with smoke. The wind was perfect for our purpose, and allowed us to leave a narrow corridor clear of smoke along the southern shore, while the rest of the Firth was filled with smoke. This gave the Commander-in-Chief the choice of using the narrow clear channel, but in which he had not the room to deploy his whole force against us before we were able to develop an attack, or go through the smoke. He chose the latter.

Luck was with us from start to finish. We spent more than two hours filling the Firth with smoke, which the wind and atmosphere helped to keep exactly right for our purpose. White CS smoke from all our floats, black smoke belching from the funnels of all our ships, and all mixing together beautifully, made a solid screen over an area of at least eight by fifteen miles. Visibility was down to about 100 yards.

At the right moment ACQ ordered our 5DF to attack with torpedoes. Obviously it was going to be a decidedly dicey run, and we felt that we required all the good luck which he laconically signalled to us just before we entered the smoke screen at high speed. The first thing I saw was the topmasts of the enemy battleships above the smoke. We appeared to be right on top of them, and only just had time to order a turn to fire and retire. Turning the flotilla and the divisional leaders together, the remainder in succession, at high speed in nil visibility, was in itself an exciting manoeuvre, but it worked, and we withdrew highly elated and without any disastrous mishaps. All of this was of course before the advent of radar and R/T.

There can be no doubt that the whole concept of this small episode contained an element of risk, if not danger, but I cite it for two reasons, both of which are important:

(a)   It's just one example of the type of risk which Pound was prepared to take in peacetime in order to provide realistic training for

76

war. There are some historians who have criticized Pound for being, amongst other things, overcautious. Some of these criticisms are justified; others are not. In the highest position as First Sea Lord for the first four years of war, of course he made some errors, some great. Who did not? But to accuse this man of being overcautious is ludicrous, and those who have done so did not know him.

(b)   My second point about this risky form of training is really a corollary to the first. Luckily for the Navy, and the country, the admirals and captains commanding in the main fleets between the wars were largely men who had learned the lessons of the first war. Their doctrine was simple: one can't make an omelette without breaking eggs. Calculated risks in peacetime training had to be taken. This doctrine permeated throughout the fleets. Night fighting, at close range, between completely darkened heavy ships, called for steady nerves, as did the job of light forces, of cruisers and destroyers, to locate, shadow, report and attack. To serve in close proximity to men like Chatfield, WW Fisher, and Pound, and others, was an infectious experience.[12]

His time as ACQ was due to finish in the spring of 1931 when he would complete the normal span of two years' sea command. Towards the end of 1930 he went to see Chetwode to discuss what had been settled for his future. This was that Pound would go as President of the Royal Naval College, Greenwich, and Vice Admiral commanding the War College. For some reason Pound had gained the impression that it might have been thought that he had been pulling strings through Chatfield, and he evidently wrote to Chetwode to remove any such suspicion. Chetwode replied early in January:

My dear Dudley,

Chatfield did mention you to me in a letter he wrote about something else some time ago, but that is the only time that your name has ever been mentioned to me by anybody outside the Admiralty, and you need not have bothered to have told me that you had not been pulling strings, as I know perfectly well that you would never do such a thing. Incidentally there is no need for you to pull any, or for anyone to try to pull them on your behalf, as the Sea Lords know all about you and your future career causes me no uneasiness.

The intention of the present Board in sending you to the War College was twofold. One was to make use of the knowledge that you have acquired as Chief of Staff, and in command of the Battle Cruisers, and the other was that you should be able to relieve Fisher as Commander-in-Chief in the Mediterranean. No Board can pledge its successors, but I have no doubt in my own mind that future Boards will be of the same opinion as the present.[13]

The reference in the letter to relieving Fisher in the Mediterranean was the first mention of plans for Pound's future after his next appointment. Fisher had not yet even taken over as Commander-in-Chief, and in the event Pound was not to relieve him until 1936. However, as is still the case today, such high appointments have to be thought about some years in advance in order that the right man should be in the right place at the right time with the necessary experience. A sudden death, or a major incident, could upset all such plans, and both of these were to do so for Dudley Pound.

Pound had been promoted to Vice Admiral in May 1930 and during the Easter leave period in 1931 he turned over his command to Wilfred Tomkinson. He said farewell to the squadron in Gibraltar after the combined fleet manoeuvres before they dispersed to their home ports. On the night of the traditional fleet pantomime in the disused coal shed on the South Mole Pound was dined out on board his old command *Repulse*, by Captain Dickens, and when the party came on deck after dinner there was a railway train drawn up alongside:

For some days the Commander and the Engineering staff under Jan Orr, the Engineering Commander, had been organising this train. It consisted of a dockyard engine and two coaches, and was christened the "Now and Then Express". A complete railway staff had been collected. Jan Orr as the Guard, a warrant engineer as the porter, and Engineer Lt. Comdr. Matheson, commonly known as "The Ref" was the ticket collector. When Admiral Pound came on deck from the Captain's cabin after dinner this astonishing train was alongside the ship, ready to take the Admiral and his staff to the coal shed, some 100 yards away, with the Admiral's flag hoisted over his compartment. The Admiral had himself commanded *Repulse*, and I think this little piece of buffoonery thoroughly amused him, and happened at the right moment when he was feeling perhaps a little

78

sad at the thought of giving up his fine command. He certainly told the ticket collector that he wanted a return ticket to *Repulse*.[14]

The end of Pound's time as ACQ also coincided with the paying off of the oldest ship in the squadron, *Tiger*, veteran of Dogger Bank and Jutland and destined for the breakers' yard. One of Pound's last acts as ACQ was to transfer his flag temporarily to *Tiger* for her last entry into Plymouth Sound flying her paying off pennant. It was the only time that *Tiger* had flown an admiral's flag. It was a fitting way for Pound to end his first flag appointment afloat.

★

Admiral Chetwode's planning for Pound's future career had been fairly precise, but the whole plot for senior commands in the Royal Navy was irreversibly altered by events in September 1931. Happenings in the Atlantic Fleet had a long fuse and were directly related to the problems of the Labour and National Governments in their wrestlings with the economy. Faced with economic collapse and rising unemployment in the aftermath of the Wall Street Crash the Labour cabinet felt bound by the economic orthodoxies of the time and insisted on balancing their budget. In order to maintain the gold standard and foreign confidence in sterling they were forced to reduce government spending. The May Committee recommended, among other economies, a cut of 20% in unemployment benefit. By the end of June 1931 there was a run on the pound. The Labour government collapsed in August 1931 over the issue of cutting government expenditure by £78 million and Ramsay MacDonald formed the National Government on 24 August. They immediately balanced their budget by imposing a £70 million cut in expenditure, which secured foreign loans. The economies imposed were, of course, not just on unemployment benefit, but also on the salaries of all government employees, which included the armed forces, and were to be cut by 10%. The cuts were not uniform; thus the police escaped with 5%, but teachers suffered 15%.

The new First Lord in the National Government was Austen Chamberlain, who had been Foreign Secretary in the 1924–29 Conservative ministry. He had only been in office for a few days before he was faced with the cuts. He was not helped by the fact that many of his board were on leave. The First Sea Lord, Field, was unwell and on leave throughout early August. The Second Sea Lord, Fuller, and the DCNS, Dreyer, both went on leave early in August, the former returning for the Board meeting on 27 August, and the latter on 3 September. The highly experienced Permanent Secretary, Sir Oswyn Murray, was also on leave from 10 August to 5 September. In other words, only junior members of the Board were present when the government demands for cuts in expenditure and pay were made, as each ministry had to respond to the May Committee. Put simply, Chamberlain was not properly briefed and did not fight hard enough in cabinet for the Royal Navy. He accepted that all those who had enlisted before 1925 and were paid on the 1919 rate of pay would be placed on the lower 1925 rate. This would come into effect on 1 October and was to be announced in the budget on 10 September. It amounted to a 25% pay cut for Able Seamen.

The Admiralty sent signals warning of this to all Commanders-in-Chief on 3 September, but unfortunately that to the Atlantic Fleet went astray. It went to Admiral Sir Michael Hodges on his flagship *Nelson*, but he was on sick leave ashore. Instead, his second-in-command Rear Admiral Wilfred Tomkinson, was in command as Senior Officer Atlantic Fleet (SOAF). Four months earlier this would have been Pound. Tomkinson saw the warning signal on 7 September, but did nothing about it. The paper explaining the government cuts was finally sent out on 10 September, on the same day that the national media received it. However, the Atlantic Fleet was at sea on its way to Invergordon and not due to arrive until 11 September. There was certainly widespread discussion of the potential cuts, and the press had speculated on the possibility of the move to the 1925 rates, so it is reasonable to assume that the lower deck was alive to what was in the wind. Certainly they could work out that an Able Seaman on the 1919 rate was to have his basic rate cut from 4/- to 3/- per day. 25% was not even close to the 10% of the May Committee. If the lower deck could work this out, then senior officers could surely do the same.

The first signs of disturbance in the Atlantic Fleet were on the evening of Sunday 13 September, when there was trouble in the Fleet canteen, and a specific warning was given that there would be trouble when four of the capital ships were due to put to sea for exercises at 8:10am on Tuesday 15 September. There were again disturbances in the canteen on the Monday, and yet still Tomkinson did nothing. His first major mistake was not to use the opportunity of a dinner in his cabin in *Hood* for the admirals and captains present at Invergordon to cancel the programmes of exercises. His second mistake was to signal to the Admiralty that night that it might prove difficult to get the ships to sea. This was the first that the Admiralty knew of trouble. On the Tuesday morning *Nelson*, *Rodney*, *Valiant* and *Hood* all failed to put to sea due to the mutiny of their crews.

Tomkinson sent Hodges' Chief of Staff, Colvin, to the Admiralty that evening to explain what had happened. The Admiralty signalled to him that "Their Lordships entirely approve of the action you have taken".[15] Since Tomkinson had done very little and the Admiralty was not yet entirely sure of what was going on this was quite a message. All that Tuesday Tomkinson did nothing and waited on events. Meanwhile in London both the Board of Admiralty and the cabinet were discussing matters, and the former had directed the Fleet "to proceed to their home ports forthwith to enable personal investigations by Commanders-in-Chief and representatives of the Admiralty with view to necessary alleviations being made".[16] By allowing ships to depart individually Tomkinson managed to get the fleet away from Invergordon by midnight of 16 September.

Meanwhile the Admiralty was trying to decide what to do. The First Lord spoke in the House of Commons on Thursday 17 September saying: "It is in the interests of everyone in the Royal Navy or out of it to forget [the mutiny]. I am not going to look back. I am going to look forward".[17] It was decided by the Board that the three home port Commanders-in-Chief would investigate the whole affair. On 21 September the Prime Minister announced in the House of Commons that the pay cuts would be strictly limited to 10%, except for higher ranking officers and that men on the 1919 rate were to receive their current rate less 10%. Married men under 25, who did not receive a married allowance, were to be assisted by help from the Royal Naval Benevolent Fund. The latter was a charity and to qualify men had to undergo a means test. It shows how badly affected young married men were and why they were likely to have made common cause with the senior men. 21 September was thus a complete climb-down by the government.

The first sign of the expected clean-out of affected people was the appointment of a new Commander-in-Chief Atlantic Fleet, Sir John Kelly, who was, of course, in a position to name his own terms. He claimed, and obtained, a free hand to make a completely fresh start, demanding the discharge of all men involved in fomenting the mutiny before he took over. The First Lord, Chamberlain, retired in November after one of the shortest spells in the Admiralty ever known. The Admiralty had probably briefed him poorly, but even so he must take much of the blame. The Board itself indulged in a prolonged spell of exculpation, led by the DCNS, Dreyer, who was determined to become First Sea Lord. To achieve that he had to be certain of avoiding any blame for the mutiny. Kelly investigated the Atlantic Fleet's morale and discipline, with the aid of two senior captains who were both renowned for their good relations with the lower deck, who later became Admiral Sir John Tovey and Admiral of the Fleet Sir James Somerville. Kelly reported to the Admiralty on 22 October that "having drawn on every available source . . . one thing stands out beyond everything else: that officers and men alike, from the highest to the lowest, appear to attribute the mutiny . . . directly to the actions of the Admiralty in accepting the cuts as first promulgated. . . . Complete confidence in the administrative authority will not be restored so long as the present Board of Admiralty remain in office."[18] The Admiralty, of course, could not agree, and Dreyer spent some twenty-nine pages placing the blame elsewhere, eventually on Tomkinson. Although confirmed in his appointment as ACQ and promoted to Vice Admiral on 16 February 1932, Tomkinson was relieved the next day, first hearing of his relief over the BBC. Fuller, the Second Sea Lord, and, as such, the Chief of Naval Personnel, was allowed to finish his appointment, but offered nothing after it, and Dreyer was not to receive one of the two main fleets, but instead went to become Commander-in-Chief China, thus making sure that he could not become First Sea Lord. It may well be argued that at least the Navy personnel were still employed while three million civilians were unemployed by 1932. However, few critics have been able to defend the performance of the Board of Admiralty.

What meanwhile had Dudley Pound been doing while these seismic events were going on? Although he had turned over the Battle Cruiser Squadron some four months beforehand, it touched him indirectly and the aftermath concerned him directly. Had his reputation not been so high, and had Kelly's investigation revealed a lack of discipline in the Atlantic Fleet, then blame could well have been apportioned to him. As was usual in those times after a command afloat Pound was on what was called "gardening leave". He was living on half-pay, awaiting his next posting, to the Greenwich War College, in a rented house near Lyndhurst in the New Forest, and had spent most of the summer playing tennis, squash and golf. At the time of the mutiny he was away "somewhere inaccessible" fishing, and on return he summoned a neighbour and fellow serving officer, Commander Charles Norris, to bring him up to date with events. Norris was subjected to a searching cross-examination and explained how the admiral in command of the cruiser squadron, Rear Admiral E.A. Astley-Rushton, had gone to London to report to the Admiralty, [In fact Tomkinson had sent Hodges' Chief of Staff, Rear Admiral Colvin.] He added the comment that this showed that the situation in that squadron was particularly bad. "On the contrary," replied Pound, "no admiral would leave his squadron if the situation was bad. It indicates that the situation there is comparatively good."[19] Indeed it is possible to see a trait emerging here, which was to be seen later. Pound considered inaction to be the only really serious crime: an honest mistake was perfectly acceptable; to do nothing and await events was always wrong.

The Admiralty having decided that Fuller should see out his time as Second Sea Lord had to decide with whom to replace him, and the choice fell on Pound. That would not be until August of 1932 and there was little point in his taking over at the Greenwich War College for so short a time. In the meantime he was sent as British Representative on the League of Nations Permanent Advisory Commission on Disarmament in Geneva, a singularly unrewarding spell for somebody of his nature, but it certainly gave him a further insight into high level politics and the utter hopelessness of attempting disarmament in the face of German revanchism.

Eventually he came back to London in August 1932 and became Second Sea Lord in a reconstructed and greatly more efficient Board of Admiralty. The new First Lord was Sir Bolton Eyres-Monsell, a former naval officer, who listened to advice and was respected by both politicians and sailors. Although Field continued as First Sea Lord until January 1933, there was no dispute as to who was to be his successor. Chatfield, who had commanded both major fleets and was widely respected, succeeded him. His principal aim in office was to restore the morale of the Royal Navy after Invergordon, and also to repair some of the major material problems which it faced in an increasingly aggressive world. The former of these problems was principally in the hands of Pound, but Chatfield took a major hand as well. To give an example, it had always been the policy of the Board of Admiralty to wear frock coats and top hats on paying official visits. This inevitably led to a lessening of understanding between fleets and Board. Chatfield insisted that the Board would wear uniform whenever they paid official visits.

Many of the welfare reforms which were carried out over the next three years were pushed through by Pound and there was a complete overhaul of the manning procedures at the home ports. He was rarely in his office if he could help it and took the opportunity to visit naval shore establishments, depots and training schools all over the country. At almost all of them he spoke, and what he said was frequently reported in both local and national press. There were official Board visits in 1934 to the Plymouth Command and also to the Combined Fleet exercises in Gibraltar, at both of which Pound much enjoyed meeting old friends, and refreshing his mind with contact with seagoing officers. Betty frequently accompanied him, and launched the destroyer *Fame* at Barrow-on-Furness. They played a relatively full part in the hectic social life of London. For instance the court circular of 9 March 1934 notes that Vice Admiral and Lady Pound had dined with the Prince of Wales. Later that year he dined at the Japanese embassy as the guest of a visiting Japanese admiral. Pound had, of course, been awarded a Japanese decoration, the Order of the Rising Sun, after the First World War. He had an unusual experience in 1935 when during a routine visit to his dentist a tooth fell out and became lodged in his lung, and could not be recovered. The episode was reported in much of the press, and after 48 hours in hospital Pound was released back to his duties. The tooth apparently remained in the lung.

The family lived at Chiselhurst, which was within easy commuting distance of the Admiralty. The house was not very large, but had a small garden and a tennis court. Pound, of course, was not there very much except at weekends. During the week he left the house at 7:15 am and did not return before 7:00 pm, usually working after dinner until well after midnight.

One matter which came across his desk was the matter of his friend and successor as ACQ, Vice Admiral Tomkinson. Like Pound, Tomkinson was a protégé of Keyes. Like Keyes, he did not take his disappointment lying down, although unlike Keyes he did not make a public fuss. Tomkinson and Pound were old friends and had spent much time shooting and fishing together. Tomkinson thus felt that he had a "friend at court" who would be able to secure him a personal hearing and a

84

possible restoration of his position. On 2 November 1932 Tomkinson wrote to Pound in his own hand with a record of all that had happened. This was evidently at Pound's own request after they had discussed the situation face to face, probably when they met shooting. Pound's first loyalty was to the Royal Navy, naturally, and to the Board, of which he was now the second senior serving member. He did not disagree with the decision of the Board to relieve Tomkinson, although he may well have disapproved of the way that it had been done, and he almost certainly disagreed with the way in which the Board had congratulated Tomkinson and then removed him from command six months later, telling him that he had not acted in a proper manner. He never gave Tomkinson any encouragement to think that he would support his case, or that he considered Tomkinson's handling of the mutiny had been faultless. A lesser man could well have dissembled and said that he understood Tomkinson's position, assured him of his support and then passed the whole question up the ladder to the First Sea Lord, knowing that the Board was unlikely to change its mind. Pound did not follow that course. He obviously believed that Tomkinson had erred in not taking immediate action. He appears to have felt that Tomkinson should have taken firm disciplinary action; however, that could have led to disaster in the circumstances of September 1931. Whatever, he refused to support Tomkinson.

Although Tomkinson suffered in silence, he did write to Keyes in fairly vitriolic terms about the whole affair. He appeared to believe, according to his letter, that his personal friendship with Pound should override loyalty to the Royal Navy. Conversely, Pound held, as he had done since he joined the Royal Navy, and was to do until his death, that the Service came first, at whatever cost to friendship. That friendship did die, only to be rekindled on Pound's deathbed when Tomkinson wrote to him to offer his condolences for his enforced retirement and hoping that they could again go shooting together. The parallels with the Dudley North affair in 1940 are striking. In both Pound was involved in the removal of a senior admiral, not for taking the wrong decision, but for, in his view, taking no action at all.[20]

★

Towards the end of his time as Second Sea Lord Pound's thoughts must have turned towards his future. Chetwode had told him in January 1931 that the plan was for him to succeed Fisher in the Mediterranean. Because of Invergordon things had changed, but he could reasonably expect to take over either that fleet or the Home Fleet, as the Atlantic Fleet had been renamed. Field had written a report on Pound before he retired in which he had said, "A most able 2 SL. An offr. of v. strong personality. Recomd. for comd. of one of the principal Fleets in due course".[21] Fisher had been in the Mediterranean since 1932 and was therefore due to be relieved before a spell as Commander-in-Chief of one of the home ports, and then, presumably, taking over as First Sea Lord from Chatfield in 1938, when the latter was finally due to retire. Boyle was in command of the Home Fleet, having taken over from Joe Kelly in 1933. Roger Backhouse was likely to take over that command, having been second-in-command to Fisher since 1932. Thus it was not altogether surprising when the First Lord's formal letter arrived on 28 November 1934 offering Pound the Mediterranean Fleet.

The appointment was publicly announced on 1 April 1935 and on 30 September Pound handed over to Vice Admiral Sir Martin Dunbar-Nasmith his office at the corner of the Admiralty building overlooking the Mall and St James's Park. He must have believed that he had seen the last of the Admiralty and was never to return there. Instead he turned his eyes towards the Mediterranean and the finest command that the Royal Navy had to offer.

7

MEDITERRANEAN FLEET COMMAND

Before Pound arrived in the Mediterranean another crisis had arisen which, yet again, caused a change in his projected career. The Mediterranean Fleet was the largest Royal Naval command, but it is sometimes difficult to decide exactly what its role was in the 1930s. Throughout the decade its obvious, and eventual, enemy, Italy, was considered to be a potential ally by the Foreign Office. This desire to have Italy on our side had two natural causes. Firstly, Italy had fought on the Allied side in the First World War, despite an initial wobble, and, secondly, she would be a useful balance against Nazi Germany, who by 1935 was openly rearming. The desire for Italian friendship reached a culmination with the Stresa Agreement of April 1935. By this Britain, France and Italy agreed to resist Hitler's renunciation of the Treaties of Versailles and Locarno, and to work together against Germany. However, this attempt at international cooperation was almost immediately torpedoed by the Anglo-German Naval Agreement of June 1935, which allowed Germany to have a navy 35% the size of the Royal Navy. The Baldwin government probably agreed to this on the grounds that they finally understood the Admiralty problem of being called to face three major potential enemies. The nightmare that the Royal Navy faced throughout the 1930s was war in Europe against both Germany and Italy, and, at the same time, war in the Far East against Japan. Somehow this apocalyptic vision had to be dispersed while Britain was as weak as she was in the early 1930s. Japan simply could not be appeased, and therefore some sort of accommodation had to be reached with Germany, while doing almost anything not to provoke Italy into war.

When Italy finally did invade Abyssinia on 3 October 1935 it came as no real surprise. The Italian build-up had been going on for some time, and this open defiance of the League of Nations had been expected. There was an expectation, too, that Mussolini could well try a preemptive strike against the Mediterranean Fleet in Malta, which was within easy reach of the Italian airfields. As a precautionary measure the Fleet was ordered to Alexandria at the end of August and was reinforced. At the same time the Home Fleet was ordered to Gibraltar to guard the Western basin of the Mediterranean. British policy had to take account of four constraints. Firstly, if Britain became involved in a war, the Japanese would almost certainly move against her, necessitating the despatch of a battle fleet to the Far East. Secondly, somewhat improbably, Italy was still seen as a potential ally against Germany. Thirdly, the Royal Navy could ill afford the possible losses a war against Italy would probably incur, even if the overall result was not in doubt, particularly when French support was not totally certain. Most importantly, was Abyssinia really an issue over which to go to war? Was it not, as Chamberlain was so memorably to say a little later about Czechoslovakia, "a faraway country of whom we know little"? All of these considerations pushed the government towards supporting the League's economic sanctions, but not to include the crucial oil within those sanctions, as this would probably tip Italy over the brink into war. It also pushed them towards the infamous Hoare-Laval Pact. With the advantage of some 50 years' hindsight, it is easy to say this was a crucial turning point on the road to war.

The crisis was at its height when Pound arrived in the Mediterranean to relieve Fisher in October 1935. This was not the moment for change in such a crucial post, particularly for an admiral who had been in command for three years. Pound accepted this and suggested that he should serve as Fisher's chief of staff until the crisis had passed and he could take over. This suggestion was accepted and, although a full Admiral (he had been promoted on 16 October 1935) and Commander-in-Chief designate, he served loyally as chief of staff until March 1936 when he hoisted his own flag. The arrangement worked well for two very good reasons. Firstly, the Admirals were close and old friends. Secondly, they were determined to make it work. One of the first things Pound did was to say to the staff, "Forget my rank. Just treat me as a normal chief of staff, and regard me as accessible at any time, day or night." Not surprisingly, it worked. Pound after all, had been chief of staff in the Mediterranean before and he was a born staff officer. The Fleet Gunnery Officer, Commander (later Rear Admiral) D.M. Lees, having said how their initial misgivings were quickly overcome, went on:

After a very short period it was a real joy to work under him. When one took some problem to his predecessor there would be humming and hawing, and usually no decision would be reached; not so with DP, who was quick as lightning to hoist in the subject under consideration. Either he would make a decision himself, or he would say, "I think we ought to consult the C-in-C about this." With that he would get up from his desk and stump along to WW's cabin, always taking one with him. WW was invariably courteous and would say, "Come in Dudley. What can I do for you?" To which DP would reply, "I've brought . . . along, Sir, as he wants a decision about so and so." In front of us he always called the Commander-in-Chief "Sir", although they were of equal rank. Indeed, those were happy times for the staff.[1]

Charles Norris, waiting to take over the command of the Commander-in-Chief's despatch vessel, served as an extra staff officer, having gone out with Pound, and he recalled playing tennis with Pound in Malta when Fisher arrived to watch. Pound stopped the game until the Commander-in-Chief was comfortably settled in a chair and then carried on, all the while calling his oldest friend "Sir". Norris was impressed with the way Pound carried out what could so easily have been a difficult role.[2] Fisher wrote to the Admiralty to praise Pound's performance:

I believe it to be without precedent that an officer of his rank should have volunteered to serve as Chief of Staff. His work for me, and with me, was so wholehearted and self-effacing that I find it impossible to express the sense of obligation and gratitude that I shall feel for all time.[3]

Pound had been encouraged to write to Chatfield once he was in the Mediterranean, and indeed when he actually became Commander-in-Chief he wrote almost every month in his own hand. However, he only wrote twice while serving as chief of staff as he felt that it would be wrong to write, as it were, behind Fisher's back. As he said on 31 March, in his first letter to Chatfield as Commander-in-Chief,

You may have wondered why I have only written you one letter since I left the Admiralty. [He had in fact written two – 20 October and 22 February.] The reason, and one I think you will appreciate, is that I soon made up my mind that it was impossible for a chief of staff to write about anything of interest without poaching on the preserve of

89

his Commander-in-Chief. When I came out WW very kindly said, "We'll run this show together like two Commanders-in-Chief." But I don't think he imagined it was possible any more than I did. It was just I think to ease what he in his kindness thought might be a difficult position for me, which it never was. I enjoyed every minute of the time, and I hope you have not thought I was "champing at the bit" to take over, because I would certainly not have recommended it any sooner had I been in your place.[4]

His first letter (20 October) told of the effect of the death of Fisher's son, Neville, on the Commander-in-Chief: "WW was of course absolutely knocked out, but hid it in a marvellous way. We kept him hard at work which was about all we could do to help."[5] The other was simply to do with who should be his Flag Captain in *Warspite* when she came out as Flagship to the Mediterranean Fleet after her extensive refit. His choice was Victor Crutchley, who had won a VC with Keyes at Zeebrugge.

*

Pound hoisted his flag as Commander-in-Chief on 20 March 1936. The staff was large, much larger than it had been when he had been Chief of Staff to Roger Keyes in the 1920s, twenty-three as opposed to fourteen. At its head was his own chief of staff, Rear Admiral Edward-Collins. Fred Edward-Collins was a large bluff Cornishman who had, as we have seen, hitched his wagon to that of Pound. He had been his flag captain in the battle cruisers and his naval assistant as Second Sea Lord. Pound thus knew him well and trusted him. However, he was not a great chief of staff for the simple reason that Pound was happy to immerse himself in the details that should have been the duty of the chief of staff. The Captain of the Fleet was Captain R.J.R. Scott, who was responsible for much of the administration of the fleet. The Flag Lieutenant was Dan Duff, later to marry Barbara Pound. Along with the faithful Hemsted these formed the Admiral's cuddy in his flagship. The rest of the staff was based on Malta, but a significant number of them came to sea whenever the flagship left Valletta harbour. The leading light was the Staff Officer Operations (SOO) who arrived in April 1936, Commander Guy (later Admiral Sir Guy) Grantham. There were others who also attracted attention later, such as the Assistant to Grantham, Commander John

90

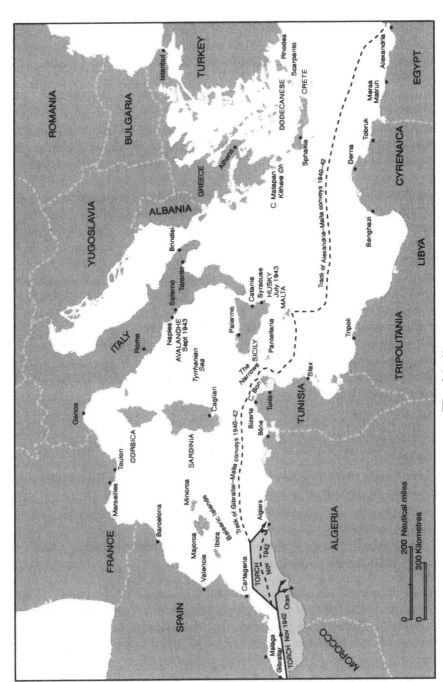

The Mediterranean

Litchfield-Speer. The second-in-command was Vice Admiral Charles Forbes, and the Rear Admiral Destroyers RA(D) was the redoubtable James Somerville.

Almost immediately Pound took the fleet to sea for exercises. The Mediterranean Fleet remained heavily reinforced, particularly with cruisers and destroyers from the Home Fleet, as well as from the China, East Indies and South America squadrons, and from the Australian and New Zealand navies. It actually consisted in March 1935 of three battle-ships, one battle cruiser, one aircraft carrier, sixteen cruisers, five flotillas of destroyers and over 100 auxiliaries. His aim in this first exercise was to test getting to sea quickly and the fleet cruising formation, as well as several specific tactical problems. He wanted to see if the new anti-aircraft cruisers, *Coventry* and *Curlew*, could protect the aircraft carrier *Glorious* against air attack when she was flying on and off, as well as some special fighting instructions to deal with encounters with the Italian fleet in the eastern Mediterranean. He also needed to try out a new signal book and experiment with the cruiser *Ajax* as a fleet flagship. The latter two projects were successful, and in the exercises he used *Exeter* as seven Italian eight inch gunned cruisers, and *Arethusa* as six six-inch gunned cruisers, as well as three destroyers each representing an Italian destroyer flotilla. He then tried to bring this force to action in a chase. As he reported to Chatfield in a letter on 31 March:

> This brought home a point I had realised all along that the D class cruisers were out of place in the Central Mediterranean Force because
>
> (a) Owing to their low endurance they would hardly ever be available in the central area.
>
> (b) If they were present they would never get into action with their low speed.
>
>   This was the only point during my time as Chief of Staff that WW and I held contrary opinions.[6]

Here we can see Pound already planning for war against the Italians. The weapon was being forged with which Cunningham would win the Battle of Matapan. The second part of the exercise showed a similar foresight. Pound, with his battlefleet, was trying to prevent a concentration of his opponent's two squadrons and tried to shadow them by night before engaging them with indirect illumination. *Glorious* shadowed *Valiant* by night with her aircraft, a first for the Fleet Air Arm, Pound claimed.

Interspersed with these sort of exercises Pound had plenty of official visits and duties. In May he had to escort Emperor Haile Selassie to exile in Haifa. He then had to attend the funeral of King Fuad of Egypt before greeting the new king, Farouk, on his arrival from England on 6 May. On 17 June Farouk went to sea with Pound to see the fleet exercising. Pound also took delivery of a new admiral's barge. Instead of the stately brass-funnelled steam barge of WW, Pound's barge was a three-engined speedboat built by British Power Boats of Southampton, and was capable of 32 knots. The young king was highly impressed.

In July Pound took the fleet back to Malta and it was from then that the size of the fleet was reduced to normal. It was reviewed by King Farouk on departure and the Malta newspapers all talked of the return of the Commander-in-Chief with his fleet to their home.

> There is a saying in the island that, if you want to know whether there is trouble in the Mediterranean, look at Admiralty House, which, like the Temple of Janus, is closed and shuttered when the gods of war call the fighting forces away. Now its doors have been flung open once again, and one would be tempted to believe that England is no longer worried by the situation in the Middle Sea.[7]

However, this was tempting providence and, as the fleet arrived at Malta, Pound had to send his 1st Cruiser Squadron under Rear Admiral Max Horton to Spain as the first rumblings of the Spanish Civil War were heard. Within a week Pound was off to the western Mediterranean in the fastest flagship available, *Galatea*, normally the flagship of his RA(D), while his own flagship, *Queen Elizabeth*, followed as fast as she could. By 4 August 1936 Pound had thirty-seven warships in Spanish waters ready to transport refugees from the civil war. This heavy commitment for the fleet was to continue until the eve of Pound's departure nearly three years later.

His command was the principal fleet in the Royal Navy; it also involved a diplomatic role, calling for political judgement. There were frequent goodwill visits to countries surrounding the Mediterranean, which were much sought after by HM ambassadors. Pound was engaged in crises at each end of the Mediterranean during his time, in both Spain and Palestine. His shore headquarters was the historic Castile, the old palace of the Knights of St John, which overlooked the Grand Harbour. Pound would often ascend the signal tower with his flag lieutenant and watch the arrival of his ships, assessing with his critical eye the performance of his captains as they manoeuvred their great ships in the narrow confines below. The main staff office, below, was cool, airy and congenial to work in.

Pound lived in some style in Admiralty House, where he replaced the normal Royal Marine guards with two blue-jacketed sailors. He was determined that no visitor should be in any doubt as to who lived there. He had a small office there where he worked happily, but his principal office was at the Castile. He was not an early riser, except for his shooting, and after breakfast with the family would appear in the office at around 9:00. In the evenings after dinner, like Churchill, he usually retired to his office to work until the early hours, although, unlike Churchill, he did not summon his staff officers in the middle of the night. Frequently he would go for a drive before going to bed, finding that this helped him clear his brain and relax. He was a notoriously fast driver in Malta, telling his own driver "not to drive like me". When the Italian fleet paid a courtesy visit in 1938 he took their admiral for a drive. The Italian returned in deep shock, Pound commenting afterwards, "Always useful to get the measure of one's enemies".

Afloat, Pound had three flagships, all of the same class, *Queen Elizabeth*, *Barham* and *Warspite*, which all had palatial flag quarters. Right aft there was a large day cabin with access to a stern walk. Forward of this was a dining room, which also extended the whole width of the ship, and then a small sleeping cabin and a steward's pantry. When at sea the vibration right aft was so severe that Pound usually occupied a small sea cabin in the bridge structure. He also had at his disposal his despatch vessel, the sloop *Aberdeen*, commanded by Commander, later Vice Admiral Sir, Charles Norris. Her principal roles were twofold. Firstly, she would precede any foreign visit and make all arrangements in advance. Secondly, she transported the Pound family and their guests. These ranged from the First Lord, Sir Samuel Hoare, and later Duff Cooper, to Noel Coward and Sir John Reith.

The Pounds' social life was hectic when he was in Malta. There were social events almost every evening, and Pound regarded them as part of his job. His own parties in Admiralty House were designed to be enjoyed rather than to impress. He enjoyed dancing enormously, preferably with a young beauty, but he always did his duty with his guests. The sight of him piloting the wife of the governor round the dance floor was said to be an awe-inspiring spectacle. Pound also took every opportunity to shoot, and the cruises of the Mediterranean Fleet in the Aegean were frequently planned around the famed Shooting Guide written when chief of staff to Keyes. In all of this social life Betty played her full part. The family was reunited in Malta, as George was serving in the fleet in the destroyer *Cossack*, and was married in Malta in 1939, while Martin, having survived four years at Pangbourne Nautical College, had been commissioned into the Royal Marines in *Sussex*, part of the 1st Cruiser Squadron. Barbara was still young enough to be living with her parents at Admiralty House.

Pound suffered a severe loss when his secretary James Hemsted, who had been with him since his time as ACNS in 1926, collapsed and died on the tennis court at Alexandria in May 1936. Paymaster Captain Cull replaced him until April 1939, but Pound did not find an adequate replacement until he arrived at the Admiralty in July 1939 and met up with Ronald Brockman. Equally tragic were, firstly, the death of his second Captain of the Fleet, Charles Hotham, who died in Malta in 1939, and, secondly, the invaliding out of the service of Geoffrey Blake. The latter was particularly close to Pound, who had been pleased to secure him as second-in-command and Vice Admiral Battle Cruiser Squadron in January 1937. In June of that year Blake suffered a stroke while pulling a skiff round the Grand Harbour in Malta. Pound was upset to lose him and asked for a purely temporary replacement, saying in a letter to Chatfield "[Blake] needs more sea experience before becoming a commander-in-chief, for which he is so eminently suited".[8] Tragically that accident coincided with the death of W.W. Fisher, Pound's oldest naval friend. He continued his letter to Chatfield:

It is really too sad about WW. As I told you, he looked desperately ill the night he dined with me, but I never for a moment imagined he was so bad as he must have been. It was madness his taking the salute on the King's birthday, but I suppose no one could control him.

Anyway, a great personality passes from the Service, and one who has added to its prestige in so many ways. Poor Lady Fisher, two tragedies in so short a time, and she worshipped William so.

Blake was succeeded by the redoubtable Andrew Cunningham as second-in-command, and he and Pound established an easy relationship, which

95

was to continue unabated until Pound's death and Cunningham's succession as First Sea Lord. The only thing harder than having Cunningham as a superior officer was having him as an inferior one, but in spite of their differing styles they got on famously. As one of Cunningham's biographers says:

> Their first private exchange set the tone for all that was to follow. Pound made it clear that he considered that a second-in-command had a duty to tell his chief what he thought, particularly if he disagreed with a decision or felt anxiety about any shortcoming in the fleet. That was exactly Cunningham's view of the matter.[9]

Other members of Pound's team of admirals were Max Horton, commanding the 1st Cruiser Squadron, another eminently forceful and able character, and James Somerville as the RA(D). The latter was a particular favourite of Pound's, who treated his often outrageous signals in rather the same way that a schoolmaster tolerates a naughty but favourite schoolboy whom everybody loves. For example, on a visit to Morocco he was offered the use of the royal concubines, which he refused "on the grounds of marital fidelity and the consequences for his promotion".[10] There was also Charles Forbes, Blake's predecessor as second-in-command, and Jack Tovey, who succeeded Somerville as RA(D). All four of these were future Admirals of the Fleet. Among his Captains were John Godfrey, of *Repulse*, later to be Director of Naval Intelligence, Philip Vian of the *Arethusa* and George Creasy commanding the 1st Destroyer Flotilla; the latter two also became Admirals of the Fleet. The Mediterranean Fleet thus contained much of the cream of the pre-war Royal Navy. Pound worked well with his fleet and, although he did not always have complete agreement over his methods, his obsession with detail, and the length of his written orders for example, there was almost universal admiration for his abilities and his integrity. Certainly, when the Second World War came the Mediterranean Fleet that Pound had handed over to Cunningham had never been better trained for war. It was a first-class fighting machine, highly trained for night action and ready for war in all respects, except possibly anti-aircraft work, in which it was an accurate reflection of the whole Royal Navy.

★

96

As mentioned earlier, Pound had despatched Horton's 1st Cruiser Squadron to Spain as the Fleet was returning to Malta, in order to protect both British residents and commercial interests. The Home Fleet looked after the northern coast and the Mediterranean Fleet the southern coast of Spain, based on Gibraltar. By 22 June there were fifteen ships at Spanish ports and Pound obviously had to take personal command. On his rapid dash from Malta to Gibraltar on board *Galatea* he issued instructions that attacks by aircraft were to be resisted by force, and by surface ships as well, if they were persisted in after remonstrance had been made. The Admiralty refused to sanction Pound's further recommendations that fire from shore batteries should be returned. One major problem facing him was the shipment of arms from Russia to the Republicans through Barcelona. One estimate was that out of 164 ships sailing from Black Sea ports to Barcelona thirty-nine were British, thirty-four Soviet and seventy-one Spanish, but these figures are of German origin and are not totally reliable.[11] However, it was Franco's stated intention to blockade Barcelona and stop this trade. Pound was determined to allow it to continue.

He delegated authority to whichever admiral was on duty in the western Mediterranean, giving clear instructions on British policy and encouraging them to act on their own initiative. Periodically he would visit the Spanish coast and meet the British diplomats and consular officials. Usually this took the form of them being brought out to his flagship and discussing matters as they steamed to the next port. The diplomat would then be returned to his own port by destroyer as the next one met Pound. In this way little time was wasted. He was determined that the Mediterranean Fleet was not to forget its principal purpose, and training went on, notably on the big ships; it was the cruisers and destroyers that bore the brunt of the work in Spanish waters. As a result Pound would take, for example, his Battle Squadron to sea with a cruiser squadron and two destroyer flotillas, and exercise them all the while moving from Malta to Gibraltar. The cruisers and destroyers would then exchange, he would carry out investigations and enquiries, and then exercise all the way back to Malta.

By early 1937 the situation was deteriorating. British ships were bombed in February and mined in May. In August the destroyer *Havock* was attacked by torpedoes. Since she did not immediately retaliate Somerville ordered her to "pursue the hunt with the utmost energy, and try to make up for your astounding lack of initiative".[12] Signals flew between *Havock*, RA(D), Commander-in-Chief Mediterranean Fleet and the Admiralty. It was in London that cold feet developed, almost certainly along Whitehall from the Admiralty, and Pound was ordered to call off the attack, in case an "innocent" submarine was attacked. The Admiralty intervention in an operation which was being controlled by the Commander-in-Chief and conducted on the spot by a flag officer in accordance with approved policy was not a good precedent, though Pound loyally kept his feelings to himself. Somerville's, it was reported, were unprintable. Here we can see Pound suffering the same fate as he was to inflict on others when he became First Sea Lord.

Early in September, after a British merchantman was torpedoed, Pound sent an appreciation to the Admiralty,[13] and it was after this that the Nyon Conference was held. This conference, completed in under a week, aimed at outlawing the submarine piracy with which Pound was contending, and it divided the Mediterranean into areas of responsibility, he being responsible for the lion's share from Gibraltar to Majorca in the western basin, as well as the Malta Channel and the northern Aegean. At the time of the conference Pound was visiting Greece in *Barham*, where he as usual indulged his passion for shooting. His abrupt departure, 48 hours earlier than anticipated, was commented on in the press, and the reason given was that he wished to hold the Fleet regatta at Mudros Bay before greater disruption scattered the fleet. Once that was completed *Barham* sailed for the western Mediterranean at 20 knots.

In order to coordinate the Nyon patrols Pound called at Oran to discuss matters with the French Commander-in-Chief, Admiral Esteva. Among other matters they arranged for a British flying boat squadron to be based at Arzeu, and a British depot ship for destroyers to be at Oran to act as a coordinating base with the French. At the same time Pound was insisting to the Admiralty upon full operational control of the flying boats.[14] The Nyon patrols were operational within a week of the end of the conference, an excellent example of political achievement being carried through by the people on the spot. What was notable was that the French had no plans themselves. Pound and his staff had put the whole organization on paper while on passage from Mudros to Oran, heavy vibration in the stern of *Barham* notwithstanding.

Six weeks later, on 30 October 1937 there was a tripartite meeting at Bizerta, when Pound and Esteva were joined by the Italian Admiral Bernotti, in order to incorporate Italian patrols into the Nyon system.

Pound much enjoyed the embarrassment of the Italians, who were discussing operations against submarines, which everybody round the table knew were Italian.

The Nyon patrols produced a large workload for the Mediterranean Fleet in terms of ships committed. For example, in October 1937 this consisted of two battleships, two battlecruisers, several cruisers, over thirty destroyers, two repair ships, a depot ship, a hospital ship, and a number of fleet auxiliaries, all of whom were away from their base at Malta. For the staff too it was hectic and Pound's secretary recorded that 100,000 sheets of A4 were expended by the Commander-in-Chief's office in a single month in 1937 and signal traffic and ciphering reached a peak in September 1937 with 47,000 cipher groups sent. However, the Nyon patrols were successful, and while the patrols were retained submarine attacks fell away.

By the spring of 1939 the Spanish civil war was over and the last Nyon patrol was withdrawn on 19 April. The Royal Navy had enhanced its international reputation for humanitarian aid. Pound and his flag officers and captains by their temperate actions under enormous provocation upheld all the best traditions of the Royal Navy. Pound was superb not only in influencing government policy, but also in carrying it out. The trust which the Royal Navy's firmness and impartiality won from the Spanish may well have had a bearing upon Franco's decision not to enter the Second World War on the Axis side.

★

In May 1937 the Mediterranean Fleet, except for those ships left behind in Spanish waters, returned to Britain for the Coronation Review. Pound led the fleet in *Queen Elizabeth*, which was due to start a complete refit afterwards, and took the fleet through the difficult Needles Channel to Spithead in fog. On the morning of the review Pound and Roger Backhouse, the Commanders-in-Chief of the Mediterranean and Home Fleets were awarded the GCVO on board the royal yacht *Victoria And Albert*, commanded by a man later to be a *bête noire*, Vice Admiral Sir Dudley North. This visit was to be the last occasion on which Pound was to meet his old friend W.W. Fisher, who as Commander-in-Chief Portsmouth had carried most of the load of organizing the Review. He was to die on 24 June.

Sadly the replacement for *Queen Elizabeth* as flagship by *Warspite* could not take place as the latter was not yet ready. Instead, Pound returned to the Mediterranean on board *Barham*. He was not happy with *Warspite*'s performance. She had been completely rebuilt at the cost of well over £2 million, but her sailing had been twice delayed by defects found during her trials. These were finally held in July when damage was done to the couplings linking turbines and gearing. These faults were not remedied until January 1938. Meanwhile there were also problems with her crew, who came from Chatham, even though the refit was being completed at Portsmouth. Discontent with leave arrangements resulted in an 'incident', as a result of which three ratings were dismissed, nine others were drafted to other ships and three officers were relieved. Sadly, one of these, the commander, was D.H. Everett who had been Pound's flag lieutenant when he had been ACQ. (He went on to distinguish himself in *Ajax* at the battle of the River Plate, and to retire as a Rear Admiral after brilliant war service.)

Pound was, not surprisingly, upset by the non-arrival of his flagship, writing to Chatfield frequently on the issue. Thus, on 7 August 1937:

> Her delay is a great blow and has upset many arrangements, but as long as she is really right when she comes out that is a small matter ... I am more perturbed by the reports of unrest in *Warspite* getting into the papers, as, though it is denied in the next paragraph, it doesn't do the Service any good. It is a rotten start for a ship, and I do not think Crutchley is quite happy about some of the men, but he and Everett will know how to deal with them.[15]

The next month he returned to the matter, writing on 28 September 1937,

> *Warspite* gives one many shocks, and their insubordination will I am afraid have undone a great deal of the good work of the fleet's during the last eighteen months in pulling the Navy back into its proper place in the esteem of the country.
>
> I wish it had been possible to give as the reason for relieving three officers that they had not acted with sufficient firmness, rather than that they had mishandled the situation, as the latter can be interpreted in two ways. Her continual breakdowns are annoying at the moment as I have not room for all the staff in *Barham*, and *Resource* has to follow me around with the remainder.

100

If *Warspite* is not here in time to do her working up before *Barham* has to go home about the first week in December the situation will become more than annoying as I do not think there should be less than two efficient battleships on the station, with the Mediterranean situation as it is.[16]

Warspite finally arrived in Malta on 14 January 1938 and, once she had finished her working-up firings and exercises, Pound went on board his new flagship on 6 February. As was customary the Commander-in-Chief addressed the crew, but instead of a welcome they were given what can only be called "a dressing down".[17] There are two descriptions of this. The first, from Pound, is in a letter to Chatfield on 7 February in which he says:

I witnessed a march past of *Warspite*'s ship's company yesterday, and as I could not just slip into a fleet flagship with a record like *Warspite*'s as if nothing had happened, I told them very plainly what we all felt out here that whilst we were all struggling and making great headway by our work on the coast of Spain to put the navy back where it was before the mutiny of 1931, they had let the side down and retarded the progress we had made. That closes the incident, and they start fair. Naturally I did not go into any details of the incident, but dealt with it on the lines of the effect it had had. All the signs in the short time that they have been out here are that they will do well.[18]

One of his staff officers saw it differently, and recorded the incident later:

When *Warspite* eventually arrived in Malta, looking a picture as she made her entrance into Grand Harbour, Pound repaired on board. Instead of welcoming, as had been expected, his new flagship to his command, he addressed the ship's company in terms which reduced her gallant Captain, Victor Crutchley, VC, almost to tears. They had come, Pound told them, with a bad name and he would not stand for indiscipline in his fleet, and he even mentioned Invergordon. It was an unhappy speech that misjudged the fine spirit of both officers and men, who were proud of their great ship and had spared no effort to make her worthy of wearing his flag and to win his approbation on arrival.[19]

Whatever the truth of the episode, and one is inclined to the second, Pound soon came to appreciate that his remarks had been unjustified and

101

he probably regretted his speech, for *Warspite* proved to be a smart and happy ship. Nor were there any lasting hard feelings as Pound soon became respected on the mess decks. By August *Warspite* had really earned her acceptance by a masterly display of main armament and anti-aircraft firings, which destroyed both high-speed battle-practice targets and the towed drone. Pound was delighted by this, and he went to the lectures on the results given to the ship's company.[20]

The gunnery officer of *Warspite* was Commander Roskill, later the distinguished Official Historian of the Royal Navy in the Second World War. An incident occurred during *Warspite*'s working up which coloured the feelings between Pound and Roskill. After anti-aircraft firings had been completed "a very junior midshipman at one of the multiple pom-poms then opened fire of his own accord"[21] and a stream of shells landed on an army range on Malta, luckily causing no casualties. Undoubtedly Pound blamed Roskill for this episode, since he was the responsible officer, fairly or unfairly. Roskill also believed that Pound was wrong in his criticisms of *Warspite* when she arrived and puts the blame for the 'incident' of 30 June 1937 obliquely on Pound's nominees: Crutchley and Everett. Undoubtedly Roskill was a difficult man, who was rather too inclined to speak his mind, particularly when at the Admiralty early in the war. As a result he was posted to the New Zealand-based *Leander* in 1941, when he might reasonably have expected a destroyer command nearer the centre of operations at home. There was also an undeniable anti-Semitic prejudice in the Royal Navy, as in the whole of society of this time, and this would not have helped his progress. However that may be, Roskill obtained his revenge on Pound in his Official History.[22]

Pound was equally wrong in his initial judgement on two destroyer captains, those of *Gallant* and *Gipsy*. These two destroyers were due to accompany the fleet to Gibraltar for the Combined Exercises with the Home Fleet. Destroyers were thin on the ground owing to the calls of the Nyon patrols, and both ships were damaged by a gale and were re-quired to go into dock for repairs, meaning they could not leave Malta. Pound was irrationally put out by this and believed, for whatever reason, that the two young commanding officers were to blame. There and then he ordered them to be paraded in front of him on the quarterdeck of *Galatea*, the flagship of RA(D). He ordered James Somerville to court-martial them both, while, according to one eyewitness, "frothing at the mouth". Somerville prevailed upon Pound to order a Board of Inquiry first, which exonerated them. On receipt of the Board's findings Pound made an *en clair* signal by radio, which would have been picked up by the whole fleet:

RA(D), D1, *Gallant, Gypsy*. The Commanding Officers of *Gallant* and *Gipsy* are exonerated of any blame whatsoever for the damage suffered by their ships in the recent gale.[23]

On return to Malta from the exercises Pound held a repeat performance on the quarterdeck of *Galatea* at which he told the two young officers that he completely exonerated them. The Captain of *Gipsy*, Richard Onslow, was shortly promoted Captain, becoming one of the most successful destroyer captains of the war, winning four DSOs and finally retiring as an Admiral.

This episode showed a rare loss of Pound's cool and is an instance of him acting without the advice of his staff, who would have told him that the fault lay with the dockyard. He similarly acted out of character when a party of seamen failed to salute him when he was in his official car, in uniform and with flag flying. Instead of leaving the matter to his Captains to deal with, he ordered patrols to be landed each night from every ship to pick up future offenders. The next morning a queue of senior officers was waiting to see the Commander-in-Chief about this, and Pound quietly rescinded the order. His own staff was certainly not immune from this side of his character either and, in the best example of this, he actually court-martialled Commander Norris, commanding his own despatch vessel *Aberdeen*.

Pound had offered Norris this command in April 1935 while on the naval staff course. In an interview Norris remarked, "He added that if ever I put a foot wrong in this job I could expect nothing else than 'three times the stick' . . . that he would serve out to others".[24] *Aberdeen* had been damaged when she dragged her anchor during a mistral on to a lee shore at St. Tropez. Although the ship was refloated without serious damage, and Norris had been cleared of any blame at the subsequent Board of Inquiry, Pound decided to have Norris court-martialled. The trial was held in Pound's day cabin in *Warspite*, while Pound went for a drive along the coast, nervously stopping every hour or so to see if the court-martial flag was still flying. Norris was duly acquitted, and returned to the *Aberdeen* to be greeted by Lady Pound on the gangway, and by the Commander-in-Chief below decks clutching a bottle of champagne. He told Norris that he had had him court-martialled for three reasons:

> Firstly because he would be suspected of favouritism if he did not. Secondly, because there had been a number of incidents recently and this would set an example and warning to others. Thirdly, because someone in the Admiralty would always hold it against Norris if he were not thoroughly cleared.[25]

★

Sadly, there can be little doubt that Fred Edward-Collins was not a great Chief of Staff to Pound. As authoritative a source as Guy Grantham said:

> [Pound's] first instinct was to do things himself, but if challenged he would relent and decentralise. He and Roger Backhouse were certain that they could do every job better than anybody else, and this led to them grabbing everything into their own hands.[26]

Despite this, all administrative matters were left to the captain of the Fleet, Scott, Pound, in effect, satisfying himself with operational matters. This is not totally surprising as when Chief of Staff to Keyes, Pound had really run the fleet, while Keyes played polo. He had then been Chief of Staff to W.W. Fisher, and in Edward-Collins he had his own choice as Chief of Staff who was an agreeable companion, who not only understood his ways and would not question his decisions, but would carry them out effectively. However, in January 1938 Edward-Collins returned to the United Kingdom and was replaced by a very different sort of man, Rear Admiral (later Admiral of the Fleet Sir) Bruce Fraser.

Fraser had just finished commanding the carrier *Glorious* and, unlike Edward-Collins, he had the full confidence of all his ex-brother Captains. He was, however, very different to Pound, a great centralizer, in that he was always a great delegator. However, he worked hard and devotedly for Pound for twelve months, respected him greatly, without imitating him, and indeed was to work with him almost continuously for five years both in the Mediterranean and at the Admiralty. Sadly for Pound Fraser was called home in March 1939 to replace the dying Reggie Henderson as Third Sea Lord and Controller at the Admiralty. Pound wrote to the Captain of *Barham*, Algernon Willis, on 3 January 1939 as follows:

My Dear Willis,

Fraser will shortly be required for a command and will have to be relieved in May. If you would come as my Chief of Staff I should be delighted as I am sure you possess all the qualifications.

It will I know be a wrench for you to leave *Barham* but from the Service point of view you will be of greater service as Chief of Staff.[27]

Willis did not relish the appointment, as he was much enjoying being captain of *Barham*, but the new job involved promotion to Commodore and was a challenge. He certainly found Pound's methods of working difficult, writing many years later:

When the staff was disembarked at the Castile, Malta, Pound would spend much of the forenoon in my office (his own was in Admiralty House), which hampered me in my work, and he would deal with the day's "In" signals, writing out the answers in his own hand, instead of waiting for the staff to produce draft replies and then approving or amending them as he wished. The latter method was in accordance with the generally accepted staff system and was more likely to produce the right answers as the staff officers concerned in drafting the replies would have looked into the back history of the matters in question.

Pound kept very late hours and when embarked in *Warspite* seldom went to bed before 2 am and was often up at 6 am to go ashore for some activity, such as shooting. When I became Chief of Staff I said to him "I like to get to bed about 11 pm. I hope you won't send for me after that unless it's urgent". He was very considerate and didn't.[28]

This illustrates another side to Pound, that when somebody stood up to him with good arguments, like he was to do to Churchill later, he was quite happy to give way. Here is a distinct difference to Roger Backhouse, who was to become First Sea Lord in February. When Commander-in-Chief Home Fleet he was an even worse centralizer than Pound, and his chief of staff, Bertie Ramsay, one of the Royal Navy's most gifted officers, had remonstrated with him. Ramsay was told by Backhouse that he could not change his habits and, if he didn't like them, he (Ramsay) had better go. Ramsay resigned and was placed on the retired list. Happily, he was recalled by Pound in September 1939 as Vice Admiral, Dover, and had a most distinguished war record.

★

Throughout his time in the Mediterranean Pound corresponded regularly with the First Sea Lord, Chatfield, and then with Roger Backhouse. These hand-written letters are fascinating as they show us Pound's innermost thoughts. They had no secrets from each other and the letters are a mixture of daily chitchat, serious discussions of tactics and strategy, information about flag appointments and the daily affairs of the fleet. For example, on 23 October 1936[29] Pound's letter included paragraphs on the shooting at Suda Bay in Crete, the Fleet visit to Greece, comments on the British ambassador in Athens ("He is pomposity itself, and at times his manners are as bad as his French."), the future visit of the Turkish fleet to Malta and Pound's decision to include Warrant Officers at official Fleet dances.

They demonstrate Pound's desire to improve the training of the Fleet as a whole. For example, on 18 February 1937 he wrote:

> At the present time anyone can tell you who won the regatta in his squadron, or the marathon, or who is likely to win the football league, but if you ask anyone except the flag officers in command of the squadrons or the captains, or their Lt G's [Gunnery Officers] who is the most efficient fighting ship I am sure they could not tell you. This is, of course, all wrong, and to try to put fighting efficiency in its proper and permanent position all the flag officers, at my instigation, have introduced a system of efficiency badges for the guns and also for the control. These badges will be awarded after each firing practice.
>
> *My cruise to Gib in January.* We had a wonderful four days exercise each way and got through the whole of our programme each way. It gave me an opportunity of impressing on the flag officers the essentials of good fleet work, and they are going like a magnificent team. They are off the mark like a shot out of a gun the moment they get an order.

Both Pound and Chatfield spent much of their time trying to plan future flag appointments and making sure that candidates for the highest posts

106

had both sufficient sea time and the right shore-based appointments. We have already seen the consternation caused by the death of W.W. Fisher and of the illness of Geoffrey Blake, and here is Chatfield, writing on the 2 July 1937, explaining to Pound how appointments will now move:

Of course William Fisher's death and Geoffrey Blake's illness have been distracting to me and upset things that were previously in my mind. However, it's an ill wind that blows nobody any good, and in consequence Cork goes to Portsmouth for two years, i.e. he will finish Fisher's time there. He will also become an Admiral of the Fleet in January. Cunningham, as you know I think, I had designated to relieve Geoffrey Blake in August '38, and therefore he will be well placed in a temporary appointment. I have no doubts it will be upsetting to the squadron and to you.

On 7 February 1938 Pound wrote to Chatfield

I was very interested in the list of future appointments which Naval Secretary sent me for my personal information. I shall be very sorry to lose Cunningham, but it is no doubt very necessary for him to get Admiralty experience. Layton should do very well in his place [as second-in-command of the Mediterranean Fleet]. Binney will I am sure do admirably at the I.D.C. Kennedy-Purvis will not I imagine be over-pleased at A.C.R. [Admiral Commanding Reserve Fleet].

Pound also commented upon individual Captains in his fleet, who were up for promotion. On 7 August 1937 he wrote about Captain (later Admiral) John Godfrey:

As you will remember I had to furnish a special report on Godfrey. I am enclosing a letter he wrote to me on his return from Corfu and Haifa as I think it shows how well he handled both situations. I had a very nice letter from the king (Greece) saying how grateful he was for the ship being sent and how much he had enjoyed *Repulse*'s visit. I shall never have any hesitation in sending Godfrey on detached service.

This is particularly interesting given the circumstances of Godfrey's later dismissal as Director of Naval Intelligence when Pound was First Sea Lord.

There was also the whole question of British naval strategy and its global

107

implications. Here Pound was at one with Chatfield in their worry about the overcommitment faced by the Royal Navy. Pound was not worried by the threat of the Italians, saying to Chatfield in his last letter to him as First Sea Lord on 24 August 1938, "I think our opinion of their efficiency, as a result of their visit, was exactly as it had been before, just second rate". Far more worrying was the threat from the Far East and the possibility of having to send a heavily reinforced Mediterranean Fleet through the Red Sea. In December 1937 Pound had been briefed about the possibility of this in the same letter that Chatfield told him that Backhouse would be the next First Sea Lord, and told that he would command this Main Fleet. Pound replied to Chatfield on 7 February 1938 saying how delighted he was at having been selected for this command,

... but leaving aside the personal side one hopes it will not be neces-sary as we can ill afford practically to denude European waters with the situation as it is. Our German and Italian friends would be delighted to see the Fleet on the other side of the Canal. To send out reinforcements only and not the Main Fleet would be simply playing into the hands of the Japanese.

This, of course, was being wise before the event, as was to be shown in December 1941.

★

Chatfield retired in November 1938 and was thus still at the helm of the Royal Navy at the time of Munich. The government accepted the urging of the First Lord, Duff Cooper, and mobilized the fleet on 28 September, which left the Royal Navy a mere four days before the German deadline of 1 October. This compares unfavourably with the ten days it had enjoyed in August 1914, to say nothing of the flying start it had been given before that by the Spithead review. Although the country rejoiced at the "deliver-ance" of Munich, there was little rejoicing either at the Admiralty or in the two main fleets. Pound and Fraser sent in a report which stressed that the Mediterranean Fleet would have to fight with its peacetime com-plements, at any rate initially, as reinforcements would never arrive in time. The reinforcements which had arrived in September 1938 had trav-elled overland to Marseilles, and then by liner to Alexandria. The report highlighted shortages of ships and ammunition, the almost total absence of any local defence for the Mediterranean stations, and, more importantly than any of these, a complete absence of planning, either with the French, or with the other services. The fleet had been prepared for war. Ammunition had been fused and all preparations made for action. Pound had planned for the fleet to sweep the eastern Mediterranean and bombard Tobruk. The Munich climbdown was greeted with anticlimax, rather than relief, in Pound's fleet.

Pound had been expecting to be moved from the Mediterranean after the normal period of three years, in the spring of 1938. There had been speculation about who would be Chatfield's successor, but Pound was quite certain in his own mind that he did not want the job and told his family and his Flag Lieutenant so.[30] He wrote to Chatfield on 18 February to tell him:

> My definition of disappointment is that one does not get something one hopes for, and that being so I can honestly say that the announcement of R[oger] B[ackhouse]'s appointment caused me not the slightest disappointment. I have such a great admiration of RB that even had we both been of equal seniority and both unemployed I should have expected him to succeed you. His being senior to me clinched the matter as it is unthinkable that he should have been passed over. Personally I consider that I have been amazingly lucky. I have achieved my greatest ambition to command the Mediterranean Fleet. I have had a wonderfully interesting two years, and it does not look as if the rest of my two years in command will be any less interesting.
>
> Also, as you have entrusted me with the command of the Main Fleet under certain circumstances, the future may give me something infinitely greater than any shore appointment.
>
> What your letter has done is to make me proud to think that I was considered fit to hold the great position that is now yours, and the tribute you paid me in the last sentence is one I shall never forget. I do appreciate your having found time to write to me as you did.

The plan had originally been for him to become Commander-in-Chief Portsmouth in July 1939 and hand over command of the Mediterranean Fleet to either William James or Charles Forbes, the latter transferring from the Home Fleet. However, with the shortage of high-class senior officers so evident, plans yet again had to be changed. The deaths of

W.W. Fisher and of Reggie Henderson, the invaliding of Geoffrey Blake from the Mediterranean, and then James Somerville from the East Indies Fleet with suspected TB, along with the resignation of Bertie Ramsay, undoubtedly caused a major hiatus in command arrangements. In November 1938 Pound was summoned back to the Admiralty for conferences, one of which concerned his own future. He returned to the Mediterranean overland and was greeted at Marseilles railway station by Charles Norris, who, like many, was agog to hear the news:

> After the meal DP started to talk of his future. "Well Charles, I can hardly believe my luck. It's exactly what I would have hoped for, but never expected to get. Just think, I am not to be the First Sea Lord, but instead am to stay with the fleet for another extra year. An extra year, and they tell me they will then make me an Admiral of the Fleet, and I can retire straight from the sea".[31]

In celebration of this extension of his command of the Fleet until May 1940 he had bought himself a brand new shotgun. Norris again explains:

> I hurried to the platform just in time to greet DP stepping from the train. He was carrying a gun case which, naturally, I made to take from him. "No, no, thank you. Nobody's going to carry that gun except me." I explained that I had done my best to avoid a French reception committee, but that there was a rear admiral outside eager to greet him. "Look here," said DP. "This is the first gun I've ever had which is brand new and has been fitted for me personally. I'm damned if I'm going to let anyone else handle it even for the whole of the French navy." When you come to think of it that was a surprising statement to be made by a man in his position and as keen on shooting as he was. DP's advancement in the service owed nothing to any outside assistance of any kind. He had little or no private means.[32]

★

So, throughout 1939 the training went on and the Mediterranean Fleet was gradually honed to as perfect an instrument of war as it was possible to make it. Pound was aware of the main weakness of the fleet, which was its very poor capacity for anti-aircraft fire. This was confirmed by

110

the new Fleet Gunnery Officer, Commander (later Vice Admiral Sir) Geoffrey Barnard:

> When the Munich crisis occurred and came to nothing, much against my wishes I was appointed FGO Med Fleet [sic]. Admiral Pound was acutely conscious of the need NOT to be caught with our trousers down, as the Americans later were at Pearl Harbour. As a result during the meeting of the Home and Mediterranean fleets at Gibraltar in 1939 we always had precautions, such as half the ships' companies at anti-aircraft stations, a destroyer patrol off the approaches etc., and this got some publicity at the time. From my personal point of view as FGO I knew enough technically to know that the fleet was totally incompetently equipped to deal with air attack, because of an old-fashioned system called High Angle Control System Mark I, which was quite incapable of shooting down aircraft, and it was too late to change it.[33]

The Nyon patrols were wound down, but the involvement of some sailors at Haifa in Palestine continued, as well as visits to foreign ports. However, nobody was in any doubt that war was on its way, nor that Italy would join Germany in that war if not at the start, then at a moment that suited her best and Britain worst. Flag officers came and went. In January 1939 Cunningham went to the Admiralty as DCNS, to acquire the necessary staff experience, and was replaced as second-in-command by Geoffrey Layton. Somerville went to command the East Indies Station, before his invaliding home, and was replaced in April 1938 as RA(D) by Jack Tovey. The two cruiser squadrons were now commanded by J.H. Cunningham, and H.R. Moore. All of these admirals were to pass through the Admiralty when Pound became First Sea Lord.

Finally, in the early summer of 1939 news began to filter through to Pound that Backhouse was not a well man. Cunningham, with mounting difficulty, was trying to do the work of both First Sea Lord and DCNS, and had been doing so since March. He got Vice Admiral Charles Kennedy-Purvis, who was serving as President of the Royal Naval College, Greenwich, to move to the Admiralty to relieve him of the normal run-of-the-mill DCNS work. On 9 May Pound was formally offered the post of First Sea Lord and Cunningham that of Commander-in-Chief Mediterranean Fleet. A new DCNS had thus to be found and, after rapid consultation by signal between the Admiralty and *Warspite*, Rear Admiral

Tom Phillips was chosen. He relieved Cunningham on 23 May and Cunningham arrived in Marseilles on 31 May, sailing post-haste to Alexandria in *Penelope*, arriving there on 5 June. Pound and Cunningham had only that evening to exchange news of their jobs. In the afternoon Pound said farewell to his fleet as they sailed past him standing on the bridge of *Warspite*, and at sunset on 5 June 1939 Pound struck his flag as Commander-in-Chief Mediterranean Fleet after three years, two months and sixteen days. They both rose early, as Pound left by flying boat at 4:00 am for London.

8

FIRST SEA LORD

There was little alternative to Pound succeeding as First Sea Lord in succession to Backhouse. He had been the only other option in 1938, but was passed over. Thus his appointment to the top job was both unplanned and unexpected. With Cunningham moving to the Mediterranean there was naturally great disturbance at the Admiralty.

It has been said, notably by Roskill, that Pound was not fit for command when he took over as First Sea Lord. Roskill says that Pound was suffering from 'a long standing osteo-arthritis of the left hip with consequent shortening of the left thigh', which caused 'a painful condition and prevented comfortable sleep and rest'.[1] Roskill followed this up by saying that his ill health meant that he could not stand up to Churchill, and cites his hip, extreme fatigue, insomnia and, perhaps, the brain tumour that was to kill him in 1943. There are continual references throughout his book *Churchill And The Admirals*[2] to this, viz:

> Pound . . . was certainly not a fit man, and it is well known that anyone who loses normal sleep as a result of osteo-arthritis is liable to have some very bad days. (Referring to July 1940) – p. 165.

> For Pound, whose health and vigour were steadily deteriorating, the early months of 1942 must have been a bitter experience – p. 204.

> One wonders whether the physical and mental exhaustion which Pound increasingly showed at this time [1942–43] were not exacerbated by the bombardment to which he was subjected [by Churchill] – p. 210.

> The failure [to alert Churchill to the shortage of shipping] undoubtedly derived in part from the fact that by 1943 Pound was a very sick man indeed, and quite unfit to carry his great responsibilities – p. 230.

There are plenty of other references, but significantly the vast majority concern the period after May 1940, when Churchill had ceased to be the First Lord.

It is therefore necessary to ask whether Pound was fit to take over as First Sea Lord in 1939. The answer has to be an unequivocal "Yes". Marder cites, among others, Vice Admiral Sir Charles Norris, then a Captain, who had left the Mediterranean Fleet in April 1939. He says that Pound was 'in top form then. I saw him again, *en famille*, on his recall to the UK in June/July. He was his usual self.'[3] His bad hip did not hamper him too much, and never stopped him taking a full part in any shooting expedition. Admiral Norris also disposes of his sleeplessness. He says that Pound 'never slept like the majority of people. . . . He was a master of catnapping'. This was well known to the immediate family, who have all separately confirmed it to the author. It was also well known to his staff in the Mediterranean. The fact that he appeared to sleep in meetings has been frequently commented on, usually to his detriment. However, even Roskill is forced to admit that as soon as any mention was made of naval matters, then he was immediately alert. An expert witness is Admiral Schofield, who, as Director of the Trade Division, was in regular contact from March 1941 until August 1943 both within the Admiralty and at special meetings such as the Atlantic Conference of August 1941, Casablanca, January 1943, and Washington, May 1943. On the way to the Atlantic Conference on board *Prince of Wales* there were numerous conferences and he

> became familiar with Pound's habit of closing his eyes in order the better to listen to what was being said. . . . I never once saw Pound unable to cope with what was going on.[4]

This is confirmed by Sir Ian Jacob, who saw Pound at Chiefs of Staff meetings almost daily, as well as at staff conferences on voyages to conferences in August 1941, December 1941, and August 1943. He states:

> From the beginning of the war Pound gave the impression of being half-asleep at meetings, and yet, as Ismay says, really very much alive if naval matters were mentioned. We knew he was a night bird, and had always worked late so as to be able to shoot and fish, so we weren't surprised to see him as he was. As time went on he seemed to get worse in this respect, but the war was having an effect on

114

everyone. When did his deterioration in health begin to affect his work? I can't really say. Unless you know a man is ill, you tend to put down a degree of slowness or lack of sharpness just to fatigue. I believe that in 1943 we thought that he was beginning to show his age. He never spoke much at COS meetings, and he still drove his fast Bentley [one foot hard on the accelerator], and he seemed full of keenness on the voyage to Halifax [Quebec conference, August 1943]. I had no idea he was ill, but thought he was wearing out. If I had to make a definite statement it would be that Pound's illness affected not more than the last year of his life, and was barely detectable even then.

Both Admiral Fraser, in correspondence to Marder, and Vice Admiral Brockman, in correspondence to Marder, and in conversation with the author, categorically state that there were no indications of ill health when Pound took over in June 1939. The latter states that the first time that Pound told him that he was suffering from ill health was in July 1943.

There is some indication that by the summer of 1943 Pound was suffering from the brain tumour that was to kill him eventually, but modern thinking indicates that the tumour could well have been present for only a month or six weeks. The absence of a post-mortem leaves much unconfirmed. It can, however, be stated that in 1939 Pound was as fit as anyone in his circumstances aged 63. How his health changed after that we shall look at later. The best comment on Roskill's criticisms is contained in a letter to *The Daily Telegraph* in 1970:

> I wonder what Captain Roskill would have made of a one-eyed, one-armed Admiral of unstable temperament. Unfit for command at Trafalgar?[5]

Who else was there anyway who might have taken on the job of First Sea Lord in the emergency of June 1939? The loss of two such brilliant men as Fisher (June 1937) and Backhouse within so short a time was crucial. Both, intriguingly, died of the same illness that was to kill Pound in 1943. Ramsay had resigned in 1935 after his clash with Backhouse and been placed on the retired list in 1938. Blake had been invalided out after his stroke in 1937. Henderson was forced to resign through ill health in May 1939 and Somerville, as we have seen, was also invalided out with traces of tuberculosis in 1939. Ramsay, Blake and Somerville all made crucial contributions during the war, but they were not available in 1939, and anyway were too junior and not yet experienced in both Admiralty matters and fleet command. Chatfield's correspondence from 1936 shows that he was acutely aware of the need to select future Commanders-in-Chief and Sea Lords, and, as we have seen, he frequently canvassed the views of such as Pound.

In July 1939 there were thus very few options open to the First Lord, Earl Stanhope. His chief advice would have come from his Naval Secretary, only appointed in June 1939 himself. Admiral Sir Charles Forbes was a possibility, but he had only recently taken over commanding the Home Fleet (April 1938). The only real alternative was to recall Chatfield. This is the option put forward by Roskill in his *Naval Policy Between The Wars*.[6] He argues that, firstly, he had only given up the post seven months before. Secondly, although four years older than Pound, he was a very fit man, and indeed he lived to be 94. Thirdly, he understood the problems and knew the politicians. Roskill suggests that he could have held the fort until 1942 when his hero, Cunningham, would have been ready to take office. This sounds a simple solution, but there are two drawbacks to it. Firstly, Chatfield may have known the politicians, but he was to make an unconvincing Minister for Co-ordination of Defence. Secondly, and more importantly, in 1914 a similar option had existed upon the resignation of Prince Louis of Battenberg, and Jackie Fisher had been brought back at the age of 74. That episode had ended with the resignation of both First Lord and First Sea Lord in May 1915, and nobody wanted a repetition of that painful trauma. The fact remains that in June 1939 there was nobody else who could possibly fit the chair. 'Pound was not bred for the role he was asked to assume, like Jellicoe had been. But he was, I think, arguably the best the Navy had to offer.'[7]

It is necessary to describe in some detail the set-up which Pound found at the Admiralty, and which he was to adopt and to control until his death. He knew his way around the corridors of power well after his previous spells at the Admiralty. Firstly, it is important to draw a distinction between the two titles which Pound held. As First Sea Lord he was the professional head of the Royal Navy and ran every aspect of it. As Chief of Naval Staff (CNS) he was head of an operational centre and also a member of the Chiefs of Staff Committee. He had to be prepared to deal with operational problems from all over the world at any time of the day or night, as well as provide advice to the government on defence policy as

116

a whole. In addition to this he was required to sit on other committees and provide expert advice when required by the Cabinet or War Cabinet. This meant that he had little opportunity, or one suspects desire, to keep his colleagues on the Board of Admiralty fully informed of current or future operations. However, each of them had their own separate spheres of activities which they would inform him about as they saw fit.

The different divisions of the Naval Staff, such as Plans, Operations, Intelligence and Trade, were all responsible to the CNS, via the Deputy Chief of Naval Staff (DCNS), and the three Assistant Chiefs of Naval Staff (ACNS), through the Director of their particular division. Thus plans and operations were discussed daily to review the previous 24 hours' actions and to consider the unending series of signals arriving from all over the world. This was frequently referred to as "The Midnight Follies", as the meeting was usually well after 11:30pm. The Director of Plans sat on the Joint Planning Staff (JPS), with the equivalent from the Army and RAF, and they reported directly to the Chiefs of Staff (COS). Similarly, the Director of Naval Intelligence sat on the Joint Intelligence Committee (JIC), later chaired by a representative from the Foreign Office, and they also reported direct to the COS.

The members of the Board of Admiralty all had their own specific areas of responsibility, with various divisions of the Naval Staff under them. Thus, as we have seen already, the Second Sea Lord was responsible for all matters pertaining to personnel. In 1939 this was Admiral Sir Charles Little, succeeded in 1941 by Vice Admiral Sir Jock Whitworth. The Third Sea Lord, or Controller, was in charge of the design, construction and delivery of all warships and their machinery, weapons and equipment. In 1939 this was Rear Admiral Bruce Fraser, who had, of course, until March 1939 been Pound's Chief of Staff in the Mediterranean. The Fourth Sea Lord dealt with the procurement and distribution of stores and supplies, and had since 1937 been Rear Admiral Arbuthnot. The Fifth Sea Lord was in charge of all matters to do with naval aviation. When Pound came to London it was Vice Admiral Sir Alexander Ramsay, and he was replaced in November 1939 by Vice Admiral Royle, who had been Pound's Rear Admiral (Air) in the Mediterranean. The other members of the Board were the DCNS, the three ACNSs, and five civilians: the Controller of Merchant Shipbuilding and Repairs (Sir James Lithgow), the Parliamentary and Financial Secretary (Geoffrey Shakespeare), the Civil Lord (Captain A.U.M. Hudson RN ret), the Secretary to the Board of Admiralty (Sir Archibald Carter), and, chairing the whole Board of Admiralty, the First Sea Lord.

This is obviously a greatly simplified account of the duties of the Board of Admiralty, but it is important to understand that it was the First Sea Lord who had the sole control of operations in his capacity as CNS. To an extent this could not exist in either the War Office or the Air Ministry. The Admiralty through the use of radio had control of both fleets and individual ships around the world. Since intelligence came direct to the Admiralty, and since ships were usually keeping radio silence to avoid direction finding, it was natural that the Admiralty would on occasion take executive control. This is a topic which we will examine in the next chapter, where it very much relates to Pound and his relationship to the First Lord.

Presiding over the whole of the Admiralty was the person of the First Lord of the Admiralty. When Pound arrived in June 1939 it was the 7th Earl Stanhope, but on the outbreak of war in September 1939 it became Winston Churchill, succeeded in May 1940 by the Labour politician A.V. Alexander. In general terms, although the First Lord carried the responsibility in Parliament, the First Sea Lord expected to have the last say in all matters of naval strategy and operations. Much of course depended on personalities. Churchill was unlikely to allow himself to be ridden over and the famous signal to the fleet on 3 September 1939 'Winston is back' was as much a warning as a greeting. It is worth making the point here that it must have been Pound who sent this signal out, although Churchill's biographer Martin Gilbert claims never to have found a copy of the signal.[8] Alexander was a different kettle of fish. He was, to be fair, a politician of the second rank, but with an enormous capacity for getting on with people. He did, though, in the Navy have a reputation of being a 'rubber stamp', who would do what the Prime Minister and First Sea Lord told him to do.

When Pound arrived in the Admiralty in June 1939 he had no permanent secretary. After the tragic death of Hemsted in May 1936, Pound had chosen Paymaster Commander Cull, but he did not take him to the Admiralty. Instead he took over both of Backhouse's secretaries, Barrow, and his assistant Brockman. In December 1939 Barrow had a heart attack and Brockman moved up to be Pound's principal Secretary, probably on the advice of Captain Guy Grantham, whom Pound had brought to the Admiralty with him. Brockman was to remain as his secretary for his whole time as First Sea Lord, and eventually moved on with Mountbatten when he went as Supreme Allied Commander South East Asia, and then Viceroy in India.

What, it should be asked, was the relationship between the First Sea Lord and the First Lord? This was partly a matter of chemistry and partly a matter of doctrine. In 1871 George (later Viscount) Goschen had laid down the idea of the First Lord's final and individual responsibility: the final say belonged to him and him alone. Operational matters were not referred to the board, since they were the province of the Naval Staff. A wise First Lord chose and relied upon his professional advisers in the shape of the Naval Staff, but doing so did not absolve him from the ultimate responsibility for all the actions of the Royal Navy. Nobody could have been more cognizant than Churchill of all that this implied. He had, after all, the memories of 1915 as a permanent reminder of what could happen when First Lord and First Sea Lord fell out. When two dominant personalities met the results had been cataclysmic, costing Churchill his ministerial career. One of the reasons for there being no Chiefs of Staff Committee in the First World War was that the two political heads of the armed forces, Churchill at the Admiralty and Kitchener at the War Office, were both dominant figures who were inclined to originate strategy and dominate their advisers. There was little chance for either of the two newly created staffs to become involved in the decision-making process. Their role had been to carry out the instructions of their political masters.

However, by 1939 things were different. Certainly Churchill was prepared to instigate operational details, as we shall see in the Norwegian campaign, when he should not have done so. However, Pound was not prepared to force the issue when the two of them agreed on so much. At the heart of the relationship was Pound's belief that a head-on collision merely increased Churchill's obduracy. They had reason to distrust each other from the outset, as Churchill had heavily criticized Pound's disposition of the Mediterranean Fleet in March 1939 when Mussolini had invaded Albania. However, in a very short time Churchill had formed a very great attachment to, and trust in, Pound. In the words of Marder 'Pound feared neither God, man, nor Winston Churchill'.[9] Churchill was prepared to accept Pound's judgement. Pound saw that Churchill's qualities of leadership were so exceptional that it was necessary to accept him 'warts and all'. He wrote to Admiral Forbes:

119

I have the greatest admiration for Churchill, and his good qualities are such, and his desire to hit the enemy so overwhelming, that I feel one must hesitate in turning down any of his proposals.[10]

In particular, whatever Roskill may have said, Pound handled Churchill extremely well. He was not prepared to contradict him at meetings and would only fight him on really vital issues, in other words 'not to present a brick wall, unless something is vital'. Thus, for example, when Churchill proposed Operation CATHERINE, sending a fleet without air cover into the Baltic in the winter of 1939–40, Pound had the operation appreciated by the Naval Staff, the forces necessary assessed, the scale of expected losses added, and finally showed where the forces would have to come from, and what their removal would mean. 'Thus,' as Admiral Waller sums up the matter, 'Churchill was brought to the point of saying (nearly) "Who thought up this damn fool project anyway?" and it was then as dead as a dodo.'[11] Pound himself said to Admiral Moore, his VCNS from November 1941, 'Never say a direct "No" to the PM at a meeting. You can argue against it, and as long as you don't exaggerate your case the PM will always let you have your say.'[12] This is confirmed by Mountbatten, when he said, 'Pound was never prepared to give way to the PM, and always expressed himself forcibly'.[13] There was a difference to this pattern during the Norwegian campaign, as we will see in the next chapter. Above all, Churchill must have kept at the back of his mind the events of May 1915. It is important to remember that Pound had been Naval Assistant to Jackie Fisher in 1915 and been a close observer of the clash of the titans. It is not fanciful to suggest that when the two met in September 1939 Churchill recalled how not to handle a First Sea Lord and Pound how not to handle a First Lord.

Mention should be made here of the way in which policy was decided upon once war had been joined. Although the COS were supposed to give strategic/military advice to the government, the Chamberlain government interposed the Military Co-ordination Committee between the COS and the War Cabinet. This was initially under the chairmanship of Lord Chatfield, as Minister for Co-ordination of Defence, and comprised the three Service Ministers and the Minister of Supply, with the three Chiefs of Staff to give expert advice. This was referred to by General Ironside, the CIGS, in his diary on 19 April 1940, as the Decontamination Committee . . . Whatever we do, we have to appear in front of committees to justify the military recommendations we have made. Strategy is directed by odd people, who collect odd bits of information. This is discussed quite casually by everyone. When the General Staff puts anything up, it has to be justified in front of the wretched Decontamination Committee – composed of civilians, who will not listen to the military arguments, and then leave the details alone. It is a ridiculous situation.[14]

Ismay, the Military Secretary to the War Cabinet and later Chief of Staff to Churchill in his capacity as Minister of Defence, was equally critical of it and comments in his memoirs

I believe that most of us, whether ministers or officials, who were cogs in the machine, felt that it would fail to secure the necessary speed of decision once the war started in earnest.[15]

This was borne out when it became necessary for the Prime Minister to chair the committee because the meetings were, in Ismay's words, becoming 'more frequent, more controversial and . . . more acrimonious'.[16] This problem was not solved until Churchill assumed the office of Minister of Defence along with that of Prime Minister and put relative nonentities into the Service Ministries, thus allowing himself to control the military aspects of the war from both the War Cabinet and COS.

★

Pound lived almost totally in Admiralty House. While the family lived in a number of houses both in London and in Hertfordshire, and he managed to get back home for the occasional day, it was essential that he stayed in touch within the Admiralty. He would appear in his office at about 8:00 when Brockman would have all the overnight telegrams for him. He would read them and then reread the papers for the COS meeting, while having a cup of coffee instead of breakfast. The COS meeting was usually at 10:30 and would normally take all morning. Lunch was often taken in his office on a tray, or he would walk to the Army and Navy Club. After lunch he would invariably have a 20–30 minute sleep in his chair, a lesson he had learned in the Mediterranean Fleet, and the remainder of the day was spent on paper work and on the telephone. Any Captain or Flag Officer returning from sea and passing through London would see Pound, allowing him to keep up to date with the Fleets. The Cabinet met at 6:30 and usually finished by 8:00, depending often upon who was chairing the meeting, Churchill or Attlee. The Chiefs of Staff agenda would be published at about 9:30 and this allowed the Director of Plans or the Director of Operations (Home) to prepare briefs for him, as at 10:30 the Defence Committee of the Cabinet met. On his return from that Pound would hold his 'midnight follies' as they became known, in which he would be briefed for the morrow's meetings by officers such as Charles Lambe, the Director of Plans. There would frequently be a late-night call from Churchill, either in person or more likely on the telephone. An interesting sidelight on this aspect of Churchill's way of working is provided in the diary of the diplomatic correspondent of *The Times* on 4 May 1940:

> After this Norway breakdown there is of course a lot of criticism of the government and general despondency. MPs are especially disenchanted. There is a drive against Chamberlain. I can't quite see who can advantageously take his place. Curiously enough, what is really wanted is that Winston should be made to take a rest. He is overdoing himself and taking the strain by stoking himself unduly with champagne, liqueurs etc. Dines out and dines well almost every night. Sleeps after luncheon, then to the House of Commons, then a good and long dinner and doesn't resume work at the Admiralty till after 10 pm and goes on until 1 or 2 am. He has got into the habit of calling conferences of subordinates after 1 am, which naturally upsets some of the admirals who are men of sound habits. So there is a general atmosphere of strain at the Admiralty, which is all wrong. Yet Winston is such a popular hero and so much *the* war leader that he cannot be dropped. But he ought somehow to be rested.[17]

At least once a day, and often more regularly, Pound went down to the OIC, in the basement of that ivy-covered monstrosity squatting on the edge of Horse Guards' Parade, frequently referred to as Stalin's tomb, where Operations and Intelligence were married. There he was briefed by the staff on the latest position of any particular operation, and he would frequently drop into the Submarine Tracking room to find out how their struggle in the Atlantic was progressing. Similarly he talked almost every day to Vice Admiral Geoffrey Blake, either on the phone or in person.

Blake was ACNS (H) until December 1940 and then ran the shadow Admiralty (in case the Admiralty was destroyed by a bomb), before becoming the Flag Officer (Liaison) to the US naval forces in Europe (FOLUS) in 1941. Pound also wrote regularly to Cunningham, both in the Mediterranean and when he went to Washington. By 1941 it was certain to all that Cunningham was his heir apparent. Pound kept all their correspondence in his own desk and they had no secrets from each other.

It became very obvious by the early months of 1940 that Pound was driving himself into the ground and that he needed some form of relaxation. This was provided by an American, Commander Paul Hammond, USNR, who was introduced to Pound by Geoffrey Blake, and remarked that 'your First Sea Lord wants a little high angle gun practice'.[18] Hammond organized a shoot in a delightful part of the country near Luton, where a Mr. Dewar lived, but was away on tank production business in the USA. Most Sundays Pound would drive out in his Bentley, covering the 25 miles in well under 40 minutes, and spend the afternoon and early evening shooting. By 1941 he had introduced a rule that everybody serving in the Admiralty should have at least 24 hours off every fortnight.

Pound had one other relaxation. Every evening at 7:10 he would leave his office and drive to the flat of Lady Poynton. The only people who knew where he went were his driver, Moth, who sometimes took him there, Ronald Brockman, and his Assistant Secretary, Paymaster Commander John Stanning. It is, of course, pure speculation, but the primary purpose of the visit was relaxation, aided by gin and tonic. It was an opportunity to talk about anything other than naval affairs. As far as Brockman can remember on only one occasion did he have to ring through saying that the Prime Minister was after him urgently.[19] Pound had always had an eye for pretty girls and much enjoyed dancing with them. Whether Lady Pound knew about the friendship is open to question; certainly the family know about it and have no doubts about his continued love for his wife.

*

The most important appointment to the Admiralty that Pound was involved in was that of Tom Phillips. When Pound was offered the post of First Sea Lord and Cunningham went to the Mediterranean, the latter was DCNS, and so a new officer was needed for that position. Pound and

123

Phillips had served together twice. From June 1923 to November 1924 they had worked together in the Plans Division, when Pound had been Director of Plans, and they had both moved to the Mediterranean Fleet in 1925, Pound as Chief of Staff and Phillips as Staff Officer (Operations). They remained there together for two years. In the 1930s they had both served at the Admiralty, but in different parts. In 1938 Phillips had been posted as Commodore Home Fleet Destroyers under Admiral Forbes. Here, therefore, was somebody who had experience of both staff work and of commanding ships, if not yet of commanding a fleet. Like Pound, Phillips was a centralizer, hated delegation and worked excessively hard. He could be abrasive and was decided in his likes and dislikes. Like Pound, he revered the Royal Navy and had few interests outside it. He inspired great loyalty amongst those working for him, both officers and seamen. The popular view of him has been of an intellectual staff officer, but he had had two periods of roughly five years commanding destroyer flotillas and one year as flag captain in the Eastern Fleet, commanding the cruiser *Hawkins*.

There was therefore a logic in selecting him as DCNS in June 1939 (the title changed to VCNS in April 1940). He was an experienced staff officer, with good sea appointments as well, intellectually well above average (he had five firsts in his sub's exams) and personally known to Pound. Certainly he had only just been promoted to Rear Admiral, and he had not commanded a Battle Squadron, but that was not a prerequisite for DCNS. Cunningham, after all, had never served in the Admiralty before becoming DCNS. There is no doubt that the appointment provoked jealousy, but, given the circumstances of his appointment in the hurry of getting Cunningham out to the Mediterranean, it is not a totally surprising one. Other admirals were definitely upset by his jump to Vice Admiral and many officers in the Admiralty found Phillips to be a poor listener and, unlike Pound, impatient and rude. Pound, however, totally trusted him.

A vast amount of Admiralty business passed across Pound's desk: signals from the fleets and commands, the work of the staff divisions, intelligence appreciations and Ultra decrypts in their buff boxes. The First World War had shown the necessity for a Deputy First Sea Lord (DFSL) when Jellicoe had shown that it was almost impossible to carry out the work single-handed. Wemyss had been brought in in September 1917, and then succeeded Jellicoe in December 1917 as First Sea Lord. Plans were in place for a DFSL to be appointed on the outbreak of war.

124

Brockman recalls that it would have been 'Daddy' Brind, but that Phillips persuaded Pound not to make the appointment as the DFSL would be senior to him, only an acting vice admiral. Instead Phillips suggested a senior captain should be appointed as Chief Staff Officer. Amongst those who filled this appointment were Captains William Tennant and George Creasy, but it was not a success as they had no authority to sign off files, and the appointment was phased out in 1940, becoming combined with that of Naval Assistant to the First Sea Lord. The job, as Pound explained to Cunningham, was simple: "he has no papers whatever, and [he] is to see that immediate action is taken on anything that requires it."[20] It was not until July 1942 that a DFSL was appointed, significantly after the death of Tom Phillips and after PQ17.

There was one major change at the Admiralty in 1939 from when Pound had served there as Second Sea Lord. Instead of the magisterial figure of Sir Oswyn Murray there was a new Permanent Secretary. Sir Archibald Carter had arrived in 1936 and, fatally, had no Admiralty background. He had come from the India Office and did not enjoy being at the Admiralty, expressing his delight when he was relieved at the beginning of December 1940. This weakness of firm civilian management at the heart of the Admiralty did much to deprive the Admiralty of good advice on a number of occasions, not least that concerning Dudley North.

Pound made certain that he had around him at least one familiar face. He took with him as Naval Assistant Captain Guy Grantham. His job was simply to devil for Pound on any matter which needed following up. But he left in May 1940, quite naturally, for a sea command, and from early 1942 that job was filled by retired officers. Otherwise he took over the Admiralty as it was. Indeed he wrote to Cunningham on 13 June 1939, 'I arrived at the Admiralty at 1800 on Friday, and at 1801 I found myself immersed in the *Thetis* disaster'.[21] He went straight to the Admiralty from the airport, taking no leave at all. He had started, if not as he wanted, then as he would be forced to go on.

9

NORWAY

The Phoney War, as the period between September 1939 and May 1940 came to be called, was not a phoney war for the Royal Navy. The Army might sit in France and dig trenches on the Franco–Belgian border, and the R.A.F. might bomb Germany with leaflets while refraining from bombing the Black Forest because it was private property. For the Royal Navy, however, the war started in earnest from the first day.

Unlike the First World War the importance of convoying appears to have been remembered at once. However, there were two major lessons of that earlier war that had to be relearned. First was the use of airpower with convoys, and second was the use of anti-submarine hunting groups. Towards the end of 1918 it had been effectively shown that a properly escorted convoy, with air cover, was a very difficult target to attack. What the Royal Navy found difficult to accept, for perfectly understandable reasons, was that for a trade war to be won it was not in fact necessary for any submarines to be sunk. All that was necessary was that all the merchant ships should arrive unscathed at their destination. This, of course, ran counter to all the aggressive instincts of both the Royal Navy and its First Lord, Winston Churchill, and all the traditions which had been built up over centuries. While the professional naval officers were to be found in the battleships, if they could, or in the fleet destroyers (those that escorted the battleships), the hostilities-only officers were usually posted to the escort craft, the corvettes, the sloops and the escort destroyers. Immediately war was declared convoys were instituted for all merchant shipping. That lesson had been learned in 1917–18. However, Churchill initially encouraged the use of hunter groups, which would be formed to roam the shipping lanes and to look for submarines, entirely separate from the convoys. When the Second World War broke out there was no Anti-Submarine Division of the Naval Staff. The A/S represen-

126

tation at the Admiralty was doubled, from one commander to two, the day before war was declared. These two officers constituted the A/S Section of the Local Defence Division of the Naval Staff. It soon became obvious that anti-submarine warfare was much too large a subject to be dealt with in this way and a separate A/SW Division was created on 2 October 1939.

Any doubts about how the Germans were going to "play the game" were immediately resolved. The *Athenia* was torpedoed (against Hitler's orders) on 3 September 1939. The first convoy sailed on 6 September. The Admiralty immediately organised a 3-fold attack on the U-boats: convoys, the arming of merchant ships, and counter-attack methods. What enabled the latter, they believed, to succeed was the growth in effectiveness of asdic. Here they were wrong. There was a widespread exaggerated confidence in asdic (renamed sonar in 1943) probably due to using as data the results obtained by a small group of dedicated experts in limited conditions off Portland. Submarine officers of the interwar period such as Captain Jackie Broome always knew that "asdic was never the infallible weapon we cracked it up to be".[1] There was equally, of course, an inability to spot a U-boat on the surface at night without any form of high-definition radar. Churchill urged on the naval staff the formation of "attacking groups" or "hunting groups" at the expense of convoy escorts, to seek out and destroy the U-boats. He proposed this in a minute to Pound on 20 November 1939:

First Lord to First Sea Lord.   20.xi.39

> Nothing can be more important in the anti-submarine war than to try to obtain an independent flotilla which could work like a cavalry division on the approaches, without worrying about the traffic or U-boat sinkings, but could systematically search large areas over a wide front. In this way these areas would become untenable to U-boats, and many other advantages would flow from the manoeuvre.[2]

It is interesting to note that Churchill here includes in his *History Of The Second World War* a footnote, "This policy did not become possible until the later phase of the war".[3] Presumably this refers to the formation of escort groups and thus shows how Churchill had still failed to grasp the basis of anti-submarine warfare. Escort groups were designed to go to the aid of convoys under attack, or threatened by attack; they were not

127

independent flotillas sweeping the Western Approaches. Pound was forced to accept these hunting groups despite the opposition to them from the DCNS and the DA/SW. It was not until 1942 when the proof of the efficacy of the convoy system had been finally demonstrated that Churchill accepted it without reservation. Meanwhile the navy had lost *Courageous*, one of only six aircraft carriers, as a direct result of her being involved in an A/S hunting group. She was sunk on September 17 in the Bristol Channel.

While Pound was against the idea of these hunting groups, he was in favour of attempting to repeat the infamous Northern Barrage of 1918, which he had been instrumental in planning as DOD. This was a mine-field laid down between the Orkneys and Norway, which was supposed to have accounted for six U-boats in six weeks at the end of the First World War, but had in fact only accounted for four. Pound proposed it to Churchill, who eventually agreed to it, but it was inefficient and was never a real threat to German U-boats even when moved to the Faeroes–Iceland gap after the fall of Norway. This is not surprising when it is considered that the depth here was about 200 fathoms. The result was dismal: one U-boat was sunk, *U702*, in September 1944. One would have expected Pound, as a torpedo expert (i.e. an underwater weapons specialist), to know something about the failure of the 1918 barrage. However, his excuse, given to Captain J.S. Cowie, a mine specialist, then a commander in the Ops. Division was:

> The Admiralty would never have been forgiven had they failed to make the attempt to mine these waters. He also emphasised that the minefields, in addition to being no more than a hazard to U-boats, were intended to have a restrictive influence on the operation of enemy surface shipping in the Atlantic. This they undoubtedly did, as well as acting as a flanking protection to the Iceland convoy.[4]

Pound had less involvement in the thorny question of how many U-boats had been sunk, but it is an important, if minor, episode for the light it shows on Churchill himself. Churchill broadcast frequently and wanted to show the Royal Navy in the best possible light. On 20 January 1940 he claimed in a broadcast that "It seems pretty certain tonight that half the U-boats with which Germany began the war have been sunk".[5] The correct figure, we now know, was six out of fifty-seven; the NID estimate was six out of sixty-six. Churchill got his figure by combining the sixteen 'probably sunk' with the nine 'known sunk', and adding in eight for good measure, supplied from Professor Lindeman's statistical section. Churchill, it is understandable, wanted to show the Royal Navy, and hence himself, doing their job well and was keen to build up Allied morale. What better way could there be than telling the free world how excellently the Royal Navy was dealing with the U-boat menace? However, this does not explain Churchill's role in the sacking of Captain A.G. Talbot, the DA/SW since 15 November 1939. The latter was the head of the Assessment Committee, whose job was to make an accurate assessment of the U-boats sunk, and he abstained from wishful thinking. He claimed more modest figures and was almost exactly right, as we now know. However, he argued the toss with the First Lord too often and too publicly. On 24 April 1940 he reported the U-boat fleet on 10 March as: destroyed nineteen, (actual figure fifteen), under repair two, available forty-three. Pound believed there were twenty-two available, and Churchill that there were only twelve. Churchill's minute to Pound (25 April) was flagged with an Action This Day sticker, and ended, "This conclusion leads me to think that it might be a good thing if Captain Talbot went to sea as soon as possible".[6] This was cruel injustice, but Pound had the sense not to fight it. He made sure that Talbot was given a good command, the aircraft carrier *Furious*. There was no point in creating a crisis unless it was over a really vital issue and a change of the Director of a Staff Division was not vital.

★

Pound, as First Sea Lord, cannot be blamed for the poor defences of Scapa Flow in 1939. The blame here rests squarely on the Treasury. From 1938 Admiral Sir Charles Forbes (Commander-in-Chief Home Fleet) and Rear Admiral Thomson (Flag Officer Rosyth) had moved heaven and earth to get the Scapa Flow defences improved. The consequences of the neglect ("Where is the money to come from?" had been the invariable response to demands) was the sinking of *Royal Oak* (torpedoed 14 October 1939), the mining of a valuable new cruiser *Belfast* (21 November 1939) and of *Nelson* (4 December 1939). A crisis meeting was held on board *Nelson* on 31 October 1939 between the First Lord, the First Sea Lord and the Commander-in-Chief Home Fleet, where a decision was eventually reached to improve the Scapa defences. Pound

129

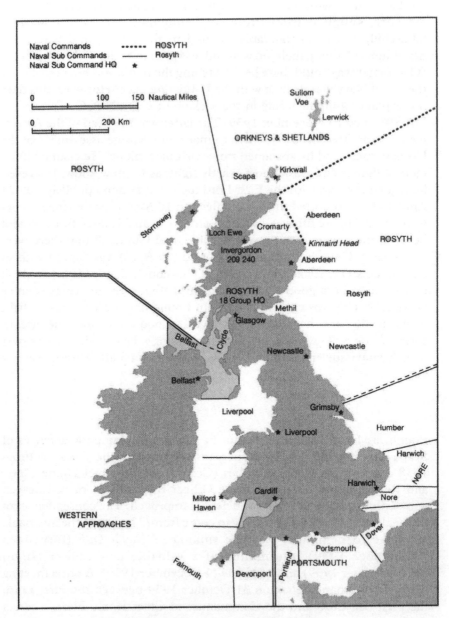

Naval Home Command Areas, 1939

was pushed hard on this by Churchill to ensure that all was going forward at the utmost speed.

> Experience shows that contractors are much more ready to book work for Government than to carry it out punctually. I therefore wish to know how many men are at work at Scapa, and how many will be working every Monday in January. Also reports whether in fact that number are at their posts. . . . My general impression is that we are making very little progress. Two and a half months have passed since the *Royal Oak* was torpedoed. What, in fact, has been done since? How many blockships sunk? How many nets made? How many men have been at work for how many days? . . . I thought we settled two months ago to have a weekly report.[7]

Pound must have thought back to that gruelling three weeks in November 1914 when he had built anti-submarine netting at Scapa Flow and had inveighed against Admiralty inefficiency. He, and indeed the whole Admiralty, was working flat out. Somerville, brought out of enforced retirement and working at the Admiralty, wrote to Cunningham on 12 February 1940:

> In the workhouse everyone is very immersed. DP (sic) seems to be bearing up. Tom Phillips always looks like death and tries to do too much. Curious shadows move behind the throne – Bill Tennant, Grantham, etc.[8]

While Pound was spending all his time attempting to accustom the Navy to war again, and it was not an easy task, Churchill began to cast his eye around for some way in which he could mount an offensive. His fertile imagination never ceased to conjure up, and to press on his advisers, ideas for carrying the war more effectively to the enemy. On the positive side it had a tremendous effect on morale. However, on the debit side it was exhausting for the Naval Staff. Pound though, as explained, never saw it as worthwhile giving a firm "No". The best example of this was Operation CATHERINE.

Churchill put forward Operation CATHERINE in a minute to Pound to 6 September 1939. It proposed "to force a passage into the Baltic and to maintain there a naval force".[9] Pound could see little in favour of such an exercise. What after all were they likely to achieve, except for the cutting off of the iron ore supplies from Sweden to Germany, and at a likely cost

131

of the entire expedition? However, he made the Naval Staff carry out a full appreciation and allowed Churchill to bring in Admiral of the Fleet Lord Cork and Orrery to carry out the detailed planning. Pound did not declare the project unfeasible; instead he laid down certain conditions as being necessary. For example, he insisted that Russia must not join with Germany and that Swedish "active cooperation" should be forthcoming. Gradually through October and November further pressure was brought to bear on the plan. Many of the ships could not be spared from their present duties: for example the battleships were needed for convoy protection. The RAF could not provide fighter cover at that range. The German Army could seize control of Denmark and could command the Kogrund Channel and the Belts with artillery fire.

By December the Naval Staff was almost totally against the plan. Despite Churchill's claim in his *History Of The Second World War* that "I had strong support in all this from the DCNS, Admiral Tom Phillips. . . . and from Admiral Bruce Fraser, the Controller and Third Sea Lord",[10] there is almost no evidence to back this up. As regards Phillips' support, Admiral Godfrey, then DNI, says tersely "Nonsense".[11] Admiral Fraser had effectively torpedoed CATHERINE in October when Churchill asked, "How are you going to get these ships into dockyards' hands [to strengthen their blisters and armoured decks] with all your other troubles?" The simple answer, which Fraser provided to Pound, was that it wasn't possible. Pound apparently said to Captain Daniel, the Director of Plans, "Don't worry. It will never take place".[12] By the end of December Pound was sending to Churchill a minute "CATHERINE is a great gamble. . . . I consider sending a fleet of surface ships into the Baltic is courting disaster." Finally, on 10 January 1940, Pound submitted a paper to the First Lord "calculated" says Marder, "to make his flesh creep",[13] which concluded:

> Our first object must be to win this war, but it is important that we should if possible end the war with our sea supremacy unchallenged. Even if we lost the whole of the submarines we sent into the Baltic it would not really matter, whilst if we lost a considerable part of our surface fleet the story would be a very different one.

Churchill eventually conceded defeat on 15 January and agreed that Operation CATHERINE would not be practicable. The German invasion of Denmark and Norway in April ended any hopes of the operation being carried out, much to the relief of the Naval Staff, and Pound in particular. Pound had won his point, but it had been an exhausting struggle.

★

There were other Churchilian flights of fancy at this time, all of which cost the Naval Staff a great deal of hard work to stop. There was his "Cultivator Number 6", a trench-cutting tank, which he wanted developed for the Army. There was Operation Royal Marine, his plan to float mines down the Rhine, Meuse and Moselle. This at least was carried out, and between 10 and 31 May over 3000 mines were launched, but the operation involved Churchill and the Naval Staff in hours of work, battling against the French government, the War Cabinet and the legal adviser to the Foreign Office.

However, the important point about most of these schemes was that they did not concern naval deployments. Such planning as Operation CATHERINE was for projected operations and, at the early stages of the war, Churchill was not prepared to challenge Pound's supreme authority on naval operational matters. A good example of this came with the action against the *Graf Spee* off the River Plate. Churchill took a keen interest in any operation which was concerned with a commerce raider or blockade runner. He would haunt the Duty Captain's office, or the OIC, and would frequently suggest opinions, as was his right.

> The First Sea Lord normally would appear to agree with what Winston proposed: he would never argue that such proposals were impracticable, or that less force would be adequate. After leaving the Map room, Pound would work out with the Naval Staff what could be done, and would then signal the necessary operation orders. He was always ready to face afterwards any complaint of Winston's that changes had been made.[14]

Graf Spee had completed a highly successful commerce raiding cruise in the South Atlantic and the Indian Ocean, but had been engaged by Commodore Henry Harwood with his three smaller cruisers on 13 December. She then sought shelter in Montevideo after suffering damage, and eventually scuttled herself on the evening of 17 December outside the harbour rather than face what she believed to be overwhelming odds. Churchill spent all of 13 December in Pound's Map Room. It became the

133

centre of action, with First Lord, First Sea Lord and Director of the Operation Division sitting round the table watching the chase being plotted. Much of the information came from American broadcasting sources, while Commodore Harwood's signals took about six hours to come, due to decipherment and retransmission via the Falklands Islands, Sierra Leone, Gibraltar and Whitehall. Churchill was keen to send suggestions to Harwood based on what the US radio reports said, but Pound insisted that Harwood should be left to make his own dispositions. This is confirmed by both Grantham and Godfrey, who explain how Pound insisted that the Admiralty signals should be confined to reinforcements being sent, the positioning of oil tankers, etc. Once *Graf Spee* had sunk Churchill immediately sent messages of congratulations to Harwood, promoting him to Rear Admiral and awarding him a KBE, and to Pound and the Naval Staff, followed up by a long signal recommending how the ships should be redisposed!

It is worthwhile considering here what Pound saw as the correct relationship between the Admiralty and the Commanders-in-Chief of the various British fleets, principally the Home and Mediterranean Fleets. Shortly after he took over as First Sea Lord (18 August 1939) Pound wrote a letter to Admiral Forbes.

> There is one point I wanted to raise with you about the Admiralty possibly having to give orders to your Fleet. The normal procedure would be for the Admiralty to give you all the information they possess and leave you to make your dispositions.
>
> On the other hand there may be occasions when you are at sea keeping W/T silence when later information makes it necessary to alter your dispositions. This can only be done by the Admiralty. Similarly if the Fleet had steam up it might be necessary to tell you in what direction to steer whilst passing the necessary information to you.
>
> I suggest therefore that it be recognised that at times it will be necessary for the Admiralty to order dispositions, but that Admiralty control will cease as soon as possible and that, to avoid any misunderstandings, the Admiralty will always make "Admiralty has ceased control" when they do so.[15]

Forbes replied on 22 August with general agreement, but concluded: "It must be left to my discretion at the time whether I carry out those orders".[16] He believed that the man on the spot must have the last word, as the Admiralty could not always be aware of the conditions prevailing many hundreds of miles away.

This difference of opinion was not satisfactorily resolved before war broke out. Indeed it could be said never to have been resolved. Pound wrote to a colleague in October 1939 stating "Why have Commanders-in-Chiefs and do their work for them? If they are not capable of doing it they must make way for someone who can."[17] Pound would have had little belief in an Admiralty which had interfered with his dispositions of the Mediterranean Fleet when he was Commander-in-Chief. Yet throughout his time as First Sea Lord he did tend to issue orders not just to Commanders-in-Chief, but even to individual ships and convoys, most notably in the case of the disaster to PQ 17. This is a topic we shall return to.

The *Graf Spee*'s supply ship *Altmark* managed to get as far as Norway on her return to Germany before being intercepted by the Royal Navy. However, she was in Norwegian territorial waters. Churchill intervened decisively here in operational matters by sending a signal directly to Captain Vian in *Cossack* with direct orders to board and search *Altmark*. According to the Duty Captain in the War Room, Churchill was there "accompanied by his PPS and by Tom Phillips, then VCNS",[18] and he makes no reference to Pound being there. Churchill in his account does not mention Pound in the context of his signal, simply stating

> When this information reached the Admiralty I intervened, and with the concurrence of the Foreign Secretary, ordered our ships to enter the fiord. I did not often act so directly.[19]

He goes on to say "Admiral Pound and I sat up together in some anxiety in the Admiralty War Room"[20] while waiting for the results of *Cossack*'s action. Roskill makes the point that

> The Admiralty did not confine its signals and instructions to the decision of policy: it also sent operational messages to Captain Vian over the Commander-in-Chief's head. Though no untoward events occurred on this occasion, Admiral Forbes later pointed out to the First Sea Lord that as Captain Vian was operating under him the Admiralty's messages might have caused a conflict of orders.[21]

Although Roskill is correct in theory, what was needed was an immediate decision at a political level. This could only come via the Admiralty, and from the First Lord. Probably the signal should have gone from First Sea Lord to Commander-in-Chief Home Fleet, but no damage was done, and speed, in this case, was of the essence.

The *Altmark* episode is not particularly significant in itself, except insofar as it shows Churchill trespassing upon Pound's domain of operational affairs for the first time. The follow-on to the *Altmark* episode is a much more serious matter, where Churchill's hand can be seen far more often. The Norwegian campaign has been the subject of enormous controversy, and in particular the extent, or lack of it, of Churchill's involvement. On the one side is Professor A.J. Marder, who claims that Churchill hardly interfered at all in the conduct of the campaign ("possibly in one or two instances"[22]). On the other hand is Captain S.W. Roskill, the official historian, who believes that the majority of signals emanating from "First Lord and First Sea Lord" were written by Churchill. The fact that the disagreement between these two eminent historians reached an almost schoolboy level of one-upmanship is regrettable.

The Norwegian campaign has its origins in the shipment of iron ore from the Swedish orefields at Gallivare to Germany. In the summer months little could be done to intercept this trade as it came through the Baltic (one of Churchill's reasons behind the aborted Operation CATHERINE). However, when the Baltic froze in winter the ore was taken by railway to Narvik in Norway and shipped from there to Germany down the Norwegian coastline. In view of the British emphasis on the economic side of the war Churchill decided that this had to be stopped. His initial method was to be through aid to Finland who had been embroiled in war with Russia since 30 November 1939. The admiration which was felt for the way in which the Finns were holding out against the Red Army led Churchill to plan to send them aid and at the same time stop the ore traffic, since the easiest way to send the aid was via Narvik and Gallivare. This was put to the Cabinet on 16 December, but little support for it was found, not surprisingly, as it would have resulted in Britain fighting against Russia as well as Germany, and invading two neutral countries, Norway and Sweden. Churchill was also determined to mine the Leads, the "thousand-mile protected Channel" of Norwegian territorial waters, which would force the German ore carriers and blockade runners out into international waters where they

136

Norway, 1940

could be intercepted by the Royal Navy. Throughout this genesis Churchill was supported by Pound and the Naval Staff in the desire to mine the Leads.

Pound was opposed to any operations within the Baltic, which might be caused by the military occupation of the Gallivare area and wrote to Churchill on Christmas Day, not only about Norwegian operations, but also, of course, about Operation CATHERINE, which was not yet dead:

> The only manner in which Naval action could ensure against any reinforcements reaching the head of the Gulf of Bothnia by sea would be to send into the Baltic a sufficient force to beat or contain the German Fleet. Owing to the great hazards to which it would be subjected during its passage into the Baltic, and by submarines, mines and aircraft after its arrival, we must be prepared to write off this force and be quite certain that we cannot lose the war at sea with the reduced forces we should have outside the Baltic.[23]

Because the Royal Navy was so fully stretched by the needs of convoy escorts and the U-boat menace, Pound concluded "I am unable to visualize therefore, a situation in 1940 in which we could spare the necessary forces to enter the Baltic, unless we are assured of Russian cooperation and could enter the Baltic at the invitation of that country".

By 27 December Churchill was in favour of sending destroyer forces into Norwegian waters to intercept the ore traffic, but this then clashed with the latest thinking of the Chiefs of Staff, who by 31 December were in favour of an expedition to the ore fields via Narvik. By 14 February the Finnish resistance to Russia had so encouraged British optimism that the Chiefs of Staff had put forward a plan to land a force in Narvik, capture the Gallivare ore fields and aid the Finns from Northern Sweden. British forces would also occupy the southern Norwegian ports of Stavanger, Bergen and Trondheim. This plan was about to be put into operation and the expedition was about to sail when, on 12 March, the Finns signed an armistice. In retrospect it is easy to sigh with relief, as the projected operation would have involved us in the occupation of two neutral countries and fighting Russia as well as Germany, a prospect that Churchill may well have enjoyed, but the more sober members of his staff viewed with some horror. Amazingly, Churchill wished to carry on with the operation, but the War Cabinet in effect cancelled the plan. Churchill then thought up various other options, including one for sending merchant ships equipped with a ram to sink German merchant ships in the Leads. Pound turned this one down, as well as others, both at the Admiralty and at the Chiefs of Staff Committee.

Suddenly, however, the Supreme War Council, that is representatives of the War Cabinet and the French cabinet, gave approval for the laying of mines in Norwegian waters, and for the occupation of Stavanger, Bergen, Trondheim and Narvik. The mines were laid (Operation WILFRID) early in the morning of 8 April, but on the same day the Germans invaded and occupied Oslo, Stavanger, Christiansand, Bergen, Trondheim and Narvik. Such was the genesis of the Norwegian campaign. As Marder has said, "It is perhaps the most completely researched operation of the war. . . . It was largely order, counterorder, disorder".[24] The actual conduct of the campaign is easily examined. The Germans secured all the major ports and airfields; the British, with some assistance from the French, were left to attack where they could. On 10 April British destroyers attempted to attack Narvik, but were driven off, leaving the Germans to be finished off on 13 April by Admiral Whitworth in *Warspite*, but there were no troops available for an immediate occupation of the town. Trondheim could not be taken by a direct assault, and so troops were landed north and south of it, at Namsos (14 April) and at Andalsnes (16 April) in order to take it by a pincer movement. However, such was the German superiority in air power and equipment that both these forces were evacuated by 3 May. Narvik was eventually captured on 28 May, but by then events in France were of more importance and it was evacuated by 8 June. During the later evacuation *Glorious* was sunk by *Scharnhorst* and *Gneisenau* on that final day.

What was the role of the Admiralty, and what of Pound and Churchill in all of this? The disagreement between Marder and Roskill here is at its most vituperative and there is little to be gained by recapitulating the details of their successive attacks upon each other, while they quote more and more sources in support of their case. To put it simply, Churchill was allowed to intervene in operations far more than Pound should have been prepared to accept. There are countless examples of this. Perhaps the most serious of them was the appointment of Admiral of the Fleet Lord Cork and Orrery as Flag Officer Narvik. The fact that he was under the Commander-in-Chief Home Fleet but senior to him in the Naval List was difficult enough, but, more importantly, Churchill had a private line of communication with him, which totally bypassed the First Sea Lord, the Naval Staff and the Home Fleet in order to send him separate orders. For example the Director of Operations (Home), Captain RAB Edwards, wrote in his diary:

> *21 April.* I have just discovered that Cork and First Lord have their own private line of communications, and they exchange all sorts of messages without the Admiralty having the slightest idea of what is going on. I have reported it to the First Sea Lord.

> *29 April.* C-in-C Home Fleet and Lord Cork are having their usual bicker. They are both incorrigible . . . Winston entered the fray and decided against the recommendation of the Naval Staff. This interference is appalling, and we don't appear strong enough to stand up to him. The Admiralty are quite hopeless, and the C-in-C worse.[25]

Where Marder appears to have erred in his article,[26] I think, is in the realization that Churchill had learnt an important lesson from his experiences in the First World War where he had sent personal instructions to admirals afloat (notably in the pursuit of *Goeben* and *Breslau* in 1914, and in the Dardanelles campaign). In the Norwegian campaign he undoubtedly dictated messages sent in the Admiralty's name, though he generally showed them to the First Sea Lord and had them sent in their joint names. That they were in Churchill's hand cannot be doubted.

> Pray regard this telegram as my personal opinion (19 April).

> It seems to me that you can feel your way, and yet strike hard (21 April).

> I shall be glad to share your responsibilities (4 May).[27]

These were all sent to Lord Cork, but there were others as well. Captain Warburton-Lee signalled to C-in-C Home Fleet before the first battle of Narvik that the strength of the Germans there was greater than originally thought and added, "Intend attacking at dawn high water". It is a long-established naval custom that when a junior officer signals a senior officer stating "intend" no reply is expected unless the senior officer disapproves. The Admiralty signalled directly to Captain Warburton-Lee on the evening of 9 April "You alone can judge whether, in these circumstances,

140

attack should be made. We shall support whatever decision you take".[28] This was over the head of both C-in-C Home Fleet, Admiral Forbes, and the Flag Officer Battle Cruisers, Vice Admiral Whitworth, who was Warburton-Lee's immediate superior, and the language itself is indicative of its author.

Lord Cork, although keeping Churchill reasonably appraised of the evacuation from Narvik, failed to keep Admiral Forbes informed, and this was a contributory factor in the success of *Scharnhorst* and *Gneisenau*. Forbes complained about the Admiralty not keeping him informed of Lord Cork's movements. Finally, when Churchill became Prime Minister, he signalled on 14 May.

> Although I am leaving the Admiralty I shall as Minister of Defence preserve that close personal contact with you which has I trust has been a help.[29]

All of this surely makes it clear that Churchill constantly interfered with operational matters.

★

There is also the matter of command appointments which must be here considered. We have already seen the appointment of a retired Admiral of the Fleet to an operational command, namely that of Lord Cork and Orrery to Narvik. This can possibly be explained as needing an experienced figure who could control both naval and army forces, but the effect upon some junior flag officers can but be imagined as they saw old war horses being brought out of retirement. Lord Cork was supposed to be "offensive-minded". Presumably the other available officers were not. Pound and Churchill were also under great pressure from another Admiral of the Fleet, Lord Keyes, to use his services, and this was a battle which went on for some time and needs to be looked at in some detail.

Pound had been criticized in some quarters for not mounting a full-scale attack on Trondheim by the main strength of the Home Fleet. The coastal defences had not, at that stage, been taken over by the Germans, but the port lay 50 miles from the open sea and any assaulting force would have been open to attack from the air in a very enclosed space in the fjord. Both Pound and Forbes were becoming fully aware of the effects of air power and the limitations which this imposed upon their operations. Roskill observes.

> To have hazarded a great proportion of our naval strength on an operation which could not have decidedly affected the outcome of the war at a time when the threat in the west was becoming more and more plain would, it now seems, have been to court a more serious setback than the loss of central Norway.[30]

This, however, was not the view of Sir Roger Keyes. He had had a long and distinguished career, but had, as we have seen, failed to be appointed First Sea Lord in 1927 in succession to either Beatty or Madden, for which, as we know, he blamed Pound. Initially, in July 1939, he wrote to congratulate Pound upon his appointment, but by 18 September he was writing to Admiral Sir William Hall:

> Of course, I *know* I ought to be CNS with Pound as my deputy. We have worked together since 1917 when he was my Flag Captain for a short spell in *Colossus*. . . . He is an admirable Staff Officer, but his judgement has not always been good. . . . Perhaps he can accept big responsibility, I hope so, but don't feel sure. Anyway, in war time there is too much for the CNS and 1st SL (sic) to do, and the CNS ought to be free from all Departmental worries. . . . I believe Winston, Pound and I would be a good combination.[31]

The sheer egoism of this, and subsequent letters, take away the breath, but, like many other senior officers who had retired before the war, Keyes felt deeply frustrated at his inability to contribute. This was particularly so as Pound had so often been his subordinate. From 1 October 1939 onwards Keyes was almost apoplectic in his comments on the Naval Staff, their refusal to give him a position, and in April 1940, their refusal to mount the attack on Trondheim.

In a letter on 4 October to Churchill, who was an old friend from before the First World War, he wrote:

> I do not know who was responsible for the idea of duplicating the First Sea Lord, but there is a good deal to be said for it in wartime.
> Pound is 4 years younger than I, and succeeded to the rank of Admiral of the Fleet at the age I was retired from it! . . .
> As I told you, I had formed a very high opinion of him as a Staff

officer, although I had good reason on more than one occasion to doubt the wisdom of his judgement on policy.

If circumstances arise which make you feel that the policy adopted in the last war should be repeated, I hope that you will bear me in mind, as Pound and I have worked together in harmony for some years and were a good combination.

I quite appreciate that this might be very difficult for you to arrange, but it is worth thinking about! I know I am not popular with the Government, but after all neither were you!

This letter is of course *for your eye only* and had better be destroyed.[32]

Again on 1 November he wrote to Churchill:

You never give me an opportunity of talking to you, and I daresay you won't even bother to read this! However, I hope some day you will remember that my unique experience is not being made use of in any way, to the astonishment of my friends, when I have to confess to them that I know nothing and have no connection with the Admiralty, after two months of war with you as First Lord!

People who don't love you told me you would let me down, but I still have faith in you and my star.[33]

Keyes was relatively quiet from then until the Norway campaign, except for some intriguing in favour of Coastal Command and the Fleet Air Arm at the expense of Bomber Command. However, on 16 April he exploded on paper with complete incomprehension that neither Churchill nor Pound had re-employed him. What particularly riled him was the appointment of Lord Cork. In a letter to his wife he spoke about an unsatisfactory meeting he had, at last, had with Churchill. He began by telling Churchill how to deal with Italy:

He did his weary Titan again – discredited my theory, told [Seal] later it was out of the question. . . . Can you imagine anything so foolish, if he really thinks that is the answer he ought not to be allowed to have anything to say about operations! What he really did not like was that I should have suggested something his tired staff had not thought of. . . . He rang the bell half way through and said he was sorry he was tired and must rest.

Winston gave me a chance of hitting back when he said I was not

143

fit for command, I had been unemployed so long. That is of course
what D Pound and Co. (sic) must be saying. I said don't think I am
jealous of Cork. I commend you for your appt. (sic). Of course it isn't
a big enough appt. for me – I could be much more use than that if I
weren't barred from helping – Cork was 7 or 8 years junior to me and
less than a year younger.[34]

In particular it was the attack on Trondheim which Keyes advocated,
sending a detailed plan for the attack to Churchill on 23 April. But he was
to be bitterly disappointed when he was firmly put down by Churchill on
the next day:

> It astonishes me that you should think that all this has not been exam-
> ined by people who know exactly what resources are available, and
> what the dangers will be. I will however ask the First Sea Lord
> whether he can receive you.
>
> You will, I hope, appreciate the fact that I have to be guided by my
> responsible Naval advisers, and that it is not open to me to make the
> kind of appointments you . . . have in mind on ground of friendship.[35]

Nevertheless, Keyes persuaded Pound to see him on 25 April, and he
wrote to Churchill to describe the meeting on the 26th:

> After my conversation with Pound yesterday, I cannot believe that he
> does not trust my judgement – or my ability to carry this business
> through successfully – so don't delay . . .
>
> Can't you see my vision? It has been my constant companion for
> days; I have tried so hard to open your overworked tired eyes to see
> the immense possibilities which lie ahead of us, and which are worth
> some risk.[36]

He also wrote to Pound the same day:

> I can't believe that the First Lord would object to making use of me
> now, in view of my past services and experience. I hope that you are
> not preventing it in this hour of peril?
>
> After all I have had more experience in making war and in
> combined operations of this kind than anyone in the Navy. If you are
> blocking me now, you are taking a very heavy responsibility on your
> shoulders.
>
> I would like to remind you of some advice you gave me some years

144

1. HMS *Britannia*, Summer 1892. Cadet Pound extreme right of back row in front of the standing figure.

2. HMS *Britannia.*

3. HMS *Britannia*. Dudley Pound, front row second from right, as Cadet Captain, 1892.

4. 1896. Pound as a newly promoted Sub-Lieutenant.

5. Officers' skiff race, Vancover, British Columbia, 1904. Dudley Pound and
Lieutenant Soper winning, coxed by a Miss Pitts.

6. HMS *Repulse*, c. 1921. Dudley, on left, and Betty Pound, seated right.

7. Commodore Dudley Pound, Chief of Staff to Admiral Keyes, Commander-in-Chief, Mediterranean Fleet.

8. The Pound family home, 1928-31, Shiplake, at Buckland Monachorum.

9. HMS *Renown* flying Vice Admiral Sir Dudley Pound's flag as ACQ in Nigg Bay, Cromarty Firth, 12 July, 1930.

10. Battle Cruiser Squadron in line ahead. Note the cars on deck on the extreme right.

11. Dudley Pound on skis.

12. Skiing trip at Obergurgl, 1934. Pound, sixth from left, front row.

13. The Second Sea Lord pays a visit. Vice Admiral Sir Dudley Pound being piped aboard.

14. Admiral Sir Dudley Pound as Commander-in-Chief Mediterranean Fleet.

15. Cis, Betty Pound's sister, Noel Coward and Lady Pound.

16. Dudley Pound relaxing in the Mediterranean: King George of Greece, Dudley Pound, Dan Duff, Charles Norris, Barbara Pound, Cis Whitehead, Betty Pound.

17. Pound on a shooting expedition. Charles Hotham, Captain of the Fleet, Pound, Victor Crutchley VC, Captain of *Warspite*, Commander Oliver Gordon, Master of the Fleet, Lieutenant Commander Dick Ryder, Dan Duff, Flag Lieutenant.

18. Admiral Sir Dudley Pound says farewell to the Mediterranean Fleet from the bridge of HMS *Warspite*. On the left his flag Captain, Victor Crutchley, V.C.

19. Admiral of the Fleet Sir Dudley Pound in his office at the Admiralty.

20. The Chiefs of Staff at the outbreak of war: General Sir Edmund Ironside, Air Chief Marshal Sir Cyril Newall and Admiral of the Fleet Sir Dudley Pound. Note the gasmask holders.

21. The Chiefs of Staff between October, 1940 and December, 1941: General Sir John Dill, Admiral of the Fleet Sir Dudley Pound and Air Marshal Sir Charles Portal.

22. The First Sea Lord with Admiral Darlan, head of the French Navy, in 1940.
    Pound later referred to him as "a twister".

23. Aboard HMS *Prince of Wales*, during the voyage to Placentia Bay, Newfoundland,
    August, 1941. Harriman, Beaverbrook, Dill, Churchill and Pound.

24. Pound and the US High Command inspect a Royal Marine guard of honour on HMS *Prince of Wales*, August, 1941. From left, Marshall, Pound, Arnold, Stark, Turner and King.

25. Pound speaking at a dinner. From the right, Portal, Stark, Pound.

26. Casablanca, January, 1943. Churchill with his Chiefs of Staff and advisors. Front
    row: Portal, Pound, Churchill, Dill, Brooke. Back row: Lieutenant Commander
    Thompson, Brigadier Dykes, Alexander, Martin, Mountbatten, Ismay, Leathers, ?,
    Macmillan, Leslie Rowan and Jacobs, ?

27. Casablanca, January, 1943. King and Pound in apparent agreement.

28. Casablanca Conference, King, Marshall, Arnold, Dykes, ?, Wedemeyer, Ismay, Mountbatten, Pound, Brooke, Portal and Dill.

29. Washington, May, 1943. Churchill and Roooosevelt with their advisers. From left, Dill, Ismay, Portal, Brooke, Pound, Leahy, Marshall, King, ?

30. The funeral procession. Churchill, followed by A.V. Alexander and the Board of Admiralty.

31. Martin and George Pound cast their wreaths into the Solent from HMS *Glasgow*.

ago, which was very unfortunate [here he tells Pound that he was responsible for Keyes not becoming First Sea Lord] . . . It wasn't good advice . . .

I think you owe me and the Navy some reparation, and you can do this by giving me the opportunity of running this inshore combined operation, and give the navy the benefit of my experience and power of leadership.

I ought not to have had to *force* a plan on the Naval Staff's notice or to remind you, of all people, of my fighting qualities.

I should not have ignored you if our positions were reversed![37]

Pound replied in a most courteous way three days later, ignoring the comments about his being 'responsible' for Keyes not being First Sea Lord:

I cannot imagine what caused you to suggest in your letter that I had been, as you put it, "blocking" you, and very much resent the suggestion that I should do such a thing either in your case or that of any other officer.

In making recommendations to the First Lord for appointments, I am guided by one thing and one thing only, and that is that the officer should be the most suitable for the appointment.

Both the First Lord and I have been fully aware of your burning desire to serve and how much you must feel in not being in the thick of things. You will realise, however, I am sure, that appointments for Admirals of the Fleet are not easy to come by.[38]

That same day (29 April) Keyes sent a long letter to Churchill summing up his feelings about the whole episode. It referred to "the shocking in-action of the Navy at Trondheim, for which you and your pusillanimous, self-satisfied, shortsighted Naval advisers must bear the responsibility". It ended, "For God's sake put your trust in me and don't waste any more time".[39] He sent copies of this letter to the Prime Minister and four other leading Cabinet ministers. The following day another letter was sent to Churchill, which included the following:

When am I going to be allowed to take a hand in the conduct of the Naval War? I know I represent the fighting spirit of the Navy. . . . If my advice had been followed in 1915 when I fought on, almost single-handed, to be allowed to force the Dardanelles (which is now

145

accepted as having been a feasible operation) the flower of the Turkish Army would have been cut off and decisively defeated. . . . Bacon and Jellicoe had to be got rid of by the Lloyd George Govt. (sic) before I was allowed to wage war in the Dover Straits and on the Belgian Coast. Is my Great War experience to be made no use of because the air factor has become more formidable? [There then follows another diatribe against Pound for stopping him becoming First Sea Lord.]

Give me the small force I asked for and the Royal Navy and its Sea Soldiers will show the world that they can stand up to any German air attack.[40]

Eventually Keyes' frustrations boiled over in his speech on 7 May in the House of Commons during the debate on the Norway campaign, which brought down the Chamberlain government. The result of that, of course, was to see Churchill move from the Admiralty to 10 Downing Street, and one of his first actions as Prime Minister was to send Keyes, as his personal representative, to the King of the Belgians, safely out of the way of interfering in Admiralty affairs.

What, however, should Pound have done? We may, surely, doubt whether he protested to Churchill about his interference in operations. What was the point, in that the entire campaign was a disaster from the moment the Germans seized the airfields? It was, anyway, just as much an Army and Air Force disaster as a Royal Naval one. Whatever the Naval Staff might do there was little that could have been done to make certain of a victory in Norway, and although we suffered heavy losses to our destroyers and carrier force, the German Navy was extremely heavily damaged (the implications for the summer of 1940 are important). The system for prosecuting the war had been seen to be hopelessly incompetent and the most important result of the campaign was the removal of Chamberlain and his replacement by Churchill as Prime Minister and, crucially, as Minister of Defence. This was the only beneficial result of the campaign. What was dangerous was the precedent that had been created. Although by the end of the campaign Churchill was no longer at the Admiralty, and the much less overpowering A.V. Alexander had been installed as First Lord, Pound had been seen by the Royal Navy to interfere with the men on the spot. A chain of command had been set up which simply defied not only belief, but also logic, and old retired ad-

146

mirals had been brought back on to the stage rather than make use of youthful service officers. Mercifully Keyes had been deflected. The thought of two retired Admirals of the Fleet being brought back for active commands passes comprehension, and Pound did well to resist the importunings of his one-time mentor. However, junior officers at the Admiralty, of whom Roskill was one, were evidently alarmed by what they had seen.

10

THE FRENCH AND THEIR FLEET

The problems of Norway started to fade into insignificance when on 10 May 1940 the Germans launched their long-awaited western offensive. The B.E.F. had been escorted to France at the outbreak of war with virtually no interference at all. The advance parties had sailed on 4 September and the first main landings took place on 10 September. By 7 October 161,000 men, 24,000 vehicles and 140,000 tons of stores had been transported to France without any loss. It was one of the few operations of the war which was conducted entirely according to plan.

Relations with the French were, on the whole, good. This was particularly so at the operational level. The French Navy had agreed to be responsible for the western basin of the Mediterranean, a logical decision given their bases in southern France and North Africa, while the Mediterranean Fleet, based on Alexandria, would look after the eastern basin. The French also based a powerful squadron, the *Force de Rade*, on Brest for operations in the eastern Atlantic, which would work in close conjunction with the Home Fleet. The military deterioration that had affected the French high command and army, and had been noted by Churchill and others, had not affected the French Navy. It was the second largest in Europe and was a disciplined and highly integrated force under the rigid control of Admiral François Darlan. Its main units consisted of five old battleships of 1914–18 vintage, of which three had been extensively modernized in 1932–35; two modern battlecruisers, *Dunkerque* and *Strasburg*, completed in 1937–38, at least the equal of *Scharnhorst* and *Gneisenau*; two powerful modern battleships, *Jean Bart* and *Richelieu*, both nearing completion; and a host of cruisers, armed with both eight-inch and six-inch guns, destroyers, submarines and smaller craft. Except for the old battleships none of these craft were more then fourteen years old, and the destroyers were among the fastest and best armed in the world. As Marder says:

> It was in general a homogeneous fleet, the guns and the communication equipment of the warships excellent, and the crews well disciplined and well trained. 80% were long-service personnel.[1]

They had proved themselves to be competent in various Allied operations, such as the Norwegian campaign, convoy escorting in the Atlantic, mine laying in the Channel and safeguarding communications in the Mediterranean. Relations were not quite so good at the highest level. Pound did not think a great deal of Darlan or of the French Admiralty, but at the operational level, given the difference of outlook and temperament, the co-operation was perfectly adequate, if not better.

★

The German campaign of May 1940 was so devastatingly successful that it was not surprising that it resulted in chaos in the orders issued to subordinate commanders by the Admiralty. So, on 19 May, at the same time as considering the evacuation of 45,000 troops, they were also considering transporting troops to the continent. There were few in the Cabinet who grasped the scale of the collapse in France. The Vice Admiral, Dover, Bertram Ramsay, appears to have been one of the few senior officers who saw what was coming and anticipated the likely size of the evacuation. Ramsay had been placed in command of the possible evacuation on 19 May and had started making preparations then. Operation DYNAMO was only ordered from the Admiralty on 26 May.

There was little that Pound, the Naval Staff or anybody at the Admiralty could do to help operations at Dunkirk. There were two keys to the success of the operation. The first was the weather. Any form of choppy weather would have stopped many of the small boats working at all. But almost throughout the course of the evacuation the sea was calm. In 1588 "God blew and they were scattered"; on this occasion God did not blow and they were saved. The second key was lifting capacity. This involved not just the Royal Naval vessels but the merchant marine and the "little ships" of the Dunkirk legend. A total of over 900 boats passed under Ramsay's control.

149

Pound sent his own Chief Staff Officer, Captain W.G. Tennant, to serve under Ramsay. He went straight to Dunkirk, where he performed heroics as the Senior Naval Officer. Ramsay was also well served by the Rear Admiral, Dover, W.F. Wake-Walker. Tennant and Wake-Walker were responsible for the day-to-day operations. It was Tennant who took the crucial decision to embark troops from the East Mole and so increase the nightly lift capacity substantially.

Pound took a number of important decisions to support the man on the spot. He put an extra thirty-nine destroyers at Ramsay's disposal, one fifth of the Navy's remaining destroyer strength. Given Britain's world-wide commitments, this was a brave decision and one about which the Naval Staff were worried. Secondly, and crucially, Pound sent Vice Admiral Sir James Somerville to help Ramsay and relieve him of some of the strain. Somerville, like Ramsay, had been retired from the Royal Navy, in 1939, in his case through ill health, but had returned on the outbreak of war to help the development of naval radar. As the Inspector of Miscellaneous Weapons and Devices he had gone over to Calais from Dover in response to a demand from Churchill to send naval 12 pounders to Calais. On return he had met up with his old friend Ramsay and had relieved him during the forenoon of 26 May to allow Ramsay to grab some much-needed sleep. When he returned to the Admiralty to report to Pound, he suggested that he should go back to Dover to alternate with the desperately overworked Ramsay in taking control of the evacuation. Pound saw the need and agreed with the idea. Somerville's contribution to the success of Operation DYNAMO has usually been overlooked. Without his help, Ramsay could well have lost his grip on things. Somerville, however,

> managed that most difficult of things, taking over the running of an unplanned and frantic operation at odd hours without ever threat-ening the authority of the commander, or allowing any break in the pattern or style of orders to be seen.[2]

Pound also had to take an unplanned decision when on 29 May he with-drew all the modern fleet destroyers from the Dover command. He did this because without such ships the Atlantic convoys could not be protected and Britain's long-term survival depended on this. This was the first occasion in which Pound can be seen to be following the dictum which he was later to make the foundation of his policy over the Atlantic

150

in his battles with the Air Ministry: "If we lose the war at sea, we lose the war." Ramsay, on this occasion, objected strongly, since it left him with only fifteen destroyers, many of them of 1914–18 vintage. After strong verbal representations by both Ramsay and Somerville, the modern destroyers were returned to Dover Command on 30 May. Pound could well have felt that his worst fears were justified when on 1 June five destroyers (one of them French) were sunk and four damaged. In total nine were sunk and nineteen damaged in the course of the whole operation.

On 4 June the Admiralty formally closed Operation DYNAMO. The losses to the Royal Navy were the equivalent of a major engagement. Her destroyer strength had dropped to only seventy-four available for duty. However, the losses in the spring campaigns of 1940 to the German Navy were even heavier, which was sufficient to prevent any realistic plans for invasion without total air supremacy. The German surface navy had been reduced to three cruisers and a handful of destroyers. Apart from the evacuation of the BEF, that was the real 'miracle' of Dunkirk.

The Admiralty was not only seriously alarmed by the destroyer shortage but also by the capital ship situation in June 1940. Although Britain had a numerical superiority over the Germans of eleven to two, with five and two building respectively, this position was misleading. Battleships had to escort the Atlantic convoys in case the *Scharnhorst* or the *Gneisenau* came out to attack them. Six battleships had to remain in the Mediterranean to watch the Italian fleet. There were none to spare for the Far East in case of war with the Japanese. The cruiser strength was equally bad, with the Royal Navy conveniently forgetting that this had been due, among other reasons, to Churchill's economic policies when he had been Chancellor of the Exchequer in the 1920s. Similarly, the destroyer shortage was, as we have seen, potentially disastrous. Given these conditions, the loss of co-operation of the French Fleet would have constituted a most serious threat to British hopes for victory. The joining of the French Fleet with the German one would have definitely constituted what could well be called a mortal threat. The ability of the Royal Navy to maintain control of sea communications would have been in jeopardy. It was for these reasons that the potential surrender of the French fleet to the Germans proved such a tremendous problem for the British and came to dominate their thinking in the days after Dunkirk.

151

*

Already, by 7 June, with the Germans 70 miles still from Paris, the problems of the disposition of the French Fleet, in the event of France pulling out of the war, was causing disquiet in London. Pound expressed in a meeting at the Admiralty the opinion that "the only practical way to deal with the matter is to sink the French Fleet".[3] What he wanted was for Darlan to scuttle the ships in advance of armistice negotiations, so that the Germans could not put pressure on the French by, for example, threatening to destroy Paris if the Fleet was not handed over intact. Pound believed that Darlan might accept this as he would be reluctant to surrender his ships to the Germans, but equally reluctant to sail his ships to British harbours.

By 11 June Pound had brought the matter up at the Chiefs of Staff Committee and a report to the War Cabinet expressed their concern over the French Fleet. They envisaged the collapse of French resistance and stated the main points that Pound had made on 7 June, giving two alternatives:

a)   to attempt to persuade as many French ships as possible to join our Fleet. We cannot expect such efforts to meet with much success.

b)   if a) fails, to press the French to sink the whole of their Fleet.[4]

It was with this advice from their military advisers that the British government had to decide on their policy towards France. Their basic problem was to decide between two differing courses: either to keep France in the war and give her what aid could be spared, or to prepare for her collapse and rescue what was possible, in particular their Fleet. Between these two stools the Churchill government fell with spectacular ineptitude and achieved neither of their desired aims. When the War Cabinet met at 10:15 on the morning of Sunday 16 June it had received a request from the French Prime Minister, Paul Reynaud, for permission to seek the terms of an armistice agreement from the Germans. The two governments had agreed on 28 March not to make a separate peace. Campbell, British Ambassador to France, and Spears, Churchill's personal representative to Reynaud, reported that if Reynaud resigned he could not guarantee that his successor would regard the surrender of the Fleet as an unacceptable condition for an armistice. Equally, if

152

Britain refused to permit the request for an armistice, Reynaud would resign. Their conclusion was that if Britain wished to safeguard the French Fleet it would be best to allow the request for terms to go ahead. The choice before the British War Cabinet and its military advisers was then between acceptance of the French proposal, as the best way of safeguarding the French Fleet, and its rejection in an attempt to hold the French to their obligations.

The War Cabinet discussion is enlightening since there was almost total agreement that the French must be allowed to ask for terms, since Reynaud was the only leader who might be able to guarantee the safety of the French Fleet. The discussion centred on the wording of the acceptance. Churchill wished to make it an absolute condition that "the French Fleet should sail forthwith for British ports pending any discussion of armistice terms". The full telegram, no 368, which was eventually despatched at 12:35, is worth quoting in full since it is central to the unfolding drama:

> Our agreement forbidding separate negotiations, whether for armistice or peace, was made with the French Republic, and not with any particular French administration or statesman. It therefore involves the honour of France. Nevertheless, provided, but only provided, that the French Fleet is sailed forthwith for British harbours pending negotiations, His Majesty's Government give their full consent to an inquiry by the French Government to ascertain the terms of an armistice for France. His Majesty's Government being resolved to continue the war, wholly exclude themselves from all part in the above-mentioned inquiry concerning an armistice.[5]

Although some people were unhappy about this, notably Spears and Vansittart, the British position was totally clear. It was not enough for them to be assured, as Reynaud and Darlan had done, that the surrender of the French Fleet would be considered unacceptable; the British wanted it under their own hand. This position might be criticized, but it could never be misconstrued. However, at this point, on what was already a dramatic day, the spectacular proposal of a union between Britain and France was made. Here the two strands of British policy started to interweave, since the proposal of union could only be seen as a means of keeping France fighting. This was how Spears, Campbell and Reynaud

153

saw it, Reynaud declaring that with such a proposal he could carry the day in his cabinet and continue fighting. He concluded, reasonably, that the proposal of union put the earlier British conditional acceptance of his request to seek terms in a completely different light.

> The proposal, if accepted, meant that France would go on in the war united with Great Britain. The disposal of the Fleet would then be a question of strategy to be settled by the joint staffs.[6]

Reynaud therefore presumed, with the enthusiastic agreement of Campbell and Spears, that Britain's latest offer superseded telegram 368.

Reynaud's reasoning was correct, up to a point: certainly the offer of union was intended to supersede the previous telegram; however, it was not intended to render Britain's conditional consent to seeking armistice terms null and void, if the proposal of union was rejected by the French cabinet. As Churchill pointed out:

> If the French Council of Ministers were rallied by it, the greater would carry the less, and the removal of the Fleet from German power would follow automatically. If our offer did not find favour our rights and claims would revive in their full force.[7]

However, this aim, so vital to the British, who were determined not to see the French Fleet go to the Germans, whatever else might happen, was not made clear. Churchill's telegram to Campbell instructing Reynaud to delay action on, and Campbell and Spears to suspend action on, the previous messages was received by Campbell and Spears only after their return to their hotel after Reynaud had left to read the offer of union to President Lebrun. A message was therefore sent to Reynaud at the Council of Ministers to inform him that "the two telegrams should be considered as cancelled". In a totally British understatement Churchill remarks that "possibly 'suspended' would have been a better word". Campbell and Spears, in their hurry to paraphrase the telegram, had unwittingly undermined the entire British strategy. This mistake, moreover, was compounded either by their rush to withdraw or by Reynaud's overwillingness to hand back the two documents and by his eagerness to interpret the British government's latest move as a revocation of its consent (and its conditions) and as a change of policy, rather than a change of tactics. As Eleanor Gates has said:

The exact chronology of successive events on 16 June resists precision, and the full story of the disappearing telegrams must remain one of the more intriguing mysteries of that historic day.[8]

In many ways the fate of the French Fleet was sealed in the mix-ups of that day, since Reynaud resigned that evening and at 12:30am on 17 June, less than seven hours after the receipt of the offer of union, Paul Baudouin, the new Foreign Minister, asked the Spanish Ambassador to transmit to Germany a request for terms of an armistice and for peace.

On 17 June the War Cabinet despatched Pound with the First Lord and Lord Lloyd, the Colonial Secretary, to Bordeaux in order to try to impress upon Darlan, now Minister of Marine, and the whole Pétain government, the necessity, as Britain saw it, of keeping the French Fleet out of the hands of the Germans. The two new battleships, still under construction, *Jean Bart* and *Richelieu*, had already been sailed from their ports to Casablanca and Dakar respectively, both voyages involving very considerable feats of seamanship, since for both of them it was their first time at sea. Pound received solemn assurances that the Fleet would not fall into German hands, but no more ships moved out of French harbours beyond the reach of the rapidly advancing German armies. Pound told the French that any ships would be received in British ports with open arms and received an explicit promise from Darlan that nothing would ever induce him to surrender the Fleet and it would go on fighting until an armistice was called. If the Germans insisted on its surrender as a condition, there would be no armistice. Pound knew that the French Fleet was continuing hostilities against the Italians, but even so he was beginning to distrust the repeated assurances that the Fleet would never surrender. However, when they left they were satisfied that the ships would remain French or would be destroyed. They had no doubt of Darlan's tight control over his Fleet.[9]

The conclusion of the armistice between France and Germany and Italy destroyed the Franco–British alliance and it only remained for the British to consider if anything could be salvaged from the wreckage. Fears that Germany would seize the French warships were considerable, since the lessons of Norway, Holland and Belgium were fresh in everyone's minds. The Germans had promised not to seize the French Fleet, but against the background of German ruthlessness Article 8 of the Armistice looked sinister in the extreme. Under this article all French warships were to return to their peacetime ports, where they were to be demobilized and disarmed under German control. For about two-thirds of the French Fleet this meant their return to ports in the German-occupied part of France, such as Brest or St Nazaire. It was thus not surprising that Churchill, in the House of Commons, on 25 June, said:

> From the text it is clear that the French war vessels under this armistice pass into German or Italian control fully armed. We note of course in the same article the solemn declaration of the German government that they have no intention of using them for their own purpose during the war. What is the value of that? Ask half a dozen countries what is the value of such a solemn assurance.[10]

The French Admiralty did not share the British view of the situation, although Darlan thought it likely that the Germans would try to seize the fleet. To this end he issued appropriate instructions, which he considered would be effective. French warships were sailed from ports threatened by the advancing German forces before the Armistice, as already noted; indeed not a single French warship fell into German hands and all dockyard facilities were destroyed. On 20 June Darlan signalled that commanders were to fight to the last unless the independent government of France indicated otherwise and on no account were ships to be handed over to the enemy, or, significantly, to any other government. On 22 June he ordered that every ship should have secret plans for scuttling, and on 24 June, in the last message he could send in secret cipher, Darlan told all his commanders that under the terms of the Armistice all ships were to remain in French ports in French hands. Should the Armistice Commission decide that the ships were not to remain in French hands they were to be sailed to the U.S.A. or scuttled without further orders. In no circumstances were they to fall into enemy hands intact.

Before he left for Bordeaux on 17 June Pound had been involved in an important discussion with the Naval Staff and the Joint Planners over whether to withdraw completely from the Eastern Mediterranean. With the French out of the war and the Italians into it on 10 June, the whole balance had shifted in this crucial area. Both Cunningham and Churchill opposed the move, but Pound had suggested that a part of the Mediterranean Fleet should move direct to Gibraltar, while the rest moved via the Cape, so as to secure the crucial Atlantic trade route. The Joint Planners were against it for "political, economic and military reasons" and the Chiefs of Staff never recommended it, but it was an option which had to be considered. This is a decision which we shall come back to as it had crucial implications for the development of British strategy.

It was necessary to organize immediately some force at the western end of the Mediterranean, and so came into being the famous Force H, which performed so many and so varied and wide-ranging a collection of tasks. On 23 June *Ark Royal* and *Hood* arrived, and on 28 June Force H was officially formed from these two ships and the battleships *Valiant* and *Resolution*, the light cruiser *Arethusa* and four destroyers. On 30 June Vice Admiral Sir James Somerville hoisted his flag in *Hood*. The Admiralty described Force H as "a detached squadron". The ambiguity of this description and its precise relationship to the Flag Officer, North Atlantic, based in Gibraltar, Admiral Sir Dudley North, we can leave until later.

Pound and the Naval Staff had also to ponder on the threat which was now posed to Britain's trade routes. In the 1920s and the early 1930s when Italy had been an ally it had always been assumed that if (or when) Japan threatened Britain the Admiralty would be able to move the Mediterranean Fleet to the Far East and leave the Mediterranean in the care of the French. Now, with France knocked out of the war and Italy into it as an enemy, the resources of the Royal Navy were terribly stretched. They simply did not have the means to keep all the French warships under surveillance and a Japanese move did not bear thinking about.

Before reaching a decision on the problems of the French Fleet, the British War Cabinet went through a week of indecision, to which many influences combined. Mainly this was due to the chaotic conditions in which both 10 Downing Street and the Foreign Office operated. Thus Sir Alexander Cadogan, the Permanent Secretary at the Foreign Office, noted in his diary:

19 June No 10 hall is like behind the scenes at the circus and every crank in the world is getting hold of the P.M. and getting half-baked decisions. I won't go on unless this is stopped.

22 June Don't remember what happened (writing on 23). I have had a most scarifying 48 hours . . . Went to bed at 1:00. Everyone all over the place and W.S.C. endorses any wild idea.[11]

While the Armistice was being negotiated there was hope that some form of French resistance could be continued, which was helped by Admiral Godfroy's force at Alexandria taking part in a bombardment of Bardia on 21 June.

There was also Pound's strong desire to trust Darlan, which caused the Germanophobe Vansittart to write on 26 June "Admiral Darlan has turned crook like the rest. I hope this will be put in its true light to Admiral Pound, who has a deal too much confidence in old friends and sailors of other races."[12] Various forms of actions were put forward which would avoid the use of force, but they promised little result. One such possibility was to buy the French Fleet for £100 million. An intriguing picture results of the British Treasury haggling with the French (after all, they were used warships), while the Germans looked on in amused tolerance. The Treasury wrote to the Foreign Office to say that "discussion should begin *well below* £100 million" and the Foreign Office pointed out that the money would anyway go straight to Germany.[13] From 22 June, when the news of the signing of the Armistice reached London, to 27 June, when a decision was finally reached, the solution was never grasped. Pound was, naturally, the most influential voice, and he preferred to trust Darlan's assurances than consider violence against a former ally.

The situation changed dramatically on 25 June when news came through that *Richelieu* had left Dakar at 2:15 that afternoon. This brief northward sortie (she returned to Dakar on 27 June), with the obvious danger that she was returning to a French port, decided the Cabinet. Cadogan noted on 26 June that there had been hesitation about using force as it would be difficult to catch all the ships and it had been hoped that Darlan could be relied upon to scuttle them. "However, when *Richelieu* sailed, it was felt that we could no longer trust entirely to Darlan's pledges, and action has been ordered".[14] When the War Cabinet met at noon on 27 June Pound could report that *Richelieu* was returning, but he now advocated action against the French squadron at Mers-el-Kebir, where both *Strasburg* and *Dunkerque* lay. The discussion which followed was no longer an argument about whether to take action; rather it was to decide what action to take. It was decided that, if necessary, force must be used, but that the French Fleet was to be dealt with on 3 July. Over the next few days the French government, through their ambassador in London, Corbin, and the head of the French Naval Mission to the Admiralty, Admiral Odend'hal, sought to get their warships in British harbours released, while they also tried to persuade the Germans and the Italians to make concessions. It was too late. As Churchill commented: "Discussions as to the Armistice conditions could not affect the real facts of the situation".[15] Neither Vichy French ports nor North Africa were considered safe

158

from the threat of a German coup de main. By 1 July the British government was being asked to reverse a judgement it had already given.

There can be little doubt that throughout these discussions the driving force had been Churchill's. He had, from the very start, advocated a bold course and had carried along the initially hesitant War Cabinet. However, both Pound and Alexander were right behind him in their desire for decisive action. Senior officers in both the Admiralty and the Air Ministry attest to Churchill being the leading voice, and the DOD(H), Captain Edwards is characteristically frank in his diary when he says:

> *1 July*   W.C. wants to take drastic action for the glorification of W.C., and the discomfiture of his erstwhile friends. He always was the protagonist of France and feels their defection badly.[16]

It must be remembered that at this time Edwards rarely spoke well in his diary of anybody in a position of authority.

What was Pound's contribution to this debate? At the heart of his policy was his belief that "the best place for the French Fleet was at the bottom of the sea",[17] preferably by their own hand. He said this to the D.N.I., Godfrey, who had been instrumental in making Pound come round to the conclusion that Darlan was not just a straightforward sailor but, in the words of Lord Tyrrell, passed on to Pound by Godfrey on the eve of his departure to Bordeaux on 17 June, "Darlan is a twister". Brockman, Pound's secretary, stated that he had "seldom seen the First Sea Lord so determined as he was then".[18] The VCNS, Tom Phillips, was as aghast as the Admirals at Gibraltar were about the dangers of antagonizing the French, but the Naval Staff were not asked to contribute to the discussion, nor were the Joint Planners, nor the Chiefs of Staff until after the decision in principle had been taken on 27 June. The Joint Planners were asked to consider the question on 28 June. Their report, which was against taking action, was considered by the Chiefs of Staff on 30 June and, in effect, rejected. Instead the Chiefs of Staff submitted their own report on 30 June, after long discussions at which, to emphasize the importance of the decision, all three Vice-Chiefs were present. Their conclusion was

> To sum up, we consider that, from a military point of view, Operation CATAPULT should be carried out as soon as possible.[19]

This decision was crucial and the memorandum also formulated the options to be offered to the French.

Pound's frame of mind can be seen from the briefing that he gave to James Somerville at 3:30 pm on 27 June, after the War Cabinet decision for action had been taken. After telling him that he was to command Force H, Somerville was told that his initial task would be "to secure the transfer, surrender or destruction of the French warships at Oran and Mers-el-Kebir so as to ensure that those ships did not fall into German and Italian hands". Pound stated in absolute terms that no concessions were to be made. The French must accept the British terms or face the consequences. Somerville met Pound and Alexander again that afternoon, before sailing in the evening, when it was stated that "whilst every preparation was made to employ force . . . it was hoped that the necessity would not arise."[20] The First Lord, Alexander, commented later:

> He understood clearly the position and what had to be done. He said to me in my room at the Admiralty: 'I quite recognise that, however repugnant this job may seem, the Government know it has got to be done, in the interests of the safety of the nation.'[21]

Both the two Admirals concerned, Cunningham at Alexandria and Somerville at Gibraltar, were appalled at what they were being asked to do. However, both were firmly rapped over the knuckles when they objected. The Admiralty reply to Somerville stated that it was "the firm intention of H.M.G. that if the French will not accept any of the alternatives which are being sent to you their ships must be destroyed. The proposals in your 1220/1 are not acceptable."[22] At 6:00pm on 1 July the War Cabinet met with Pound and Phillips to finalize the ultimatum to be delivered. Pound, still with a faint belief in the French,

> took the view that demilitarisation was the measure which was most likely to appeal to the French navy. If their ships were demilitarised, they would hope to get them back after the war.
> The view taken on this point was that, while we should not offer demilitarisation, the Flag Officer should be authorised to accept it if the other alternatives were refused, in order to avoid bloodshed.[23]

i.e. if the French offered to demilitarize their ships it would be accepted. That night Churchill and Pound together wrote the four long signals sent to Somerville giving him his final instructions and orders on what to do in almost every eventuality. The orders to Somerville read as follows:

160

(A) French Fleet at Oran and Mers-el-Kebir is to be given four alternatives:

(1) To sail their ships to British harbours and continue to fight with us.

(2) To sail their ships with reduced crews to a British port from which the crews would be repatriated whenever desired.

In the case of Alternatives (1) and (2) being adopted, the ships would be restored to France at the conclusion of the war or full compensation would be paid if they are damaged meanwhile. If French Admiral accepts Alternative (2), but insists that ships should not be used by us during the war you may say we accept this condition for so long as Germany and Italy observe the Armistice term, but we particularly do not wish to raise the point ourselves.

(3) To sail their ships with reduced crews to some French port in the West Indies such as Martinique. After arrival at this port they would either be demilitarised to our satisfaction or, if so desired, be entrusted to United States jurisdiction for the duration of the war. The crews would be repatriated.

(4) To sink their ships.

(B) Should the French Admiral refuse to accept all of the above alternatives and should he suggest that he should demilitarise his ships to our satisfaction at their present berths, you are authorised to accept this further alternative provided that you are satisfied that the measures taken for demilitarisation can be carried out under your supervision within six hours and would prevent the ships being brought into service for at least one year, even at a fully equipped dockyard port.

(C) If none of the above alternatives are accepted by the French you are to endeavour to destroy ships in Mers-el-Kebir, particularly *Dunkerque* and *Strasberg*, using all means at your disposal. Ships at Oran should also be destroyed if this will not entail any considerable loss of civilian life.[24]

The second signal gave the text of the communications to be made to the French. The third offered Somerville "suggestions" which were intended as a guide in case of discussions with the French Admiral, and the fourth offered advice on what to do if the French Fleet was met at sea. Those to Cunningham were a little different, principally because he was dealing with a French force within his own harbour at Alexandria. The choices to be offered to Admiral Godfroy were firstly to put his ships at the disposal of the British government. Secondly, to put his ships in a condition in which they could not go to sea. Thirdly, to take his ships to sea and sink them in deep water. Both Somerville and Cunningham were enjoined to finish the whole business on 3 July. In Britain, French warships were to be seized by armed boarding parties at dawn on 3 July. In both Alexandria and Britain everything was to be done to prevent the ships being scuttled in harbour.

The actual events of 3 July need not be related in detail. In Portsmouth and Plymouth all French warships were seized by the armed boarding parties in the early morning, all of them provided with phonetically spelt phrases so as to give instructions to the crews. The only serious fighting occurred on the huge submarine *Surcouf* where some French officers resisted and the chefs in the galley refused to discontinue preparing breakfast. The officers "retired to their wardroom where they intimated their intention of drinking the wine rather than have it sullied by contact with the uncultivated palate of perfidious Albion".[25] At Alexandria both sides had little room to manoeuvre either physically or diplomatically. Godfroy's squadron was in a British-controlled harbour and unable to put to sea; neither Cunningham nor the Admiralty wanted to risk a battle in the harbour. Both commanders were thus constrained to negotiate and their friendly relationship made this possible. At differing times they both turned a Nelsonian eye to signals from their own governments, Godfroy ignoring a signal instructing him to put to sea and Cunningham ignoring one which ordered him to ensure that the French began disembarking their crews before dark on 3 July. This signal ended with the words "Do not, repeat not, fail." In retrospect Cunningham described this as "a perfect example of the type of signal which should never be made", because it showed no understanding at all of the explosive situation in Alexandria harbour. He later wrote "At the time I did not believe that signal emanated in (sic) the Admiralty, and do not believe it now."[26] By which, of course, he meant that Churchill had originated it, not Pound. Cunningham ignored it and reached a settlement with Godfroy on 4 July, which resulted in signals of congratulation from Pound and Alexander, if not from Churchill.

Events at the other, western, end of the Mediterranean were more tragic. Pound had attempted, on the morning of 3 July, to draft a signal authorizing Somerville to accept demilitarization of the French ships where they lay. However, the War Cabinet turned this down as "this would look like weakening".[27] Somerville decided to send Captain L.V. Holland of *Ark Royal* to talk to the French Admiral, Gensoul, since Holland had previously been naval attaché in Paris. Godfrey had warned Pound against this as he believed that "attachés . . . almost always tended to identify themselves too closely with the nation to which they were accredited".[28] Holland failed to impress on Gensoul that action really would be taken; Gensoul simply reiterating that the French Fleet would never be allowed to fall into German hands. The difference here was one of timing: Somerville's orders required Gensoul to take immediately certain actions which the French admiral might be willing to take at some future time, if there was a German threat. To have accepted this latter course would have involved delay and prolonged uncertainty, and, since the British government was decided on rapid action to finish the matter, the divergence of views was decisive. Gensoul made the situation worse by informing the French government (not knowing that the British were reading his ciphers) that the British ultimatum was to sink his ships or be fired on; he did not set out the full range of options open to him. His message read

Ultimatum sent: sink your ships within six hours or we will force you to. Reply: French ships will meet force with force.[29]

Although this message raised feelings in the French government, it is doubtful if in fact it had much effect on the outcome, since all the British alternatives entailed a violation of the terms of the Armistice. The chances of getting the approval of the German Armistice Commission would have been negligible, and had the French accepted one of the alternatives it would, almost inevitably, have resulted in the German occupation of the remainder of France. The fact is that Gensoul had to choose between accepting one of the British proposals or standing on his honour and his existing orders. He chose the latter. Somerville, too, was bound by his orders and when Gensoul finally declined to accept any of the British proposals Force H opened fire. In the 10-minute bombardment one battleship was sunk, one badly damaged, along with the battlecruiser *Dunkerque*. However, the other battlecruiser, *Strasburg*, got away with three destroyers to Toulon. It is possible that with a little more patience and diplomacy the desired result might have been achieved, but haste was implicit in the operation from the start. Marder summarizes:

> Yet, when everything has been said, I consider it extremely improbable that, even if Gensoul had signalled a full summary of the British terms, and there had been more time for discussion, anything short of a direct order from Darlan would have changed his mind on 3 July.[30]

★

The possibility that France might declare war on Britain was seriously considered. A report by the Joint Planners on 4 July assessed the capacity of the French to take significant military action. By and large it was not considered to be too great. Darlan's immediate reaction to the events of 3 July was furious. However, the Vichy government opposed any sort of military action and contented themselves with breaking off diplomatic relations. In the House of Commons on 4 July M.P.s received Churchill's statement with a remarkable demonstration of support, the first he had really received from Conservative M.P.s since he became Prime Minister. The press did not exult in the action, but praised it as "a necessary action". In the Royal Navy itself there was little pleasure. After the war Cunningham wrote to then First Sea Lord, Admiral Sir Bruce Fraser (who had then been Third Sea Lord), that "90% of senior naval officers, including myself, thought Oran a ghastly error, and still do".[31]

Neutral opinion, and particularly that of the U.S.A. was of primary importance. Indeed, it was one of the principal reasons for Operation CATAPULT. As Churchill made plain in the second volume of his *History Of The Second World War*, "It was made plain that the British War Cabinet feared nothing and would stop at nothing."[32] At Chequers the following January Harry Hopkins, special adviser to President Roosevelt, told Colville that Oran had convinced the President, in spite of Ambassador Kennedy's defeatist opinions, "that the British really would go on fighting, as Churchill has promised, if necessary for years, if necessary alone".[33] When the French ambassador met Roosevelt on 4 July he was told:

> Even if there were only the most remote possibility that your fleet would pass into German hands, the British government had reason to act as it did. I would not have acted otherwise. I am a realist.[34]

164

Elsewhere, too, the opinion of other neutrals was favourable. Only in Madrid and Tokyo was opinion, as was to be expected, violent in its condemnation, but the Imperial Japanese Navy "understood, and regarded it as inevitable". Even the Italians, although not saying so, could understand. Ciano noting in his diary that the action "proves that the fighting spirit of His Britannic Majesty's fleet is quite alive, and still has the aggressiveness and ruthlessness of the captains and pirates of the seventeenth century".[35] Ciano was never a great historian and presumably meant the Elizabethan age, a century before!

Volume 2 of the Official History *Grand Strategy*, by Professor Butler, makes a point of showing the parallel with Copenhagen in 1807. It is worth quoting in full:

> 'Denmark's safety', wrote George Canning in July 1807,' is to be found, under the present circumstances of the world, only in a balance of opposite dangers. For it is not to be disguised that the influence which France has acquired from recent events over the north of Europe, might, unless balanced and controlled by the naval power of Great Britain, leave to Denmark no other option than that of complaisance with the demands of Bonaparte, however extravagant in their nature or repugnant to the feelings and interests of the Danish Government.'
> Read France for Denmark, Germany for France, west of Europe for north of Europe, Hitler for Bonaparte, and the parallel is striking. It was as essential in 1940 as in 1807 that the naval power of Great Britain should not be endangered.[36]

And yet who can fail to be moved by Darlan's *cri de coeur* in his letter to Churchill three weeks before his murder, three weeks after the Germans had taken over the unoccupied part of France, and one week after the French Fleet at Toulon had scuttled itself. He wrote:

> I admit having been overcome by a great bitterness and a great resentment against England (sic) as the result of the painful events which touched me as a sailor; furthermore it seemed to me that you did not believe my word. One day Lord Halifax sent me word by M. Dupuy that in England my word was not doubted, but that it was believed that I should not be able to keep it. The voluntary destruction of the

Fleet at Toulon has just proved that I was right, because even though I no longer commanded, the Fleet executed the orders which I had given and maintained, contrary to the wishes of the Laval Government.[37]

This is the whole of the French case. Events proved that the British should have taken the French Navy and Government at their word. There is no evidence that the Germans intended at that time to man, or put into service, any of the French ships. It would have been almost impossible to provide enough specialists as they were all needed in the German Navy. However, it is more important to look at what the British government and their military advisers knew at the time. The threat of the French Fleet, and the necessity to show the whole world that they were determined to continue the war, come what may, make it a necessary decision. It took extraordinary moral courage on the part of Churchill and Pound to act in the way that they did. I include Pound because throughout Churchill based his political decisions on the naval advice given by Pound and it was the two of them together who controlled and stage-managed the action. Operation CATAPULT was a mixed blessing for the British, but necessity had dictated their harsh course of action.

★

Immediately after Operation DYNAMO Pound, along with the Chiefs of Staff, had to look at the question of a possible German invasion. As early as 25 May they stated that the Royal Navy could not hope to operate in the North Sea and the Channel in the face of overwhelming air superiority. Once that superiority had been lost the Navy could only prevent an invasion 'for a time', but not indefinitely.[38] Despite this Pound and the naval Staff had to make their dispositions for the repelling of a German descent on the southern coastline. Unlike the last three periods of major invasion threat – 1588, 1803–05, 1914–18 – the enemy fleet was relatively insignificant. Both major surface units had been damaged in the Norwegian campaign, although the Admiralty did not know it for certain, two cruisers were available (we believed it to be two heavy and possibly four light), seven to ten destroyers, and twenty-eight U-boats (as opposed to the forty–fifty we believed to be operational). Hence the Germans dependence on air superiority. The Admiralty's plan was first to try to disrupt the build-up of invasion barges in their anchorages by bombing, shelling and mining. For this intelligence was crucial. Secondly, it would be attacked 'at the point of arrival', and thirdly, the Admiralty considered 'the happy possibility that our reconnaissance might enable us to intercept the expedition on passage'.[39] For the latter two eventualities they believed that four destroyer flotillas, plus supporting cruisers, were necessary, to be based in the Humber, at Harwich, Sheerness, Portsmouth or Dover.

The problems implicit in this were that Western Approaches and the Home Fleet would be almost totally denuded. The Nore Command at the end of July had thirty-two destroyers and five corvettes, and on 4 July Admiral Forbes had signalled to the Admiralty asking them to inform him which cruisers of the Home Fleet could be considered as coming under his command. The key was the amount of advance warning which could be given, as the Germans were highly unlikely to mount an invasion attempt until they had defeated Fighter Command. Forbes believed that he could move his forces south given 24 hours' notice; the Commanders-in-Chief covering the invasion coast wanted to have and to hold all the destroyers and cruisers they could get. GCCS had not yet broken the German Naval Enigma, although they had broken the Luftwaffe's. However, after the French campaign the amount of radio traffic slackened as much of the traffic now passed on land line. The Joint Intelligence Committee was alarmed at what it read and offered mid-July as a putative invasion date. Military Intelligence in the War Office agreed with this, suggesting the unlikely scenario of a fleet of motor launches carrying individual tanks. The DNI, Godfrey, scorned the idea, but Pound, supported by Phillips was prepared to accept it.

Late in August indications from photo-reconnaissance and Sigint all started to indicate a projected invasion, and on 7 September GHQ Home Forces issued the codeword 'Cromwell', bringing all forces to immediate readiness to repel a landing. In fact, Hitler postponed SEALION on 14 September and on the following day, in the climactic mass attack of the Battle of Britain, the Luftwaffe was decisively beaten. It was Forbes, not the Admiralty, who read the situation correctly, judging as early as 15 September that Fighter Command had 'removed the threat of invasion completely', and on 28 September he demanded that

the Navy should be freed to carry out its proper function – offensively against the enemy, and in defence of our trade – and not be tied down

167

to provide passive defence to our country, which had now become a fortress.[40]

By October Pound was in agreement, and Enigma decripts and other sources agreed as well.

★

The problem of the French Fleet had not been solved and, after the botched job at Mers-el-Kebir, there was still a sizeable force in southern France. The Admiralty wanted to make quite certain that these ships did not return to German-held French ports, but held less objection to them going to French North African ports, such as Casablanca, or West African, such as Dakar. However, by August it had been decided to mount Operation MENACE, an attempt to seize Dakar so as to bring Senegal and the other French West African colonies over to the side of de Gaulle's Free France. Neither Dudley North nor James Somerville, both at Gibraltar, knew the precise details of the operation, but they knew enough to know what the objectives were. Their formal relationship was very complicated in that North was senior in rank, but Somerville was commanding Force H as a detached squadron, not under North's command, and Force H's movements were always ordered by the Admiralty or Somerville, never by North. The Admiralty instructions instituting Force H on 28 June 1940 only referred to actions against the Italian Fleet, and said nothing about actions to be taken against the French. Both Somerville and North always acted on the assumption that Force H was under the direct operational control of the Admiralty, and this was certainly confirmed by operational signals being sent by the Admiralty direct to Somerville, not to North. Roskill comments that the chain of command was 'ill defined' and 'operationally dangerous'.[41]

Early in the morning of 11 September six French ships (three cruisers and three super-destroyers) were sighted steaming from Toulon towards Gibraltar. They passed south of Europa Point at 0845 and lit the touch paper of a complicated and long-burning fuse. It is not necessary to go over all the details of the Dudley North affair. That has been done in at least three exhaustive books.[42] However, it is necessary to explain why Pound thought it necessary to relieve Dudley North of his command. There can be little doubt that North had seriously compromised his

168

position by two unfortunate letters to the Admiralty. In June he had written to say that 'Gibraltar could before long be untenable as a naval base,' and that 'it will be impossible to base large ships on Gibraltar once the enemy are in a position to attack the fortress from the land, or from nearby air bases'. That may well have been truthful, but it was fairly obvious, and was not what Pound wanted, or needed, to hear. Similarly, at the same time as James Somerville wrote to his wife explaining his horror at Operation CATAPULT, North took the unwise step of signalling on 4 July to the Admiralty his dislike of the operation. He might have got away with this before the operation, but not afterwards. He received an icy blast on 17 July. There can be no doubt that the Admiralty as a whole had lost confidence in North by that stage. When in 1950 Vice Admiral Sir Peter Gretton, as Naval Assistant to the First Sea Lord, was asked to carry out an examination of the records of the North affair he recorded

> I got the firm impression that Dudley Pound lost confidence in Dudley North quite early on in his time at Gibraltar, and thought he was not imbued with the offensive spirit.[43]

On 2 October, three weeks after the French force had passed through the Straits, North was asked to supply "a report in writing . . . as to why no action was taken". He replied that same day and showed his signal to Somerville, who agreed with all that he said, but on 25 October a "secret and personal" letter arrived which concluded

> Their lordships cannot retain full confidence in an officer who fails in an emergency to take all prudent precautions without waiting for Admiralty instructions. They have accordingly decided that you should be relieved of your present command at the first convenient opportunity.

Pound had written a long minute on the matter, which is worth repeating in full as it demonstrates his thinking.

> The general tenor of [North's letter of 2 October] gives one a most unfavourable impression as it depends on [an] attitude of mind that is always waiting for orders instead of wishing to take the initiative and forestall any orders from the Admiralty. What he ought to have done was to order *Renown* to sea and at the same time inform the

Admiralty what he had done. If the Admiralty did not like what he had done they could recall him. Under the circumstances Admiral North no longer retains my confidence. Flag officers are of no value if they do not possess initiative and accept responsibility.

There are two alternatives.

(a)   To relieve Admiral North at once.

(b)   To order him to haul his Flag down and proceed home at the first suitable opportunity.

I am in favour of (b).

It is interesting that, although Alexander accepted Pound's recommendation of (b), it was subsequently changed to (a). The Secretary to the Board, Sir Archibald Carter, recommended that the letter say as little as possible as "this would provide the minimum of surface for purposes of future controversy". However, Pound overruled him and a full explanation of the Admiralty case was made to North. A stronger secretary would have stopped Pound making this mistake, as the North controversy rumbled on until 1957. North was replaced at the end of 1940 by Pound's old follower Fred Edward-Collins, referred to by Somerville in derogatory terms in many of his letters as 'Fat Fred', and North returned to England in January 1941.

Soon after his return North had a most unpleasant interview with Pound. We only have North's account of it, who says that Pound was "furiously angry . . . and very contemptuous in his manner".[44] North charitably attributed that to poor health. Brockman was not in the room, but remembered the occasion well:

1 SL was hopping mad. North must have been a very vain man if he imagined he was going to be received with sweetness and light [Pound] was as tough as old boots, and it was certainly characteristic of him that he should deal harshly with an Admiral whom he considered had failed.[45]

Pound's case against North was that he had not taken any action at all, but had waited for orders from the Admiralty. As a result it would have been possible for the French ships to have gone north to German-controlled ports. To a certain extent, though, the French ships were irrelevant. It was the lack of action that Pound was so angry about, and it

170

was because of that lack of action that North was relieved. It was exactly the same as Tomkinson at Invergordon in 1931. The error made by Pound was in trying to give reasons. It would have been much better to have simply said that North had lost the confidence of the Admiralty and arranged for his relief in due course. A stronger Secretary to the Board than Carter would have stopped Pound doing just that, and it is instructive that on 3 December 1940 a new Secretary to The Board of Admiralty was in place, Sir Henry Markham. Unlike Carter, Markham had spent his whole career in the Admiralty.

11

MID-WAR CRISES

By the middle of the summer of 1940 the Royal Navy was faced with a position it had not wanted, indeed a position it had actively counselled against. Throughout the 1930s it had kept reminding politicians that above all they must avoid a position where they were faced by a coalition of Germany, Italy and Japan. By July 1940 two of these protagonists were lined up, and it appeared as if the third would enter when it suited them best and Britain least. Added to this, the loss of France decisively shifted the balance against Britain. At a stroke the Mediterranean no longer remained *Mare Nostrum*, with a large, but containable, enemy fleet in the middle separating two Allied Fleets. However, Pound had ensured that, instead, two British forces at either end were commanded by two of the most successful of Britain's fighting admirals, Cunningham at Alexandria with the Mediterranean Fleet and Somerville at Gibraltar with Force H. In Britain the first twelve months of the war had produced nothing but defeat and retreat, even if it could be portrayed as deliverance, and occasionally even as triumph. Even the Battle of Britain was really a negative victory, in that it stopped Germany invading rather than ensuring a British victory. Churchill was desperate for a British victory and would stop at nothing to achieve one. He was prepared to be ruthless in his drive for this victory, and personal considerations would come second. It also appeared as if naval orthodoxy would be ignored to that end as well.

On 25 November 1940 Force H left Gibraltar to escort a convoy through the Mediterranean to Malta and Alexandria. These 'club runs', as they became known, were planned with considerable care and attempts were always made to deceive the enemy, even if with little success. Force H always turned back before reaching the mine- and E-boat-infested waters of the Sicilian Narrows, dominated by aircraft based in Sicily, Sardinia and the southern Italian mainland, before handing over to the

Mediterranean Fleet, who escorted the convoy on the last half of its passage to Egypt. Operation COLLAR was a typical 'club run' with reinforcements for Malta as well as corvettes and MT ships for Alexandria. On 27 May Somerville ran into an Italian force of two battleships, seven cruisers and sixteen destroyers. Force H ultimately consisted of *Renown* and *Ramilles*, *Ark Royal*, five cruisers and fourteen destroyers. Somerville's actions were a classic case of convoy defence against a superior enemy. When the enemy were sighted, the convoy made off at best possible speed, while Somerville attacked the Italians. The latter, after an initial exchange of fire between *Renown* and the Italian cruisers, and an unsuccessful torpedo strike from *Ark Royal*, turned tail for their base, hotly pursued by Somerville. *Renown* was reduced by a hot bearing to 27 knots, while *Ramilles*, whose principal role by this date was solely that of convoy escort, was lumbering along at 20 knots, 30 or so miles behind. By 1300 the action had died away with the Italians out of range. Somerville had to decide what his priorities were and correctly decided that "the safe and timely arrival of the convoy" was the most important, particularly since "I was being led towards a dense smokescreen in close proximity to his air, submarine and light forces base at Cagliari."[1] There was no chance of another torpedo strike from *Ark Royal* for three and a half to four hours and two of Somerville's five cruisers were packed with RAF and Army personnel in transit for Malta and Alexandria. Somerville was justified, in that by 30 November the convoy had been successfully passed through to Cunningham and both Force H and the Mediterranean Fleet were back in their harbours without any loss. In a letter to his wife, written on 28 November, i.e. while still at sea, Somerville wrote.

> I shouldn't be surprised if some [people?] at the Admiralty don't argue that I should have continued the chase. . . . Occasionally I get a bun from T[heir] L[ordships] but usually it is carping criticism and I feel that if they don't feel that I am the right one for this job then they had better get rid of me.[2]

Sure enough, it came as little surprise to Somerville when he returned to Gibraltar to find out that the Admiralty had ordered a Board of Enquiry into his decision to abandon the chase of the Italian fleet. Admiral of the Fleet the Earl of Cork and Orrery arrived in Gibraltar by 3 December, and Somerville was engaged with him, rather than the Italians, until 6 December.

There is some evidence that the idea for this Board was not Pound's. It was actually ordered by A.V. Alexander, and "it seems clear that Churchill was the prodding force behind it".[3] Arrangements had been made to supersede Somerville with Vice Admiral Harwood, the victor of the River Plate and a favourite of Churchill's, and a letter to that effect had been written. However, Geoffrey Blake wrote to Pound deploring the change, both on the grounds that Harwood had only just worked himself in as ACNS(F), and also in support of the abilities of Somerville.[4] The actual details of who started what is unclear, but it seems likely that Pound decided on a Board of Enquiry in order to forestall anything worse. He could hold Churchill off by telling him he could do nothing until the Board reported, confident that the Board would justify Somerville. Certainly it fits with his policy of never giving a firm negative to Churchill's proposals when Churchill was First Lord, but frustrating him in other ways. This view is reinforced by a letter to Somerville by Lord Cork and Orrery, written after he had finished the Board, before departing for England:

It is possible however that you take rather too harsh a view of the Admty. (sic) action for the following reasons.

There are always critics ready to raise their voices and suggest what might have been done although they are quite ignorant of what really happened or of the prevailing conditions.

These people, impatient for results, exist both in and out of the Admty., and in high quarters (I speak from personal experience) and no doubt have raised their voices on this occasion and the most expeditious way of silencing them has in this case been adopted.

As a result I do not think you need anticipate hearing anything further. This is as far as I can judge and sincerely hope.[5]

The indications are that the very idea of the Board was opposed by others at the Admiralty. Somerville received a letter from Vice Admiral Royle, the Fifth Sea Lord, in which he said:

. . . You would have smiled to see us sitting round and talking about your action and whether there was the remotest possibility of doing anything more. Whether you should have held on any longer with your very inadequate force, etc., etc. I think most chaps were fed up with the whole business and reckoned you and the FAA had done magnificently not only in your lap at the enemy but also in getting the convoy safely to its destination.

... Those d—d politicians who know nothing of the real difficulties are responsible for most of these stunts.[6]

The price of this episode was the loss of confidence by James Somerville in the Admiralty. He already had a low opinion of Churchill and Tom Phillips. Now his regard for Pound dipped, not helped by the actual despatch of the letter relieving him, which had to be returned unopened. It was an unfortunate way to move into 1941 and the dark depths of the naval war.

At much the same time as Somerville was fighting off his Board of Enquiry the Italians were receiving a very bloody nose at Taranto from Cunningham. Here the Fleet Air Arm changed the course of naval history by severely damaging three Italian battleships by torpedo in a night attack in their own harbour. The original idea for this attack had been conceived in 1935–36 during the Abyssinian crisis, when Pound had been Chief of Staff to Fisher, and had been resurrected during the Munich crisis in 1938 when the Captain of *Glorious* had been Lyster, but had then been quashed by Pound, as Commander-in-Chief. In August 1939 Pound had written to Cunningham:

When we attack Italy itself ... then I think there is a great deal to be said for making an attack by air on the Italian fleet at Taranto. One reason for this is that I do not believe *Glorious* will be able to remain in a serviceable condition in the Mediterranean for very long, what with air and submarine attack, and it might be a good thing to get the most one can out of her before she is placed *hors de combat*.[7]

When Lyster returned to the Mediterranean Fleet in September 1940 as Rear Admiral (Air) the plan was brought up again. Pound thoroughly approved of the plan and it was brilliantly carried out on the night of 11–12 December with the minimal loss of only two Swordfish aircraft. More damage was inflicted than had been suffered by the Germans at Jutland, and, combined with the victory in the Western Desert in December 1940, the Italians were decidedly forced on to the back foot.

Pound was not wholly satisfied that Forbes was in control of events in the Home Fleet. He believed that he had lost the confidence of his fleet and therefore looked around for a replacement. His first choice was

Horton, at that time Vice Admiral (Submarines). However, he turned it down in a most interesting letter, believing that as Commander-in-Chief he would not have sufficient control over various parts of the RAF, which he deemed necessary. He further commented that "the Commander-in-Chief Home Fleet did not enjoy that independent judgement and action which seemed to me to be essential to the full discharge of the responsibilities of this Command".[8] In other words, he was not prepared to be interfered with as Pound had interfered with Forbes. Pound instead chose Vice Admiral Sir John Tovey, at that time Second-in-Command Mediterranean Fleet, and Vice Admiral Light Forces.

★

If the early weeks of 1941 brought a false dawn in the Mediterranean for the Admiralty, so too did events in the Atlantic. Between January and May there were three different forms of attack on the British convoys. On the surface there were raids by *Scharnhorst, Gneisenau, Hipper* and *Scheer*, which resulted in the loss of forty-eight ships. The policy of escorting convoys by battleships was vindicated in January when *Scharnhorst* and *Gneisenau* sighted convoy HX 106, but made off as soon as *Ramilles* started to work up to her full speed (all of 20 knots compared to the Germans' 32). In the air Göring was persuaded to station KG 40 with their four engined Kondors in western France to co-operate with the U-boats. They were only reasonably effective in their other role of attacking the Freetown – Gibraltar – Britain convoys. Far more effective than either of these was the U-boat attack, which was assuming critical weight in December 1940. The Commander-in-Chief Western Approaches, Admiral Dunbar-Nasmith, wrote to Pound on 22 December explaining why "the convoy system is now failing to obtain similar results [to 1914–18, or to the first half of 1940]."[9] He explained the reasons for this: shortage of escorts, lack of time for training, poor methods of attack and an inability to find the U-boats both on the surface and under it. All of these criticisms were echoed by Admiral Sir Percy Noble when he took over at Western Approaches at the end of February 1941. Coastal Command too was struggling. Its only squadron equipped with Very Long-Range (VLR) aircraft, not formed until July 1941, was allowed to wither away due to wastage and transfer. Anyway, it had no effective way of either finding, let alone attacking, a U-boat until the

176

operational use of the Leigh light and ASV came in at the end of 1941.

There were, however, two aspects which helped the British. On 15 February 1941 Coastal Command was placed under the operational command of the Admiralty. This meant that naval Commanders-in-Chief could issue operational requirements direct to their opposite numbers in Coastal Command. Indeed, Noble and Air Vice Marshal Robb, commanding 15 Group, shared a new HQ at Derby House in Liverpool. At the top level Churchill formed a War Cabinet Committee, the Battle of the Atlantic Committee, to oversee the problems, presided over by himself, on which Pound, naturally, sat. March was a critical month for the U-boats. Doenitz lost three of his most experienced commanders, Prien, Schepke (both sunk) and Kretschmer (captured). Henceforth Doenitz switched entirely to the wolf pack tactics in the Atlantic.

Spring 1941 also saw a major development in signal intelligence. On 4 March the trawler *Krebs* was captured with her Enigma material intact, followed by the two weather ships *Munchen* and *Lauenberg* on 7 May and 28 June respectively, and finally on 9 May *U-110* was captured intact. As a result of these successes, and a lot of hard work, Bletchley Park achieved total mastery over the enigma 'Home Waters' code, which it retained until the end of the war. Consequently OIC could effect expert convoy re-routing. Added to which was a raising of the minimum speed of independently-sailed ships to fifteen knots, and the supply of end-to-end escorts. As a direct result, from June to August only three convoys were attacked.

Pound's involvement in all of this was at the least peripheral and at the most critical. The problem of control of Coastal Command had been raised as early as November 1940 when Lord Beaverbrook proposed in the Defence Committee that Coastal Command should be removed from the RAF and be converted to a separate Naval Air Service. Pound was not impressed by this idea and, along with Portal, the new CAS, simply wanted a better provision of air cover for the Atlantic. Beaverbrook's suggestion was defeated early in December 1940 and the Defence Committee simply emphasized that "operational control of the U-boat war must continue always to rest with the sailors".[10] This became known as Coastal Command's Charter. In fact the partnership of Coastal Command and Western Approaches is as excellent an example of inter-service co-operation as one could hope to find.

★

One of the critical moments of the naval war occurred in May 1941 when the German battleship *Bismarck* emerged into the Atlantic. Grand Admiral Raeder believed he could deal a mortal blow to the British supply system by operating *Bismarck* and her sister ship *Tirpitz* with *Scharnhorst* and *Gneisenau*. Indeed, such a combination would have been devastating. However, *Tirpitz* was still completing trials and working up, and *Gneisenau* had been severely damaged in Brest by a torpedo. Raeder was not prepared to wait and *Bismarck* left Gdynia on 18 May in concert with *Prinz Eugen*. The first news to reach the Admiralty about this came from an unconventional source: via Sweden. The Swedish cruiser *Gotland* passed on news of the sortie and this was immediately passed on to the British naval attaché in Stockholm. By 2100 on 20 May the Admiralty was informed that *Bismarck* was out and they asked Coastal Command to search the Norwegian fjords the next morning. Sure enough, two hours after *Bismarck* and *Prinz Eugen* dropped anchor at Bergen they were spotted by Photo Reconnaissance Spitfires from Wick. By 1828 OIC had alerted all commands: "It is evident that these ships intend to carry out a raid on trade routes."[11]

Sir John Tovey, the Commander-in-Chief Home Fleet, now ordered his dispositions. He already had the 1st Cruiser Squadron of *Norfolk* and *Suffolk* watching the Denmark Strait, north of Iceland, and *Manchester* and *Birmingham* between Iceland and the Faroes. He sent his Battle-cruiser Force of *Hood* and the newly completed but unworked-up *Prince of Wales*, under Vice Admiral Holland, to support 1st Cruiser Squadron. Pound now took a hand by detaching *Repulse* and *Victorious* from a Middle East troop convoy and placing them at the disposal of Tovey, who remained at Scapa Flow as long as possible. That way he could remain in touch by telephone with the OIC; at sea he would need to maintain radio silence. On the evening of 21 May, after nearly nine hours, *Bismarck* and *Prinz Eugen* left Bergen and headed north. Not until 2000 did Tovey receive news from Coastal Command that his quarry had left harbour. By 2245 he had left Scapa Flow in *King George V* with *Victorious* and 2nd Cruiser Squadron, joined by *Repulse* the next morning.

There was nothing to do at this stage except wait, both in the Home Fleet and at the Admiralty. This wait ended on 23 May at 1922 when *Suffolk* sighted *Bismarck* in the Denmark Strait. Admiralty received her's and *Norfolk*'s sighting reports at 2103. While Tovey steered the Home

Fleet to support Holland some 600 miles from his present location at his best speed of 27 knots, the Admiralty had to look at the whole of the Atlantic plot. In the War Room Pound and Phillips could see on the wall map that there were eleven convoys at sea in the North Atlantic, five outward bound and six on their way to Britain. There was a critical troop convoy for the Middle East from which *Repulse* and *Victorious* had been removed and was now only protected by two cruisers and five destroyers. Shortly after midnight on 24 May Pound ordered Force H into the Atlantic to meet this convoy. By 0200 Somerville was at sea with *Renown*, *Ark Royal*, *Sheffield* and six destroyers.

At 0535 *Hood* sighted *Bismarck* and *Prinz Eugen*. Both sides opened fire at 0552 at 25,000 yards. At 0600 *Hood* was sunk by *Bismarck*'s fifth salvo, and by 0613 the action had been broken off. Although *Prince of Wales* had received seven major hits, *Bismarck* had been hit twice with critical results. The first caused her to lose fuel and ship some 2,000 tons of water, and the second damaged an engine room. As a result of this *Bismarck* opted to make for Brest in France. For the Royal Navy, three admirals had to make critical decisions. Rear Admiral Wake-Walker in *Norfolk* had to decide what to do with *Prince of Wales*: engage *Bismarck* again or shadow her. He opted for the latter, believing it to be his principal job to maintain contact with *Bismarck* and deliver her to the Commander-in-Chief, arguing that *Bismarck* had driven off the combined power of *Hood* and *Prince of Wales* and would thus be able to deal with *Prince of Wales* alone, supported by only two cruisers. Tovey, steering to intercept *Bismarck*, had to decide whether she was making for the Atlantic or back to Germany. At the Admiralty Pound had to fight on two fronts.

Correlli Barnett in his book *Engage The Enemy More Closely* claims that Churchill "had now become a more or less permanent fixture [in the Admiralty War Room] because of his fascination with the hunt for the *Bismarck*".[12] In fact Churchill had been told about the loss of *Hood* early on the morning of Saturday 24 May while at Chequers. He did not leave Chequers until 12:30 on Monday 26 May and thus could not have reached the Admiralty War room until 1400 at the earliest. Certainly he would have been in constant touch with the Admiralty, and very probably with Pound, and Colville says in his diary:

The P.M. cannot understand why the *Prince of Wales* did not press home her attack yesterday and keeps on saying it is the worst thing

179

since Troubridge turned away from the *Goeben* in 1914. He rates the First Lord and the First Sea Lord continuously.[13]

Certainly Pound needed little encouragement from Churchill to prod Wake-Walker, demanding to know how he was going to employ *Prince of Wales*. In fact, Wake-Walker's reply that he doubted if *Prince of Wales* had the speed to force an action infuriated Pound, and after the action he wrote to Tovey demanding that Wake-Walker and Leach (captain of *Prince of Wales*) be court-martialled for not re-engaging *Bismarck*. Much to Tovey's credit he refused to do so, and no more was heard of this.

The remainder of 24 May saw the Admiralty redeploying all of the Royal Navy's far-flung strength to catch *Bismarck* before she came under the Luftwaffe umbrella. *Rodney* was taken from escort duty, as had been *Ramilles* already, and ordered to close the Home Fleet. *Revenge*, in port at Halifax, was ordered to sea. By that evening the Royal Navy had deployed four battleships (*Prince of Wales*, *King George V*, *Rodney* and *Ramilles*), two battlecruisers (*Revenge* and *Renown*), two aircraft carriers (*Victorious* and *Ark Royal*), twelve cruisers and a mass of destroyers. Much of this was co-ordinated by Tom Phillips who was "right on the ball the whole time".[14] That evening Tovey tried to slow *Bismarck* by attacking with torpedoes from *Victorious'* aircraft, but, despite achieving one hit, *Bismarck* was not slowed. That night at 0306 on 25 May *Suffolk* lost contact with *Bismarck*, and another Admiralty nightmare started to look as if it might come true. *Bismarck* was in the Atlantic undetected.

That Sunday, 25 May, was spent in frantic worry at the Admiralty. Churchill certainly was regularly on the phone from Chequers. Tovey was convinced *Bismarck* was steering for Germany via the Denmark Strait, principally because of false computing of HF/DF readings in his flagship. The Admiralty was certain by as early as 1023 that *Bismarck* was making for Brest and signalled to both Force H and Wake-Walker to proceed on that assumption. This was confirmed by a German signal at 1812, which told the Luftwaffe that *Bismarck* was making for Brest. Tovey thereupon turned south-east, but with no realistic hope of catching her unless she was slowed by *Ark Royal*'s aircraft.

Early on the morning of 26 May (0200) the Admiralty ordered Philip Vian and his 4th Destroyer Flotilla to leave the convoy he was escorting and to join Tovey, who had been forced to send his destroyers back to refuel. Coastal Command did find *Bismarck* at 1030 and by 1125 she was spotted by Force H aircraft. Pound ordered Somerville not to engage *Bismarck* with *Renown* unless *Bismarck* was already engaged by *King George V* or *Rodney*. There was little purpose in allowing *Renown* to follow *Hood*, which would assuredly have happened if *Bismarck* was not already damaged. Pound knew James Somerville too well, from his time as his RA(D) in the Mediterranean Fleet. Certainly by the early afternoon Churchill would have been in the Admiralty, and equally certainly Pound was instrumental "in restraining him from sending impulsive signals to Tovey and others engaged in the operation".[15] That evening *Ark Royal* managed to obtain the critical strike on *Bismarck* in her one really vulnerable spot (her rudders) and, as darkness descended on the eastern Atlantic, *Bismarck* was wallowing at 7 knots head into the wind, moving directly towards Tovey and her fate.

The final destruction of *Bismarck* between 0847, when *Rodney* opened fire and 1036 when *Bismarck* finally sunk, was not affected by the Admiralty, except by one signal urged by Churchill, but despatched by Pound:

> We cannot visualise situation from your signals. *Bismarck* must be sunk at all costs, and if to do this it is necessary for *King George V* to remain on the scene then she must do so even if subsequently means towing *King George V*.[16]

This signal was sent at 1137, by which time Tovey was on his way back. In his despatch Tovey did not comment on this, but instead praised

> The accuracy of the enemy information supplied by the Admiralty and the speed with which it was passed were remarkable, and the balance struck between information and instructions passed to forces out of visual touch with me, was ideal.[17]

A vivid eyewitness of the hunt for the *Bismarck* at the Admiralty is given by Lieutenant Commander (later Vice Admiral) B.L. Austin, USN, who was attached to the US Naval Mission to London under Rear Admiral Robert Ghormley at that time. He and his admiral were summoned to the Admiralty War Room to see the last part of the *Bismarck* episode and he described his visit in a report back to America. Their visit was not unprecedented.

But today was not a normal day in the war room, nor was it really necessary for all the lights to be on the wall charts. The attention of the entire staff was centred on a small area of the Atlantic where one of the war's most dramatic scenes was being enacted, where the unsinkable new German battleship *Bismarck* was about to be sunk. The chart of this area was near the middle of the north wall of the war room. Between it and the window on the east side of the room sat the First Sea Lord and the First Lord with their advisers around a small table. To them were being taken signals as they came in, reporting the progress of this grim last act for the *Bismarck*. Around the room in little groups stood those whose expert opinion or advice might be needed. From time to time a name would be called . . . [a] member of the staff would hasten to the little table.

A signal had come in saying that *Bismarck* could not be sunk by gunfire. Slowed and battered by five torpedo hits, she still absorbed the tons of shells from the *Rodney*'s guns. An eight-inch cruiser added her guns to the effort, and yet the *Bismarck* floated. It was decided to send in a cruiser for torpedo attack. Then a wait while the gunnery experts in the war room answered the friendly jibes of their fellow officers with smiles, which emphasized the weary looks caused by the strain of the last forty-eight hours without sleep. There was a tenseness in the air not unlike that at an Army–Navy game when the score is tied and a play has been fumbled near the goal line in the last minute of play. But the tired lined faces of Admiral Pound, Vice Admiral Phillips, Rear Admiral Power, Admiral Max Horton, Rear Admiral Lyster, Captain Daniels, Captain Bellairs and the others who had followed and directed the hunt and chase since early morning on the twenty-fifth, when the *Bismarck* had dealt the Royal Navy a staggering blow by sinking the *Hood*, all reminded one that this was no football game but a grim game with high stakes. Already one British destroyer had been bombed with little information in on damage and a flight of sixty Junkers eighty-eights were reported heading for the scene.

Anxiously we all waited and hoped. Then an officer rushed in with the news that a telegraph message had been received from the flag officer in command at Rosyth, saying that he had intercepted a message that the *Bismarck* had been sunk at 1101, or 0901 Greenwich Civil Time. Then at a run came Captain Brocking, head of the

182

Admiralty Press Division, to say that Reuters had it from New York before the Admiralty that *Bismarck* was sunk. About ten minutes later the official signal was brought in and the First Sea Lord read aloud "*Bismarck* sunk 1101, Lattitude 48°–09' N longitude 16°–07' W." Smiles lighted tired faces from which bloodshot eyes sparkled again as the First Sea Lord put on his cap, reached for his cane and limped out to tell the Prime Minister, who was making a speech in the Commons. He came back and called his Vice Chief of the Naval Staff, diminutive but able Vice Admiral Phillips, to the door to give hasty instructions for orders to the various units involved in the drama on which the curtain had just fallen.[18]

The loss of *Bismarck* and the damage to *Gneisenau* at Brest were instrumental in causing Hitler to end the attempt to stop Britain's Atlantic trade via surface action. He had little further belief in the ability of these ships, but it was not until the end of the year that he sacked Raeder and promoted Doenitz. Meanwhile Pound and the Admiralty could ponder a job well done. Pound wrote to Cunningham on 19 June:

> In the battle for the *Bismarck* we were both unlucky and lucky, and I cannot remember any 48 hours in which I jumped so frequently from great hopes to black despair. It was a sickening moment when it was reported that *Hood* had been sunk, and the partially effective *Prince of Wales* who had barely got through her teething problems was left to deal with *Bismarck* alone. There is no doubt that *Hood* with her third salvo got two or three hits on *Bismarck* and I think this started leaks in her oil tanks . . . These [FAA] attacks must have been an example of magnificent flying as there was a very heavy sea running.[19]

Pound was not to know when he wrote this that in fact the hits on *Bismarck* obtained in the Battle of the Denmark Strait had been by *Prince of Wales*. One of his more enjoyable tasks after the *Bismarck* episode was that of increasing and balancing out the awards and medals between the different forces involved, most of which he deputed to Geoffrey Blake.

★

Within six weeks the Admiralty was in a major flap. On Sunday 27 July 1941 Pound announced to his private office that he was to go with the

Prime Minister and the Chiefs of Staff on *Prince of Wales* to meet President Roosevelt at Placentia Bay in Newfoundland and that they had less than a week to prepare for their departure. The files demonstrate that Brockman did most of the organization for this and he insisted that the Executive Officer and Purser of *Prince of Wales* fly down to the Admiralty to make the arrangements, swearing them to secrecy. Pound took with him an officer from both the Trade and Operations Divisions of the Naval Staff, as well as Brockman, whose principal job would be to act as chief cypher officer for the entire party. Two retired officers also came to set up a travelling War Room. As Colville put it "The PM left for the north with a retinue which Cardinal Wolsey might have envied."[20] The whole party ate well, a welcome change from the wartime fare in London. On Monday 4 August their train arrived at Scrabster, and by noon all were on board *Prince of Wales*, where they met Roosevelt's personal representative, Harry Hopkins, hot foot from Russia with a large supply of vodka and caviar.

That afternoon *Prince of Wales* cast off and the party settled into a simple routine. Every morning the Chiefs of Staff met at 10:30 and usually also in the afternoon at 4:00. After dinner the whole party watched a film in the wardroom. There can be little doubt that there were two benefits from the four and a half-day voyage. Firstly, the Chiefs of Staff were able to present a united front to the Americans. Over the course of the voyage they could thrash out what the British view was on how the war should be conducted. By comparison, the American Joint Chiefs appeared to be uncoordinated. Secondly, a breath of sea air and a taste of good food acted as an excellent short holiday. As Churchill said, "The voyage was an agreeable interlude."[21]

Pound certainly enjoyed the chance to be at sea again. Apart from crossing the Channel to France in 1940 it was his first time at sea since he had left the Mediterranean Fleet in the summer of 1939. On their first morning at sea the weather was so rough that their accompanying destroyers could not keep pace. On Pound's orders *Prince of Wales* ploughed on alone. The Chiefs of Staff appeared to do very little actual work, but discussed things in general terms. Ian Jacob recalled in his diary for 5 August:

The Chiefs of Staff met at 10.30am, and Jo [Hollis] and I were present. They seemed in quite good shape, but no more inclined to

184

rattle through their business than they are on land. During the night a telegram had arrived, mostly filled with political stuff which did not get a very good reception. The second telegram contained the morning news summary and was short and to the point. Though still keen on hearing news, the Prime Minister on board ship seems quite content to forget about what is going on elsewhere and simply to enjoy himself, so we have not been at all troubled.

After lunch we had time for a bit of 'shut eye', and resumed our meeting at 4 o'clock, by which time the ship had settled down to steady going and everyone was feeling all right. We had tea in the course of our meeting and the Prime Minister joined us in very skittish form. He asked the Chiefs of Staff what they were doing, and said it did him good to see them working. He then moved into the other half of the room where he and Harry Hopkins settled themselves down to listen to the wireless. I think this must be the first Chiefs of Staff meeting held to the accompaniment of Bruce Belfrage's dulcet tones. We stopped work at 7 o'clock, very little business having been done.[22]

One of their chief distractions was Professor Lindemann, who "frequently succeeds in buttonholing one of the Chiefs of Staff for a long discussion of figures, just when the latter particularly wants to go off and have a sleep. He is, therefore, not entirely popular."[23] Pound insisted that *Prince of Wales* enter Placentia Bay at the correct time. Sir Alec Cadogan recorded in his diary for 9 August:

Up at 7 and breakfast about 8. Then found that by US ship's time it was only 6.30! A long day. We had to put out to sea to kill time, and eventually came in through lines of US destroyers and dropped anchor by the *Augusta*, with the *Arkansas* lying beyond.[24]

There were three principal purposes to the meetings for Pound. Firstly, it was a chance to meet his opposite number. Secondly, it was an opportunity to co-ordinate a number of naval matters of importance, and thirdly, as a member of the Chiefs of Staff it was necessary to gain agreement to the "Germany first" strategy. Pound had a one-to-one meeting with President Roosevelt on the Sunday afternoon, after the memorable church service on board *Prince of Wales*, and he had several meetings with the three chief American naval officers at the conference: Admiral Harold

185

Stark, the Chief of Naval Operations, Admiral Ernest King, Commander-in-Chief Atlantic Fleet, and Rear Admiral Richmond Turner, Director of the War Plans Division. He established particularly good relations with 'Betty' Stark, who was soon to transfer to London, and perfectly adequate relations with the formidable Ernie King, who succeeded Stark.

In fact many of the decisions reached here had already been decided in the highly secret staff conversations which had been held in Washington in January–March 1941 and were effectively ratified at this meeting. To these conversations Pound had sent a strong naval team of the retired Rear Admiral Roger Bellairs (who had been Director of Plans in the early 1930s) as chairman, and Captain Victor Danckwerts, who had been Director of Plans from 1938 to January 1940. Both had excellent brains and wide experience. The most important agreement they had reached with their American partners-in-secrecy had been 'Germany first', described by S.E. Morrison as "the basic and vital decision , based on an estimate of the then global situation, and on a correct anticipation of the future".[25] Fundamentally, all the decisions reached in August 1941 stemmed from that decision. The Americans were in a similar position to that of Britain in 1938 and were to repeat many of the same mistakes. Experience is the only teacher of the harsh lessons of war and, no matter how often Pound would have liked later to tell Ernie King what to do, that proud man understandably was not prepared to be told. Pound wrote to Andrew Cunningham on 3 September.

> This was most interesting and I am sure did good in many ways, particularly through our meeting our opposite numbers. I like Admiral Stark very much, but there is no doubt that his Director of War Plans, who is an Admiral called Turner, is the driving force in their War Staff.
>
> I formed a very good opinion of Admiral King, the C-in-C of their Atlantic Fleet.
>
> They are all longing to get into the war but I don't think there is much sign of America coming unless there is some incident.[26]

As a direct result of the Placentia Bay meeting the US Atlantic Fleet took over escorting all convoys to the Mid-Ocean Meeting Point south of Iceland. The pressure on the Royal Navy began to ease and this was helped by the launching in September of the first of the new escort carriers, HMS *Audacity*.

In the summer of 1941 sinkings by U-boats had fallen, principally but not solely owing to the use of Enigma Intelligence and the evasive routing of convoys. The advent of US escorts was critical in allowing Pound to set up escort groups under Sir Percy Noble at Western Approaches and the fruits of this were seen in November, when convoy HG76 was successfully fought through from Gibraltar against a mass U-boat attack. Four U-boats were sunk, as against two merchant ships, principally due to the use of *Audacity*'s aircraft and the close control of Commander F.J. Walker, the non-pareil U-boat hunter. By the end of 1941 the figures of merchant shipping lost in the Atlantic that year stood at over four million tons, bad enough, but not as bad as the seven millions which had been projected. Thirty-five U-boats had been sunk. Pound could be reasonably well pleased that a method of combating U-boats was emerging: close co-operation between Western Approaches and Coastal Command, well trained and professional use of close escorts and the use of escort carriers, all backed up by the critical use of intelligence from Bletchley Park and evasive routing ordered by the OIC.

*

Within Whitehall Pound was still facing one of his sternest critics, his one-time patron and now the Director of Combined Operations (DCO), Sir Roger Keyes. For fifteen months, since his appointment in June 1940, Keyes had agitated for more power, even suggesting in October 1940 that he become Churchill's deputy and preside over the Chiefs of Staff Committee. Certainly both Ismay and Colville believed that one of the reasons for his original appointment was nepotism. Unsurprisingly Pound had not been in favour of it, given their relationship over the Norwegian episode, and he wrote to Cunningham on 12 December 1940:

> I pointed out to the PM that the employment of an officer of RK's age on a job of this kind was entirely opposed to the policy which we were urged to adopt of only employing young officers at sea. However, the PM is as pigheaded as a mule over these things and his reply was that RK was full of the flame of war etc.[27]

The principal problem was Keyes' rampant ego. He aimed to build up an empire and to that end one of his first moves was to move his headquarters from the Admiralty to Richmond Terrace. Colville called him "a mega-lomaniac".[28] An effective DCO had to have the trust of all three services and this Keyes signally failed to achieve. His outspoken attacks on the Admiralty, and on Pound personally, in April and May 1940 meant that Pound was unlikely to view Keyes' demands favourably. Matters came to a head over Operation WORKSHOP, Keyes' plan to seize the island of Pantelleria, located between Sicily and Tunisia, about 150 miles north-west of Malta. This saw Pound and Cunningham present a united front of opposition to the plan on every possible grounds. The Army disliked Keyes firstly for his defence of the King of the Belgians (perfectly correctly as it turned out) over his role in the defeat in France in 1940, and secondly for his retaining control of the Commandos, instead of them being under the command of the Commander-in-Chief Home Forces, Sir Alan Brooke. The RAF had suffered under the lash of Keyes' tongue in the House of Commons over their retaining control of Coastal Command.

The final nail in Keyes' coffin was a message from the Mediterranean to Pound from Admirals Somerville, North and Cunningham, which said:

> They all personally liked and admired Roger, but felt that he was too old, too out of date, and too reckless for the job . . . Further objections were that besides being Winston's personal friend, to have an Admiral of the Fleet loose in the Mediterranean could hopelessly complicate their tasks.[29]

In particular they were worried about WORKSHOP, as was Pound, who wrote to Cunningham in the letter already quoted:

> The WORKSHOP plan started the wrong end as RK put up the suggestion without having made any investigation of it whatsoever. The next step was that a half-baked plan was put before the COS and of course when we criticised it, it was insinuated that we were trying to kill it and to do nothing. As you will realise as soon as you have anything to do with him, RK is not capable of making out a plan and you would certainly be very unwise to allow him to do so.

Cunningham wrote bluntly to Keyes telling him his views on WORK-SHOP and saying that it was impracticable. This all gelled together and WORKSHOP was stopped. It was this lack of trust that really brought about Keyes' dismissal by Churchill on 5 October 1941. Pound could breathe more easily.

If events in the Atlantic and at home appeared to be relatively hopeful towards the end of 1941 this was very much not the case in the Mediterranean. Indeed, by the end of the year events had reached the nadir of the war from a naval point of view. 1941 had started well, reaching a climax in March with the victory at Matapan. Although Cunningham had suffered a severe loss in the crippling of *Illustrious* in January, which surely confirmed Pound in his belief in the vulnerability of aircraft carriers, the Mediterranean Fleet dominated the Eastern Basin in the same way that Force H did the Western Basin. This naval dominance allowed Britain to transfer troops to Greece in March after the defeat of the Italians in North Africa at Beda Fomm in February. The Chiefs of Staff were not in favour of this and only reluctantly accepted it as a political necessity on 24 February. Sure enough their worst fears were vindicated when the Germans attacked Yugoslavia and Greece on 6 April, and by 24 April Operation DEMON, the evacuation of Greece, was under way.

Meanwhile in North Africa the Western Desert Force was under enormous pressure. Cunningham eventually agreed to the bombardment of Tripoli on 19 April, a most hazardous operation, which he did not approve of, due to the considerable distance from friendly air cover. He had been under increasing pressure from Churchill to mount operations to relieve pressure on the Army. Churchill wanted Cunningham to sacrifice *Barham* in order to block Tripoli harbour. Here again it is possible to see Pound's method of handling Churchill: 'Never say a direct NO'. On this occasion the implications of the action were spelled out by Cunningham, not by Pound, and they forced Churchill to drop the idea. The blocking of a harbour had not been effective at Zeebrugge in 1918 and in this case would also have resulted in the loss of most of *Barham*'s crew. Instead, Cunningham took the Mediterranean Fleet to bombard Tripoli for 45 minutes. A week before, a destroyer flotilla from Malta had annihilated an Italian convoy off Sfax. Both operations showed Churchill how effective the Mediterranean Fleet could be if left to its own devices.

Churchill was determined to reinforce Wavell in Egypt with Britain's latest tank production. In 1940 the Chiefs of Staff had persuaded him to send a convoy of tanks round the Cape; this time he prevailed, and

Operation TIGER entailed a highly complicated series of linked manoeuvres around the movement of five fast ships carrying the 250 tanks, as well as separate fast and slow convoys, and reinforcements for Cunningham. Amazingly the operation went off with minimal loss, mainly due to poor weather. Thus early May saw morale high, but it reached its lowest point at the end of that month with the loss of Crete.

Almost all concerned saw the key role in the defence of Crete being held by the Royal Navy. Nobody believed that it would be possible for German airborne troops to capture the island without seaborne reinforcements. Thus "the destruction of the reinforcing troop convoys would eventually win the day".[30] Cunningham accepted this view, but realized that without air cover (Crete was over 400 miles from Alexandria) his fleet would be at the mercy of the Luftwaffe. On Crete there were nine RAF planes (all put out of action before the battle began) and *Formidable* was reduced to four serviceable planes. Thus Cunningham decided he could only operate north of Crete with cruisers and destroyers, and only at night. He also reluctantly decided that he would have to control his widely scattered forces from Alexandria, not afloat. Sure enough on the night of 21–22 May the Mediterranean Fleet destroyed three German troop convoys, but the cost of the two days was traumatic: two cruisers and one destroyer sunk, two battleships, two cruisers damaged and all severely short of ammunition.

On 27 May Wavell ordered the evacuation of Crete and Cunningham was involved in yet another withdrawal, which was completed, insofar as it was possible, by 1 June. The results were equivocal, to say the least. Although 16,500 soldiers were rescued, the cost had been the equivalent of a major fleet action: two battleships badly damaged, *Formidable* out of action for five months, three cruisers sunk, five damaged, six destroyers sunk and seven damaged. Cunningham wrote to Pound on 30 May:

There is no hiding the fact that in our battle with the German Air Force we have been badly battered. I always thought we might get a surprise if they really turned their attention to the Fleet. No A/A fire will deal with the simultaneous attacks of 10–20 aircraft . . . I would not mind if we had inflicted corresponding damage on the enemy but I fear we have achieved little beyond preventing a seaborne landing in Crete and the evacuation of some of the Army there. I feel very heavy hearted about it all.

I suppose we shall learn our lesson in time that the navy and army cannot make up for lack of air forces. Three squadrons of long range fighters and a few bombing squadrons would have saved Crete for us . . .

I hear that the PM has removed Longmore [AOC Middle East] . . . It may be that he or the Admiralty would like a change in command of the Fleet out here. If this is so I shall not feel in any way annoyed, more especially as it may be that the happenings of the last few days have shaken the faith of the personnel of the fleet in my handling of affairs.[31]

Despite this offer Pound kept faith with Cunningham, who was undoubtedly the right man in the right place.

Throughout the summer the Mediterranean Fleet and Force H were fully committed to running convoys through the Mediterranean, taking reinforcements to Malta and on to Alexandria. As a result Malta's defences were at last put into a proper state of repair. She could thus operate as an offensive base and Pound was instrumental in the formation of Force K on 21 October 1941. Although both RAF and submarines had been effective in attacking the Italian naval convoys, it was really Force K, composed of two cruisers and two destroyers, which cut the supply route to North Africa to under 40% of that despatched. Despite these successes the year ended with four catastrophes. On 13 November *Ark Royal* was torpedoed and sunk within 30 miles of the safety of Gibraltar. On 24 November *Barham* was also torpedoed and sunk, with heavy loss of life. Early in December Cunningham lost two cruisers to U-boats and mines, and finally on 19 December the two remaining battleships of the Mediterranean Fleet, *Queen Elizabeth* and *Valiant*, were sunk in Alexandria harbour by Italian impact mines attached by divers who rode into the harbour on human torpedoes, a most valiant exploit. As a result the Fleet was reduced to three light cruisers, while Force H was reduced to *Malaya* (unmodernized), *Argus* (obsolete) and one cruiser. In the course of the year the Royal Navy had lost (within the Mediterranean) one battleship sunk and four damaged, one carrier sunk and two damaged, seven cruisers sunk and ten damaged, sixteen destroyers sunk and twelve damaged, one monitor sunk and five submarines sunk and three damaged.[32]

Worse, on 7 December 1941 the ultimate calamity occurred which

191

successive First Sea Lords had warned about since the 1920s: the Japanese entered the war on the side of Germany and Italy. On 10 December *Prince of Wales* and *Repulse* were sunk off the east coast of Malaya. Not only was the Mediterranean stripped bare, but so was the Far East. Pound had to face the fact that Britain was very nearly bankrupt in naval matters.

12

FORCE Z

In August 1941 Churchill had asked the Chiefs of Staff to consider what active steps could be taken to deter Japanese expansion. The only possible action was naval and the Royal Navy was already fully stretched. The only effective battleships in the Home Fleet were *King George V* and *Prince of Wales*. In the Mediterranean Fleet *Warspite* was being repaired in the USA and Cunningham's battle fleet consisted of *Barham*, *Valiant* and *Queen Elizabeth*. Force H possessed *Nelson* and *Renown*. Refitting in Britain were *Malaya*, *Repulse* and *Royal Sovereign*, while *Rodney* and *Resolution* were refitting in the USA. *Ramilles* and *Revenge* were useful only for convoy protection in their unmodernized state. Knowing that *Tirpitz* was ready for operations, and that the Italians were numerically superior to Cunningham, Pound and the Naval Staff could see that the Royal Navy were stretched to the limit. Their recommendation, confirmed by the Chiefs of Staff, was that by September one battleship should be sent east from the Mediterranean Fleet and that all four of the R-class (all of which were unmodernized) should follow by the end of the year. They should be accompanied by an aircraft carrier, probably *Eagle*. The Chiefs of Staff stated that the purpose of this force was not to fight the Imperial Japanese Navy, but to prevent disruption to trade in the Indian Ocean. It was purely the first step to an Eastern Fleet, which would ultimately consist of seven battleships and an aircraft carrier.[1]

Pound had looked at this problem as far back as 1940 when he had stated: "There is no object in sending a fleet to Singapore unless it is strong enough to fight the Japanese Fleet. Singapore is inferior to Trincomalee as a base from which to protect our trade in the Indian Ocean."[2] What he therefore proposed was a fleet of old slow heavy ships, i.e. the Rs, to protect the Indian Ocean trade, based on Ceylon. However, as a result of the ABC-1 planning conversations in Washington in early 1941, the USA agreed to help the Royal Navy defend the Atlantic and this allowed Pound eventually to write to Churchill on 28 August 1941 proposing an Eastern Fleet of *Nelson*, *Rodney* and three of the Rs, *Ark Royal*, and *Renown*, ten cruisers and thirty-two destroyers.[3] This, of course, was delayed by repairs and modernization to the relevant ships and led to upset within the United States Navy, who were insistent on this force operating north of the Malay Barrier, rather than concentrating on trade defence in the Indian Ocean.[4] Pound's proposed fleet having a slow speed, but reasonable protection and range of gun, was purely defensive and was not capable of threatening the Japanese main fleet, which could evade battle if it so wished. Pound's concept was thus trade defence, while Churchill viewed the problem as one of deterrence. Churchill saw the effect that *Bismarck* had had and *Tirpitz* was having on the Home Fleet. He believed that the Japanese would not dare attack to the south if threatened by the US Pacific Fleet on their eastern flank at Pearl Harbor and Manila, and a British fast squadron at Singapore. His view is best summarized in a memo to Pound on 25 August 1941:

> It should become possible in the near future to place a deterrent squadron in the Indian Ocean. Such a force should consist of the smallest number of the best ships. We have only to remember all the preoccupations which are caused us by the *Tirpitz* – the only capital ship left to Germany – to see what an effect would be produced upon the Japanese Admiralty by the presence of a small but very powerful and fast force in Eastern waters . . . This powerful force [he proposed *Duke of York*, *Repulse* or *Renown* and a fast aircraft carrier] might show itself in the triangle Aden–Singapore–Simonstown. It would exert a paralysing effect upon Japanese naval action [5]

Pound then took up his normal procedure with Churchill: 'Never say a direct No'. He instructed the Naval Staff to prepare briefs as to why it was not sensible to send out any of the *King George V* class unworked-up. Churchill had proposed that *Duke of York* should work up while on passage to the Far East. Pound replied to Churchill on 28 August with a long paper in which he explained the need to work up battleships in close proximity to a dockyard and then commented on the problems of the capital ship situation. He was prepared to send out by the beginning of

1941 *Nelson*, *Rodney*, *Renown* and *Hermes*, with *Ark Royal* to follow in April 1942. The force would go to Singapore, but retire to Trincomalee if war broke out, and would be backed up by the 4 Rs engaged on convoy escort in the Indian Ocean. This deployment, it was hoped, would "go some way to meet the wishes of Australia and New Zealand for the Far East to be reinforced".[6]

Churchill replied the next day (29 August) in a long memorandum in which he argued against Pound's dispositions. In particular he deplored the use of the Rs, which he described as "floating coffins", and compared Pound's retention of the three *King George V*'s to protect against *Tirpitz* with the potential effect of his proposed "fast squadron" upon the Japanese.[7] Here, obviously, was a direct clash between the Prime Minister and the Admiralty, between the political will and naval expertise, between Churchill's concept of a "high class" squadron which would deter Japanese aggression and the Admiralty's concept of two larger forces of older capital ships, also to deter the Japanese, but principally to protect British trade in the Indian Ocean.

Little happened for six weeks on the naval front, until matters moved on the political front. Early in October a new Japanese Prime Minister was appointed, the expansionist General Tojo. This sufficiently alarmed the Foreign Secretary, Eden, to write to Churchill on 16 October: "You will recall that we discussed some little time ago the possibility of capital ship reinforcements to the Far East. The matter has now become urgent, and I should be glad if it could be discussed at the Defence Committee meeting tomorrow afternoon."[8]

Thus the matter came to a head at the Defence Committee on 17 October. Pound was visiting the Home Fleet, not on leave as suggested by Barnett,[9] and so Tom Phillips represented the Naval Staff, but the Admiralty case was put by the First Lord, A.V. Alexander. Churchill proposed that *Repulse*, escorting a convoy to India, should be diverted to Singapore, and *Prince of Wales* should be detached to join her. Alexander fought hard with the arguments put forward for him by Pound and Phillips, but to little effect. Phillips reported to Pound that Churchill "was scathing in his comments on the Admiralty attitude to this matter".[10] Churchill was powerfully backed by Attlee and Eden, the latter commenting that a modern ship like *Prince of Wales* "would have a far greater effect politically than the presence in those waters of a number of the last war's battleships. If the *Prince of Wales* were to call at Cape Town on her

195

way to the Far East, news of her movements would quickly reach Japan and the deterrent effect would begin from that date." Churchill summarized by inviting the Admiralty:

> to consider the proposal to send out as quickly as possible one modern Capital Ship, together with an aircraft carrier, to join up with *Repulse* at Singapore. He would not come to a decision on this point without consulting the First Sea Lord, but in view of the strong feeling of the Committee in favour of the proposal, he hoped that the Admiralty would not oppose this suggestion. The Committee would take its final decision on Monday 20th October.[11]

The final critical meeting was held on that day, which Marder describes as "essentially a dual between Churchill and Pound".[12] In fact the really critical meeting had been the Chiefs of Staff meeting that morning, with the Prime Minister in the chair. Pound was under desperate pressure to bend to the political necessity. He reiterated the problems if the Home Fleet was weakened and explained that

> the deterrent which would prevent the Japanese from moving south-wards would not be the presence of one fast battleship. They could easily afford to put four modern ships with any big convoys destined for an attack in Southern waters. What would deter them, however, would be the presence at Singapore of a force (such as the *Nelson*, the *Rodney* and the R-class battleships) of such strength that to overcome it they would have to detach the greater part of their fleet and thus uncover Japan.[13]

Pound tried to argue with both operational necessity for the Home Fleet and possible requirements in the Far East, even being prepared to use the four R-class as the nucleus of a battlefleet. By this stage Pound realized that he was in much the same position as one of the R-class (14" guns, 21 knots and an unmodernized First World War veteran) faced by the *Yamato* (18" guns, 27 knots, completed 1941) and gave way.

> He fully realised the value of a report from Cape Town of the arrival there of the *Prince of Wales*. He suggested that she should be sailed forthwith to that destination, a decision as to her onward journey being taken in the light of the situation when she arrived at Cape Town.[14]

The Chiefs of Staff agreed, and this was ratified later that day by the Defence Committee on the grounds that the political need was so urgent "as to outweigh objections hitherto advanced by the Admiralty on strategic grounds".[15] The decision as to *Prince of Wales'* subsequent movements from Cape Town was not mentioned. Yet in a signal to all concerned the very next day (21 October) Pound explained that she was to go to Singapore. A message was also sent to the US Chief of Naval Operations, Stark, saying that *Prince of Wales* "will leave the UK this week for Singapore via the Cape".[16] Rear Admiral Fraser, who was at that time Third Sea Lord and Controller, wrote to Professor Marder, "It was understood when *Prince of Wales* sailed from the Clyde that her destination would be Singapore."[17]

Yet there is also evidence to show that no such decision had been made. On 1 November Churchill wrote to Pound, "If it is decided that *Prince of Wales* should go to Singapore . . ." and Pound replied on 2 November, "It is my intention to review the situation generally just before *Prince of Wales* reaches the Cape." In other words he would consult with the Prime Minister over that decision.[18] But by 7 November Pound in reviewing the naval situation with Allied admirals stated that Tom Phillips in *Prince of Wales* "was on his way to Singapore".[19] Phillips was actually ordered to Singapore on 9 November and on 11 November to RV with *Repulse* at Ceylon before proceeding to Singapore. Almost certainly a meeting with Churchill, probably late at night, had reached this decision, but no record of it has come to light.

It had been agreed that an aircraft carrier would accompany *Prince of Wales* and the choice was *Indomitable,* working up in the West Indies. Unfortunately, she ran aground off Jamaica on 3 November and, although repaired at Norfolk, Virginia, by 19 November, by that time the situation had changed again: *Ark Royal* had been sunk (13 November). *Illustrious* and *Formidable* were both under repair in the USA after major damage in the Mediterranean. *Furious* was undergoing major refit in Britain. *Eagle* and *Hermes* were too old and slow, and *Argus* was even worse, all three only carrying between twelve and eighteen aircraft each. Thus all the lessons of the war were, in effect, being tossed aside. *Prince of Wales* would operate with no aircover, no cruiser screen, an inadequate destroyer escort (four), moreover, in an area where they did not know the strengths or capacities of the potential enemy.

One final piece remains to be slotted into place: the choice of the

197

commander of this minimal fleet (two capital ships and four destroyers). Pound chose his Vice Chief of Naval Staff, Tom Phillips. It was a decision not universally approved. Both Cunningham and Somerville disapproved of it on the grounds that Phillips had had no experience of active warfare since the start of the war, Somerville writing to Cunningham on 21 December, with, of course, the advantage of hindsight:

> The *Prince of Wales* and *Repulse* affair seems to have been a thoroughly bad show. No air support, but in any case fancy relying on quite untried shore based air for cover! Why the hell didn't they send *someone* out there who has been through the mill and knew his stuff.[20]

There were two reasons why Pound chose Phillips. Firstly, Phillips had served as VCNS for over two years and was due to be appointed to an important sea-going command. Secondly, there is some evidence that, although Phillips and Churchill had got on excellently, by 1941 this was no longer the case. The change came because Phillips had opposed the expedition to Greece in April of that year. He had wanted to concentrate on the North African campaign and thus secure airfields in order to protect Malta and cover naval operations in the Mediterranean with shore-based air cover. He had spoken his mind bluntly and Churchill, it is said, hardly ever spoke to him again.[21] These two factors, combined with Pound's high opinion of Phillips, make the appointment understandable. Pound wrote to Phillips on the eve of his departure:

> My dear Tom,
>
> This is a very sad moment for me as it means the breaking up of what I hope has been a satisfactory combination. I have been lucky enough, or wise enough, to make sure I had your assistance whenever it was possible . . . You have done magnificent work during the last two years and I cannot adequately put into words how grateful I am personally . . . it will be a great comfort to know that there will be someone in the Far East who will make the most of the slender resources available and in whom we have complete confidence.
>
> Yours,
>
> Dudley.[22]

The clearest comment on the decision to despatch *Prince of Wales* and *Repulse* was made by Vice Admiral K.G.B. Dewar: "British naval policy

198

in Far Eastern waters was based on unrealistic threats and imaginary deterrents, conceived in Mr Churchill's strategical cloud cuckoo land."[23] Certainly this is true of the naval aspect. Politically it made some sense, but even there it was a case of too little too late. Pound did eventually give way to Churchill's pressure. He told the DNI, Admiral Godfrey, that the Prime Minister "had worn him down".[24] One extra-ordinary event did take place, probably sometime between the two Defence Committee meetings. Pound had not been present at the first meeting, as we have seen, being on a visit to the Home Fleet, and, after a full briefing from Phillips, he called a meeting of all the Sea Lords and other naval members of the Board of Admiralty. The meeting was apparently not minuted, but was recorded by Rear Admiral Sir Rowland Jerram, who was then Secretary to the ACNS (Home), Captain A.J. Power, and is confirmed by Brockman.[25] The unanimous opinion of the naval officers was that the despatch of *Prince of Wales* and *Repulse* was strategically unsound and it was so expressed in a minute to the First Lord, A.V. Alexander. Alexander directed the Permanent Secretary, Markham, to draft a memorandum from the First Lord to the Sea Lords reminding them that Pound had given his professional opinion and there the matter must now rest. Power expected that Pound might feel bound to resign, but resignation in time of war is never a realistic option (as Fisher had demonstrated so vividly in 1915). Pound and the Naval Staff were simply overruled on political grounds and a political decision must nearly always outrank a strategic one.

★

Phillips arrived in Singapore on 29 November, leaving *Prince of Wales* and *Repulse* to steam across the Bay of Bengal and arrive on 2 December. Steaming north to intercept a Japanese invasion fleet, *Prince of Wales* and *Repulse* were attacked by land-based torpedo and bomber aircraft on the morning of 10 December and were both sunk by 1320 that afternoon, local time. Pound received the news shortly after 8:30 that morning, and immediately telephoned Churchill, who recorded how he received the news:

I was opening my boxes on the 10th when the telephone at my bedside rang. It was the First Sea Lord. His voice sounded odd. He

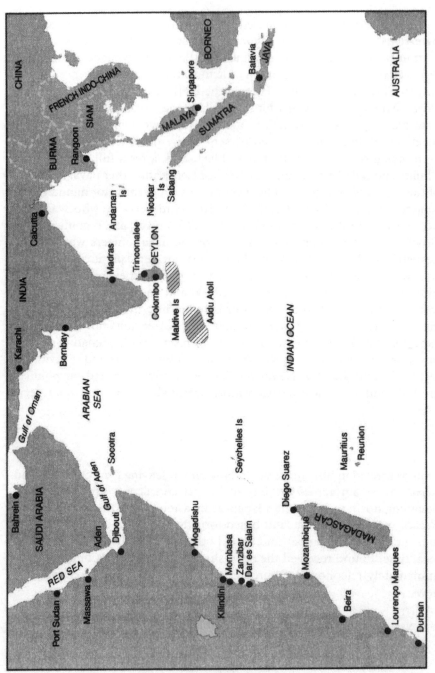

The Indian Ocean Area

gave a sort of cough and gulp, and at first I could not hear quite clearly. "Prime Minister, I have to report to you that the *Prince of Wales* and *Repulse* have both been sunk by the Japanese – we think by aircraft. Tom Phillips is drowned." "Are you sure it's true?" "There is no doubt at all." So I put the telephone down. I was thankful to be alone. In all the war I never received a more direct shock . . . As I turned over and twisted in bed the full horror of the news sank in upon me. There were no British or American capital ships in the Indian Ocean or the Pacific except the American survivors of Pearl Harbour, who were hastening back to California. Over all this vast expanse of waters Japan was supreme and we everywhere were weak and naked.[26]

When he made a statement in the House of Commons that afternoon announcing the news he was plied with a number of questions, inevitably the most hostile being from Keyes. Pound's reaction was much the same as it had been when *Hood* had been lost: stoical and philosophic. He was, however, profoundly shaken by the loss of Phillips. Brockman, in a letter to Marder in 1975, recalls:

I do not think I have seen Dudley Pound so distressed at the death of anyone as when the *Prince of Wales* and the *Repulse* were lost. He had a small meeting in his room at the time and he asked me to read out the signal from Singapore announcing the loss, and Admiral Phillips's death. The meeting finished shortly afterwards and Dudley Pound picked up his cap and stick and went to walk around the lake in St James's Park for three-quarters of an hour. Although the loss of the two ships was a disaster, there was no doubt in my mind that it was the loss of Tom Phillips which affected Dudley Pound so keenly.[27]

This is confirmed by what Pound wrote to Phillips' widow on 30 January: "His death is one of the tragedies of the war – much more so, infinitely more so, than the loss of those two ships. In time we can replace those ships – we can never get another Tom . . . His loss is a blow to the Service of the first magnitude and one which is irreparable. In the P. of Wales [sic] incident I regret nothing except Tom's loss . . . I personally know I have lost one of my greatest friends".[28]

The Admiralty investigated as far as they were able to do. There was an internal inquiry by two senior Captains on the staff. Their findings formed the basis of a report to the Board by Phillips' replacement as VCNS, Vice Admiral Sir Henry Moore, along with Pound's own memorandum, dated 25 January. In this Pound reviewed all the options and came to two conclusions:

> The decision to send an unbalanced naval force to Singapore was taken in the hope primarily of deterring the Japanese from starting the war, or, failing that, of deterring them from sending convoys into the Gulf of Siam. This hope was not fulfilled.
>
> To sum up, it is clear that Admiral Sir Tom Phillips knew the risks he was taking, took what steps he could to mitigate them, and when these failed, abandoned his original attack. Only subsequently, at long range from enemy air bases, did he again proceed to a newly threatened area. It is considered that the risks he took were fair and reasonable in the light of the knowledge he had of the enemy, when compared with the very urgent and vital issues at stake and on which the whole safety of Malaya may have depended.[29]

Pound wrote to Cunningham on 29 January and commented on the attacks that occurred on the Royal Navy in general and on himself in particular in both the press and the House of Commons:

> I do not know, but both the House of Commons and the Public seem to think that the sinking of an important ship is a crime, whilst nobody takes any notice of the loss of 30 or 40 bombers in a night due to innacurate metereological reports, or to the many failings of the Army.[30]

What, though, had been Dudley Pound's options over the whole episode? Firstly, he could have offered his resignation rather than despatch what he knew to be an unbalanced fleet. However, there can be little doubt that Churchill and Alexander would simply have appointed somebody who would have done their bidding. Cunningham was not yet ready to be moved from the Mediterranean. Indeed, only recently he had offered his own resignation if the Admiralty had desired it. Thus Pound had little option but to bow to political pressure, as is correct: politicians must ultimately take the decisions in war. Secondly, he could have tried to send out a balanced force. However, given the losses of the Royal Navy in late 1941, there was little or no prospect of this. He was faced with the prospect of what had become a one-ocean navy trying to fight a three-ocean war. Thirdly, he could have sent out an experienced admiral. Here there are more valid grounds for criticism. He could have sent Phillips either to Force H or to the Mediterranean Fleet, and sent either Somerville or Cunningham to Singapore, or even have sent Phillips as second-in-command to either of them. However, it is reasonable to ask whether either Somerville or Cunningham would have acted very differently in the circumstances of 8 December. Would either of them have taken their fleet to Trincomalee, rather than going to the help of the Army and the RAF in Malaya? Indeed, Cunningham, a critic of Phillips, said in May 1941 of his decision to continue the evacuation of Crete "It takes the Navy three years to build a ship. It would take three hundred years to rebuild a tradition." As Marder hypothetically asks "Which would have been better, the fall of Malaya and Singapore due to [Phillips'] inactivity, or the fall of Malaya and Singapore due to the loss of his fleet? The former is two good ships better. This is the logical answer, but surely 99% of Royal Naval officers would have done what Phillips did."[31]

13

ALLIES, ENEMIES AND FRIENDS

On the evening of Sunday 7 December 1941 Winston Churchill was at Chequers with the American ambassador, John Winant, and Roosevelt's Special Representative, Averell Harriman, when they heard on the radio of the Japanese attack on Pearl Harbor. Immediately receiving confirmation from the President by telephone, Churchill was enormously encouraged by his comment "We are all in the same boat now." Two days later he decided that it was imperative that he and Roosevelt meet, and proposed a second trip across the Atlantic. The news of the disaster off Malaya arrived on 10 December, just as Churchill's party was preparing to leave.

Churchill's retinue was even larger than for the August meeting. He took with him Lord Beaverbrook, Pound, Portal, who had relieved Newall in October 1940, and Dill, who was in the process of handing over as CIGS to Brooke. Brooke was to be left to "mind the shop" in London and to read himself in. All three of the Chiefs of Staff took with them various staff officers. In Pound's case it was Captain Charles Lambe, who was the Deputy Director of Plans and an officer whom Pound trusted totally. There was the usual large number of hangers-on as well. They left London on 12 December by overnight train from Euston to Greenock, where they boarded the new battleship *Duke of York*, which was to be allowed to work up on her voyage. Churchill, Beaverbrook and Pound had cabins in the bridge superstructure, while the rest were accommodated aft. *Duke of York* left the Clyde at noon on 13 December and the party rapidly settled into the same routine as on the August trip, with the Chiefs of Staff meeting each morning and afternoon. There was also, as before, a film each evening.

It was originally hoped that the journey would take seven days at 20 knots, but, unsurprisingly, winter weather intervened and delayed them. Their route was southwards across the Bay of Biscay and the Admiralty advice was to keep their escorting flotilla of destroyers due to the large number of U-boats around. However, so bad was the weather that the destroyers could not keep up. On the night of 13/14 December Pound took the decision to press on alone, as he had done with *Prince of Wales* on the earlier crossing: they were more likely to ram a U-boat than to be torpedoed by one. The sea was so heavy that all ports and doors on the upper deck had to be closed and fastened. Beaverbrook complained that it was like crossing the Atlantic in a submarine. By 16 December the weather had moderated and it was possible to walk on the quarter deck.

The principal purpose of the voyage was to prepare papers for the meeting with the American Joint Chiefs. Far more so than the previous crossing this voyage was essential in preparation for their discussions. To that end the Chiefs of Staff frequently met for a third meeting, after the evening film, starting usually at 11.30, and sometimes not finishing until 2.15 in the morning. The original plan for *Duke of York* to proceed up Chesapeake Bay was ruined by their late arrival due to the bad weather. They eventually disembarked at Hampton Roads late on 22 December, at the entrance to Chesapeake Bay, and Churchill and the Chiefs of Staff flew to Washington at 1.30 on the morning of 23 December.

During the voyage the Chiefs of Staff started by discussing strategy in the Far East. Here Pound saw that there was nothing to do but remain on the defensive. Britain could not attack until she had built up a fleet. (The Joint Planners proposed nine capital ships and four carriers.) With the losses suffered at the end of 1941 this would not be possible for some time. With this argument the others could not but agree. The Prime Minister wrote three remarkable papers for the Chiefs of Staff to discuss during the voyage, in which he correctly foretold the broad outlines of how the war would be fought. As Ismay was later to write, "In his grasp of the broad sweep of strategy . . . he stood head and shoulders above his professional advisers."[1] However, the Chiefs of Staff were more concerned with the practicalities of co-operation and alliance. Once in Washington the two sets of military chiefs met in the Federal Reserve Building, next to the White House, chaired by Stark. The discussions were long and hard, but eventually there were three fundamental decisions reached. Firstly, the ABC-1 decision of "Germany first" was confirmed. Secondly, the Combined Chiefs of Staff organization was set up, with British representatives sitting in Washington as the British Joint Staff Mission, and with a full supporting staff organization of Combined Staff Planners and a Combined Secretariat. Thirdly, the principle of unified command in theatres was established by the creation of ABDA. Of these, the most important was the acceptance by the Americans of a secretariat. Sir Ian Jacob provides an example of what could happen in his diary of 23 December 1941.

> On the following day the US Chiefs of Staff met ours in their first formal meeting at the Federal Reserve Building. There was no agenda, and the first thing Admiral Stark, who was in the chair, did was to run through the notes he had made on the previous days' meeting. General Marshall had also dictated, on his return to his office, his idea of what had happened. We of course had our minutes prepared, and it was a complete waste of everyone's time to go all over the ground again. . . . We found this lack of system extended right throughout.[2]

New Year was spent in Washington and the time there allowed Pound to get to know the senior officers of the United States Navy. Betty Stark, known to the more junior officers of the Joint Staff Mission as "Tugboat Annie", was an easy man to get on with. Ernie King on the other hand was a difficult man to like. He had recently become Commander-in-Chief US Fleet and was effectively in charge of the day to day running of the US Navy, leaving the grand strategy to Stark. This arrangement did not really work, and in March Stark moved to London as Commander-in-Chief US Naval Forces Europe, while King became both C-in-CUS and CNO. Nobody ever found King an easy man. He appeared prejudiced against all things British, but was probably better described as a ferocious Americanophile. He considered that any deployment of American forces in Europe, or, worse, North Africa was wasted as it detracted from the main theatre of the US Navy, the Pacific. His biggest dislikes were mixing US and Royal Navy ships in a combined force, or allowing US Navy ships to serve under foreign, especially British, command. His feelings can best be summed up in a letter he wrote to Stark in November 1943:

> The seeming helplessness of our cousins strikes me as amusing when it is not annoying. I am sure that what they wish in their hearts is that we would haul down the Stars and Stripes and hoist the White Ensign in all of our ships. What particularly irks me is their strong liking for

mixed forces, which as you know approached anathema to me. I am willing to take over additional tasks – and we have done so – but I cannot be expected to agree to help them cling to tasks that they themselves say they are unable to do unless we lend them our ships and other forces. I think we have done enough for them in their Home Fleet.[3]

When in the New Year Churchill went to Ottawa to discuss the matters with the Canadian government Pound went to New England to visit several of his mother's relatives, spending a day there. Churchill, Beaverbrook, Pound and Portal flew down to Bermuda where they were due to board *Duke of York* for the return voyage. Churchill suggested flying back to Britain in the plane which had brought them from Washington. Pound and Portal were initially against the idea, thinking the risk wholly unjustifiable. Churchill later wrote

It occurred to me that both these officers thought my plan was to fly myself and leave them to come back in the *Duke of York*, so I said, "Of course there would be room for all of us." They both visibly changed countenance at this.[4]

The flight was not without incident; they nearly flew over the German anti-aircraft batteries at Brest, only just turning north in time. Pound wrote to Cunningham on 29 January describing the trip.

As you may have gathered from the papers I have been away from here for nearly five weeks, of which nine days were spent in a gale getting to the Chesapeake, three and a half weeks at Washington and two days flying home via Bermuda. . . . We only expected to be in Washington for a week, but things move very much more slowly than you would imagine, as they have really no organisation. Before we left we had got a Combined Chiefs of Staff, Combined Planning and Combined Intelligence on a satisfactory footing and it is working well.

I took 24 hours off and flew up to Boston to see some relatives, and one afternoon had a look at Washington's home at Mount Vernon, but otherwise we were kept at it pretty consistently, though one did get to bed before midnight instead of 3am![5]

★

207

Almost immediately after his return from Washington Pound was faced with an apparent catastrophe right on his own doorstep. On 12 February 1942 the two German battlecruisers *Scharnhorst* and *Gneisenau*, along with the heavy cruiser *Prinz Eugen*, steamed up the English Channel from Brest to Wilhelmshaven. They were undetected as far as Boulogne and were only attacked once they were well past Calais. This episode was so close to the hearts of many Englishmen that *The Times* declared

> Vice-Admiral Ciliax has succeeded where the Duke of Medina Sidonia failed. Nothing more mortifying to the pride of sea power has happened since the 17th century.[6]

Singapore fell three days later, but there is no doubt which event hurt the Royal Navy most. As a direct result both Pound and Churchill came under increasing attack in both the House of Commons and in the press, leading, among other episodes, to the attempted vote of No Confidence in the government in July.

It had been appreciated by the Admiralty, and by the Home Fleet, that the Germans would not be able to keep their three major units at Brest indefinitely without them being heavily damaged by the RAF. They had been there for eleven months and caused enormous worry by their threat to the Atlantic convoys. The Germans decided to bring them back to Germany because Hitler was convinced that the British were threatening Norway (much to Admiral Raeder's disagreement). The problem for the Royal Navy was deciding which route they would use. It became obvious that they would try to use the Channel, as Intelligence sources provided various pieces of information, such as the redeployment of fighter units along the north French coast. Pound was not prepared to risk a battleship from the Home Fleet in the narrow waters of the Channel under the close attentions of German air power, giving the lie to those critics who claim that he did not understand the threat of air power. Nor did he have much in the way of small craft to offer to the Flag Officer, Dover, still Vice Admiral Ramsay, but he sent six destroyers and six MTBs from the Nore Command. Flag Officer Submarines, Admiral Max Horton, had stationed a submarine off Brest to give some warning and to have a go at the German ships as they emerged. Clearly much would depend on what the RAF could do, since the Royal Navy could only oppose the capital ships with destroyers and MTBs, and would be lucky to sink them with their torpedoes. Here, then was an excellent opportunity for the RAF to justify their taking over of the Royal Naval Air Service in 1918. Not only was it their task to man various radar sweeps across the western end of the Channel, but it was Bomber Command's task to mount the principal attack on the ships, along with some Fleet Air Arm torpedo-bombers which were to be flown south from Scotland as soon as the German ships were sighted. There was also an untrained Fleet Air Arm squadron of Swordfish torpedo-planes under Ramsay's control at Manston, near Ramsgate. In theory the German ships should never have been able to make it up the Channel against such a concentrated collection of air power.

In effect, everything that could go wrong did go wrong. The submarine *Sealion* had withdrawn to seaward to recharge her batteries at exactly the moment the German squadron emerged. The two ASV-equipped Hudsons of Coastal Command covering the western Channel broke down and were not replaced. Nobody bothered to pass this information on to Dover. A Spitfire dawn air search at 06.00 missed them, by which stage the German ships were past Cherbourg. Snow on various Scottish airfields prevented the transfer of RAF Beaufighter torpedo-bombers to the south. Only at 10.45 did shore-based radar pick them up and Coastal Command eventually identified them at 11.05, but did not pass this information on until 11.24. The attacks which were then carried out lacked nothing in bravery, but everything in co-ordination and skill. When Bomber Command tried to knock out the German ships only thirty-nine out of 242 aircraft managed to locate and attack the enemy. Not one scored a hit. The Fleet Air Arm squadron at Manston attacked with suicidal bravery at 12.30, achieving no hits and all being shot down. Five destroyers from Harwich attacked with torpedoes. All missed and, to add insult to injury, were attacked by the RAF. The only British success of the entire day was that both major ships hit mines dropped by Bomber Command earlier that day, but these failed to prevent the German squadron making a triumphal entry into their ports that evening. Bomber Command did salvage something that night by hitting *Gneisenau* and effectively destroying her in dock at Kiel.

To what extent does the Admiralty and Pound have to accept blame for this débâcle? They have to do so insofar as they were the responsible service, but the shortage of effective destroyers cannot be laid at the door of Pound. His decision not to allow Home Fleet battleships into the enclosed waters of the Channel was surely correct, given the threat of

Tirpitz and the shortage of battleships at that precise period. The Admiralty had produced a highly accurate intelligence appreciation by OIC, which alerted both naval and air force commands. The main blame has to be laid at the door of the RAF and their total lack of training for operations over the sea in the inter-war years. Not only could they not hit their targets, but they could not identify them: the Harwich destroyers were bombed, machine-gunned, shelled and torpedoed. If the episode demonstrates anything, it shows that the independence of air power is a fallacy and that effective air support of both the army and the navy required specialist training. The comparison to the Japanese performance off Malaya is striking. All that can be said is that, although the Germans could claim a tactical victory, as at Jutland it was a strategic victory for the Royal Navy. Having the German squadron in Germany, or even in Norway, meant that it could be covered from Scapa Flow; in Brest they could have attacked the Atlantic convoys whenever they wanted.

★

The fiasco of *Scharnhorst* and *Gneisenau* undoubtedly fed a feeling in the public and in the House of Commons of dissatisfaction with the leadership of the Royal Navy and with the general direction of the war itself. Indeed there is reason to believe that there was some dissatisfaction within the Navy itself with Pound's leadership. Churchill himself was upset at the episode, and, when telephoned by Pound to inform him of the ships' escape, simply and crushingly asked, "Why?" An eyewitness described the scene:

> Admiral Sir Dudley Pound lifted the private telephone which connected him with 10 Downing Street. Around him, several senior staff officers gazed intently at maps on the War Room wall, not caring to watch his face.
>
> "I'm afraid, sir," the Admiral said, "I must report that the enemy battlecruisers should by now have reached the safety of their home waters."
>
> He was silent while the waiting officers tried to imagine what the Prime Minister was saying. It must have been brief, for quickly the receiver was replaced and at an inquiring look from another Admiral present, Sir Dudley said,

"I think there's going to be some trouble about this. The Prime Minister was quiet for a bit. He said quite simply "Why?" Then he put the phone down."[7]

Undoubtedly this was one of the factors which influenced Churchill to ask the new CIGS to take over as Chairman of the Chiefs of Staff Committee. Brooke had become CIGS on Christmas Day 1941, although he had been in the office since 1 December. On 5 March Churchill nominated Brooke to be chairman. He had written to Pound the day before. The correspondence is worth quoting in full as it shows that Churchill recognized the implications for the First Sea Lord of also being the Chief of Naval Staff, i.e. of being an operational officer, unlike the CIGS and the CAS.

My dear Pound,

1. You are in a different position to the other two Chiefs of Staff because you are conducting the Naval War over its whole spread in direct contact with the enemy, and are in fact a Super Commander-in-Chief. I must say I consider this your first duty as First Sea Lord. Now that the war has invaded so many theatres and the work of the Chiefs of Staff Committee has been so vastly extended and complicated I am clearly of the opinion you should lighten your load. If therefore you were to represent this to me I would arrange for Brooke, as it is the army's turn, to preside over the Chiefs of Staff Committee so that you could attend or not as you chose and for the rest manage the movements of the Fleet and all the other aspects of Admiralty business confided to you. You know I have the greatest confidence in your judgement and in your handling of the Fleet . . .

2. . . .

3. Pray give these matters your careful consideration.

Yours sincerely,

Winston S. Churchill.

Pound replied the next day:

My dear Prime Minister,

As you are aware the Admiralty have to exercise general operational control over the Naval forces and from time to time have immediate situations to deal with which require my undivided attention.

211

As Chairman of the Chiefs of Staff Committee I am naturally even more reluctant to absent myself from their meetings than I should be if I were not Chairman.

This alone would not have moved me to ask that I should be relieved of the Chairmanship of the Chiefs of Staff Committee, but taken in combination with the fact that I have been Chairman for nearly a year and a half, I should like to suggest that the Chairmanship should be taken over by one of the other services. As the Army has not held the Chairmanship during the war it would seem appropriate that they should have a turn.

Yours very sincerely,

Dudley Pound.

The next day, 6 March 1942, Churchill wrote to General Ismay, copying Pound's letter:

I have received the attached letter from the First Sea Lord, and in consequence I appoint the CIGS as Chairman of the Chiefs of Staff Committee. At the same time I wish to place on record my appreciation of the very great service which the First Sea Lord has rendered to the Chiefs of Staff Committee and to His Majesty's Government, and my admiration of the manner in which he has been able to combine these ever-growing duties with his direct responsibilities in regard to the Fleet.[8]

Churchill's understanding of the First Sea Lord's dual role is interesting and it was quite correct that the Chiefs of Staff should be chaired by somebody who did not have direct operational control of forces. It is also fair to say that in the desperately dark days of early 1942 it was not a bad idea to have a new figurehead. Pound had many virtues, but he was not an expeditious chairman of either the Chiefs of Staff, or of the nascent Combined Chiefs of Staff. Brooke on the other hand, was superb. March 1942 really was the nadir of the Allied cause. In the Far East Singapore had surrendered, Rangoon had been captured, the Japanese had invaded New Guinea, and accepted the surrender of the Allied forces in Java, while in India Gandhi preached non-co-operation. In the Mediterranean Cunningham was left without a battleship or aircraft carrier and had just failed to get a convoy through to Malta (every ship had been sunk), and Malta was down to its last reserves of oil. In the Atlantic the U-boats had

212

fallen on the easy prey of American shipping on the east coast and were enjoying their second 'happy time'. Nothing appeared to be going right and an injection of fresh blood and leadership was certainly required. Brooke provided exactly that.

Brooke took the chair for the first time at the Chiefs of Staff meeting on 9 March 1942 and recorded in his diary that night: "First C.O.S. in which I took the chair. Went off all right, and both Portal and Pound played up very well." Later he was to add:

> This is putting it mildly. Dudley Pound was usually late for our C.O.S. meetings and I rather dreaded taking his chair in his absence, but to my surprise dear old Dudley on this morning made a point of arriving before the appointed time, and I found him already sitting in my chair with his chairman's seat empty. This was typical of the man. I feel certain this gesture on his part was done on purpose to make matters easier for me, and to impress on me how ready he was to serve under my chairmanship. I was deeply grateful to him.[9]

Brooke's appointment as chairman was accompanied, at Churchill's insistence, by the promotion of Lord Louis Mountbatten from 'Adviser on' to 'Chief of Combined Operations'. Since his appointment as Adviser in October 1941 Mountbatten had attended meetings of the Chiefs of Staff Committee about once a week, whenever an item concerning Combined Operations was on the agenda. On 4 March Churchill invited Mountbatten to Chequers and told him he was to become Chief of Combined Operations, and to have the acting rank of Vice Admiral, Lieutenant General and Air Marshal. He wrote to Pound that evening, in the same letter quoted above,

> I consider that Mountbatten should join the Chiefs of Staff Committee as an equal member while retaining control of the Commandos etc., and assuming the title of Chief of Combined Operations. The rank of this office would be raised appropriately in all three services, but not personally to the individual.

By the time he wrote to Ismay on 6 March this had been subtly altered so that Mountbatten should attend the meetings of the C.O.S. Committee "whenever larger issues are in question and when his own Combined Operations or any special matters in which he is concerned, are under discussion. His title will be Chief of Combined Operations, and his position upon the C.O.S. Committee when present will be that of full and equal membership irrespective of rank."[10]

Pound was not happy with this and wrote to Churchill, one assumes after speaking to him:

> I hope that you will not mind my returning to the charge about granting Mountbatten the acting rank of Vice-Admiral. I feel, however, that I must put certain facts before you.
>
> Three days ago I had a private letter from a Commander-in-Chief in whom I have great confidence, in which he was giving a review of the state of feeling amongst the officers in his command. He said that one of his captains had come to him and said that there was great anxiety because: "There is a firm belief that the Prime Minister overrides the advice of his Naval Advisers or has done so. They cannot believe, for example, that the Naval Advisers to the Cabinet really wanted Admiral Keyes as Director of Combined Operations – yet they feel that the Prime Minister just insisted on doing what the whole Navy knew to be wrong."
>
> I am afraid that there is a very widespread belief, not only in the Services but also in the country, that you do override the opinion of your professional advisers and it is doing a great deal of harm in undermining the confidence in the Service leaders.
>
> I can honestly say that in no case do I feel that my advice has been overridden in anything that matters.
>
> I certainly did not like Roger Keyes being D.C.O., but I did not feel very strongly about it.
>
> Other incidents which are widely quoted in which you have overriden my advice are the sending of the *Prince of Wales* and *Repulse* to the Far East and the sending of the R class battleships to the Indian Ocean.
>
> In the above cases, I have been able to say quite definitely that it was in accordance with my advice.
>
> If Mountbatten is made an acting Vice Admiral, it will be attributed to one of three things:-
>
> (a) That it is on my advice. I am afraid I feel so strongly that it is wrong that I cannot shoulder this responsibility and, if I do so, it would reduce confidence in my leadership.

(b)   That it has been done contrary to my advice. Naturally, I could not say this and consequently people must be left to think what they like, and I am very much afraid that it would be taken as another case of you overriding my advice.

(c)   That it is his Royalty. This would naturally do him harm in the Service.

Apart from the above, the Service will not understand the junior Captain in a shore appointment being given three steps in rank [in fact only two], and if he is to change his uniform again it will undoubtedly cause publicity.

The question of his rank will not make the slightest difference to the weight which is given to the opinions he expresses at the C.O.S. meetings.

I did not bring this up at the C.O.S. meeting this morning, because if he is to be given honorary rank in the Army and Air Force, the rank he is given in these Services will not have anything like the effect it will have in his own Service.

I must apologise for writing at such length, about what may appear a small matter. It is only because I feel the reactions will be so great that I have done so.

Yours sincerely,[11]

However, he was to be overruled. Churchill, writing to Ismay to formalize Mountbatten's position, added as a postscript that the Chiefs of Staff were welcome to discuss the issue, "but I trust they will find themselves generally able to agree". To Ismay himself he was even blunter, saying that they could discuss the details "but I cannot have the plan seriously affected".[12]

It took some months for Mountbatten to be accepted and it was not until later in the summer that the secretariat took to minuting him as a full member of the Chiefs of Staff Committee. Pound's comment that he did not believe that he had been overruled is surprising, particularly given what had occurred over Force Z, and certainly shows a greater degree of loyalty than of accuracy. One wonders what Churchill made of the letter. There is no evidence of a reply.

★

However, if Pound did not find Mountbatten an ally, March saw the arrival in London of one who very definitely was. On Thursday 30 April Admiral Harold Stark arrived in London as the Commander United States Naval Forces in Europe (COMNAVEU), and was greeted at Hendon airport by Pound. The significance of his arrival, along with that early in 1941 of John Winant as the American Ambassador in place of the defeatist Kennedy, is hard to overstate. Back in November 1940 it had been Stark, then CNO, who had written the famous Plan Dog, his assessment of how the Allies should fight a global war when and if the USA and Britain were faced by a coalition of Germany, Italy and Japan. Annoyed by the President's inability to think things through logically, Stark believed it was essential that the USA have a statement of national defence policy and intended to write one. In 1940 the only War Plan the USA had was the Orange Plan (Rainbow 3), of which the Commander-in-Chief Pacific Fleet said, "He knew of no flag officer who wholeheartedly endorsed it".[13] Stark drafted his memorandum in one 24-hour period in October 1940 and over the next week refined it with a select group of staff officers, principally Turner. The plan was approved by General Marshall and stated that they believed that the correct course for the USA was "Germany first". Put simply, "If Britain wins decisively against Germany, we could win everywhere; but . . . if she loses, the problem confronting us would be very great; and while we might not *lose everywhere*, we might, possibly, not *win anywhere*."[14] Although he did not expect, and did not get, an immediate endorsement from Roosevelt, Stark showed a copy of the memorandum to the British naval attaché on 29 October and sent a copy to the Special Naval Observer in London, Admiral Ghormley, but expressly forbade him to show it to the Admiralty. Roosevelt almost certainly approved the memorandum by the end of November, although this approval was never expressed in writing. However, the Joint Planning Committee reviewed and approved it on 14 December. This also led to the ABC-1 joint staff talks, which began on 29 January 1941. Thus the "Germany first" strategy was Stark's brainchild.

By February 1942 Stark was in the uncomfortable position of knowing that he had an overmighty subject in Ernie King as Commander-in-Chief US Fleet. The separation of function between CNO and Commander-in-Chief was unsatisfactory, and Stark believed that King was the right man to be a wartime CNO. Thus, on 9 February he wrote to Roosevelt suggesting that King become CNO and that he (Stark) move to London

216

to head the naval command there because of his experience in negotiating with the British and because he had served there in 1917–18 with Admiral Sims. Roosevelt saw the sense in this and in effect Stark became the equivalent of Sir John Dill in Washington. He was wholly immersed in Allied strategy. He knew the exact state of American forces and he knew the British leaders. The key to his liaison with the British lay with Dudley Pound.

Pound took the critical decision that Stark should know everything that he knew. He, and indeed the whole Board of Admiralty, knew how much they already owed to Stark and as a result Pound wanted something more than just the normal liaison. After all, they would be meeting very regularly to discuss matters of enormous consequence. What was essential was that Stark should receive the very latest operational information. Indeed, this should not be limited to naval matters, but was to include the whole war situation. Pound decided that Stark should be as well informed as a member of the Chiefs of Staff Committee, so that when they met they would be talking from a common background. As a result on 30 April 1942, the day of his arrival, Pound offered Stark Vice Admiral Geoffrey Blake as his personal liaison officer. It is difficult to think of a better choice. Not only was Blake Pound's closest surviving naval friend, who had been his second-in-command in the Mediterranean until invalided in 1938, he was already serving in the Admiralty as ACNS and thus knew all that was going on. He had also served in Washington as a naval attaché after the First World War. Indeed it suited Blake perfectly. He had written to Pound in September 1941 saying, "I've been here for so long, can I go to a command? I accept not afloat, but what about Rosyth?"[15] Here was the perfect solution.

This offer was immediately accepted by Stark and Blake started at once as Flag Officer, Liaison United States Navy (FOLUS), moving into the American HQ at 20 Grosvenor Square on 18 May. There was already a routine courier service bringing a vast number of British despatches, reports, letters etc. from the Admiralty to Grosvenor Square, but it soon became evident that much information was not being received and it was this system that Blake set out to repair.

Blake gained access to the more exclusive distribution lists, including all HUSH MOST SECRET despatches, and all the despatches routed through the Admiralty Registry. The selection of these latter was critical and the head of the War Registry, J.G. Lang, achieved almost perfection

217

in this. Blake also obtained access to the Cabinet War Room Record, a summary on never more than two sheets of the preceding 24 hours' Naval, Military, Air and Home Security events, and to the First Lord's Report, prepared every morning by the Director of the Operations Division for the First Lord and the King, summarizing all naval events in the preceding 24 hours. Out of these three sources Blake composed a daily report of the events of the war. The series was known as SH, standing for HUSH, and they were only seen by Stark, his Chief of Staff and Flag secretary. They are an outstanding summary of the critical operations of the war and still make interesting reading. Indeed the history of FOLUS shows the truism that "Liaison is about personalities" to be correct. Pound's choice of Blake was inspired.

From his office Stark would meet regularly with Pound. A sign of his visible importance is that his first weekend in England was spent at Chequers with the Churchills, and in his first week he was given a formal lunch by the Board of Admiralty, at which Alexander, Pound and Churchill, in that order, all spoke. He made formal calls throughout his first week, to every department within the Admiralty, as well as the other Service Chiefs and the Foreign Office. However, not all was pleasantries. Within 48 hours he was asked by Pound to come over to the Admiralty late in the evening to help draft a telegram to Washington which Pound and Churchill had been wrestling over. Pound saw the advantage of having a high-powered American admiral in London and, much as he liked and respected Admiral Sir Charles Little, head of the British Admiralty delegation in Washington, he knew that he really needed a tough battle-hardened admiral to talk to King on relatively equal terms. To that end he wrote to Cunningham in March asking him to move there from the Mediterranean. He knew full well the respect in which Cunningham was held by the US Navy and that this would be critical if they were to be held to the "Germany first" principle. Cunningham had also been Commander-in-Chief for nearly three exhausting years and a break was probably opportune.

Nowhere was the tension that existed between London and Washington better exemplified than in the North Atlantic. When the USA entered the war their navy was not yet ready for the realities of modern commerce warfare. It is another truism that the lessons of war can only be learned by experience and cannot be taught on paper. The Royal Navy had learned their lessons the hard way as to how to cope with the U-boats.

Their remaining problem in 1942 was that they did not have the industrial base to produce the necessary new equipment, or repair the existing equipment that was damaged in conflict. The combination of excellent intelligence and evasive routing, VLR aircraft, escort carriers, escort and support groups, and new weapons, as well as determined leadership was seen as the way ahead. However, the VLR aircraft and most of the escort carriers had to come from American factories and shipyards. The Americans had yet to learn their lessons and while they were doing so the U-boats enjoyed their second "happy time" off the east coast of the USA. For various reasons the US Navy did not institute convoys immediately. Nor did they impose a blackout on this coast. U-boats were thus presented with plentiful unescorted targets, frequently silhouetted against the lights of the coastal towns. Pound did what he could to warn, encourage and advise, but Ernie King, understandably, would not be told, particularly by an Englishman. The convoy battle was not helped by the Germans introducing a fourth wheel to their U-boat Enigma encoding machines on 1 February, leading to an intelligence blackout, and at the same time the Allied convoy cipher was broken. All of these factors led to mounting losses, which Pound could do little about.

The critical factor, however, was that, at last, the one-power navy of 1939–41, which had been faced by the task of taking on three powers, had had her responsibilities reduced. By agreement at Washington in December 1941 the Royal Navy would look after the eastern Atlantic, the Arctic convoys, the Mediterranean and the Indian Ocean. However, the two navies calculated that together they were short of 810 escort craft.[16] Although most of these would be built in American shipyards, the unpredictable factor was the German U-boats. It was Pound in March 1942 who said "If we lose the war at sea, we lose the war".[17] Here he made what is probably his most important single contribution to Allied strategy in the whole war. Compared with what happened in the North Atlantic almost all else was irrelevant, whether it be the Army in North Africa, Cunningham in the Mediterranean, Somerville in the Indian Ocean, or the RAF's bombing campaign. None of them could operate if Britain herself became untenable, and Doenitz's U-boats could very well do that. Ultimately no cross-Channel invasion could ever be mounted if the German U-boats in the Atlantic could not be mastered. Pound saw this more clearly than anybody else in Britain, even than Churchill.

The first U-boats arrived off the east coast of the USA on 13 January

1942 and in the first two weeks they sank 100,000 tons. In February the rate increased. In March the total sunk on the east coast of the USA and in the Gulf of Mexico and the Caribbean was only just under 250,000 tons, and critically oil tankers made up 17% of that total. No defensive measures were taken before April. Pound was desperately worried by this, and remembering the American loan of fifty old destroyers in 1940, promptly offered the US Navy the loan of twenty-four anti-submarine trawlers, which in the words of the American Official Historian "were a great help".[18] The Royal Navy also helped by training American crews in anti-submarine techniques, which produced a note from Stark paying tribute to "the outstanding work done by the training schools".[19] Pound also wrote to King that he "regarded the introduction of convoys as a matter of urgency". King took little notice replying that "inadequately escorted convoys were worse than none". Roskill comments that it was "the exact opposite of all that our experience has taught".[20] However, by June the lessons that Pound and Doenitz had been teaching began to be heeded and King introduced a convoy system on the east coast. However, the U-boats continued their attack on shipping in the Caribbean, sinking ships at an unprecedented rate. In June 1942 the Allies lost over 704,000 tons in all theatres. By the end of June, however, Allied defensive measures had forced Doenitz to recognize that the *Schwerpunkt* of the naval war was back in the North Atlantic.

*

While the U-boats were enjoying their second "happy time", the Royal Navy was under desperate pressure in the Mediterranean. Much centred around the continued British hold on Malta. The arrival in January 1941 of Fliegerkorps X in Sicily, which specialized in anti-shipping bombing, had rapidly shown the dangers of operating in the enclosed waters of the central Mediterranean. By early 1942 it had become impossible to maintain Force K at Malta, and by April it had left. The submarine flotilla was reduced to submerging in daylight hours in order to survive and by mid-April the dockyard and the surrounding areas were virtually defenceless. The Chiefs of Staff decided on 27 February that it was not possible to run a convoy to Malta from the west "due to the general naval situation". However, Malta became a symbol of British defiance, as seen by the award of the GC on 16 April. Churchill asked Pound to write to the island's

220

governor, Lord Gort, and assure him that "the Royal Navy will never abandon Malta".[21] Cunningham faced a similar problem in the Mediterranean as Pound faced in the Atlantic: a shortage of trained aircrews capable of co-operating with the Royal Navy. Not only that, but for most of 1942 the airfields of Cyrenaica were held by the Germans and thus any attempt to run convoys to Malta was attacked from both north and south by air, even if not by the (substantial) Italian surface fleet. In turn, the RAF could not attack Rommel's supply convoys, from Italy to Africa, from Egypt. The problems were immediately to be seen in February 1942 with the first attempt to run a convoy of three fast merchant ships through to Malta. The escort consisted of three light cruisers, an anti-aircraft cruiser, seven Hunt class destroyers and eight fleet destroyers. Despite this large escort not one ship got through, although four empty merchant ships managed to get out from Malta to Alexandria unscathed.

The Chiefs of Staff ordered Cunningham to mount another convoy and to regard it as the Mediterranean Fleet's primary commitment. He used his entire remaining strength of three cruisers, one anti-aircraft cruiser, ten fleet destroyers, seven Hunts, as well as one cruiser and one destroyer from Malta, to escort four merchantmen. This convoy, MW10, was brilliantly fought through as far as Malta by Rear-Admiral Vian, despite the attention of the Italian battle fleet, but heartbreakingly all four of the merchant ships were sunk either in harbour or within reach of Malta itself. It was the loss of the two ships to bombing in Malta harbour that persuaded Pound and Cunningham that surface ships could no longer survive there.

It was at this point that Pound opted to send Cunningham to Washington. Few could deny that Cunningham needed a break, but Churchill did not see the matter in this light, believing that he should go to Washington for a short time. He wrote to A.V. Alexander on 4 June 1942.

First Lord

As you know, I do not think that the arrangement of Commands is the best that could be made. I thought that Cunningham should command the Home Fleet, Admiral Noble should go to Washington, and that Admiral Tovey should go to Liverpool and manage the Western Approaches. I am sure that this is what the true interests of the Service and the war require, and I hope it may be brought about.

2.   However, I think there are advantages in Admiral Cunningham paying a short visit to the United States, as they will pay great attention to what he says on account of his having actually handled ships against the enemy so frequently and on so large a scale. I hope that in, say, a couple of months he will be put in his rightful place as the Head of the Home Fleet. All that you say about him shows how wrong it is to send him off out of the war. You know well that all-important Anglo-American decisions are taken between the First Sea Lord and Admiral King.

Pound was not prepared to accept this and wrote a most firm response on 8 June for Alexander to reply to Churchill.

First Lord

With reference to the Prime Minister's Minute No. M. 227/2. The question of who should command the Home Fleet at the expiration of Admiral Tovey's period of command cannot be settled until nearer the time when he would normally be relieved, as so many things may happen before then.

2.   The normal period of command of the Home Fleet is 2½ years.

3.   Admiral Forbes held the command for one year and seven months, the last seven months being as an Admiral of the Fleet. The reason for Forbes being relieved was that I had reason to believe that he had not got the confidence of the Fleet, and I therefore recommended to you that it was desirable that he should be relieved and you accepted my advice.

4.   Assuming that –

(a)   our main object is to win the war;

(b)   the Navy is the one Service which can lose it;

(c)   battles are unlikely to be won if the officers and men do not have a leader in whom they have confidence;

The premature removal of a leader, who not only has the confidence of the officers and the men of the Fleet, but who has proved himself a capable and, when the supreme test came (as in the action against the *Bismarck*) a successful leader, would cause the Navy to lose all confidence in Admiralty administration.

5. For the above reasons I am entirely in disagreement with the contention of the Prime Minister that the appointments are in the true interests of the Service. It is most unwise to attempt to fight a war with a Navy which has lost confidence in the Admiralty administration.[22]

Nothing more was heard from Churchill on the subject. This is a classic case of Pound knowing when it was correct to stand up and say "No" to Churchill.

There has been much argument over the choice of Cunningham's successor. Pound chose Sir Henry Harwood, the victor of the River Plate action in 1939, who had been serving as ACNS (F) at the Admiralty. Put simply, this was a poor choice. Harwood had been a good commander of a small cruiser squadron, but he was out of his depth as Commander-in-Chief Mediterranean, a post which required diplomatic, political and inter-service skills, beside the requisite naval ones. He had already, according to Roskill, been passed over for Flag rank before the war.[23] The appointment was not a success, despite the running of a large convoy through to Malta from Gibraltar in August. Ultimately Harwood would fall foul of the Commander-in-Chief of Eighth Army and was relieved of his command in January 1943.

Cunningham arrived back in England on 9 April. He was met at Paddington by the entire Board of Admiralty, with the solitary exception of Pound, who sent a note to greet him:

Welcome back! Sorry we cannot give you the official welcome you deserve but the longer the ITi's [sic] are in ignorance of your having left the better. Please excuse my not meeting you which I certainly should have done had not Betty had another major operation yesterday and I am seizing the only chance of dashing down to Gerrards Cross to see her. Kindest regards to your lady. Much looking forward to seeing you.[24]

Betty Pound had just had an operation for cancer at a nursing home in Gerrards Cross. Cunningham found Pound under intense pressure. After the war he wrote to John Godfrey:

When I came home in 1942 to go to Washington I found Pound in great distress. He asked me if I thought he ought to resign and I said certainly not. He also told me that Winston was thinking of getting rid of him and putting Mountbatten in as First Sea Lord! Naturally I told him to glue himself to his chair, but he was much worried about it.[25]

The only evidence of Pound's feelings about the possibility of being replaced by Mountbatten comes from his daughter. Barbara remembers very clearly her father coming home one evening in April 1942 and

> without taking off his greatcoat exploded. . . . He said he would have to resign if that was what Winston wanted. I don't remember what happened to the rest of the evening, but it was never mentioned to us again. At that moment I think he was more hurt and angry, and dismayed, at the idea of Mountbatten taking over. Distressing it must have been, but once over I think he would have put it behind him.[26]

What evidence there is of Churchill's intention is not clear, but it may well have stemmed from Mountbatten spending time at Chequers. However, there can be no doubt that such a proposal (at this time) would have been seriously objected to, not least by Cunningham. Hence his reply to Pound. Pound also persuaded Cunningham to accept a baronetcy, if not for himself, then for the Mediterranean Fleet. Cunningham eventually left for Washington on 23 June.

Pound needed a strong presence in Washington as it was important to have continual pressure on the US Navy to make them understand the problems that the Home Fleet had. In March Churchill told Roosevelt that an expedition was to be mounted to take over Madagascar and asked for US Naval help with support in the Atlantic, while Force H was away from Gibraltar. King sent Task Force 39 (later renamed TF 99), consisting of two battleships, *Washington* and *North Carolina*, the carrier *Wasp*, two heavy cruisers and a destroyer squadron. They arrived at Scapa Flow, having unfortunately lost their admiral, Rear Admiral J.W. Wilcox, overboard in a storm, on 8 April. The hope of both Admiral Tovey and Rear-Admiral Giffen was that they might encounter *Tirpitz*, but the Germans did not oblige. *Wasp* was twice used to ferry Spitfires to Malta before Pound received a message from King, via Stark requesting that she leave for the Pacific. The correspondence is worth quoting in full in that it shows how the two navies liaised at the top level:

My dear Admiral,

The Commander-in-Chief, United States Fleet, informs me that the situation in the Pacific, as to aircraft carriers, requires the *Wasp* to be sent there and that it is his intention to withdraw the *Wasp* and two destroyers when they have returned from the mission on which they are now engaged.

The *Ranger* will remain on the western side of the Atlantic when she has completed her plane ferrying service.

Sincerely yours,

HR Stark.

Pound replied the next day, 10 May:

My dear Admiral,

Many thanks for your letter of 9th May. I quite understand the necessity for the transfer of *Wasp* to the Pacific and have informed C-in-C. H.F. accordingly. I look forward to hearing of a brilliant success of your forces in the Coral Sea as soon as we know the details.

Yours ever,

ADPR Pound.

Pound followed up this note with a letter to Stark, once *Wasp* had left the Home Fleet, on 19 May:

My dear Admiral,

Now that *Wasp* has left the United Kingdom, I feel I must write to express my appreciation for all that she has done since she has been over this side. You are well aware of the important position that Malta holds in our Imperial strategy, and the services of *Wasp* in keeping the island supplied with Spitfires have proved invaluable, as has been shown by the recent results of successes against enemy aircraft.

Those two operations in which *Wasp* was concerned were carried through successfully and efficiently, and I should be glad if you would convey my thanks to Admiral King and to say how much we appreciated having such an efficient ship working with us.

Yours ever,

Dudley Pound.[27]

Wasp was accompanied by part of TF99, *North Carolina* and two cruisers, Pound asking that *Washington* remain behind until *King George V* was fully refitted so as to retain the three to one battleship superiority deemed necessary to deal with *Tirpitz*.

*

At the same time further events encroached on the gloom in London. The Japanese, after marauding through the Pacific, launched their fast carrier force into the Indian Ocean. Immediately after the sinking of *Prince of Wales* and *Repulse* Pound appointed James Somerville from Force H to command the Eastern Fleet. The latter came back to London and spent most of January briefing his successor in Force H, Syfret, and battling with Pound to obtain the admirals whom he wanted. In this respect he was successful, insisting on having men with experience of air power and, if possible, recent combat. To that end he got Vice-Admiral Willis as his second-in-command, Rear-Admiral Danckwerts as Deputy Commander-in-Chief (in effect Chief of Staff Ashore), Commodore Edwards as Chief of Staff afloat, and Tennant, recently of *Repulse*, as Rear-Admiral commanding the 4th Cruiser Squadron. Edwards had been due to be with Tom Phillips on *Prince of Wales*, but had luckily been ashore having major dental work. Admiral Layton, meanwhile, was holding the fort as Commander-in-Chief, Ceylon. He was one of the few men who had come out of the disaster in South-East Asia with any credit. Both Layton and Somerville were convinced that the Eastern Fleet, as then constituted, could not tackle the Japanese. Although it might appear as an undistinguished role, it was critical that the Eastern Fleet remain 'in being'. Somerville wrote to Pound on 11 March:

> The best deterrent, and the best counter, too, is to keep our Eastern Fleet in being and avoid losses by attrition . . . I feel . . . that we must avoid having our Fleet destroyed in penny packets by undertaking operations which do not give reasonable prospects of success.[28]

The Chiefs of Staff agreed, signalling to Wavell, the Commander-in-Chief ABDA: "Policy of our Fleet will be to act as a Fleet in being, avoiding unnecessary risks, crippling losses and attrition."[29]

Sure enough, the Japanese swept into the Bay of Bengal on 4 April sinking the cruisers *Dorsetshire* and *Cornwall* that day, and the carrier *Hermes* on 9 April. The two cruisers were sunk "in fifteen minutes in an

226

attack of clinical efficiency".[30] Equally true to form Churchill criticized the Royal Navy in the House of Commons casting doubt on Somerville's dispositions. Pound wrote to A.V. Alexander on 6 June saying, "I do not think this can be allowed to go unchallenged",[31] and drafted a long statement for him to send to Churchill, which mollified the Prime Minister. Luckily the Japanese did not mount an all-out attack on Ceylon; instead they returned to the Pacific, where in June they were worsted in the Coral Sea, and then decisively defeated at Midway.

★

It was at this stage, in April, that a key American visit to London took place, to try to come to some form of agreement on strategy. On 8 April Harry Hopkins and General George Marshall arrived to ensure that the British were committed to an invasion of the continent in 1943 (ROUNDUP). The Americans appeared happy with the British commitment at this stage, although the Chiefs of Staff were worried about any prospect of a cross-Channel invasion unless the Germans were sufficiently weakened to guarantee success. The Americans did not really understand the British position until Professor Lindemann observed to Marshall, "You are arguing against the dead of the Somme."

Late in April Pound went to Washington to discuss matters with the US Navy and in particular the running of the Russian convoys. This was a trip without Churchill, or any of the Chiefs of Staff. There must also have been discussion about where the Americans would join the fight. They believed that there was only one place to fight in Europe: the direct route to Berlin across the Channel. Marshall was the exponent of this. King, on the other hand, was prepared to ditch Europe completely and fight the war in the Pacific against the Japanese. He viewed any diversion from this, the principal US Navy theatre, as a waste. From his point of view if the Combined Chiefs of Staff could not come to an agreement he would be free to use the massive resources of the US Navy in the Pacific. Hence Marshall's and Hopkins' visit to London in early April. The British were, at this stage, happy to consider ROUNDUP, but not an invasion in 1942 (SLEDGEHAMMER), which was only to be considered if Russia was on the point of collapse. Although they were prepared to sign up for ROUNDUP, and Marshall went back to Washington with that belief, the Chiefs of Staff had no doubts of the problems of such a

227

continental commitment. Brooke maintained that he would only mount a cross-Channel invasion when the balance of forces was such as to ensure a minimum loss to the invading force. However, what was to be done in 1942?

Churchill was keen on JUPITER, the invasion of northern Norway, and the Chiefs of Staff adopted a Poundian strategy of analyzing it and showing how impossible it was. There was effectively only one other option, one that Churchill had initially proposed to the Chiefs of Staff during the voyage to the ARCADIA conference, back in December 1941. This was GYMNAST, the invasion of French North Africa. By July the Chiefs of Staff were pushing for this, aided by Cunningham from Washington, who wrote, "It would go a long way towards relieving our shipping problem once the short route through the Mediterranean was gained. . . . [It would] jeopardize the whole of Rommel's forces and relieve anxiety about Malta. It would shake Italy to the core and rouse the occupied countries."[32] The Joint Chiefs of Staff now saw this as diluting their entire war strategy of concentration on what they saw as the decisive point: Northern France. As a result Marshall, King and Hopkins flew to London on 18 July to try to reach a decision. The British position was helped by the defensive victory achieved by Auchinleck at Alamein. In effect the British ruled out a cross-Channel invasion in 1942, while Roosevelt insisted on some sort of Allied operation that year. The only operation that satisfied both of these positions was the invasion of French North Africa. Brooke took the lead in arguing this case, realizing only too well the paucity of British resources on their own. Ultimately the Americans accepted this, but it was not to their liking. The Americans were entertained to dinner at 10 Downing Street, where Churchill was moody and grumpy until Mrs Churchill told him not to be difficult, whereupon he became his more normal charming self! The visit came to a rousing finish with a dinner given to the Americans at the Painted Hall in Greenwich on 24 July. The chief guests went by launch from Whitehall, no doubt purposefully allowing them to see how much the City of London had suffered, and there was a vast gathering of naval officers. Most of the senior officers then on duty in London and all the senior US Naval officers then in London attended. Marshall and Eisenhower did not attend, but Hopkins and Churchill were delighted to be there. Our only account of this was given by one of Churchill's private secretaries, John Martin, who wrote to his parents on 26 July:

An unusual evening on Friday, when we went down by river to Greenwich to a dinner given by the Admiralty in honour of certain visitors. Fortunately it was a fine day and the river and the Hospital looked their best in the soft evening light. . . . I have never seen so many admirals. Their Lordships gave us an excellent dinner, after which we went to the young officers' gun-room, where the PM toasted Admiral Jackie Fisher's grandson who was one of them and happened to be celebrating his twenty-first birthday. Alexander, the First Lord, then sat down at the piano and for about an hour thumped out I should think every song in the "Students' Song Book" and conducted community singing with great gusto. The room was crowded with sub-lieutenants, admirals and Wrens, . . . all singing at the tops of their voices (not excluding the PM), the most cheerful party I have seen for a long time. Altogether a memorable evening, which the Americans obviously enjoyed enormously. It ended with 'Auld Lang Syne' and the two National Anthems. One of the highlights was Admiral Stark, of the USN, singing 'Annie Laurie' solo. Even the grim Admiral King thawed.[33]

While all of this jollification had been going on, as well as deep discussions of future strategy, the Royal Navy had been involved in one of the most painful episodes in its long history, convoy PQ 17.

14

PQ 17

The first six months of 1942 had seen a gradual stabilization of the war. The Battle of the Atlantic had yet to reach a climax, but the U-boats were being driven from the east coast of America and the convoys were getting through. Planning for the invasion of North Africa was under way. In the Pacific the Americans had decisively defeated the Japanese at Midway, and although the Japanese held all of Burma their advance into India was likely to be problematical. Russia was still fighting, although the German summer campaign was awaited with some degree of worry. Bomber Command had begun, at last, to pound the German cities. However, there were still two open sores with which the Royal Navy had to contend: the running of convoys to both Russia and Malta. At the Arcadia conference Pound had accepted these as part of the Royal Navy's areas of responsibility. The Russian convoys show up Pound's relationship with the Intelligence community and highlight the problem which so many naval historians failed to grasp for so long: the Admiralty was, unlike the War Office and the Air Ministry, an operational HQ. Fully to understand what happened in the waters north of Norway in the summer months of 1942 it is necessary to look at the relationship between Pound and Naval Intelligence.

Pound had served with the Director of Naval Intelligence, Rear-Admiral John Godfrey, twice. In the early 1920s Godfrey had been a young commander in the Plans Division when Pound had been Director of Plans. They had worked together there for eighteen months. In the 1930s Godfrey, as already noted, had commanded *Repulse* for two years in the Mediterranean Fleet. Both of them had moved to the Admiralty in 1939. Godfrey had found the Naval Intelligence Division (NID) in some disarray and had achieved remarkable success in getting it ready for war, insofar as that was possible. He took the sensible precaution of getting back as many as possible of those who had served in NID in the First World War. For example, as head of the Operational Intelligence Centre (OIC) he installed Captain Jock Clayton, a retired rear-admiral who had been a watchkeeper in the War Room in 1917. Similarly, the head of the Government Code and Cipher School (GCCS) at Bletchley Park, Commander Alastair Dennison, had served in Room 40 and brought back a number of ex-colleagues from those days. Like his 1914–18 predecessor, the legendary "Blinker" Hall, Godfrey had a use for non-naval personnel, such as his appointment of the stockbroker Ian Fleming as his personal assistant, and the KC Rodger Winn as Head of the U-boat Tracking Room.

Godfrey had an independent mind. He was certainly one of the few real intellectuals in the Royal Navy and was fundamentally a shy man. He found it difficult to make friends and was better on paper than making verbal presentations. His genius, and as qualified an observer as Euan Montagu called him that[1], was as an administrator. He built the machinery and then allowed it to run. He was abrasive and took little trouble to conceal his impatience with others who either did not agree with him or who were less gifted than he was. The US Naval attaché in 1940, Captain, later Admiral, Alan Kirk said after the war:

> A man of curious character, rather inclined to be reticent and suspicious and loath to help very much. . . . There was never any real warmth of friendship between him and me, or between him and most of his officers as a matter of fact. He was a very curious man.[2]

In much of this, then, he was the antithesis of Pound. One of Godfrey's key introductions in 1939, under the direction of the DCNS, Vice-Admiral James, was the creation of the OIC. Here a young Paymaster Lieutenant Commander, Norman Denning, helped him. This was an operational HQ able to communicate directly to ships and authorities at sea and overseas. Gradually after 1939, as its sources of Intelligence grew – air reconnaissance, direction finding (HF/DF), Secret Service reports and, most importantly, signals Intelligence from GCCS at Bletchley Park – it began to exercise an influence on maritime operations never approached by Room 40 in 1914–18. Certainly, by 1942 OIC was integrating information and disseminating it so well that it can be said that Intelligence was in practice, if not in theory, controlling operations. Certainly it was laid down by the ACNS (U-boats and Trade)

231

Rear-Admiral Edelsten, in 1943, that "without reference to him no ship or convoy was to be routed without the advice of the Tracking room"[3]. No higher praise could be given to the efficiency of the system than this.[4]

Why then was Pound not more understanding of the role of Intelligence? He must have known of the role of Room 40 during 1914–18. After all he had served in both Plans and Operations Divisions in the Admiralty from 1916–20. Probably he was influenced by Keyes, who was Director of Plans at the time, and not a great admirer of the role of Intelligence. Certainly in the 1914–18 Admiralty Operations dominated Intelligence, in the persons of the Chief of the War Staff, Admiral Oliver, and the Director of Operations, Captain Jackson. Both were inveterate centralizers, who refused to delegate. Pound would certainly have been influenced by them. Between the wars he would not have had much dealings with NID as such, although the normal day-to-day running of the Admiralty would have led to some contact, but as Director of Plans and as ACNS he appeared to have little real understanding of how Intelligence worked. Certainly as Second Sea Lord he would have had almost no contact. He took over the Mediterranean Fleet where he had a Staff Officer (Intelligence), Lt Commander Oliphant, but there is no indication that he had much input. Pound consulted instead with other members of his staff, such as Grantham and Litchfield, i.e. the Operational Staff. Thus when he arrived at the Admiralty in July 1939 Intelligence would have been a relatively foreign matter to him.

Certainly Pound's conception of how to use a staff was not very advanced. Even as Commander-in-Chief in Malta he preferred to write his own papers. Grantham gave an example to Donald McLachlan in 1967:

He told me once to do an appreciation and I worked like hell on this damned thing, took a long time over it and then typed it out. It must have taken me 48 hours in all. I had just started on the final version when DP sent a signal to the Admiralty on this very same matter and, briefly, listed the points – A–L – of things that were relevant to what I had done over the last couple of days. He came to the same conclusions as I – in a long paper – had done. What was the point in my doing all the research for this paper when the C-in-C had not even waited to look at it? Edward-Collins said I should type the thing out anyway and let him have a look at it. He took it into DP, who softened and said, "I felt I wanted to get this thing off quickly. I am most appreciative of what you have done. Thank you for confirming what I thought." He had great *savoir-faire*. If we were sitting round a table in his after-cabin discussing, say, the Spanish Civil War, the tradition was that he liked to draft and send signals himself. He did it to the last.[5]

This was carried on at the Admiralty, as implied by Grantham, who again says

Pound brought in Tom Phillips as VCNS and he and the First Sea Lord concentrated everything in their hands. They became a complete bottleneck and maddened a lot of people.[6]

This method of working was not to ease until late July 1942, when Pound consented to the appointment of a Deputy First Sea Lord.

★

The quality of intelligence which Bletchley Park was producing was by 1942 quite outstanding. The introduction of the fourth rotor to the U-boat Enigmas did not affect the traffic from U-boats in the Arctic, so their radio messages could be read. There were two drawbacks evident. Only messages sent by radio could be read; in other words those messages sent by landline were immune. Secondly, there were delays in decryption. The settings of the German Home Waters Enigma were changed daily at noon. For technical reasons the second 24 hours in a 48-hour period were very much easier to read than the first. This meant that delays in decryption usually occurred every 48 hours, followed by 48 hours of increasingly current reading. Radio reception in the Arctic is notoriously difficult. Neither the British nor the Germans would receive all the signals sent in perfect order, let alone gain accurate decryptions of encoded messages. In such circumstances, more than ever the intuition of an intelligence officer is critical. In the early days of July 1942 Godfrey was away on leave, leaving matters in the hands of the Deputy Director Intelligence Centre, Captain Clayton, who as a retired regular officer was unlikely to resist or argue about orders from a serving regular officer, let alone the First Sea Lord. Serving under him were two outstanding Intelligence officers. By 1942 Commander Denning was responsible for all information on

233

German surface ships. He was later to become DNI and then DCDS (I). He had, however, to overcome the prejudice of the Executive branch officers of the Royal Navy, i.e. the seamen, to the Supply and Secretariat branch. Secondly there was Rodger Winn, a temporary Commander in the Special Branch RNVR in charge of the Submarine Tracking Room. As a civilian in uniform he had a certain freedom to voice his mind. Pound, however, despite being a regular visitor to the OIC, was not on close terms with either of these officers.

The convoys to Russia were reaching a critical phase by the summer of 1942. There were only ever three routes to Russia. The first, via the Pacific, Vladivostok and the Trans-Siberian Railway, was acceptable, if long, but had been closed by the Japanese from December 1941. The second, round the Cape of Good Hope and across neutral Persia, was not yet viable due to the poor state of communication in Persia. That only left the route through the Barents Sea to Archangel and Murmansk. However, it was tactically unsound. The climatic conditions were appalling: fog, ferocious gales, perpetual darkness for six months and daylight for six months. It was within easy reach of German aircraft and U-boats in northern Norway. Evasive routing, as practised so successfully in the Atlantic, was not an option, given the lack of sea room, with the ice to the north, Norway to the south, and an ever-narrowing funnel as the convoys neared their destination. However, political necessity made the convoys happen. It was essential that the supplies were forced through. The Russians were engaging never less than 97% of the German combat divisions between June 1941 and the autumn of 1943, when compared with the Western Allies.[7] While Churchill may not have liked the despatch to Russia of so much of the supplies that the British so desperately needed, he understood the political necessity of keeping Russia in the war.

The early convoys to Russia (PQ to Russia and QP returning) were relatively minor affairs, but the Germans steadily deployed more forces to Norway and so the necessity grew to provide greater cover, initially cruisers, and ultimately when *Tirpitz* arrived in March 1942, the Home Fleet Battle Squadron was forced to deploy. Tovey, based at Scapa Flow, had a real dilemma in that he had to face both ways: to cover the convoys to the north-east, while guarding against a German breakout to the west. He also had to balance the need for a covering force of cruisers sufficient to deal with the German pocket battleships or cruisers, but which could not hope to deal with *Tirpitz*, and keeping the Home Fleet as distant cover

234

in case *Tirpitz* emerged, while not being too close to the airfields of Norway and suffering the sort of mauling which his predecessor, Forbes, had received in 1940.[8]

Tovey also had problems of information and control. Ultra information was passed to indoctrinated officers, that is those who needed to know, by a simple means instituted by Godfrey. Messages were straight factual information, differentiated from any conclusion NID drew by the word "comment". Thus the recipient benefited from NID's view, but also had the chance to draw his own, possibly different, conclusions, based on local information not known to NID. In port Tovey's flagship was connected via scrambler telephone and telex directly to the Admiralty. Pound aimed to give the Commander-in-Chief afloat the maximum information possible, but reserved the right to send orders, on the grounds that the Admiralty might frequently know more than any admiral afloat. Such an example happened in March 1942, when PQ12 sailed from Iceland.

PQ12 was first located by German reconnaissance aircraft and then threatened by the departure of *Tirpitz* from Trondheim, both of which were immediately detected by British Intelligence. The next six days saw some highly complicated manoeuvrings. Suffice it to say that *Tirpitz* failed to find the convoy by the narrowest of margins, while the Home Fleet would not have been in a position to attack *Tirpitz* with aircraft from *Victorious* had not the Admiralty, on the basis of OIC's more correct appreciation of the situation, intervened to redirect Tovey. Unfortunately that attack failed to hit *Tirpitz*. Tovey, also, had been forced to ask the Admiralty to manoeuvre his destroyers and cruisers for him because of signalling difficulties. This episode revealed a fundamental difference between Tovey and Pound, between the Home Fleet and the Admiralty. It was inevitable that the Admiralty would be the focal point of Intelligence and thus occasions would arise when they were better informed than those at sea. Tovey insisted that instead of instructions to him based on that information he should be sent the information and left to take the appropriate action, having regard to local conditions. From Pound's point of view there came the unreliability of communications and the undesirability of Tovey breaking wireless silence, which Tovey would have to do if he was to issue orders to a detached force. As far as PQ12 was concerned, the Admiralty's appreciation of *Tirpitz*'s movements was seen to have been more correct than Tovey's, and this must have reinforced

Pound's conviction that "Father knows best". Indeed Roskill is forced to concede:

> The circumstances of the Arctic convoys do, however, appear to have been somewhat different from those earlier cases in which the Admiralty's interventions had aroused the critical comment of Commanders-in-Chief. In the first place the Intelligence derived by the Admiralty and sent to the fleet flagship was, we now know, more accurate than the appreciations made afloat. Neither the signalling of the Intelligence, nor the issue of orders when the Intelligence available in London indicated that the assumptions on which our forces' movements had been based were wrong (as happened on the evening of 8 March) is open to criticism. Secondly, communications in those waters were proved to be so difficult that Admiral Tovey himself had once broken wireless silence to ask the Admiralty to operate the cruisers and destroyers of his fleet . . . If any conclusion is to be drawn, it is perhaps that, as was suggested in an earlier context, it is the extent to which interventions are made from London, rather than the principles involved in making them, which requires watchfulness ashore.[9]

To what extent was there agreement between Tovey and Pound about the threat to the Arctic convoys, and how to defeat that threat? Basically, there was a fundamental difference in their objectives. Tovey wanted to bring *Tirpitz* to action and saw this as the principal aim of the Home Fleet. He was thus reluctant to commit the entire Home Fleet to convoy protection. Pound, on the other hand, saw the forcing through of the convoys as the prime objective, which could also bring *Tirpitz* to action, but as a bonus. Prior to PQ12 Tovey had been overridden and was informed that "Their Lordships take full responsibility for any breakout of German ships which may occur while you are covering PQ and QP convoys".[10] Tovey believed that the March operations around PQ12 had demonstrated that the Germans "will not willingly expose this unique and irreplaceable asset to any unnecessary risk".[11] He argued that he should not risk his entire battle fleet of *King George V*, *Duke of York* and *Renown*, as well as his only fleet aircraft carrier, *Victorious*, in far-distant, U-boat infested waters, where distances and the poor fuel capacities of his destroyers meant he was frequently without a screen. He believed that two battleships were enough for *Tirpitz*. Pound and the naval Staff did not accept the last point, believing that the *Bismarck* episode had shown that three were necessary. However, they accepted that the destruction of *Tirpitz* became Tovey's primary aim. The best way to bring that about was to lure her out by the fat bait of a large convoy.

Neither PQ13 nor PQ14 saw an attack by the major German surface units, although German destroyers attacked PQ13. Unfortunately a British cruiser *Trinidad* torpedoed herself due to the extreme cold. She was patched up in Russia, but was sunk on the return trip. The advent of spring and summer meant the season of perpetual light, and both Tovey and Pound were united in seeing the convoys as not being a practical operation. Pound submitted a memorandum to the War Cabinet Defence Committee on 8 April arguing "geographical conditions are so greatly in favour of the Germans that losses . . . may become so great as to render the running of these convoys uneconomical".[12] Politically it was imperative that the convoys continued, so Pound and Tovey were overruled. Churchill certainly understood the problem, warning Roosevelt about "the serious convoy situation" on 26 April and explaining that the "voyage of each of these convoys now entails major fleet operation" on 28 April, and finally on 1 May:

> With very great respect what you suggest is beyond our power to fulfil.
> . . . I beg you not to press us beyond our judgement in this operation.
> . . . I can assure you Mr President we are absolutely extended and I could not press the Admiralty further.[13]

It was in April that Pound had flown to Washington (with the returning Marshall and Hopkins) and reached agreement with King that the Russian convoys were militarily impracticable in the summer months. The month of May saw PQ15 fought through, but with considerable loss. Rear-Admiral Bonham Carter, commanding 18 Cruiser Squadron, had a second flagship sunk under him, losing *Edinburgh*, and wrote in his report of proceedings

> I am still convinced that until the aerodromes in North Norway are neutralised and there are some hours of darkness that the continuation of these convoys should be stopped. If they must continue for political reasons, very serious and heavy losses must be accepted. The force of German attacks will increase not diminish. We in the Navy are paid to do this sort of job, but it is beginning to ask too much of

the men in the Merchant Navy. We may be able to avoid bombs and torpedoes with our speed; a six or eight knot ship has not this advantage.[14]

With this all naval opinion was in agreement, from Pound and King down. However, the political pressure was intense, with the failure of the Russian spring offensive and the impending German summer offensive. Pound wrote to King on 18 May that the Russian convoys "are becoming a regular millstone round our necks and cause a steady attrition in cruisers and destroyers. . . . The whole thing is a most unsound operation with the dice loaded against us in every direction . . . but I do . . . recognise the necessity of doing all we can to help the Russians at the present time".[15] PQ16 was fought through between 21 and 30 May, and although German surface ships did not attack, U-boats and aircraft caused the loss of seven ships (20% of the total). Tovey commented that "this success was beyond expectation."[16]

The British naval attaché in Sweden, Captain Denham, had, through his contacts, managed to obtain details of the German plan for their attack on PQ17, Operation KNIGHT'S MOVE. It involved *Tirpitz*, *Lutzow* and *Hipper* attacking the convoy after it had reached the area of Bear Island. However, Intelligence could not provide Hitler's secret written and verbal order which refused permission for *Tirpitz* to operate unless and until the Home Fleet had been located and the threat of carrier based aircraft had been eliminated. To that extent, the strike by *Victorious'* Albacores in March had been effective.

PQ17 left Iceland on 27 June and consisted of thirty-four British, American and Russian merchant ships, with three rescue ships, carrying 157,000 tons of war supplies, estimated to be enough to equip at least 50,000 men. The close escort, commanded by Captain Jackie Broome, consisted of six destroyers, four corvettes, three minesweepers, four anti-submarine trawlers, two anti-aircraft ships and two submarines. The Home Fleet dispositions consisted of the cruiser covering force provided by 1st Cruiser Squadron, under Rear-Admiral "Turtle" Hamilton, of four heavy cruisers (two Royal Navy and two US Navy) and three destroyers, while the distant cover was the remainder of the Home Fleet, the battleships *Duke of York* and *Washington*, the carrier *Victorious*, two heavy cruisers and fourteen destroyers. Thirteen submarines were patrolling off the exits from the bases of the German surface ships.[17]

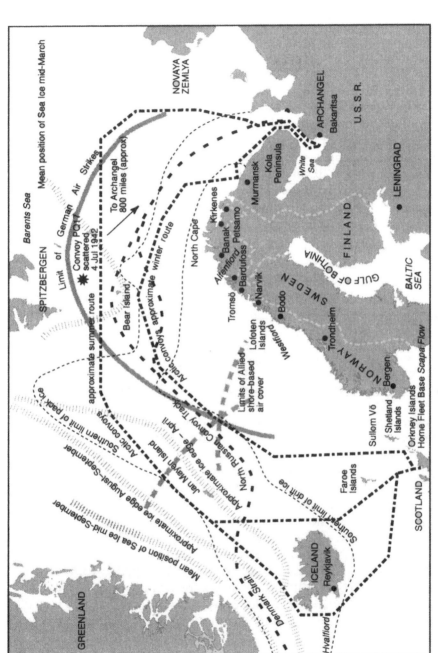

North Russian Convoys, 1941–45

Tovey planned to turn PQ17 around, if it was threatened, for between twelve and eighteen hours, so as to induce the German surface ships to come further west into areas patrolled by Allied submarines and hopefully within reach of *Victorious*. Once *Tirpitz* had been damaged by torpedoes his battleships could finish her off. However, the Admiralty vetoed this idea. Their idea was that surface forces would defend the convoy west of Bear Island, but not beyond. They emphasized that Hamilton's cruisers were not to go east of Bear Island unless the convoy was threatened by surface forces capable of being engaged by cruisers alone, in other words not if the convoy was threatened by *Tirpitz*, and in any case they were not to go beyond 25° E. Tovey had issued a new directive on 16 March, which he subsequently incorporated into the Home Fleet Instructions for North Russian Convoys, which stated

> I wish it to be clearly understood that in the event of a Russian convoy being attacked by a force overwhelmingly superior to the escort, the primary object of the escort is to ensure the enemy being shadowed to enable them to be brought to action by our heavier forces or submarines or to be attacked after dark, or under more favourable conditions, by the escort itself.[18]

Atlantic Convoy Instructions (ACIs) of April 1942 specifically forbade scattering of a convoy "until or unless the escort is overwhelmed", and on 21 June Tovey had ordered that Arctic convoys were to follow ACIs.

Tovey did not believe that *Tirpitz* would be risked after her near miss in March, and he was unhappy sending heavy cruisers into the Barents Sea after the losses of *Trinidad* and *Edinburgh*. He was dismayed during a long conversation with Pound to hear the First Sea Lord mention for the first time that the Admiralty now contemplated scattering the convoy under certain circumstances. Tovey is said to have replied that this would be "sheer bloody murder".[19] Pound appears not to have been influenced by this, as his final convoy instructions included orders for scattering, as well as orders for PQ17 to reverse course if needed.

When Tovey and Hamilton sailed they were supplied with all the Intelligence available to OIC. Thus they were kept informed of the state of play at Bletchley Park: when they expected to break the next 24 hours' traffic, when this happened, and when each period's reading had been completed. For example at 0510 on 30 June they were told

Information for 29 June now available, anticipate 30 June by about midnight.

and at 1819 on 3 July:

All important information has now been studied. Information from 1200/3 is not expected before 2359/4.[20]

Nor was it simply positive information. Late on 30 June an Ultra signal was sent to Tovey and Hamilton stating:

It appears from negative information that there was no movement of a main unit on the Norwegian coast on 27, 28 and 29 June.

Thus they were receiving every scrap of information, but were also warned that Special Intelligence could not warn them of every move.

For the first few days PQ17 was undisturbed and the convoy shook down into normal cruising routine. It was not until 1432 on 1 July that a Luftwaffe sighting report was decrypted and passed on. Air strikes were carried out on the convoy between Jan Mayen Island and Bear Island, but OIC could signal at 2349 on 2 July "No direct indications of movement of enemy units". At 0800 on 3 July OIC signalled to Tovey as follows

1.   Shadowing aircraft were still in contact with PQ at 0200/3rd. Germans stated weather conditions made it doubtful whether it would be possible to continue shadowing.

2.   At 2104/2nd British Battlefleet had not been located since 2100/1st. Unverified report had been received of a Skua 60 miles west of Trondheim at 1630/2nd, which led Germans to suggest that a carrier was possibly off Trondheim.

3.   At 0300/2nd, AOC Lofoten reported that close air escort for operation CONCERT would probably not be possible on account of weather.

4.   GAF intentions for 3 July were –

    (a)   renewed reconnaissance for convoy; and

    (b)   operation KNIGHT'S MOVE . . .

5.   U-boats were in contact with PQ during 2 July.

Comment: Operations CONCERT and KNIGHT'S MOVE are probably concerned with enemy main units.

During the course of the morning and afternoon of 3 July four more Ultra signals were sent to Tovey indicating that the German heavy units were on the move, finishing with one at 1745, which concluded

> Comment: It appears certain *Scheer* has moved northwards from Narvik, probably accompanied by destroyers. Movement of *Lutzow* is uncertain but she was independent of *Scheer*. *Tirpitz* and *Hipper* may have left Trondheim area since 0001/3rd.

That was followed rapidly by another at 1819, saying

> All important information has now been studied. Information from 1200/3rd is not expected before 2359/4th.

This meant that no reliable information, except possibly from Luftwaffe intercepts or RAF reconnaissance, could be expected just when it was most vitally needed. The RAF reconnaissance failed. At Bletchley Park, despite the crisis in North Africa (Rommel was pounding on the British defences in the first Battle of Alamein), authority was obtained to concentrate their meagre supply of bombes on the naval Enigma in order to help the defences of PQ17. Despite this it was not until 1934 on 4 July that OIC could signal Tovey and Hamilton that

> Noon 3rd to noon 5th now available.

The tension rising in the Admiralty, as well as on *Duke of York* and on Hamilton's flagship *London*, is not difficult to imagine. Denning has written how there were frequent visits to the OIC by VCNS, Moore, ACNS(H) Brind, and the Director of Operations (H) Eccles. Pound however, did not do so until late on the evening of 3 July, when Denning explained to him how it appeared that the Germans were putting into operation the plan reported by Denham. Pound listened, but left without making any comment.

By 2200 3 July the convoy was north-west of Bear Island, not yet having lost a ship, even though it was within 400 miles of the Luftwaffe bases. Hamilton and his cruisers were just to the north of the convoy, and Tovey and the Home Fleet were 250 miles to the south-west, about half way between Jan Mayen and Bear Islands. The critical moment had come when the cruisers would have to turn back. It was at this point that the RAF reconnaissance failed. At 0250 4 July OIC told Tovey that a series of as yet undeciphered German signals might "indicate the commencement of a special operation by main units". As a result the Admiralty signalled Hamilton giving him permission to stay with the convoy until it reached 25° East. Tovey at 1512 ordered Hamilton to leave the convoy when it reached 25° East, or even earlier "unless assured by Admiralty that *Tirpitz* cannot be met". At 1800 Hamilton announced his intention of withdrawing at 2200. However, at 1858 the Admiralty signalled him:

> Further information may be available shortly. Remain with convoy pending further instructions.[21]

The long wait in OIC for the decrypts from Bletchley Park was over.

Earlier, in the late afternoon, Pound had limped into Denning's office with Brind, Eccles and Clayton[22] in his wake, and asked what would be the furthest-on position if *Tirpitz* had sailed from Trondheim direct to attack PQ17.[23] Brind said she could have been within striking distance by then, but Denning pointed out that this was unlikely as she would have undoubtedly put into Narvik or Tromso to refuel her destroyers. No decision was reached, and it was shortly after this that Hinsley rang from Bletchley Park to say that the break was imminent. Hence the 1858 signal to Hamilton.

At 1900 the teleprinter in OIC began to clack out two decrypts: one saying that the Luftwaffe had located a force of one battleship and three cruisers, which by the position given the Admiralty knew was Hamilton's cruiser squadron. The second was an order timed 0740 that morning from Raeder to the Admiral Commanding Cruisers:

> Immediate. Arriving Alta 0900. You are to allot anchorage to *Tirpitz* . . . Newly arrived destroyers and torpedo boats to complete with fuel at once.[24]

Denning was in the midst of drafting a signal to Tovey and Hamilton conveying this when Pound, with Brind, Eccles and Clayton, reappeared in his office. Denning's signal contained the comment that "all indications point to *Tirpitz* and accompanying ships still being at Alta". Pound considered this to be premature and it was stripped out, leaving only the bald facts. One may well ask why Pound had not asked Denning why he thought the German ships were still at anchor. The answer appears to be pressure of time. "Get a factual signal off now, and then discuss the implications."

All decisions now rested on whether or not *Tirpitz* was at sea heading towards PQ17. Pound had to resolve that operational problem based on negative rather than positive information. Denning gave his considered opinion to Pound as to why he considered *Tirpitz* had not sailed. He based his opinion on a number of factors.

(a)   *Tirpitz*'s cautious pattern of sortie against PQ12 indicated that she was unlikely to operate until satisfied that she was not in danger from Home Fleet aircraft.

(b)   No decrypts had yet been received ordering the U-boats to keep clear of the convoy, i.e. to avoid mistaken attacks on *Tirpitz*. HF/DF showed the U-boats still in contact with PQ17.

(c)   No Luftwaffe location reports of the Home Fleet.

(d)   Patterns of German signalling did not indicate a major surface ship sortie.

(e)   British and Russian submarines off North Cape had made no sightings.

Pound listened to all this and finally asked, "Can you assure me that *Tirpitz* is still in Altenfjord?" Denning replied that, although confident that she was, he could not give an absolute assurance, but that he expected to receive confirmation in the fairly near future when Bletchley Park had deciphered the new traffic.

Pound left Denning and went to the Submarine Tracking Room to check on the latest disposition of the U-boats, and then back to his office where he called a staff meeting for 2045. Denning meanwhile at 2031 received over the telex from Bletchley Park a fresh decrypt from Admiral Commanding Group North to the U-boats operating against PQ17, timed 1130 that morning, which informed them that there were no German surface forces in their operational area and that, if they sighted British heavy units, these were to be their principal target. To Denning the implications were obvious: *Tirpitz* had not sailed in the morning since the U-boats were not being warned about her presence. He went to find Clayton and met him on his way to Pound's meeting. He gave him the message and impressed on him both the meaning and the importance. Denning's appreciation was that the Germans would not risk their only heavy battleship to attack PQ17 while the Home Fleet and its carrier were still undetected. This of course agreed with Tovey's appreciation of 14 March. He drafted a signal to Tovey and Hamilton which included the

244

comment, "Germans do not repeat not appear to be aware of position of C-in-C Home Fleet." Normally, he would have despatched this himself, but after earlier events he waited for the return of Clayton from Pound's staff meeting. Denning was then visited by Rodger Winn, who, on reading Denning's draft despatch, commented that he understood from discussion in his room that *Tirpitz* was already at sea and that there was talk of dispersing the convoy. Winn was an exceptionally astute man, used to summing up judges and juries, and although we have no record of what was said during Pound's visit to his Submarine Tracking Room, it is possible to make a judgement that some, if not all, of those present had misunderstood Denning's view, or that they had already gained the impression that Pound had rejected it.

There is also no contemporary record of what was discussed at Pound's staff meeting at 2045. Those present included Pound, Moore, Brind, Eccles, Clayton, Rear-Admiral E.L.S. King and Lambe (Director of Plans). There may well have been more. The best recreation of what happened is in David Irving's (in)famous *The Destruction of Convoy PQ17*,[25] which he wrote after interviews with Moore, Brind, Eccles and King. The first decision made was that Hamilton's cruisers should be withdrawn. They would be of no use against *Tirpitz*. Pound himself wrote the signal, despatched at 2111:

Most Immediate. Cruiser Force to withdraw to westward at high speed.[26]

The stress on "high speed" was the result of the visit to Winn in the Submarine Tracking Room, where the German change in emphasis for U-boat attack from the convoy to the cruisers had been reported to him. Unnecessarily it was given the highest priority of Most Immediate, and contained no explanation.

Once Hamilton had departed, the senior officer present with the convoy was the Escort Commander, Jackie Broome. Pound did not believe it was correct that the burden of such a major decision should be placed on the shoulders of so junior an officer. The Admiralty alone was in possession of all the information, so it must be the Admiralty which took the key decision. Pound asked all those round the table what line of action they would support for the convoy to avoid it being slaughtered by *Tirpitz*. Each officer in turn said that it ought not to be dispersed yet, except Vice-Admiral Moore, who alone agreed with Pound, adding that it should be done immediately. This, he explained, was not a similar incident to that of the *Jervis Bay* in 1940; PQ17 could only disperse to the south, because of its proximity to the ice to the north. In other words it could only head right on to the guns of the approaching Germans. If it was to disperse it must do so at once. However, what Moore did not state, or maybe did not realize, was that in the four to five hours thought to be available the ships would not be much more than twelve miles from each other. That was not much better than remaining in convoy as a defence against a surface force, but, as Tovey had pointed, out "sheer bloody murder" against U-boat and aircraft attack. We do not know what Clayton said, or whether he made use of the despatch thrust into his hand by Denning on his way to the meeting. According to Eccles:

> The way in which Admiral Pound reached his final decision was almost melodramatic: the First Sea Lord leaned back in his leather-backed chair and closed his eyes – an invariable attitude of deep meditation when making difficult decisions; his hands gripped the arms of the chair, and his features, which had seemed almost ill and strained, became peaceful and composed. After a few moments the youthful Director of Plans [Lambe] whispered irreverently, "Look, Father's fallen asleep". After thirty long seconds, Admiral Pound reached for a Naval pad Message and announced, "The convoy is to be dispersed". As he said this, he made a curious but eloquent gesture to the others, indicating that this was his decision, and he was taking it alone.

The message despatched at 2123 said:

> Immediate. Owing to the threat of surface ships convoy is to disperse and proceed to Russian ports.

No sooner had the signal been despatched than Moore pointed out that this still meant that the ships would bunch together leaving them a worthwhile target. He pointed out that the correct order should have been to scatter. Pound agreed: "I meant them to scatter." Moore swiftly drafted a second signal despatched at 2136:

> Most Immediate. My 2123B of the 4th. Convoy is to scatter.

When Clayton reached the OIC after the meeting he related to Denning what had happened. The latter urged Clayton to return to Pound and

246

explain, again, that OIC were convinced that *Tirpitz* had not yet sailed, nor was there, as yet, any indication that the Germans were planning to do so. Clayton, much against his better judgement one suspects, did return, but was told by Pound, "We have decided to scatter the convoy, and that is how it must now stay".

It is undeniable that the three messages were just about as badly drafted as it is possible to be. The recipients had been provided ever since the convoy had left with a frequent, if occasionally spasmodic, full flow of information and appreciation about German movements and intentions. They had been aware of the possibilities of *Tirpitz* making an attack. Tovey and Hamilton, though not Broome, were aware of the difficulties at Bletchley Park of breaking the traffic for the period after noon on 3 July, and the 1858 message had warned of possible new developments. Then within 36 minutes the three executive orders landed on their respective bridges. Captain Broome wrote later

> It seemed to explode in my hand. . . . Some twenty-seven years . . . later [I was asked] to describe the impact this signal made on me at the time. The best descriptive parallel I could think of was an electric shock.[27]

Tovey and Hamilton, if not Broome, must have wondered why these signals were not accompanied by any factual Special Intelligence in an Ultra signal, but there was only one conclusion to be drawn: *Tirpitz* was at sea and her masts might appear over the horizon at any moment. Both Hamilton and Broome believed that, and prepared to do or die in an attempt to protect their convoy. In the event twenty-three merchant ships and rescue ships were sunk, not by *Tirpitz*, but by the U-boats and aircraft against which as independent ships they had no effective defence. Not one Royal Navy ship was lost in the defence of PQ17.

What, though, were Pound's options in the evening of 4 July? Given that his advice not to run the convoys in the summer months had been overruled, his room for manoeuvre was slim. Three factors are at the heart of his decision: time, the fog of war and personal weakness. The time factor was crucial. Every account agrees on this. If *Tirpitz* was at sea she could have been on to the convoy very rapidly. The accounts we have of the meeting in Denning's room and the staff meeting agree that Pound was to be seen personally wielding chart and dividers calculating those eternal factors, time and distance. He felt that a decision had to be reached there and then. Hence the decision to send the 1918 Ultra message with no comment. Secondly, the fog of war factor: no operation of war is ever without it. Here the inability of Bletchley Park to decipher the critical messages in time, even though the naval operations were taking priority over the North African struggle, was crucial. Denning could not provide the positive intelligence required. Thirdly, there were two weaknesses on Pound's part. He was unable to accept negative Intelligence at its proper value. He would not have understood Sherlock Holmes and "the curious incident of the dog in the night-time"[28]. Here was an exceptional Intelligence officer, with sea-going experience, who had correctly forecast the *Scharnhorst* and *Gneisenau* Channel Dash, saying that the absence of Intelligence must be positively interpreted. It was the quality of the Intelligence received which allowed the Admiralty to act as an operational HQ. Pound ought to have relied on that intelligence. Equally, and this can be seen as a point of strength as well as one of weakness, Pound was not prepared to allow a junior officer of the rank of Captain to have to shoulder the responsibility to decide to scatter the convoy. It was Pound's duty, he felt, and he was never one to shirk duty.

Two possible courses were open to Pound, given that he was not prepared to delegate. The first was to allow Broome to continue to escort the convoy the 800 or so miles to Russia. It would have been unlikely to have suffered worse losses. The second was to reverse the convoy's course and order Tovey and the Home Fleet to steer towards PQ17. Their combined speed would have been about 30 knots. By about 0230 on 5 July, when Pound estimated that *Tirpitz* would fall on the convoy, *Victorious* would have been just about within range to strike. However, this was what Tovey had already suggested before PQ17 had left and it had been turned down then. Either way, PQ17 would have had to traverse the Barents Sea to Archangel escorted by Broome's close escort at some time, delayed or not: a perfect target for *Tirpitz* and her consorts. We can be fairly sure that she would eventually have emerged from her lair, as she did on the afternoon of 5 July, by when PQ17 was already being decimated.

Did the Admiralty learn the lessons of PQ17? The short answer is Yes. PQ18 in September 1942 was escorted by a "fighting escort" of sixteen Home Fleet destroyers, in addition to her normal close escort, and, critically, an escort carrier. Tovey ran the operation from his flagship at Scapa Flow, and although thirteen merchant ships were lost, significant damage was done to both U-boats and aircraft: three U-boats sunk, and

248

forty aircraft shot down. Then in December 1942, in the battle of the Barents Sea, convoy JW51B was attacked by the German pocket battleship *Lutzow* and the heavy cruiser *Prinz Eugen*, and was successfully defended by two cruisers and three destroyers. Finally, on 31 December 1943 *Scharnhorst* was sunk by the Home Fleet under Admiral Sir Bruce Fraser as she tried to attack JW55B, a classic case of how to use centralized Intelligence and yet not take away the initiative from the man on the spot. In total between August 1941 and May 1945 813 ships set out for Russia; 720 arrived successfully.

The whole sad story of PQ17 was investigated at the Admiralty. One of the first inquests was on 28 July when Pound and Alexander, along with the Foreign Secretary Eden, met the Russian Ambassador, Maisky and a Russian admiral, Harmolov. This bad-tempered meeting ended with Pound telling Maisky, "Tomorrow I shall tell the Prime Minister to appoint you First Sea Lord instead of myself."[29] On 1 August Pound gave an account to the Cabinet[30], which rather gives the lie to Churchill's claim in his *Second World War* that he "never discussed the matter with [Pound]. Indeed, so strictly was the secret of these orders being sent on the First Sea Lord's authority guarded by the Admiralty that it was not until after the war that I learned the facts."[31] However, as Roskill points out, Churchill did fly the next day to Cairo to investigate the Middle East Command and then on to Moscow to confront Stalin, so he did have other things on his mind.

★

Two things happened in the Admiralty partly as a result of the disaster to PQ17. Firstly Pound finally accepted the necessity of a Deputy First Sea Lord. On 11 May A.V. Alexander had suggested dividing the duties of Chief of Naval Staff and First Sea Lord, but Pound had replied that the two were bound together, possibly drawing the lessons of Stark's attempt to remain CNO, while King was COMINCH. However, he accepted that the appointment of a Deputy would reduce his workload. Brockman produced a paper[32] on the possible division of responsibilities showing that in the period 1 January to 15 May Pound had seen 227 dockets, of which 60% could have been delegated to a deputy. Finally on 10 July Pound sent a memorandum to the Sea Lords and other senior members of the Naval Staff, as well as the Commanders-in-Chief Home

Fleet, Western Approaches, Portsmouth, Plymouth, Nore, Rosyth and
FOLUS:

For some time I have come to the conclusion that a deputy First Sea
Lord was necessary to free me from some of the work connected with
the administrative side of the First Sea Lord's work. The First Lord
has therefore approved the appointment of Admiral Kennedy-Purvis
as Deputy First Sea Lord, and his duties will be as follows . . .

It has also been decided that Admiral Lyster shall vacate the
appointment of Fifth Sea Lord and on Saturday 11 July he will be
appointed Rear Admiral (Air) Home Fleet. The reason for this
sudden appointment is that an important operation will shortly be
carried out in which it will be necessary to operate three carriers
together, and it is essential to have a Flag Officer with previous experience of handling more than one carrier in command. The
appointment of Fifth Sea Lord will lapse temporarily and Admiral
Dreyer will from Saturday 11 July take on the duties of Chief of Naval
Air Service.

I am aware that there will probably be a good deal of criticism of
this appointment, but I am convinced that it requires an officer not
only with great drive but also with the capacity of getting down to
details so as to penetrate the mists which seem to surround the
production of aircraft. During the war Admiral Dreyer has been given
various jobs and has shown that he possesses these qualities to as great
an extent as he always has.

I may ask that the Service will reserve criticism for six months when
I have every confidence that the results will prove that my judgement
has not been misplaced.[33]

The appointment of Kennedy-Purvis was a great success. He relieved
Pound of a vast amount of work and allowed him to concentrate on his
important decisions in much the same way that Brooke delegated the
effective running of the Army to his VCIGS, Nye. Somerville summed it
up well in a letter to Pound on 1 September 1942:

We all welcome the appointment of KP [sic] because he has a really
fine brain, is extremely quick, and can grasp details with amazing
speed and accuracy. It is both right and proper that someone else
should have the Fleet laid on a plate for you to use, and that you

should not be bothered with details of training etc. It is very much the same reason that I want Algy Willis as my trainer in Force A when it is at full strength.[34]

The other appointment, Dreyer to be CNAS, was less of a success, and one must really question Pound's judgement here. He had been against bringing back old warhorses like Roger Keyes, and yet here he was doing the same thing. Dreyer had no experience at all of naval air work and there was hostile criticism, as Pound had predicted, in both Parliament and the Press. Somerville, in the same letter quoted above, comments:

FC D[reyer] undoubtedly gets things done, and everyone will agree that the improvement he effected in merchant ship gunnery was outstanding. This, however, is his own special line, and my only doubt is whether at his age he can switch his great brain, nimble as it was and may still be, to so different a problem. With good supporters it may work all right as he will certainly provide the drive and energy, but I imagine that in the service at large there may be some tooth-sucking over this appointment.

Sure enough the appointment never really worked. Dreyer tried to justify himself with several long letters, even trying to see Churchill, earning a stinging rebuke from Pound. As Roskill says, "Dreyer's letters to Pound strongly suggest instability of mind."[35] On 14 January 1943 Dreyer was removed from his position and replaced by Admiral D.W. Boyd who assumed the position of Fifth Sea Lord.

*

A second consequence of the PQ17 disaster came two months later, although it may be invidious to link them together. There had been a gradual increase in tension in the Joint Intelligence Committee (JIC) where Godfrey sat with the Army and RAF Directors of Intelligence under the excellent chairmanship of William Cavendish-Bentinck from the Foreign Office. As has been seen, Godfrey was not an easy man with whom to get on. Although he definitely won the loyalty and affection of his own staff in NID, he had reached loggerheads with the DMI, Major-General Davidson, the Assistant Chief of Staff (Intelligence) at the Air Ministry, Air Vice Marshal Medhurst, and the head of the Secret Service,

251

Sir Stewart Menzies. The two service Directors of Intelligence had requested their respective Chiefs of Staff to ask for Godfrey's removal. Pound was on leave between 4 and 12 September and asked his VCNS, Moore, to investigate this friction. Godfrey was in effect accused of not agreeing with the Army's belief that the Germans had a large reserve army, and of querying the RAF's ability to hit their targets. On both of these issues he was correct, but Moore's report left little doubt that the JIC would work better without Godfrey, and thus, despite his recent promotion to Vice-Admiral and a letter of confidence from Pound, he was removed from office with all too little ceremony and what can only be called a curt letter of dismissal. Nor was he given any sort of recognition such as a KCB or KBE, which his remarkable success as DNI surely deserved.[36]

★

Earlier in the summer Sir Bruce Fraser had completed an outstanding period as Third Sea Lord and Controller. He had been in that office from March 1939 to May 1942. He had, in the words of his biographer, "supervised the crucial transition of the Fleet from peace to war, and its equipment with the weapons of victory".[37] He became second-in-command to Tovey in the Home Fleet on 28 June and immediately put to sea in *Victorious* during the operations to cover PQ17. The Home Fleet had no sooner returned to Scapa Flow after that operation than it was required to lend forces to Force H for another convoy operation. This time it was to take supplies through to the beleaguered island of Malta. The last attempt had been from the east and had failed; now an attempt was to be made from the west in Operation PEDESTAL. With this operation and the imminent invasion of French North Africa the Home Fleet was going to be denuded of much of her strength, and so, once PQ18 was fought through in September, Pound managed to get the Russian convoys suspended until December, when the winter weather and shorter daylight hours made for an easier passage.

The Mediterranean operations in the Western basin were even more fraught with danger in that the German air bases in Sardinia and Sicily were closer to the routes of the convoys than they had been in north Norway. However, as Pound had foreshadowed in his letter of 10 July, it had been decided to use three carriers in support of PEDESTAL and try

252

to disrupt the Axis air effort. Not only were there to be three carriers with over seventy aircraft, but a battlefleet under Vice Admiral Sir Neville Syfret, Flag Officer Force H, in case the Italian fleet ventured out, and a strong fighting escort of three cruisers, an anti-aircraft cruiser and twelve destroyers to get the convoy through the narrow Sicilian Passage to Malta. So dangerous was it thought likely to be that the War cabinet discussed the operation.[38] Operation PEDESTAL was a success in that four out of thirteen merchant ships and one tanker, the legendary *Ohio*, managed to make it into Valletta harbour and kept the island alive; but the cost was heavy. One carrier (*Eagle*) was sunk and another (*Indomitable*) badly damaged, two cruisers (*Manchester* and *Cairo*) were sunk and two more damaged, and one destroyer sunk. However, the experiment of operating three carriers together had been proved to be a success.

Manchester was badly damaged by German E-boats late at night off the Tunisian coast to the extent that all four of her propeller shafts were out of action, three of them permanently. Her captain ordered her to be sunk the next morning when any chance of rescue seemed out of the question and the French authorities interned the crew. Among them was Dan Duff, Pound's son-in-law. When they were released in November certain of her officers, including Duff, were court-martialled for the loss of their ship. This was unusual in that the normal court of enquiry into the loss of the ship had been given court-martial powers. "This was . . . a device to save time and unnecessary duplication of much effort, especially necessary in wartime, in that the revelation of any failures of duty on the part of any survivors of the ship would necessitate a court martial to follow."[39] The court martial found that "the decision to scuttle the ship had been premature".[40] Cunningham, by that time back in the Mediterranean as Commander-in-Chief again, wrote to the Second Sea Lord, Sir William Whitworth, on 13 April 1943

> My spies tell me that the *Manchester* court martial disclosed a poor show, but I was much disturbed to hear that Dan Duff had been badly jumped on. Hadn't you better send him out here to me and I will put him in the way of rehabilitating himself. I am very sorry as I am sure he is a good one.[41]

Churchill was under intense pressure throughout the summer to produce some sort of success, and his methods of dissipating that pressure appear to be to attack and put great pressure on other parts of the war direction team, usually on the Admiralty. He unleashed:

> a flood of Action This Day minutes . . . on the hapless Pound, asking where this or that ship was and why any given ship could not sail at once into action. Churchill was now using these red-flagged documents, which required response and action on the very day received, for questions that, while important, did not concern issues on which immediate action could be taken in any operational sense. Such was his Action This Day request on 14 April asking for an explanation of why the Japanese could transport more aircraft in their carriers. Another of the same date asked for the latest information on the repairs to a number of ships, sarcastically adding, "You surely do not propose to send *King George V* for refit in the present stringency?" At the same time Churchill demanded to know why Admiral Somerville was complaining about the readiness of *Malaya*, and asked if her guns were cocked up. For good measure Churchill tossed in another barb, noting that he had found an Admiral who did not agree with one of the readiness estimates Pound had given him earlier.[42]

As Atlantic losses started to mount in the summer of 1942, principally due to the inability of the Admiralty to practise evasive routing, Churchill's anxieties increased, and he continued to bombard Pound and the Admiralty with minutes demanding detailed technical reports daily. Occasionally the Admiralty protested at this paper attack, and this should have been the task of A.V. Alexander, but he was not enough of a heavyweight to have much effect. Truly it can be said of Pound that he fought Hitler by day and Churchill by night.

It was at this stage that the Dieppe raid was launched. Pound was under vast pressure to keep the Russian convoys running, which he managed successfully to fight off, even if the Malta convoy would probably have to be repeated. The planning for TORCH was extremely difficult with the American part of the invasion coming direct from the USA. He was totally on the defensive and thus was prepared to see Mountbatten launch the raid. The Royal Navy had managed to gain some credit for the raid on St Nazaire in March, and a successful raid on Dieppe would probably gain it more, particularly given Mountbatten's genius for publicity. It was certainly desperately needed. The Soviet Ambassador Maisky was mounting a vigorous campaign against Pound, and both Sir Stafford Cripps and

254

Beaverbrook appeared to be supporting him. However, although he was prepared to support the Dieppe raid, he was not prepared to allow it to have battleship, or even cruiser, support. The loss of a battleship would have given the critics of the Royal Navy, and of Pound in particular, a field day, although, as Pound wrote to Cunningham in January 1941:

> I do not know why, but both the House of Commons and the public seem to think that the sinking of an important ship is a crime, whilst nobody takes any notice of the loss of 30 or 40 bombers in a night due to inaccurate meteorological reports, or to the many failings of the Army.[43]

As a result a Canadian division went ashore at Dieppe with pitifully in-adequate fire support and the operation on 19 August can certainly be seen as a disaster, even though very important lessons were learnt from it.

In August the US Navy suffered some severe losses in the campaign around the island of Guadalcanal. The carrier *Saratoga* was badly damaged and *Wasp* and *Hornet* were sunk. *Enterprise* was still undergoing repairs after Midway. This left the US Navy with only one carrier in the south Pacific, and this (*Enterprise*) was not yet fully fit. They estimated that the Japanese could attack with four carriers in the south west Pacific and they therefore turned to their allies for help. Despite initial confusion between King, Stark and Pound *Victorious* went out to the Pacific, arriving at Pearl Harbor on 4 March 1943, and staying there under Nimitz's and Halsey's control for six months.[44]

The planning for the invasion of French North Africa was going ahead rapidly, and there had already been considerable discussion as to who should be the naval Commander-in-Chief. The Americans had insisted on Eisenhower as Supreme Commander, and he was appointed on 14 August. His Chief of Staff, Brigadier Walter Bedell Smith, was serving in Washington as Secretary to the Joint Chiefs, and thus knew Cunningham well. It was he who asked Cunningham whether TORCH, as GYMNAST had been renamed, was a worthwhile operation. Reporting this to Pound, Cunningham wrote on 31 July:

> [Bedell Smith] told me that the reason he had come to see me was to have a naval opinion as to the effect of the capture of North Africa on the naval and shipping situation. King had apparently stated that it would have little or no effect, hence Smith's desire for an

independent opinion. I explained to him that the gain from complete success was just incalculable from every point of view. . . . Incidentally, Smith sounded me out as to whether I would take on the job of Naval Commander in the operation. I don't suppose there was anything behind his query, but he stressed it was important to get a naval officer who was wholeheartedly in favour of the operation. . . . You probably have someone already in your mind, but if it was considered that I could be of use I should be more than willing. At the same time I don't want to push myself forward.[45]

Eisenhower and King were certainly in favour of Cunningham's appointment as Allied Naval Commander Expeditionary Force (ANCXF), and he was appointed on 14 August, but the appointment was kept secret. Pound wrote to Cunningham on 24 August:

I have now come to the conclusion that not only is a Supreme Commander necessary, but also, that as the success of the operation must necessarily depend on the naval part. We should have been considered to have failed to do everything possible to make it a success if we did not put in the most suitable naval commander, and you know who that is.[46]

To replace Cunningham in Washington it was important to have somebody who could stand up to King, but was also in a position of having the necessary sea experience. One option was Somerville, but Pound was reluctant to bring him back from the Indian Ocean, and so appointed Admiral Sir Percy Noble, who had been Commander-in-Chief Western Approaches since February 1941, when Western Approaches had moved to Liverpool. Since the Atlantic struggle was approaching a climax, the opportunity to have in Washington somebody who was deeply versed in all its problems was eminently sensible. He also had the legendary charm to beguile even King! In his place Pound made the inspired choice of Admiral Sir Max Horton. Given his record in submarines in 1914–18 this was a case of poacher turned gamekeeper, and it worked superbly. Horton had been Vice Admiral, Submarines, from December 1940 and had inspired the submarine force, knowing that he always had the backing of Pound. He particularly treasured two signals from Pound. The first was within weeks of taking over as VA(S) and suffering three losses. Pound wrote on 16 January 1941.

My Dear Horton,

I must write and tell you how we all regret the loss of so many gallant lives in *Seahorse*, *Undine* and *Starfish*. . . . Losses will occur from time to time, but three submarines from one flotilla in a week is a heavy blow. I cannot say how glad I am that you are VA(S) because it is times such as these that your knowledge and reputation will be so invaluable to the S/M service.

I trust that your Command may soon have a great success to set off against this heavy loss . . .

Yours very sincerely,

Dudley Pound.[47]

The other came much later, and was recorded by Horton as "the proudest signal I ever received" and said simply

Thank God we have not to guard our convoys against the attacks of your submarine Commanders.[48]

The command set-up for TORCH was complicated by King's initial refusal to allow any US Naval task force to serve under a British commander. Only when the US Naval task force commander, Rear-Admiral Kent Hewitt, was specifically asked his opinion at a conference and indicated his willingness, and indeed pleasure, to serve under Cunningham was the matter sorted out. Pound took another key decision by appointing Vice-Admiral Sir Bertram Ramsay as Cunningham's deputy. Ramsay had been involved in the planning from the beginning and was a master of detail; Cunningham was many things, but not a noted staff officer. The mounting of the operation was highly complicated, but Ramsay demonstrated why he was probably the most competent of all British admirals in the whole of the Second World War by calmly getting his orders issued within three weeks, and by 2 October the first convoys were leaving harbour. The Admiralty knew that there were up to fifty U-boats which could converge on the convoys and Pound wrote to the Prime Minister that the U-boats "might well prove exceedingly menacing . . . to the most valuable convoys ever to leave these shores".[49] As a result the Atlantic convoy escorts were reduced and every available escort craft (over a hundred in all) was despatched for this first critical Allied offensive operation. Here indeed, as Roskill says, was "the passing of the Defensive Phase".[50]

257

On 8 November Operation TORCH opened, and within three days had accomplished its first objective of occupying French North Africa from Algeria to the Atlantic. Pound wrote to Cunningham offering his warmest congratulations, and demonstrating his relief that all had gone well:

> I am sure that you had as anxious a time as we did here. I had visions of large convoys waltzing up and down inside as well as outside the Mediterranean, with the weather too bad to land and the U-boats buzzing around. We really did have remarkable luck.[51]

Supplying the North African campaign was to take a great deal of merchant shipping, but the key fact was that the Allies had now gone over to the offensive.

15

THE BATTLE FOR THE AIR

The Casablanca Conference of January 1943 marks a point of change in the war. The Axis efforts had reached a high point and now were to wane. The invasion of French North Africa and its liberation as far as Tunisia from both east and west was a sign of things to come. The Allies were on the offensive and were to remain so, strategically, for the rest of the war. This meeting was to decide their strategy for 1943, and it was to be the last such occasion at which the British were to dominate. Within the Mediterranean the advance of 8th Army towards Tripoli meant that the RAF could occupy the airfields of Cyrenaica and as a result the first convoy to Malta from Alexandria since June 1942 could be successfully run, and surface forces could be re-established at Malta (Force K again) and a similar force at the North African port of Bône (Force Q). These two forces and two submarine flotillas now started to play havoc with the Axis shipping, starving Rommel and von Arnim of desperately needed fuel.

Two key issues had to be settled at Casablanca: firstly the allocation of resources between the Pacific and Europe, and secondly the rival merits of the cross-Channel and the Mediterranean strategies. At the Arcadia conference in Washington in December 1941/January 1942 "Germany first" had been agreed. As a result the Pacific war was receiving about 15% of the available supplies. King believed that this should be raised to about 30% and that he should be allowed to go on to the offensive so that the Japanese could not establish impregnable defensive positions. The key to this, as to most of the Allied planning, was landing craft capacity and King retained a pretty tight control over this. Allowing the problems of the Pacific to be discussed first sweetened King and made him feel that the rest of the Allied High Command was not against him (as he was inclined to believe).

259

Prior to arriving in Casablanca the Chiefs of Staff had fought a mighty battle with Churchill to ease him away from his desire to mount ROUNDUP, the cross-Channel invasion in 1943, and instead to support their preferred Mediterranean strategy. All of them deemed it necessary to clear the North African shore and then ensure a clear passage of the Mediterranean. Knocking Italy out of the war would be a bonus. A cross-Channel assault, although accepted in principal, was not deemed to be a feasible operation, as had been shown at Dieppe. Given the fact that in January 1943 Tunis had yet to be captured it would be almost certainly impossible to move the Allied armies in North Africa back to England in time to mount an invasion of northern France in that summer. Anyway, the German army in France was still too strong, not yet worn down enough by the Russians, or by bombing, to guarantee a safe invasion. Since the Allies had all those troops in North Africa it was logical to use them in that theatre. Hence the plan to attack Sardinia, Sicily, the Balkans, or wherever.

For the Americans ROUNDUP was still the correct way forward and they believed that they had reached agreement on that in their discussions in London in the summer of 1942. Here was a fundamental difference between the Allies. There were other differences, however, which did not run along national lines. Churchill in private agreed with Marshall over ROUNDUP. Portal and Arnold wanted exclusive priority to be given to the bombing offensive, believing, against all the evidence, that this would be sufficient to defeat Germany on its own. Pound and King were agreed on the primacy of the anti-U-boat campaign, while King was playing a lone hand in championing the Pacific war against the European. The British had one fundamental advantage over the Americans. This was that on the whole the British Chiefs of Staff presented a united front. They had been superbly briefed by Dill upon the American position. They had brought with them a full panoply of staff, and an HQ ship, *Bulolo*, which could provide all the communications necessary. The Americans, on the other hand, were clearly deeply divided: Marshall wanting ROUNDUP, King wanting the emphasis switched to the Pacific, and Arnold believing that bombing alone could win the war, and that this would present an unanswerable case for a separate US Air Force.

The British had arrived at their agreed position after two months of agonized debating in November and December. Churchill and Brooke slugged it out, toe to toe, until Brooke won. Churchill was deeply concerned that he had promised Stalin a second front in 1943, and even though Churchill and the Chiefs of Staff had reached agreement, Brooke was continually haunted by the worry that Marshall might win Churchill back to ROUNDUP. Pound's contribution to these debates was limited to supporting Brooke and emphasizing the fact that there was, as yet, no secure passage across the Atlantic. As far as he was concerned that was the principal problem that had to be tackled. There were fifteen Combined Chiefs of Staff meetings at Casablanca and three plenary meetings with Churchill and Roosevelt. At the first of these on 14 January all three of the British Chiefs of Staff gave an overview of what they saw as the way ahead and Pound emphasized that the main threat to any prosecution of the war in Europe was in the Atlantic, and that the key to allowing the convoys to cross the Atlantic safely was the use of very long-range aircraft. At every opportunity during the conference Pound emphasized this, trying to educate the Americans as he had educated his colleagues. He did not contribute much to the discussion on where the main weight of Allied power should be exerted; instead he managed to convince the Combined Chiefs and the two statesmen that none of their plans could work unless and until the U-boat menace was overcome. It would not be possible to mount any form of cross-Channel assault without mastery of the Atlantic and the waters around Britain.

There was plenty of relaxation alongside the hard work. On Saturday 16 January there was a dinner party attended by both Roosevelt and Churchill and most of the top-ranking military and naval officials. It was at the most difficult moment in the negotiations and Brooke was in despair at finding an agreement with the Americans. Eisenhower's aide Captain Butcher recorded in his diary:

> The President had commented that regardless of criticism of this secret rendezvous, he would hold office for three more years. Sir Dudley had then chimed in with the comment: "That's more than any other person sitting at this table can say."
>
> Sir Dudley had been fearful the Prime Minister hadn't appreciated the remark, but later conversation gave him assurance no offence was taken.[1]

The final decisions made at the conference were to mount an invasion of Sicily – HUSKY – as soon as possible, and an assault on the coast of Burma – ANAKIM – as well as operations in the Pacific. However, as

Pound warned his colleagues, "the defeat of the U-boat remains first charge on our resources" and that this might well not allow all of their projected operations to proceed as they hoped. To understand why this was so it is necessary to take the story back some way.

The loss of the RNAS in 1918 meant that the Royal Navy had no control over their own air space. Between the wars the RAF appeared to be little interested in working with the Royal Navy; instead they concentrated on building up a bomber force, believing in the doctrine of their founder Lord Trenchard that wars could be won by bombing alone. As a result two areas of naval air matters were totally neglected: firstly planes for use from carriers, and secondly planes for any operations at a distance over the sea in defence of trade. Despite the lessons of 1917–18 the RAF failed to appreciate that air power was as essential for the defence of convoys as surface escorts. Thus when war broke out in 1939 the Fleet Air Arm, only recently reconstituted in 1937, was totally ill equipped and unready for war. Nor, just as importantly, had the Royal Navy been given control of Coastal Command. All the lessons of the First World War indicated how necessary it was for one authority to control operations under, on and above the surface of the sea. To have the air element commanded, operated and supplied by a different Service was at best inefficient, at worst dangerous. Even more to the point, the RAF was wedded to the idea of bombing being a war-winner. All their thoughts and priorities went on this, to the alarm of forward-thinking naval officers.

Not surprisingly this subject was raised once the war began in earnest. In December 1940 Lord Beaverbrook commented that "the conditions of Coastal Command are a grave reflection on the Air Ministry, which starves it of equipment and has not given it the right type of aircraft". He suggested that Coastal Command be handed over to the Royal Navy, but Churchill decreed that it "would be disastrous to tear a large fragment out of the RAF. This is not the time for an inter-Service controversy."[2] As a result a compromise was reached by which Coastal Command was put under the operational control of the Admiralty, but all other aspects of it were left to the Air Ministry. Relations between Coastal Command and the Admiralty were generally excellent, but the Air Ministry did not give Coastal Command a fair allocation of equipment. In particular they lacked any of the necessary VLR aircraft to do their job properly. There was an enormous area in the middle of the North Atlantic, the Atlantic

Gap, which land-based aircraft could not reach. Here the U-boats could operate with relative immunity.

It is correct to say that the RAF "lacked the right kind of aircraft and the right kind of training and doctrine for effective co-operation with the other armed services".[3] Nor was the RAF able to carry out what it wanted to do. It was incapable of bombing by day, nor could it find its targets accurately by night until it received navigational aids early in 1943. It was the Royal Navy which had been forced to fight, without the back up of a correctly-equipped air component, and who had to pay the price for this. Even as early as the Arcadia conference in December 1941 it became evident that the key area of operations was the North Atlantic, for without control here no effective operations in Europe could be mounted. It was Pound who hit the nail on the head. It was he who identified "if we lose the war at sea we lose the war"[4] and he never lost sight of that central idea. All else depended on it and few in the RAF, other than those in Coastal Command, ever grasped it. Not only did any prospect of offensive operations depend upon it, but Britain's very survival.

By the end of June 1942 the U-boats had been driven away from their second 'happy time' off the east coast of America and the Caribbean, and were back concentrating on the central North Atlantic. Doenitz had the enormous advantages of being able on the one hand to read the main Royal Naval cipher and on the other to mask the U-boats transmissions through the fourth wheel on the U-boat Enigmas, which blinded Bletchley Park from February 1942. As a result the U-boat Tracking Room was forced to report to Pound on 9 February 1942:

> Since the end of January no Special Information has been available about any U-boats other than those controlled by Admiral Norway. Inevitably by now the picture of the Atlantic dispositions is out of focus and little can be said with any confidence in estimating the present and future movements of U-boats.[5]

Mercifully one worry was removed from the Admiralty when Hitler decided that his remaining surface raiders should be brought back to Germany. They passed up Channel in February 1942, as related in Chapter 13. Here was a true and accurate comment on the ability of the RAF to carry out operations over water. The inadequately-equipped Coastal Command and Fleet Air Arm failed totally to halt the German ships and the vaunted bombing force could either not find or not hit their

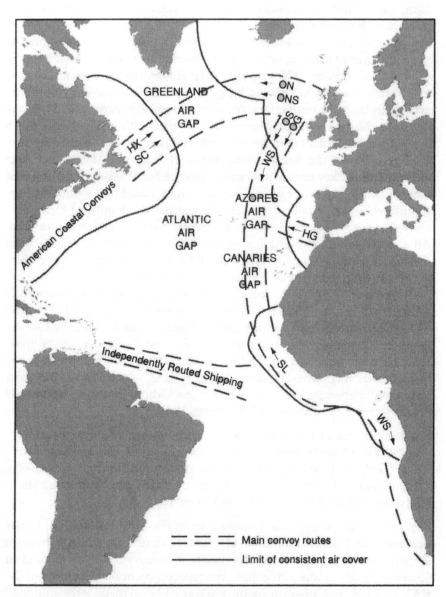

The Battle of the Atlantic, 1942

naval target. Thus as 1942 started the Admiralty could not practise evasive routing, could not determine where the U-boats were, was desperately short of suitable escorts, but was aware of vastly increased U-boat numbers in the Atlantic. As a result air power assumed a critical importance: it could drive the U-boats below the surface so that their speed was reduced to less than even the slowest convoy.

Coastal Command was acutely aware that it did not possess the necessary armoury to contribute fully. Its Commander-in-Chief, Sir Philip Joubert de la Ferté, had twice in 1941 asked that Bomber Command attack the U-boat pens in the western French ports. Twice he had been put down, on the second occasion the reply from the Air Ministry had concluded:

> There seemed no justification whatever for a return to this defensive strategy now when conditions at sea had so much improved and we were beginning to develop fully the air offensive to which we must look for winning as opposed to not losing the war.[6]

As a result of this the U-boat pens were by January 1942 all but impregnable. In February 1942 the Air Ministry, just before *Scharnhorst* and *Gneisenau* sailed up Channel, put forward a paper called "Bombing Policy" which demanded the use of all bombers over Germany. It was this paper which marked the start of what came to be called the Battle of the Air. This struggle took up far too much of both the Admiralty's and the Air Ministry's time, as Admiral Whitworth wrote to Cunningham on 15 December 1942:

> Our fight with the Air Ministry becomes more and more fierce as the war proceeds. It is a much more savage one than our war with the Huns, which is very unsatisfactory and such a waste of effort.[7]

It is true to say that the Royal Navy were not the only people to feel so strongly about the operational requirements of their air support and the indivisibility of air and naval operations. Admiral Stark and the US Navy felt equally strongly on the matter. He wrote to King on 2 June 1942 about a recent conversation with an unnamed British admiral, who had said, "We can't get anything unless the RAF sees fit to give it to us. They are fighting their own war, and it can't be done by bombing Germany alone." The month before he had written to Secretary Knox mentioning a conversation with two Royal Naval admirals over dinner:

They were opposed to a system which prevented their Navy from owning and controlling its own airforce, lock stock and barrel. One of the admirals stated, "It is difficult to get two branches of the Services, Army and Navy, to cooperate; it is practically impossible when you inject a third service." The other admiral . . . went on to state that the British Mediterranean Fleet was practically destitute of air support, and German aircraft had practically no opposition other than anti-aircraft guns.[8]

Pound promptly put in his own demand for six and a half squadrons of Wellingtons and for eighty-one American VLR aircraft, fitted with ASV. He wanted to attack the Bay of Biscay transit route with the former and close the air gap with the latter.[9] Joubert even dared to question the doctrine of bombing Germany "if England is to survive this year".[10] On 3 March Pound, after much discussion within the Admiralty, put before the War Cabinet Defence Committee a statement of "Air Requirements for the Successful Prosecution of the War at Sea". This must be among the key documents in the war, as the Admiralty identified exactly how the war might be lost: "If we lose the war at sea we lose the war. We lose the war at sea when we can no longer maintain those communications which are essential to us."[11] He explained that this could happen by losses to merchant shipping so that necessary supplies could not be imported, or by a reduction in tankers so that the armed forces could no longer operate. It was essential to "provide the necessary shore-based aircraft for the adequate protection of our convoys and shipping". He now demanded that the Admiralty be given operational control over all aircraft involved in operations over the sea, not just those of Coastal Command. He included what can only be called a shopping list of the global requirements for shore-based air support amounting to 1,940 aircraft, of which 900 were required at home, compared to Coastal Command's strength then of 519 aircraft. The Air Staff replied with their own paper expounding the principle of bombing German industry as being correct:

It remains the opinion of the Air Staff that squadrons of Bomber Command could best contribute to the weakening of the U-boat offensive by offensive action against the principal industrial areas of Germany within our range, including the main naval industries and dockyards. To divert them to an uneconomical defensive role would be unsound at any time. It would be doubly so now when we are

266

about to launch a bombing offensive of which we have high expectations and which will enable us to deliver a heavy and concentrated blow against Germany when German morale is low and when the Russians are in great need of our assistance.[12]

The two sides met head on in the War Cabinet Defence Committee on 18 March when both of these papers were discussed and both sides were asked to put forward further proposals. It was at this point that Brooke put in a paper demanding similar treatment for the Army, and in effect calling for a separate Naval and Army Air Force, alongside an Independent Strategic Bombing force. In other words, what had existed before the creation of the RAF. These opening salvoes in the Battle of the Air foreshadowed a campaign which lasted throughout the year and into 1943. The Admiralty (as well as the Air Ministry) files are filled with answers to specific questions and likely ones for use at Chiefs of Staff, Defence Committee, Cabinet and War Cabinet level. It is fair here to question the view of Portal portrayed by some historians as marked out by "his intellectual capabilities, integrity and moral courage" as well as an ability "to concentrate upon the critical issues".[13] The critical issue here was quite simply the ability of Britain to survive and Portal appears not to have been ready to grasp it.

In 1942 Doenitz's U-boats were approaching the figure he had always wanted of 400 and were sinking somewhere in the region of 450,000 tons per month in the North Atlantic. In particular he was sinking more tankers than were being built. Impartial observers, insofar as there were any, did not accept Bomber Command's thesis that it could win the war single-handed. Mr Justice Singleton was appointed by the War Cabinet on 16 April to investigate: "What results are we likely to achieve from continuing our air attack on Germany at the greatest possible strength during the next six, twelve and eighteen months?" He reported: "I do not think [the bomber offensive] ought to be regarded as of itself sufficient to win the war or to produce decisive results; the area is too vast for the effort we can put forth."[14] To Pound the spring months passed with increasing frustration. Whatever decision was taken or postponed his losses kept mounting. On 10 May he submitted a paper which conveys his sense of desperation:

What the Admiralty presses for now with all urgency is that:

(a)   The increased number of aircraft of the right type necessary to safeguard our vital sea communications should be provided.

267

(b)   The organisation of Bomber Command should be such that our bomber squadrons are capable of locating and attacking targets at sea with success.

He added in his own hand:

(c)   All types of aircraft which may be required to operate over the sea should receive such training as will enable them to do this with success.[15]

The frustration felt by Pound and the Admiralty was further fuelled by the anger in the Fleet who simply felt let down by the RAF. The best example of this was Vice Admiral Max Horton who turned down the command of the Home Fleet because of it.

Horton had been offered the command of the Home Fleet in succession to Sir Charles Forbes in October 1940 and turned it down for three principle reasons. The first was because of the lack of control of aircraft. Horton wrote:

I think it is essential that the Commander-in-Chief Home Fleet should have directly under his orders adequate air forces –

(a)   For reconnaissance;

(b)   For sea bombing;

(c)   For fighter protection

To carry this into effect bomber squadrons would have to be placed under C-in-C HF's orders, not only for bombing enemy forces at sea, but to supplement the inadequate reconnaissance machines which is all that the AOC-in-C Coastal Command can supply.

Shore based fighter protection for the Fleet is also necessary and must be under the Commander-in-Chief's orders in certain areas.

These forces should work and train together and with the Fleet continuously, and the personnel should not be subjected to constant change.

Only if the above measures are put into force do I see a chance of the Home Fleet successfully fulfilling its functions.[16]

His other two reasons for refusing the command were the belief that the Commander-in-Chief Home Fleet should operate from a shore-based HQ, and that he "did not enjoy that degree of independent judgement and action which seemed to me to be essential to the full discharge of the responsibilities of this Command."

On 2 June Pound consulted his Commanders-in-Chief and Sir John Tovey wrote afterwards to emphasize the strength of feeling. He even went so far as to suggest that "the situation at sea is now so grave that the time had come for a stand to be made, even if this led to Their Lordships taking the extreme step of resignation. I was supported in this by both Admiral of the Fleet Sir Charles Forbes and Admiral Sir Andrew Cunningham."[17] Backed up by this sort of support, Pound returned to the fray at a Chiefs of Staff meeting on 16 June, saying:

> The present threat to our sea lines of communication, on the security of which our existence and ultimate victory depended, called for an immediate increase in the strength of the land-based air forces working with the Navy.[18]

In the absence of Churchill in Washington the Chiefs of Staff could come to no agreement, and the decision was taken to ask two senior staff officers (ACNS(H) Rear Admiral Brind and ACAS(Policy) Air Vice Marshal Slessor) to examine the problem and to recommend a solution. Their recommendation was for fifty-four long-range aircraft for home waters (Bay of Biscay, Western Approaches and for support of the Home Fleet), and a further seventy-two long range general reconnaissance aircraft. They also recommended that thirty-six Lancaster bombers (two squadrons) be transferred temporarily to Coastal Command from Bomber Command. These recommendations were promptly rejected by Portal, and so the matter moved up to War Cabinet level.

Churchill also received an extraordinary document from the new AOC Bomber Commander, Sir Arthur Harris, who wrote him a personal letter dated 17 June, expounding the proper use of air power.

> We are free, if we will, to employ our rapidly increasing air strength in the proper manner. In such a manner as would avail to knock Germany out of the war in a matter of months, if we decide upon the right course. If we decide on the wrong course, then our air power will now, and increasingly in future become inextricably implicated as a subsidiary weapon in the prosecution of vastly protracted and avoidable land and sea campaigns.

It is imperative, if we hope to win the war, to abandon the

disastrous policy of military intervention in the land campaigns of Europe, and to concentrate our air power against the enemy's weakest spots . . . The success of [the 1,000 bomber raid on Cologne on 30 May] had proved beyond doubt in the minds of all but wilful men that we can even today dispose of a weight of air attack which no country on which it can be brought to bear could survive. We can bring it to bear on the vital part of Germany. It requires only the decision to concentrate it for its proper use.

As for Coastal Command, it was "merely an obstacle to victory".[19] As an example of the gospel according to Trenchard it could not be bettered!

Churchill in his judgement on 21 July tended towards Harris, despite accepting that "it might be true to say that the issue of the war depends on whether Hitler's U-boat attack on Allied tonnage or the increase and application of Allied air-power reach their full fruition first."[20] He allowed the argument to drag on through the summer, eventually instructing Sinclair to raise Bomber Command to fifty squadrons, from thirty-two, two of these new ones to come from Coastal Command. This decision reduced Joubert to despair, who wrote to Pound on 25 July:

(i)   We are losing tankers faster than we are building them.

(ii) We are losing merchant ships at the approximate rate of building, but the immense quantities of material and valuable lives lost in the sinkings are quite irreplaceable.

(iii) We are unable to conduct the offensives necessary for victory at the time, and on the scale, which are desirable.

(iv) The standard of living of the people of the Allied Nations is much reduced by inability to ship required raw materials and consumption goods.[21]

Pound, not surprisingly, took up the matter again in the Defence Committee, submitting a long paper entitled "The Needs of the Navy" on 5 October. He produced a rational review of the whole position, pointing out, amongst other things, that:

. . . we have lost a large measure of control over our sea communications. This has already had, and is having a far-reaching effect not only on the maintenance of the United Kingdom but on our ability to take the offensive . . . In fact, we have reached the point at which

270

we are unable to carry out concurrently those operations which the present state of the war so urgently demands.[22]

He demanded that industrial resources be switched to the Navy and that it be given the resources to be able to fight properly. Churchill's response on 24 October was negative. He would not change things: "At present, in spite of U-boat losses, the Bomber offensive should have first place in our effort."[23]

Portal celebrated, rather unwisely, by announcing to the Chiefs of Staff that he planned to have between four and six thousand heavy bombers to "shatter the industrial and economic structure of Germany", which would eliminate one third of German industry.[24] Not surprisingly, Pound and the Admiralty had few problems in destroying this fanciful document by pointing out that at present the Allies imported 1,250,000 tons of air fuel into the United Kingdom alone. Portal's bomber programme would require an additional five million tons, added to other demands on shipping. Pound forced the whole issue back to be examined again. He again produced the Royal Navy's case, this time to the new Anti-U-boat Committee on 18 November. He went equipped with a succinct five-page brief, which concluded:

> The key to the whole problem at the moment is to get at least 40 long-range aircraft to re-equip selected squadrons now in Coastal Command . . . Added to this we must provide 10cm. ASV for the Bay.[24]

The Anti-U-boat Committee would also have had the statistics from the Atlantic, so they could have seen that in October 1942 637,833 tons of shipping had been lost, over 500,000 of these in the Atlantic alone.[26]

Portal at last started to relent. He transferred thirty Halifax bombers to Coastal Command to strengthen it in its Bay offensive, and to replace some of Coastal Command's aged Wellingtons with more modern ones equipped with Leigh Lights and 10cm radar. However, this was a relatively hollow victory: the new Wellingtons did not come into service until March 1943 and there was no advent of VLR aircraft for the Atlantic gap. Coastal Command still had only twenty VLR aircraft. Meanwhile, in Barnett's vivid phrase, "Doenitz was continuing to torpedo his way towards final victory,"[27] with, in the three months November 1942 to January 1943, nearly half of Britain's consumption of raw materials coming from stock because of the losses in the North Atlantic.

Pound had opted to attack the U-boats in the Bay of Biscay, hoping to sink them through Coastal Command while they were in transit between their bases and their areas of operations. In the first six months of 1942 this was a total failure: not one U-boat was sunk, and 265 U-boats transited the Bay.[28] Despite the introduction of the Leigh Light and ASV II radar the Bay offensive was not markedly more successful in the next six months either. From June 1942 to January 1943 an average of 3,500 patrol hours were flown each month over the Bay. The cost was a loss of some 100 aircraft and only seven U-boats were sunk. In contrast, just over 1000 hours patrol time were flown in the North Atlantic and resulted in seventeen U-boats sunk and fewer convoys attacked.[29] There was a dreadful delay in the production of ASV II, the radar which would allow Coastal Command aircraft to pick up the U-boats on the surface without the German Metox device alerting the U-boat.

Thus 1942 had seen great verbal battles, but little success in the actual struggle at sea against the U-boats. In the twelve months the U-boats claimed 1160 ships at 6,266,215 tons. At that rate there was no prospect of any successful cross-Channel invasion, and the success of the North African invasion was remarkable. As the old year went out it was speeded on its way by a wave of ferocious gales which at least had the advantage of bringing some relief to the escorts and the merchant crews in that it blinded the U-boats.

In fact 1943 opened with all the ingredients in place which were to result in victory for the Allies by the end of May, though it could not have been seen in January. Firstly, Coastal Command was at last able to use ASV II in February 1943 and this allowed them to pick up the U-boats accurately at a range of twelve miles. Secondly, in December 1942 Bletchley Park eventually managed to break into the U-boat's 'Shark' Enigma key. This was helped by Doenitz's strict centralized control of his U-boat fleet, requiring constant signalling and relying on his conviction that Enigma was secure. These signals, both to their base and to each other, were not only a boon to Bletchley Park but also to the escorts, as they were now nearly all equipped with HF/DF equipment. Thirdly, the escorts had also been equipped with Type 271 10cm radar, which allowed them to "see" their targets as well as Coastal Command. Fourthly, escort carriers were becoming available, but were not yet being used in the North Atlantic, much to King's disgust. Although there were more escort ships available there were not yet enough for Western Approaches to form the support groups which Horton wanted. These would be able to help convoy escorts who were hard-pressed and also remain to hunt a U-boat without weakening the convoy escort. Only late in February with the release of destroyers from North Africa and the Arctic convoys were sufficient found to create four Escort Groups, three of which were centred around an escort carrier. By May the Royal Navy was at least equipped with escorts of sufficient speed and strength to be able to challenge the U-boat effectively. Newer and better weapons also began to appear in the New Year. Coastal Command was equipped with the Mark VII depth charge with a reliable 25-foot setting pistol only from July 1942. The Hedgehog (a forward-throwing mortar) first went to sea in January 1942, but by the end of 1942 only 100 ships had been equipped with it.

In January 1942 Pound and King set up the Allied Anti-Submarine Survey Board whose job was to standardize training and operational procedures, and to co-ordinate the Allies' overall pool of escorts. The appointment of Horton to Western Approaches in November 1942 was matched by the appointment of Slessor to Coastal Command in February 1943, and these two drove their two commands like a coach and horses. Horton's requirements for command (as mentioned earlier) were perfectly fulfilled. He had operational control over his part of Coastal Command. He was flying his flag ashore in Derby House, Liverpool, and Pound and the Admiralty left him alone as far as was possible. Horton was matched against Doenitz, who became Commander-in-Chief of the German Navy in January 1943, but retained his rigid personal grip of U-boat operations.

January was a deceptive month as the appalling weather and partial reading of 'Shark' allowed the Allies some success via evasive routing. However, in February German success in deciphering the Allied codes and an inability to read Shark quickly enough meant that the Germans played havoc with two convoys, SC118 and ON166. The month saw sixty-three ships sunk and a total of 359,328 tons. Early in March the Allies held an Atlantic Convoy Conference in Washington. So important did Pound believe this to be that he sent his VCNS, Moore, to help Noble combat King and the US Navy. Here King initially proposed to withdraw all US Naval escorts from the North Atlantic so as to concentrate on routes further south, i.e. to American forces in North Africa. He eventually agreed to provide a support group, complete with escort carrier, to work under British control, and to escort the critical tanker convoys from the Caribbean, while the Royal Canadian Navy and the Royal Navy took over the whole of the North Atlantic. It was pointed out to King that Coastal Command had only twenty-three VLR aircraft operational, while the US Navy controlled 112, seventy of which had been sent to the Pacific to carry out reconnaissance missions in non-combat areas, and the other squadrons were operating from airfields in California and the Caribbean. No US Liberators were operating from Newfoundland. The British, led by Noble and Moore, argued their case well, backed by figures supplied by Professor Blackett, the new Head of the Admiralty Operational Research Department. Despite all of the evidence, King would not divert a single US Navy plane, and eventually it was US Army planes that operated from Newfoundland in early April. In a cryptic aside in his HUSH report for Admiral Stark on the conference, dated 19 March, Geoffrey Blake wrote

> We are now faced with extremely heavy and increasing U-boat concentrations in the North Atlantic. Our convoys have to fight their way through. Admiralty's undertakings given at this conference have required the full use of *all* their resources. [his emphasis].[30]

March saw catastrophic losses. From 7 to 10 March SC121 was attacked by seventeen U-boats losing thirteen ships (62,000 tons) and not sinking a single U-boat. HX228 was also heavily attacked, losing four ships, but sinking two U-boats. Worse was to come as OIC tried to route HX 229 away from the clutches of the U-boats, but could do little to help SC122. From 16 to 20 March a constant battle raged and twenty-one ships were sunk in convoy for the loss of only one U-boat and three damaged. Ten other ships had been so badly damaged that they had had to put back to port or had to be sunk. In all waters over the first three weeks of March the Allies had lost ninety-seven ships, totalling more than half a million tons, 75% of which had been in convoy, which was particularly disturbing as this was supposed to be the traditional method of defending merchant ships against attack. Pound reported to the Anti-U-boat Committee on 22 March that "we can no longer rely on evading the U-boat packs and hence we shall have to fight the convoys through them."[31]

However, the final week of March saw a change in fortunes. The USS *Bogue* became the first of the new escort carriers to see action and by the end of the month the Royal Navy had three working with the convoys.

There was thus 24-hour aircraft protection, even when shore-based VLR aircraft could not be present. The need for destroyers for TORCH, and subsequent operations had finished and so at the beginning of April Horton had five escort groups ready to go into action as support groups, three of them with escort carriers. By mid-April there were forty-one VLR aircraft available and more Wellingtons were ready for the Bay offensive. Signals Intelligence was improving, even though the Germans were still reading the Allied convoy cipher.

As April unfolded it started to become clear that the U-boats were losing the will to attack and U-boat command was forced to order its commanders to press their attacks home harder. Convoys which had been losing anything up to 50% of their ships in convoy, let alone as stragglers, were now losing only two or three, and just as importantly were seeing three or four U-boats sunk by the expert working together of escorts and air power. Throughout April only fifty-six ships were sunk by the U-boats in all seas (327,943 tons), and fourteen U-boats were sunk in the North Atlantic and the Bay of Biscay. The critical convoy battle was around ONS5, which left Britain on 23 April. It was fought through by Commander P.W. Gretton against a total of forty-one U-boats. Over their three-day attack the U-boats sank twelve merchant ships, but at a price: seven U-boats sunk and five badly damaged. Throughout May the U-boats were attacked mercilessly and unrelentingly, leading Doenitz to signal to his captains on 22 May:

> If there is anyone who thinks that combating convoys is no longer possible, he is a weakling and no true U-boat captain. The battle of the Atlantic is getting harder but it is the determining element in the waging of the war.[32]

The joy on the faces of Pound and the Naval Staff and of Horton and his officers at Western Approaches as they read this can be imagined. By 31 May Doenitz had lost forty-one U-boats in that month alone and withdrawn them from the North Atlantic. Between 1 June and 18 September only one ship was lost in convoy, and fifteen in total, in the North Atlantic.

It is too easy to say that Pound had won a decisive battle: it can, however, be said that the Allies had done so. The Royal Navy, the Royal Canadian Navy, the US Navy, the Merchant Navies, Coastal Command of the RAF, the US Army Air Force and the Royal Canadian Air Force had all played their critical part. Pound, however, must take the credit for having the right man in the right place at the right time in Horton, and for forcing the RAF to ensure that Coastal Command had sufficient (but only just sufficient) VLR aircraft. He had persuaded the US Navy to put their escort carriers into the fray and, finally, as professional head of the Royal Navy, he can claim to represent the thousands of ordinary seamen, without whose courage this victory could not have been achieved.

★

In February 1943 it had been decided to reappointed Cunningham as Commander-in-Chief Mediterranean Fleet in place of Harwood. There can be no doubt that this was due to General Montgomery who had complained over the head of his superior, Alexander, direct to Brooke, about the unblocking of Tripoli harbour. In fact Tripoli harbour was cleared rapidly, but Pound evidently bowed to Churchillian pressure and removed Harwood to the Levant command. In fact Harwood was far from well and was eventually relieved there by J.H.D. Cunningham. A.B. Cunningham complained to the Second Sea Lord, Whitworth, about this: "I never thought Harwood should have gone as C-in-C Med [sic] but once there he should have been supported."[33] He also wrote to Pound suggesting that Harwood had been relieved because he withstood Churchill over the French Fleet at Alexandria and because of Montgomery's complaints, ending his letter, "Montgomery, I gather, is not given to appreciate what the Navy does for him and wants pulling up." Pound replied on 23 April, explaining Harwood's relief.

> As regards Harwood's relief, the French Fleet at Alexandria had nothing to do with it. He was relieved on my recommendation as I came to the conclusion that someone – J.H.D. Cunningham – could do the job much better. The actual job of the salvage party at Tripoli was very good and they were commended, but the staff arrangements left too much to chance which was quite unacceptable when one takes into consideration what the clearing of Tripoli means to the Army. As a matter of fact, Montgomery has been most appreciative of what the Navy has done and took the trouble to visit every ship at Tripoli. I am very sorry for Harwood, but what with blood pressure of 225, which no one knew about until after Tripoli, it is not surprising that he was not up to the mark. I am surprised at your

276

expressing such a definite opinion about his relief when you only knew one side of the case.[34]

The planning for the invasion of Sicily was very muddled and not helped by the dispersion of HQs: Cunningham had his in Algiers, Ramsay, the Eastern Task Force Commander, was in Cairo, while the Western Task Force was in Rabat. Cunningham, anyway, was far more involved in helping to finish off the North African campaign, to which he contributed with his memorable signal to the Mediterranean Fleet "Sink, burn and destroy. Let nothing pass". By 12 May the whole of the North African coastline was in Allied hands and by 17 August Sicily had also been captured. A large step on the way to eventual victory had been taken and the benefits of sea power were quite clearly to be seen. It is not too much to say that in the summer of 1943 all the benefits of the victory in the Battle of the Atlantic started to appear.

16

EBB TIDE

The summer of 1943 saw two meetings of the Combined Chiefs of Staff with their political leaders. The approaching victory in Tunis in May meant that decisions had to be made about the future. Although the Casablanca Conference had made the decision to invade Sicily and the planning for this was well advanced, the Allies had to decide how to exploit their likely victory there, as well as deciding what to do in Burma. As a result Churchill decided it was necessary for him to travel to Washington, and so he took with him a large party, including all three Chiefs of Staff. They left the Clyde on 5 May on board RMS *Queen Mary*.

Throughout April the Joint Planners, the Chiefs of Staff and the Prime Minister had been engaged in debate about how to exploit their expected victories in Tunis and Sicily. They knew that both King and Marshall would oppose them in any extension of the Mediterranean strategy, although for different reasons. Dominating all their thoughts was the knowledge that once Sicily was cleared they must do something with all of the forces in the Mediterranean theatre, rather than simply wait to employ them in northern France in 1944. There were various options, such as Sardinia and Corsica, Greece, the Dodecanese Islands and mainland Italy. Whatever they chose, Pound reminded them of the cost in assault craft and merchant shipping. The question that they had to decide was at whose expense that shipping was to come. Was it to be at the expense of an invasion of northern France, Burma or the Pacific campaign?

After considerable discussion in Washington the Combined Chiefs of Staff made two fundamental decisions. Firstly, they committed themselves to a cross-Channel invasion in the summer of 1944. Secondly, they allowed Eisenhower to exploit the success of Sicily, as he thought best within certain limiting factors. Pound saw the problems implicit in expanding the scope of operations in the Mediterranean and warned the Combined Chiefs of the shipping problems that it would cause. However, two factors militated against closing down the whole Mediterranean theatre. Firstly, the political necessity of showing the Russians that they were continuing to fight and had indeed opened a Second Front, and, secondly, the prospect of knocking Italy out of the war and exploiting their likely success in Sicily. From this trip to Washington there comes a lovely story, which shows Pound in a true light. It was reported in the *Evening Standard* on 25 May 1943:

> From Washington my correspondent sends me a story showing that the British Navy's reputation for silence is not without justification. Admiral Sir Dudley Pound was one of the higher officers attending a party in the capital. There was an assembly of admirals, generals diplomats and journalists. In the middle of the conversational hubbub one optimistic American newspaperman was heard to ask Sir Dudley, "Can you give us anything on the battle of the Atlantic? How's it really going?"
>
> Pound looked grave, stroked his chin, and chatter died away as the entire room listened for his answer. Eventually, after long consideration, he said, still with a deadly serious expression: "I can tell you this, my boy. I'd rather be Ernie King or Dudley Pound than that fellow Doenitz!"[1]

While at Washington the Combined Chiefs of Staff paid a visit to Williamsburg, the old colonial capital of Virginia. They stayed at the Williamsburg Inn, then an Army and Navy officers' club, and toured the restored town. On the Sunday morning they all went to morning service at Bruton parish church, in the middle of Williamsburg, where Pound read the lesson from the bible presented to the church by King Edward VII in 1907. No doubt he was thinking of his colonial ancestors as he toured the restored town.

While Pound sailed back on the *Queen Mary* with the vast majority of the party, Churchill flew off with Brooke and Marshal to Algiers to consult with Eisenhower and, in Churchill and Brooke's case, to press him to invade mainland Italy.

The summer of 1943 saw the first indications that Pound was not well. He had come to the Admiralty in 1939 with a bad leg and hip, and he had walked with the aid of a stick for some time. Despite what Roskill, and others, have repeatedly said, those who served with him at close quarters believed that he was fit for office in 1939. Certainly his method of working was not conducive to rest. Sleeping on a camp bed in the Admiralty cannot have been really restful. His only relaxation was his shooting on most Sundays and his evening drink with Lady Poynton. Without doubt he drove himself hard, probably too hard, and dealing with Churchill's hours of work was extremely taxing. By 1943 he was tired, of that there can be no doubt, but the appointment of Kennedy-Purvis as Deputy First Sea Lord appeared to give him a new lease of life.[2] It is probably true to say that by late in 1942 he was becoming reactive rather than proactive and that this may well account for the decision by Churchill to make Brooke the Chairman of the Chiefs of Staff. However, that does not mean to say that he was incapable of doing his job.

In June 1943 he started to have trouble with his left knee. The Admiralty Surgeon, Captain Miller, examined it and could diagnose nothing wrong with it. He simply told Pound "to ease up if he could". There was, of course, very little that Pound could do on that front, given the daily routine that he worked. In July, shortly before he left for the Quebec conference he suffered the loss of his devoted wife, Betty. She had been suffering from cancer for some time and, although she had had an operation in 1942, she had never really recovered. She finally died on 20 July after 35 years' devoted partnership. She had never been one to walk in the limelight, but instead had supported her husband in all that he did, making their home a welcome refuge. As a naval officer wrote in *The Times* on 24 July

> The friendship that she gave to all was complete. No one was more alive to the opportunities, which came to the wife of a highly placed officer. But of all personal part in these opportunities it seemed that she was unconscious and oblivious. It was the object to be attained that claimed her attention, and to which her mind and heart were devoted, not the part she took, far less the credit that might come to her . . . Assistance without interference might well have been her motto.[3]

The funeral was held at St Michael's, Chester Square, and was conducted by the former Chaplain of the Fleet, Archdeacon Peshall. It was a full occasion, with the entire Board of Admiralty present, led by the First Lord, A.V. Alexander, as well as all the Chiefs of Staff and Betty Stark.

At some point in the summer of 1943 occurred a delightful incident, which has been related by Peter Kemp, who was working in the OIC as a watchkeeper:

> One morning I found on my desk a large package containing a copy of Richard Walton's history of Anson's voyages around the world in 1740–4 – a copy which had been published in 1748. Accompanying it was a note written in the green ink which all First Sea Lords use in the Admiralty. 'I saw this in a bookseller's shop in the Charing Cross Road yesterday,' it said, 'and, knowing that you are interested in naval history, thought you might like it. D.P.' I found it deeply touching that an admiral of the fleet, and a man who bore so great a burden of responsibility, should have had the time and the thought to remember one of the more junior members of the Naval Staff at the Admiralty.[4]

As the summer progressed Pound became involved in a number of discussions, which made it clear that another Combined Chiefs of Staff meeting would be necessary, and so planning began for a meeting at Quebec in early August. He viewed the voyage there as the nearest thing to a rest that he was likely to get. Among the issues for discussion was the appointment of the Supreme Allied Commander in the South East Asia Command (SEAC). A number of candidates had been put forward, none of whom had been universally acceptable. It was Churchill who resurrected his original suggestion that Mountbatten should be appointed. Pound did not oppose the appointment; neither did he actively support it. He was happy to see Mountbatten move from COHQ to a theatre where his undoubted talents would be useful, but where he would have a highly experienced naval Commander-in-Chief, James Somerville, under him. As a result Mountbatten came to Quebec to be "inspected" by the Americans.

On the afternoon of 5 August Churchill and his advisers sailed from the Clyde in the *Queen Mary* for the QUADRANT conference. They used the five-day voyage to review every aspect of their war plans for the year ahead, knowing that their reception by the American colleagues, although physically warm, would not necessarily be strategically welcoming. Among the issues discussed on the voyage were the Mulberry harbours for the Normandy beaches and offensive operations in Burma. In order to convince the Americans that the British were in earnest in Burma

Churchill took with him Orde Wingate, who had just returned from the first Chindit operation. During the voyage news reached them of the first feelers from the Italians for peace. *Queen Mary* arrived at Halifax on 9 August and the party immediately caught their train to Quebec, which brought them there at 6.00pm on 10 August.

The whole party was accommodated in the Chateâu Frontenac Hotel, with the British on one floor, the Americans, when they arrived, on another, and the conferences on the ground floor. It was a most convenient arrangement. As soon as he arrived Churchill departed to meet Roosevelt at Hyde Park, the Roosevelt country house, while the Chiefs of Staff prepared themselves to meet their American counterparts on 12 August. By 19 August they could report to their political masters at the first plenary session on a number of key issues. They were agreed on Operation OVERLORD with a target date of 1 May 1944, that the Italian campaign should be carried on with unrelenting pressure and that a landing should be made in southern France soon after OVERLORD. The second plenary session on 23 August looked at operations in the Far East, agreeing that the new aim should be the defeat of Japan within twelve months of the defeat of Germany. There had also been agreement on the development of the atom bomb.

Pound was approached by Mountbatten and asked if, as Supreme Allied Commander, he would have the power to remove any naval Commander-in-Chief. Pound would have soon discovered that Mountbatten had asked all three Chiefs of Staff the same question. This was an understandable request in that he was still only a substantive Captain, while an Acting Vice-Admiral, and among his subordinates was Admiral James Somerville. Pound gave a similar reply as the other Chiefs of Staff: "No". Mountbatten could not simply sack a Commander-in-Chief, but if he kept in touch with the Admiralty and there were problems then they could surely be sorted out. Nevertheless in his time as SAC SEAC he got rid of four Commanders-in-Chief!

Mountbatten, ever one for the limelight and unusual ideas, had been developing Operation HABBAKUK, which was an ingenious design for the construction of a carrier from 1.7 million tons of frozen sea water mixed with sawdust and concrete. Mountbatten wished to demonstrate how tough this Pykrete (named after its inventor, Professor Pyke) was. Because it was so secret all the assistants were cleared from the room. Mountbatten asked General Arnold to try to chop a block of pykrete with a machete, and Arnold nearly ruptured his arm in attempting this, letting out a shriek of pain. Mountbatten then produced a revolver and fired a bullet at it, to demonstrate its toughness. Indeed it demonstrated that so effectively that the bullet richoched around the room, taking a chunk out of Ernie King's trousers. The thoughts of the excluded staff as they heard Arnold's yell and then a shot can but be imagined.

By 24 August the conference was finished and agreement had been reached on how the war was to be fought to a victorious conclusion. In relief Brooke and Portal decided to go fishing for 48 hours. Knowing that Pound was normally a keen fisherman they asked him to accompany them. Indeed, before the conference began all three had seized the chance to have a day's fishing together on 12 August, and they had had an excellent day. They were surprised when Pound turned them down, and he remained at the Chateâu Frontenac. Almost certainly he had had his first stroke, and, realizing that he could not cope, opted to try to harbour his strength.

Brooke and Portal left Quebec on 28 August to fly back to London, while Pound stayed on in Quebec with Churchill to have further discussions with the Canadian Navy, before travelling with Churchill down to Washington on the night of 31 August/1 September. It was here that his colleagues first noticed that something was not right. Percy Noble, writing to Cunningham after Pound's death told him:

It may interest you to know that Pound actually gave up the unequal contest with me at Washington. He asked me to come to his hotel where I found a doctor who had been flown out from England in attendance. He told me he had lost the use of his right leg while we were at Quebec, and that he now had no feeling in his right arm (he had spilt his tea all over himself the day before, which I had been rather astonished at); and that he felt it now creeping up to the right side of his head – so the long and the short of it was he couldn't go on. I got him to go and see the PM immediately, and the next day he flew up to Halifax and remained in the *Renown* until the PM embarked in her for his return to the UK. Little did I imagine when I said goodbye to him that he would be dead in under five weeks. The specialist doctor told me that he thought it was a slight stroke and that, in his opinion, he might get reasonably fit again but he would have to give up his work. It was all very sad.[5]

The night before sailing Pound dined with senior Canadian naval officers and told them that he was resigning, but nobody else was informed of this. Brockman had sent for the doctor from the Admiralty, Captain Miller, and he remained with Pound throughout his voyage. On board *Renown* he stayed in his cabin, never appearing, and, as related in Chapter 1, went straight to hospital from the Admiralty, and died on 21 October.

Once in hospital Pound was seen by two senior specialists in neurology and neurosurgery from the Army and the Royal Air Force, called in by the senior Royal Naval physician. Their reports both stated that Pound was suffering from loss of speech and paralysis of the right side, and "had a left-sided brain tumour of the most malignant form, commonly termed nowadays a *glioblastoma multiforme*". They both stated that there was no surgical or medical treatment which could effect any improvement, and continued:

> We have, therefore, a cerebral illness of some three months' duration, with a stroke-like onset – a frequent occurrence with brain tumours.' Within a few weeks of the onset of the illness the two greatest Service neurological specialists independently reached a similar diagnosis: of a highly malignant and rapidly growing tumour. Their statements are very much the same that we could make today; but nowadays the extent of the growth could be delineated by the CT scan . . . With these facts in my mind I feel quite sure that the Admiral of the Fleet died of a most malignant cerebral tumour, the *glioblastoma multiforme*, sometimes causing death within weeks rather than months of onset.[6]

Pound's performance when he returned to London was remarkable. By sheer will power and dedication to duty he forced himself to meet the Board of Admiralty to announce his resignation. Only those who met him personally, such as Blake and Brockman, were able to detect his problems, and then only when it was seen that he could hardly write. By the end of that day, 20 September, he was in the Royal Masonic Hospital. Here he refused a peerage, because he felt that the family could not afford it, but was prepared to accept the OM as it would cost little, and was a recognition of the work of the whole Royal Navy.[7] He received a formal letter from the Board of Admiralty thanking him for all of his services, which is worth quoting in full.

9th October 1943.

My dear First Sea Lord,

At their meeting today, the Board of Admiralty resolved that I should express to you on their behalf their deep regret that ill-health has occasioned your retirement from the Board and the loss of your invaluable services.

They consider that your arduous labours during the past four years of war as First Sea Lord and Chief of Naval Staff are largely responsible for the present highly satisfactory state of the war at sea, particularly in the Atlantic, and the predominant position generally of the Royal Navy, a position which has recently been emphasized by the surrender of the Italian Fleet and the reconquest of the seaways in the Mediterranean.

They are fully conscious that the high state of efficiency of all units of the Fleet at the beginning of the war and since was largely due to your untiring insistence upon training and preparation for war in all its aspects.

They wish me to say that they will miss your unfailing help and guidance on the Board and that each member individually will long continue to feel a sense of personal loss.

Yours sincerely,

A.V. Alexander.[8]

It would be fair to say that his final months are a fitting tribute to his whole career, not just his time as First Sea Lord. He drove himself out of a sense of duty and a feeling of what was right. Duty was all to him. Sometimes in life that duty means knowing when to step down, but this higher conception of sacrifice is enormously difficult to realize when things are going badly. For much of 1942 and 1943 that was indeed the case. Anyway who was there to take over from him? The easy answer is that Cunningham was the obvious choice, but that is with the advantage of hindsight. Certainly Cunningham was our premier sailor, with a great reputation in the Royal Navy, but he had extremely limited experience of Whitehall. Anyway, in much of 1942 and 1943 he was needed where he was, commanding in the Mediterranean, aside from his spell in Washington. The possibilities otherwise were very limited. Fraser had only recently escaped from being Controller and had only just taken over

285

as Commander-in-Chief, Home Fleet. A possibility was Horton, but he was essential at Western Approaches and his idiosyncratic approach would not have gone down well with everybody at the Admiralty. Neither Forbes nor Tovey would have commanded the respect of the entire Royal Navy. There was a case for putting in somebody more junior, such as Syfret or Moore, in much the same way as Wemyss had become First Sea Lord in 1917, while Beatty commanded the Grand Fleet. However, none of these possibilities really stand up to close examination. Pound must have longed to retire. He had not wanted the job in 1939, but had taken it out of duty. It was his duty to see the thing through as long as he could. There was no doubt in his mind that by early 1943 Cunningham was the man to succeed him. The only question was when. It was his own body that would decide that question.

What, then, are we to make of him? As a public servant he must stand very high. He was single-minded in his determination to make the most of what he had. His conception of duty is old-fashioned, but simple. He was not prepared for the role he had to play, as Jellicoe had been before 1914. He took the job on because there was nobody else and he shouldered the burden as best he could. He is not a Roosevelt figure; rather he is like Truman, and like Truman he stayed in the kitchen and he took the heat.

Appendix

SERVICE CAREER OF SIR DUDLEY POUND

1891	1/1	**CADET**		
		Britannia	Training ship.	
1893	5/1	**MIDSHIPMAN**		**PROMOTION**
		Royal Sovereign	Battleship	Flagship of Channel Sq.
1894	17/4	Mdm *Undaunted*	Cruiser	China.
1895	5/10	Mdm *Calypso*	Cruiser	Training Sq.
1896	29/8	**ACTING SUB LIEUTENANT**		**PROMOTION**
		R.N. College	Studying for Lt Certificates:	
			Seamanship 1	
			Navigation 1	
			Torpedo 1	
			Gunnery 2	
			Pilotage 2	
		SUB LIEUTENANT		**PROMOTION**
1897	11/10	Sub Lt *Oppossum*	Torpedo Boat Destroyer.	Devonport
1898	17/1	Sub Lt *Magnificent*	Battleship	Flagship of 2i/c Channel Squadron.
	29/8	**LIEUTENANT**		**PROMOTION**
	1/10		Flag Lt.	
1899	30/9	Lt *Vernon*	Torpedo Sch	
1902	14/1	Lt(T) *Grafton*	Cruiser	Flagship of Pacific Fl
1905	3/1	Lt(T) *King Edward VII*	Battleship	Flagship of Atlantic Fl
1907	5/3	Lt(T) *Queen*	Battleship	Staff of CoS Med Fl
1909	6/1	Lt Admiralty		Ordnance Department

	30/6	**COMMANDER**		**PROMOTION**
1911	30/5	Comd *Superb*	Battleship	Home Fleet Commander
1913	6/1	Comd *Victory*		R.N. War College Instructor
1914	21/4	Comd *St Vincent*	Battleship	Home Fleet Commander
	31/12	**CAPTAIN**		**PROMOTION**
1915	20/1	Capt Admiralty		NA 1SL
	17/5	Capt *Colossus*	Battleship	Flag Capt.
1917	6/7	Capt Admiralty		Asst. D of P
1918	1/1	Capt Admiralty		D O D(H)
	15/7		half-pay	
1920	20/5	Capt *Hood*	B/Cruiser	Special Service.
	18/10	Capt *Repulse*	B/Cruiser	Command
1922	9/5	Capt Admiralty		D of P
1925	2/5	**COMMODORE**		
		Capt *Warspite*		CoS to C-in-C Med Fleet.
1926	1/3	**REAR ADMIRAL**		**PROMOTION**
1927	20/3	R/Adm Admiralty		ACNS
1929	21/5	R/Adm *Repulse Renown*		*Commander Battle Cruiser Squadron.*
1930	15/5	**VICE ADMIRAL**		**PROMOTION**
1931	24/4	V/Adm	R.N. War College	
	1/2	Admiralty	British Naval Representative on the Permanent Advisory Commission to the League of Nations Disarmament Conference.	
1932	31/8	V/Adm	Admiralty	Second Sea Lord
	16/1	**ADMIRAL**		**PROMOTION**
1935	9/10	Adm *Queen Elizabeth*		CoS to C-in-C Med Fleet.
1936	20/3	Adm *Barham*		Commander-in-Chief Mediterranean Fleet.
		Warspite		
1939	12/6	Adm Admiralty		First Sea Lord and Chief of Naval Staff.
	31/7	**ADMIRAL OF THE FLEET**		**PROMOTION**

FOOTNOTES

CHAPTER 1. DEATH OF A SAILOR. (PAGES 1 TO 7)

1   A. Bryant, *The Turn Of The Tide*, p.698.
2   Ibid. p.721.
3   W.S. Churchill, *Closing The Ring*, p.118.
4   Pound papers, DUPO 2/4.
5   All letters in the possession of the Pound family.
6   Blake Papers, BLE/9.
7   G. Pawle, *The War and Colonel Warden*, p.253.
8   J. Colville, *The Churchillians*, p.139.
9   Stark papers, Box A2.
10 Pound papers, DUPO 2/4.
11 Melville Papers, 92/15/1.
12 Stark papers, Box A4.

CHAPTER 2. EARLY LIFE. (PAGES 8 TO 21)

1   Pound Family Newsletter, Vol I, No 3, Easter 1995.
2   R.V. Brockman, *Admiral of the Fleet Sir Dudley Pound*, 1949.
3   *Isle of Wight Mercury*, December 1890.
4   *Entry and Training of Naval Cadets* (HMSO 1914).
5   Game Book in the possession of the Litchfield family.
6   Pound papers, DUPO 7/7.
7   Ibid, DUPO 3/1
8   K. Edwards, *Men of Action*, p.163.
9   Pound papers, DUPO 3/1
10 ADM 196/44
11 Citation in family possession.
12 Pound papers, DUPO 3/1.

Chapter 3. War Service. (pages 22 to 40)

1   A.J. Marder, *From The Dreadnought To Scapa Flow*, Vol II, p.414.
2   Pound diary, Imperial War Museum, LS Box 92/53/1.
3   W.S. Churchill, *The World Crisis, 1911–1918*, Vol I, p.360.
4   Litchfield MSS p.62.
5   Churchill, op cit p.363.
6   Fisher to Pound, 22 March 1915. Imperial War Museum. Misc G6.
7   Hankey, *The Supreme Command*, Vol I, p.335.
8   A.J. Marder, *From The Dreadnought To Scapa Flow*, Vol III.
9   Marder, ibid, p.101.
10 N.J.M. Campbell, *Jutland: An Analysis Of The Fighting*, p.349–352.
11 Commander D. Joel, Memoir of Dudley Pound, DUPO 2/3.
12 R. Keyes, *The Naval Memoirs of* . . . Vol II, p.97.
13 Keyes, ibid. p.101.
14 A Temple-Patterson (Ed.) *The Jellicoe Papers*, Vol II, 1916–35, p.167.
15 Admiralty, Mss HSB 190, August 1917, quoted in Marder Vol IV.
16 Litchfield MSS, p.89.
17 C.F. Aspinall-Oglander, *Roger Keyes*, p.217.

Chapter 4. Command and Planning. (pages 41 to 52)

1   CAB 23/15, 15 August 1919.
2   Pound papers, DUPO 3/4.
3   Both reports ADM 196/90.
4   Pound papers, DUPO 3/4.
5   Quoted in S.W. Roskill, *Naval Policy Between The Wars*, Vol I, p.348.

Chapter 5. Staffwork. (pages 53 to 66)

1   Pound papers, DUPO 3/4.
2   S.W. Roskill, *Hankey: Man of Secrets*, Vol II, p.509.
3   S.W. Roskill, *Naval Policy Between The Wars*, Vol I, p.47.
4   Quoted in S.W. Roskill, ibid, p.534.
5   Pound Papers, DUPO 2/3.
6   Ibid, DUPO 2/4.
7   The best account of this extraordinary episode is R. Glenton, *The Royal Oak Affair*.
8   P.G. Halpern, *The Keyes Papers*, Vol III, p.43.
9   S.W. Roskill, op cit p.48.
10 Keyes Papers, MSS 15/20.
11 Keyes Papers, Vol II, p.268–9.
12 Pound Papers, DUPO 3/4.
13 P. Beesly, *Very Special Admiral*, p.64.

14 Pound Papers, DUPO 6/1.
15 Ibid.
16 Ibid., DUPO 2/2.
17 Both references are in DUPO 2/2.
18 Quoted in Lichfield MSS, p.134–135.
19 S.W. Roskill, *Hankey: Man of Secrets*, Vol II, p.508.
20 Keyes Papers, Vol II, p.221.
21 Ibid, p.227.
22 ADM 116/2550.

CHAPTER 6. BATTLE CRUISERS AND SECOND SEA LORD. (PAGES 67 TO 86)

1   Pound papers, DUPO 3/4.
2   Ibid.
3   Ibid., DUPO 2/2.
4   Ibid.
5   Ibid, DUPO 5/6.
6   Ibid, DUPO 2/4.
7   Ibid, DUPO 3/4.
8   This, and the two subsequent reports, ADM 196/90.
9   Keyes Papers, Vol II, p.261.
10 Pound Papers, DUPO 3/4.
11 Ibid.
12 R/Adm Sir Charles Norris, taped memories for Professor A. Marder, in the author's possession.
13 Pound Papers, DUPO 3/4.
14 Ibid., DUPO 2/4.
15 Quoted in A. Coles, *Invergordon Scapegoat*, p.129.
16 AM 1445 of 16 September 1931, also quoted in Roskill, ibid., p.109.
17 Quoted in Roskill, p.112.
18 ADM 178/89.
19 Norris taped memories.
20 All the Tomkinson papers are at Churchill College, Cambridge, TOMK.
21 ADM 196/90.

CHAPTER 7. MEDITERRANEAN FLEET COMMAND. (PAGES 87 TO 112)

1   Pound papers, DUPO 4/2.
2   Norris, taped memories.
3   ADM 196/90.
4   Chatfield papers, CHT 4/10.

5   Ibid.
6   Ibid.
7   *Great Britain And The East*, August 13 1936.
8   Chatfield papers, CHT 4/10.
9   R. Ollard, *Fisher And Cunningham*, p.76.
10   Letter to Pound, 5 May 1937. Somerville Papers, SMVL 5/5.
11   H. Thomas, *The Spanish Civil War*, Appendix 3, p.981.
12   SMVL 5/5.
13   ADM 116/3522.
14   ADM 116/3527.
15   Chatfield papers, CHT 4/10.
16   Ibid.
17   S.W. Roskill, *HMS Warspite*, p.187.
18   CHT 4/10.
19   Litchfield, MSS. p.248.
20   S.W. Roskill, *HMS Warspite*, p.189.
21   Ibid, p.187.
22   For this relationship see the Introduction to S.W. Roskill, *HMS Warspite*, by
     H.P. Willmott.
23   Litchfield MSS, p.250.
24   Norris tape.
25   Pound papers, DUPO 2/4.
26   Ibid DUPO 2/2.
27   Willis papers, WLLS 5/3.
28   Willis papers at IWM, Box p.186.
29   This and all subsequent letters, Chatfield Papers, CHT 4/10.
30   Private information.
31   Norris tape.
32   Ibid.
33   Pound papers, DUPO 8/1.

CHAPTER 8. FIRST SEA LORD. (PAGES 113 TO 125)
1   S.W. Roskill, *Naval Policy Between The Wars*, Vol II, p.463.
2   S.W. Roskill, *Churchill And The Admirals*.
3   A.J. Marder, *Old Friends, New Enemies, Strategic Illusions 1936–1941*, p.236.
4   Ibid, p.236–7, and for the following quotation.
5   *Daily Telegraph*, 11 March 1970.
6   S.W. Roskill, *Naval Policy Between The Wars*, Vol II, p.466.
7   P. Naylor, Talk to the RUSI Military History Circle, 6 May 1987.
8   M. Gilbert (Ed.), *The Churchill War Papers*, Vol I, At The Admiralty, p.6
9   A.J. Marder, *From The Dardanelles To Oran*, p.110.

10   Cunningham Papers, BM Add. Mss 52565.
11   Vice Admiral J. Ashley Waller, Naval Assistant to Pound, October 1941–June 1943, quoted by A.J. Marder, *From The Dardanelles to Oran*, p.176.
12   Ibid, p.176.
13   Mountbatten to Godfrey, 18 November 1964, Godfrey papers, GDFY.
14   R. Macleod & D. Kelly (Ed), *The Ironside Diaries, 1937–1940*, p.268.
15   Lord Ismay, *The Memoirs of Lord Ismay*, p.109.
16   Ibid., p.111.
17   Kennedy papers, LKEN 23.
18   Blake papers, BLE/9.
19   Brockman to the author.
20   Cunningham Papers, BM Add Mss 52560.
21   Pound papers, DUPO 5/1.

CHAPTER 9. NORWAY. (PAGES 126 TO 147)
1   J. Broome, *Convoy Is To Scatter*, p.79.
2   W.S. Churchill, *The Gathering Storm*, p.589–590.
3   Ibid.
4   J.S. Cowie, *Mines, Minelayers And Minelaying*, p.135.
5   Churchill broadcast of 20 January, *The Churchill War Papers*, Vol I, At The Admiralty, p.668.
6   ADM 205/6.
7   Ibid.
8   Cunningham Papers, BM Add Mss, 52563.
9   Operation Catherine is covered by ADM 205/4 and ADM 199/1928. All unattributed quotations are to be found in these.
10   W.S. Churchill, *The Gathering Storm*, p.365.
11   Godfrey, Naval memoirs, Vol vii, Pt 2, p.223, GDFY.
12   Ibid.
13   A.J. Marder, *From The Dardanelles To Oran*, p.146.
14   Admiral Sir Guy Grantham, quoted in Marder, Ibid, p.137.
15   Cunningham papers, BM Add Mss 52565.
16   Ibid, p.225.
17   Quoted in S.W. Roskill, *The War At Sea*, Vol I, p.27.
18   Alexander papers, 'Winston and the Altmark', AVAR 5/4/1.
19   W.S. Churchill, ibid p.444.
20   Ibid, p.445.
21   S.W. Roskill, ibid p.152.
22   Marder, ibid, p.137.
23   ADM 199/1928
24   Marder, ibid p.154.

25 Admiral Sir Ralph Edwards' diary, REDW 1/2.
26 A.J. Marder, "Winston Is Back: Churchill At The Admiralty, 1939–40", published in *From The Dardanelles To Oran*.
27 All three, and others, in ADM 199/1929.
28 Ibid.
29 Ibid.
30 Roskill, op cit p.187.
31 P.G. Halpern, *The Keyes Papers*, Vol III, p.8.
32 Ibid, p.15.
33 Ibid, p.16.
34 Ibid, p.23.
35 Ibid, p.32.
36 Ibid, p.33.
37 Ibid, p.34–35.
38 Ibid, p.35.
39 Ibid, p.36–40.
40 Ibid, p.42.

CHAPTER 10. THE FRENCH AND THEIR FLEET. (PAGES 148 TO 171)

1   A.J. Marder, *From The Dardanelles To Oran*, p.180.
2   M. Stephen, *The Fighting Admirals*, p.60.
3   ADM 205/4.
4   CAB 80/12 COS (40) 44.
5   CAB 65/13 WM (40) 168.
6   E. Spears, *Assignment To Catastrophe*, p.591.
7   W.S. Churchill, *Their Finest Hour*, p.185.
8   E. Gates, *End Of The Affair*, p.423.
9   ADM 205/4.
10 Hansard, series 5, vol. 362, col 304–5.
11 D Dilks (Ed), *The Diaries Of Sir Alexander Cadogan*, p.305.
12 FO 371/24348.
13 FO 371/24311.
14 FO 371/24328.
15 CAB 65/14 WM(40) 190.
16 Edwards Diary, REDW 1/2.
17 Godfrey to J.P.L. Thomas (late 1954), quoted by Marder, Ibid, p.221.
18 Brockman to Marder (22 May 1972) quoted by Marder, Ibid, p.221.
19 CAB 80/14, COS (40) 510.
20 Both quotations, Somerville Papers, SMVL 7/19.
21 Alexander in the House of Lords, 26 July 1954. Hansard, series 5 (Lords), vol. 139, col. 96.

22   Somerville Papers, SMVL 7/19.
23   CAB 65/14, WM (40) 190.
24   CAB 65/8.
25   *The Times*, 11 October 1986.
26   Viscount Cunningham, *A Sailor's Odyssey*, p.250.
27   CAB 65/14 WM (40) 192.
28   P. Beesly, *Very Special Admiral*, p.160.
29   Quoted in Marder, op cit p.245.
30   Marder, ibid, p.251.
31   Cunningham papers, MB Add Mss 52575.
32   Churchill, op cit p.211.
33   J. Colville, introduction to W. Tute, *The Deadly Stroke*, p.17.
34   Quoted in Marder, ibid, p.282.
35   M. Muggeridge (ed), *Ciano's Diary*, 1939–43, p.274.
36   J.R.M. Butler, *Grand Strategy*, Vol II, p.22737.
37   Quoted in Churchill, op cit pp.203–4.
38   CAB 66/7 WP (40) 168 and 169.
39   Quoted in Roskill, *War At Sea*, Vol I, p.249.
40   Ibid, p.257.
41   Roskill, p.311.
42   A.J. Marder, *Operation Menace*, C. and D. Plimmer, *A Matter Of Expediency*, N. Monks, *That Day At Gibraltar*. All quotations are from ADM 1/19180–19187, unless specified.
43   Letter from Gretton to Marder, 29 September 1973, quoted in Marder, p.198.
44   North Commentary, copy in Somerville Papers, SMVL 7/4.
45   Brockman to Marder, 3 November 1973.

CHAPTER 11. MID-WAR CRISES. (PAGES 172 TO 192)

1   Somerville's Report of Proceedings, Somerville Papers, SMVL 7/5.
2   Ibid., SMVL 3/22.
3   M Simpson (Ed), *The Somerville Papers*, p.66.
4   Blake Papers, BLE/9.
5   Somerville papers, SMVL 7/21.
6   Ibid., SMVL 7/21.
7   Cunningham Papers, BM Add Mss 52560.
8   M. Chalmers, *Max Horton and Western Approaches*, p.100–102.
9   ADM 205/7.
10   Quoted in J. Terraine, *The Right Of The Line*, p.243.
11   ADM 223/78.
12   C. Barnett, *Engage The Enemy More Closely*, p.298–9.

13 J. Colville, *The Fringes Of Power*, p.391.
14 Admiral Sir William Davis, Roskill Papers, ROSK 4/17.
15 Ibid.
16 ROSK 4/17. Churchill admits the authorship in *The Grand Alliance*, p.282.
17 ADM 234/322.
18 Austin papers, Library of Congress, Container 1.
19 Cunningham Papers, BM Add Mss 52561.
20 Colville, p.424.
21 Churchill, *The Grand Alliance*, p.382.
22 Sir Ian Jacob's diary, quoted in C. Richardson, *From Churchill's Secret Circle To The BBC*, pp.63–4.
23 Ibid, p.65.
24 D. Dilks (Ed), *The Diaries Of Sir Alexander Cadogan*, p.397.
25 S.E. Morrison, *The Battle Of The Atlantic, 1939–1943*, p.46.
26 Cunningham Papers, BM Add Mss 52561.
27 Ibid.
28 Colville, p.297.
29 Quoted in J. Langdon, "Too Old Or Too Bold? The Removal of Sir Roger Keyes as Churchill's first Director of Combined Operations" in *Imperial War Museum Review* No. 8, p.80.
30 ADM 234/320.
31 Cunningham Papers, BM Add Mss 52561.
32 ROSK 4/63.

CHAPTER 12. FORCE Z. (PAGES 193 TO 203)

1   ADM 234/330.
2   ADM 205/6 dated 1 August 1940, memorandum from Pound to A.V. Alexander on the redistribution of the Fleet in the event of war with Japan.
3   PREM 3/163/3. Pound to Churchill, 28 August 1941.
4   ADM 116/4877.
5   ADM 199/1934.
6   ADM 205/10.
7   ADM 205/10.
8   CAB 69/2.
9   Barnett, p.397.
10 ROSK 4/79.
11 Both quotations from CAB 69/2.
12 Marder, *Old Friends, New Enemies*, p.226.
13 CAB 79/24, COS (41) 360th.
14 Ibid.
15 CAB 69/8, DO (41) 66th.

16 US Operational Archives. Central Security Classified Records, Secretary of the Navy/Chief of Naval Operations, Secret file, (SC) A-4-3EF13.
17 Marder, p.228.
18 ADM 205/10.
19 ADM 205/7.
20 Cunningham papers, BM Add Mss 52563.
21 Marder, p.367.
22 Pound papers, DUPO 3/6.
23 Quoted in Marder, p.231.
24 Godfrey, Naval Memoirs, Vol vii, Pt 2, p.259. GDFY.
25 Quoted by Marder, p.239.
26 W.S. Churchill, *The Grand Alliance*, p.551.
27 Quoted in Marder, p.497.
28 Pound papers, DUPO 3/6.
29 ADM 199/1149.
30 Cunningham papers, BM Add Mss 52561.
31 Marder, p.501.

CHAPTER 13. ALLIES, ENEMIES AND FRIENDS. (PAGES 204 TO 229)

1 Ismay, *The Memoirs of . . .*, p.163.
2 Richardson, *From Churchill's Circle To The BBC*, p.89.
3 Letter King to Stark, copy in Simpson B. Mitchell papers for his biography of Harold B. Stark. Mss Coll 155, Box 9 File 2. Newport War College, USA.
4 Churchill, *Grand Alliance*, p.626.
5 Cunningham papers, BM Add Mss 52561.
6 *The Times*, 14 February 1942.
7 T. Robertson, *Channel Dash*, p.169.
8 PREM 3/119/6, all three letters, 4 March, 5 March and 6 March.
9 A. Bryant, *The Turn Of The Tide*, p.318.
10 PREM 3/119/6.
11 PREM 3/119/6, letter of 7 March 1042.
12 PREM 3/330/2.
13 Mitchell Simpson, *Stark*, p.141.
14 Quoted in ibid, p.144. Emphasis in the original.
15 Blake papers BLE/9.
16 Roskill, *The War At Sea*, Vol II, p.92.
17 CAB 69/4 DO(42) 23, dated 5 March 1942.
18 S.E. Morrison, *The Battle of the Atlantic*,1939–43, p.131.
19 ADM 205/18.
20 All three quotations in Roskill, *War At Sea*, Vol II, p.97.
21 ADM 205/14, 17 June 1942.

22 Both minutes are in ADM 205/14.
23 Roskill, *Churchill and the Admirals*, p.189.
24 Cunningham papers, BM Add Mss 52561.
25 Godfrey, Naval memoirs, Vol v, Pt 2, p.312, GDFY.
26 Letter from Barbara Duff to the author, 23 October 1998.
27 National Archives, Washington, Flag Files COMNAVEU.
28 Somerville papers, SMVL 8/1.
29 Quoted in Edwards diary, REDW 2/8.
30 M. Simpson, *The Somerville Papers*, p.359.
31 ADM 205/14.
32 M. Howard, *Grand Strategy*, Vol IV, p.xxi.
33. J. Martin *Downing Street. The War Years*, p.83.

CHAPTER 14. PQ 17. (PAGES 230 TO 258)

1 P. Beesly, British Naval Intelligence In Two World Wars, in *Intelligence and International Relations 1900–1945*, Eds. C. Andrew and J. Noakes, p.262.
2 Alan G. Kirk, Oral History, p.210 Newport. Rhode Island.
3 D. McLachlan, *Room 39, Naval Intelligence In Action 1939–45*, p.118.
4 For a fuller understanding of the workings of naval intelligence 1939–45 see D. McLachlan, ibid, P. Beesly *Very Special Intelligence* and *Very Special Admiral*, and F.H. Hinsley et al, *British Intelligence In The Second World War*, 4 Vols.
5 Pound papers, DUPO 8/1.
6 Ibid., DUPO 2/2.
7 J. Ellis, *Brute Force*, Tables 35 and 36, p.547.
8 For the Arctic Convoys in general see B.B. Scholfield *The Russian Convoys* and R. Woodman *Arctic Convoys*.
9 S.W. Roskill, *The War At Sea*, Volume II, p.124–5.
10 ADM 234/369.
11 Ibid.
12 CAB 69/4, DO 42 (37).
13 All three quotations from Ed. W.F. Kimball, *Churchill and Roosevelt. The Complete Correspondence*. Volume I.
14 ADM 234/369.
15 ADM 205/19.
16 ADM 234/369.
17 The literature on PQ17 is vast. Much of it concerns the experience of those who sailed in it. The most important on the decision making process, and on Pound's part in it are F.H. Hinsley, Volume II, S.W. Roskill, Volume II, D. Irving, *The Destruction Of Convoy PQ17*, J. Broome *Convoy Is To Scatter*, and D. Mclachlan, *Room 39*.
18 ADM 234/369.

19 Quoted by Roskill, *Churchill and the Admirals*, p.130.
20 Both messages and all subsequent messages from OIC are in Hinsley, Vol II, pp.686–8.
21 Roskill, Vol 2, p.138.
22 Rear Admiral E.J.P. Brind was ACNS (H), Captain J. Eccles DOD(H), Captain J.W. Clayton Deputy Director OIC.
23 There is no contemporary record of this or subsequent exchanges. The only participant who left a written account was Denning, written in 1979. It is held at Churchill College, Cambridge, ROSK 5/72.
24 Ibid.
25 D. Irving, p.116–121. The account here is based on this.
26 All three signals can be found in Roskill Vol II, p.139.
27 J. Broome, p.182.
28 Conan Doyle, *The Memoirs of Sherlock Holmes*, The Silver Blaze.
29 Maisky's memoirs, quoted in Irving, p.295.
30 CAB 65/31.
31 Churchill, *The Hinge of Fate*, p.236.
32 ADM 205/20, dated 15 June 1942.
33 ADM 205/20.
34 Somerville papers, SMVL 8/1.
35 Roskill, *Churchill And The Admirals*, p.231, footnote 21.
36 The best account of this episode is P. Beesly, *Very Special Admiral*, Chapter 11.
37 R. Humble, *Fraser Of North Cape*, p.149.
38 CAB 65/31.
39 Letter from Dan Duff to the author, 23 October 1998.
40 Roskill, Vol 2, p.306.
41 Imperial War Museum, Whitworth Papers.
42 B. Loring Villa, *Unauthorised Action. Mountbatten and the Dieppe Raid 1942*, p.107.
43 Cunningham papers, BM Add Mss 52561.
44 For this complicated episode see Roskill, Vol II, p.229–231.
45 Cunningham papers, BM Add Mss 52561.
46 Ibid.
47 W.S. Chalmers, *Max Horton And Western Approaches*, p.69.
48 Ibid, p.146.
49 Roskill, Vol II, p.317.
50 Ibid, p.322.
51 Ibid, p.339.

CHAPTER 15. THE BATTLE FOR THE AIR. (PAGES 259 TO 277)

1   H.C. Butcher, *My Three Years With Eisenhower*, p.239.
2   ADM 116/469, 4 December 1940.
3   C. Barnett, *Engage The Enemy More Closely*, p.430.
4   CAB 69/4, 5 January 1942.
5   D. Syrett (Ed), *The Battle of the Atlantic and Signals Intelligence: U-boat Situations and trends, 1941–45*, p.10.
6   AHB/II/117/3.
7   Cunningham papers, BM Add Mss 52570.
8   Both letters, Stark papers, Box 8.
9   CAB 69/4 DO(42) 23.
10 AHB/II/117/3.
11 This and subsequent quotations CAB 69/4 DO (42) 23.
12 CAB 69/4, DO(42)24, 8 March 1942.
13 E. Bramall and W. Jackson, *The Chiefs*, p.199.
14 CAB 69/4, DO(42) 47, 20 May 1942.
15 ADM 205/15.
16 W.S. Chalmers, *Max Horton and Western Approaches*, p.100–101.
17 ADM 234/578.
18 CAB 79/20 COS(42) 180, minute 12.
19 C. Webster and N. Frankland, *The Strategic Air Offensive Against Germany 1939–1945*, Vol I, p.340.
20 CAB 66/26, WP (42)311.
21 ADM 205/24.
22 CAB 70/3 DO(S) (42) 88.
23 CAB 66/30 WP (42) 311.
24 CAB 80/65 COS(42) 379.
25 ADM 205/27.
26 S.W. Roskill, Volume II, Appendix O.
27 Barnett, p.476.
28 ADM 234/578 p.103.
29 ADM 234/578, p.106.
30 National Archives II, Washington, COMNAVEUR papers. SH series, No. 140, dated 19 March 1943.
31 CAB 86/3 AU(43) 90.
32 F.H. Hinsley, *British Intelligence In The Second World War*, Volume II, p.571.
33 Whitworth papers, Imperial War Museum.
34 Cunningham papers, BM Add Mss 52561.

CHAPTER 16. EBB TIDE. (PAGES 278 TO 286)

1   *Evening Standard*, 25 May 1943.
2   Goldrick papers, Brockman to Goldrick, 14 January 1989.
3   *The Times*, 24 July 1943.
4   P. Kemp, Sir Dudley Pound, in S. Howarth (Ed), *Men Of War. Great Naval Leaders of World War II*, p.40.
5   Noble to Cunningham 23 December 1943. Cunningham papers, BM Add Mss 52571.
6   This and the previous quotation from William Goody MD FRCP, Neurological factors in Decision-Making, in J. Watt, E.J. Freeman and W.J. Bynum (Eds) *Starving Sailors*, pp.195–8.
7   Information from the Pound family.
8   ADM 196/90.

BIBLIOGRAPHY

1. Unpublished Sources.

1. *Public Record Office.*

ADM 1	Admiralty and Secretariat papers.
ADM 116	Admiralty and Secretariat Records.
ADM 178	Admiralty and Secretariat Papers.
ADM 186	Naval Staff Histories.
ADM 196	Officers' Service Records.
ADM 199	War Histories and Cases.
ADM 205	First Sea Lord's Papers.
ADM 223	Naval Intelligence Papers.
ADM 234	Naval Staff Histories.
AIR 41	Air Historical Branch, Specialist Monographs and Narratives.
CAB 65	War Cabinet Minutes.
CAB 66	War Cabinet Memoranda.
CAB 69	War Cabinet Defence Committee (Operations).
CAB 70	War Cabinet Defence Committee (Supply).
CAB 79	Chiefs of Staff Committee, Minutes.
CAB 80	Chiefs of Staff Committee, Memoranda.
CAB 86	Battle of the Atlantic Committee.
FO 371	General Correspondence, Political.
PREM 3	Prime Minister's papers, Operational Files.

2. *Churchill Archives Centre, Churchill College, Cambridge.*

AVAR   Earl Alexander of Hillsborough: political papers.

CUNN	Admiral of the Fleet Viscount Cunningham of Hyndhope: papers collected for the biography by Oliver Warner.
DUPO	Admiral of the Fleet Sir Dudley Pound: papers collected for a biography by Donald McLachlan.
GDFY	Admiral J.H. Godfrey: Memoirs.
LKEN	Captain Leo Kennedy: diaries as diplomatic correspondent of *The Times*.
NRTH	Admiral Sir Dudley North: Papers concerning his dismissal from command, Gibraltar, 1940.
REDW	Vice Admiral Sir Ralph Edwards: Naval papers.
ROSK	Captain Stephen Roskill: Historical and family papers.
SMVL	Admiral Sir James Somerville: Naval and personal papers.
TOMK	Admiral Sir Wilfred Tomkinson: Naval papers.
WLLS	Admiral of the Fleet Sir Algernon Willis: Naval Papers.

3. *Imperial War Museum.*
Admiral of the Fleet Sir Dudley Pound papers, LS Box 92/53/1, and Misc G6.
Admiral of the Fleet Sir Algernon Willis papers, Box P186.
Admiral Sir William Whitworth papers.
Vice Admiral AG Talbot papers.
Rear Admiral AD Nicholl papers.
Captain A.V. Walker papers.
Lt Col A.D. Melville papers, 92/15/1.
Gerald Pawle papers.
Joan Bright-Astley papers.

4. *British Museum.*
Cunningham papers, including a file of the papers of Sir Charles Forbes. BM Add Mss, 52559–52574.

4. *National Maritime Museum.*
BLE/	Admiral Sir Geoffrey Blake papers.
CHT/	Admiral of the Fleet Lord Chatfield papers.
COW/	Admiral Sir Walter Cowan papers.
FHR/	Admiral Sir William Fisher papers.
GRO/	Vice Admiral Baillie-Grohman papers.
HTN/	Rear Admiral Sir Louis Hamilton papers.
KEL/	Admiral of the Fleet Sir John Kelly papers.
PWL/	Admiral Sir Henry Pridham-Wippell papers.
TEN/	Vice Admiral Sir William Tennant papers.
Ms93/008	Vice Admiral Sir Peter Gretton papers.

5. *National Archives, Washington DC, USA.*
RG30   Records of COMNAVEUR.
RG38   Records of the US Naval Attaché in London 1937–43.

6. *Operational Archives Centre, Washington DC, USA.*
Papers of Admiral Alan G. Kirk.
Papers of Admiral Harold R. Stark.
Oral Histories: Rear Admiral C.W. Ansel.
                  Vice Admiral B.H. Bieri.

7. *Naval War College, Newport, Rhode Island, USA.*
MSS Coll 155   Simpson B. Mitchell papers for biography of Admiral Harold R. Stark.
Oral Histories   Admiral Alan G. Kirk.
                 Vice Admiral J.L. McCrea.
                 Rear Admiral H.B. Miller.
                 Rear Admiral E.M. Eller.

8. *Library of Congress, Washington DC, USA.*
Papers of Vice Admiral B.L. Austin.
Papers of Fleet Admiral E.J. King.

2.   PUBLISHED BOOKS.
All published in London, unless specified.

Adams J., *The Doomed Expedition*. Leo Cooper, 1989.
Andrew C. & Noakes J., *Intelligence and International Relations 1900–1945*. Exeter Studies In History, 1987.
Aspinall-Oglander C., *Roger Keyes*. Hogarth Press, 1951.
Beesly, P., *Very Special Intelligence*. Hamish Hamilton, 1977.
    Very Special Admiral, Hamish Hamilton, 1980.
Barnett C., *The Swordbearers*, Hodder & Stoughton, 1987.
    Engage The Enemy More Closely, Hodder & Stoughton, 1991.
Bell P.M.H., *A Certain Eventuality*. Saxon House, 1974.
Bennett G., *Jutland*. Batsford, 1964.
    Naval Battles of the First World War. Batsford, 1968.
Blake R. and Louis W.R. (Eds), *Churchill*. OUP, 1993.
Bramall E. and Jackson W., *The Chiefs*. Brasseys, 1992.
Bright Astley J., *The Inner Circle. A View of War at the Top*. Hutchinson, 1971.
Broome J., *Convoy Is To Scatter*. Futura, 1974.

Bryant A., *The Turn Of The Tide*. Collins, 1957.

Butcher H.C., *My Three Years With Eisenhower*. Simon & Schuster, 1946.

Butler, J.R.M., *Grand Strategy, Vol II, September 1939–June 1941*, HMSO 1957.

Calvocoressi P., *Top Secret Ultra*. Sphere, 1981.

Campbell N.J.M., *Jutland: An Analysis of the Fighting*. Conway Maritime Press, 1986.

Chalmers W.S., *The Life And Letters of David, Earl Beatty*, Hodder & Stoughton, 1951.

> *Max Horton And Western Approaches*. Hodder & Stoughton, 1954.
> *Full Cycle, The Biography of Admiral Sir Bertram Ramsay*. Hodder & Stoughton, 1959.

Charmley J., *Duff Cooper*, Papermac, 1987.

Chatfield Lord, *The Navy and Defence*. Heinemann, 1942.

> *It Might Happen Again*, Heinemann, 1947.

Churchill R.S., *Winston Churchill*, Vol II, *Young Statesman, 1901–1914*. Heinemann, 1961.

Churchill W.S., *The World Crisis 1911–1918*, 2 Vols. Odhams Press, 1938.

> *The Second World War*, Vol I *The Gathering Storm*,
> Vol II *Their Finest Hour*,
> Vol III *The Grand Alliance*,
> Vol IV *The Hinge Of Fate*,
> Vol V *Closing the Ring*. Cassell 1948–1952.

Coles A. and Briggs T., *Flagship Hood*. Robert Hale, 1985.

Coles A., *Invergordon Scapegoat. The Betrayal of Admiral Tomkinson*. Alan Sutton, 1993.

Collier R., *1940. The World In Flames*. Penguin, 1980.

Colville J., *Footprints In Time*. Collins, 1976.

> *The Churchillians*. Weidenfeld & Nicolson, 1981.
> *The Fringes of Power. Downing Street Diaries 1939–1955*. Hodder & Stoughton, 1985.

Cooper D., *Old Men Forget*. Century Publishing, 1986.

Corbett Sir Julian S., *Naval Operations*, Vol I, II and III. Longmans, 1920–1923.

Cosgrave, *Churchill At War, Alone 1939–40*. Collins, 1974.

Costello J. and Hughes T., *Jutland 1916*. Weidenfeld & Nicolson, 1976.

> *The Battle Of The Atlantic*. Collins, 1977.

Cowie J.S., *Mines, Minelayers and Minelaying*. OUP, 1949.

Cowman I., *Dominion Or Decline. Anglo-American Naval Relations In The Pacific, 1937–1941*. Berg, 1996.

Cray E., *General Of The Army. George C. Marshall, Soldier and Statesman*. Simon & Schuster (New York), 1990.

Cunningham, Admiral of the Fleet Lord, *A Sailor's Odyssey*. Hutchinson, 1951.

Danchev A., *Establishing The Anglo-American Alliance. The Second World War Diaries of Brigadier Vivian Dykes*. Brassey's, 1990.

Dear I.C.B. and Foot M.R.D. (Eds), *The Oxford Companion To The Second World War*. OUP, 1995.

Dilks D. (Ed), *The Diaries Of Sir Alexander Cadogan, 1938–1945*. Cassell, 1971.

Edwards K., *The Mutiny At Invergordon*, Putman, 1937.
   Men of Action. Collins, 1943.

Ehrman J., *Grand Strategy*, Vol V, *August 1943–September 1944*. HMSO, 1956.

Ellis J., *Brute Force. Allied Strategy and Tactics in the Second World War*. Andre Deutsch, 1990.

Ereira A., *The Invergordon Mutiny*. Routledge & Kegan Paul, 1981.

Fergusson B., *The Watery Maze The Story of Combined Operations*. Collins, 1961.

Fraser D., *Alanbrooke*. Collins, 1982.

Freedman L. et al, (Eds), *War, Strategy and International Politics. Essays in Honour of Sir Michael Howard*. Clarendon Press, 1992.

Gardiner L, *The British Admiralty*. Blackwood, 1968.

Gates E.M., *End Of The Affair. The Collapse of the Anglo-French Alliance, 1939–40*. George Allen & Unwin, 1981.

Gilbert M., *Winston S. Churchill*, Vol III, *1914–1916*. Heinemann, 1971.
   Winston S. Churchill, Vol IV, *1917–1922*. Heinemann, 1975.
   Winston S. Churchill, Vol V, *1922–1939*. Heinemann, 1976.
   Winston S. Churchill, Vol VI, *Finest Hour, 1939–1941*. Heinemann, 1983.
   Winston S. Churchill, Vol VII, *Road To Victory, 1941–1945*. Heinemann, 1986.
   The Churchill War Papers, Vol I, *At The Admiralty, September 1939–May 1940*. Heinemann, 1993.
   The Churchill War Papers, Vol II, *Never Surrender, May 1940–December 1940*. Heinemann, 1994.

Glenton R., *The Royal Oak Affair*. Leo Cooper, 1991.

Gordon A., *The Rules Of The Game*. John Murray, 1996.

Greene J. and Massignani A., *The Naval War In The Mediterranean 1940–43*. Chatham Publishing, 1998.

Grenfell R., *The Bismarck Episode*. Faber & Faber, 1953.
   Main Fleet To Singapore. OUP, 1987.

Gretton P., *Convoy Escort Commander*. Cassell, 1984.
   Former Naval Person. Winston Churchill and the Royal Navy. Cassell, 1968.

Grove E. (Ed), *The Defeat Of The Enemy Attack On Shipping, 1939–1945*. Naval Records Society, 1997.

Gwyer J.M.A., *Grand Strategy*, Vol III Pt 1, *June 1941–August 1942*. HMSO, 1964.

Halpern P.G., (Ed) *The Keyes Papers*, Vol I, *1914–1918*.
   Vol II, *1919–1938*.

Vol III, *1939–1945*. Naval Records Society, 1979, 1980, and 1981.

A Naval History Of World War I. UCL Press, 1994.

Handel M.I. (Ed), *Intelligence And Military Operations*. Frank Cass, 1990.

Hankey M., *The Supreme Command*, Vol I. Allen & Unwin, 1961.

Harper J.E.T., *The Truth About Jutland*. John Murray, 1927.

Hattendorf J.B. (Ed), *On His Majesty's Service. Observations of the British Home Fleet from the Diary, Reports and Letters of Joseph H. Wellings, Assistant Naval Attaché, London, 1940–41*. Naval War College Press, Newport, Rhode Island, USA 1983.

Hinsley F.H. and Thomas E.E., Ransom C.F.G., Knight R.C., *British Intelligence In The Second World War. Its Influence on Strategy And Operations*. Vols I and II. HMSO, 1979 and 1981.

Hill J.R. (Ed), *The Oxford Illustrated History Of The Royal Navy*. OUP, 1995.

Hough R., *The Great War At Sea 1914–18*, OUP 1983.

The Longest Battle. The War At Sea, 1939–45. Weidenfeld & Nicolson, 1986.

Former Naval Person. Churchill and the Wars at Sea. Weidenfeld & Nicolson, 1987.

Howard M., *Grand Strategy*, Vol IV, *August 1942–September 1943*. HMSO, 1972.

The Continental Commitment. The Dilemma of British Defence Policy in the Era of Two World Wars. Pelican, 1974.

British Intelligence In The Second World War. Vol V, *Strategic Deception*. HMSO, 1990.

The Mediterranean Strategy In The Second World War. Greenhill Books, 1993.

Howarth P., *Intelligence Chief Extraordinary. The Life of the Ninth Duke of Portland*. The Bodley Head 1986.

Howarth S. (Ed), *Men Of War. Great Naval Leaders Of World War II*. Weidenfeld & Nicolson, 1992.

Humble R., *Fraser Of North Cape*. Routledge & Kegan Paul, 1983.

Irving D., *The Destruction of Convoy PQ17*. Cassell, 1968 and 1980.

Irving J., *The Smoke Screen of Jutland*. William Kimber, 1966.

Ismay Lord, *The Memoirs of Lord Ismay*. Heinemann, 1960.

Jellicoe, Admiral Viscount . . . of Scapa, *The Grand Fleet, 1914–16*. Cassell, 1919.

The Crisis Of The Naval War. Cassell, 1920.

Kahn D., *Seizing The Enigma. The Race to Break the German U-boat Codes, 1939–43*. Souvenir Press, 1992.

Keegan J., *The Second World War*. Hutchinson, 1989.

Kennedy L., *Pursuit. The Sinking of the Bismarck*. Fontana, 1982.

Menace. The Life and death of the Tirpitz. Sphere, 1981.

On My Way To The Club. Fontana, 1990.

Kennedy P.M., *The Rise And Fall Of British Naval Mastery*. Macmillan, 1983.

Strategy And Diplomacy, 1870–1945. Fontana, 1984.

Kersaudy F., *Norway 1940*. Collins, 1990.

Keyes Admiral of the Fleet Sir Roger, *The Naval Memoirs of. . . Scapa Flow to the Dover Straits, 1916–1918*. Thornton & Butterworth, 1935.

Kimball W.F., (Ed), *Churchill and Roosevelt. The Complete Correspondence*, 3 vols. Collins, 1984.

King E.J. and Whitehill W.M., *Fleet Admiral King. A Naval Record*. Eyre & Spotiswood, 1953.

Lamb R., *Churchill As War Leader – Right Or Wrong?* Bloomsbury, 1993.

Law D., *The Royal Navy In World War Two. An Annotated Bibliography*. Greenhill Books, 1988.

Lewin R., *Ultra Goes To War. The Secret Story*. Hutchinson, 1978.

Love R.W. (Ed), *The Chiefs Of Naval Operations*. Naval Institute Press (New York), 1980.
The Year Of D-Day. The 1944 Diary of Admiral Sir Bertram Ramsay. University of Hull Press, 1994.

Macintyre, D., *Narvik*. Evans Brothers, 1959.
Fighting Admiral. The Life of Admiral of the Fleet Sir James Somerville.
Evans Brothers, 1961.
The Battle Of The Atlantic. Pan Books, 1969.

Macleod R. and Kelly D., *The Ironside Diaries 1937–1940*. Constable, 1962.

Marder A.J., *From The Dreadnoughts To Scapa Flow*, 5 Vols. OUP, 1963.
From The Dardanelles To Oran. Studies of the Royal Navy in War and Peace, 1915–1940. OUP, 1974.
Operation Menace. The Dakar Expedition and the Dudley North Affair. OUP, 1976.
Old Friends, New Enemies. The Royal Navy and the Imperial Japanese Navy. Strategic Illusions 1936–1941. OUP, 1981.

Marder A.J., Jacobsen M., and Horsfield J., *Old Friends, New Enemies. The Royal Navy and the Imperial Japanese Navy. The Pacific War 1942–1945*. OUP, 1990.

Martin J., *Downing Street. The War Years*. Bloomsbury, 1991.

McGeoch I., *The Princely Sailor. Mountbatten of Burma*. Brassey's, 1996.

McLachlan D., *Room 39. Naval Intelligence in Action, 1939–45*. Weidenfeld & Nicolson, 1968.

Middlebrook M. and Mahoney P., *Battleship. The Loss of the Prince of Wales and the Repulse*. Allen Lane, 1977.

Mitchell S.B., *Harold B. Stark*. New York, 1982.

Monks N., *That Day At Gibraltar*. Muller, 1957.

Montagu E., *The Man Who Never Was*. Corgi Books, 1968.
Beyond Top Secret U. Peter Davies, 1977.

Morrison S.E., *American Contributions To The Strategy Of World War II*. OUP, 1958.

History Of United States Naval Operations In World War II,
Vol I, *The Battle Of The Atlantic, September 1939–May 1943*.
Vol II, *Operations in North African Waters, October 1942–June 1943*.
Vol IX, *Sicily, Salerno, Anzio, January 1943–June 1944*.
Vol X, *The Atlantic Battle Won, May 1943–May 1945*. Little & Brown New York, 1975.

Moulton J.L., *The Norwegian Campaign Of 1940. A Study of Warfare in Three Dimensions*. Eyre & Spotiswood, 1966.

Muggeridge M. (Ed), *Ciano's Diary, 1939–1943*. Heinemann, 1947.

Mullenheim-Rechberg Baron von, *Battleship Bismarck. A Survivor's Story*. Arms and Armour Press, 1991.

Murfett M.H. (Ed), *The First Sea Lords. From Fisher to Mountbatten*. Praeger, 1995.

Ollard R., *Fisher And Cunningham*. Constable, 1961.

Pack S.W., *The Battle Of Matapan*. Batsford, 1961.

Padfield P., *Doenitz. The Last Fuhrer*. Panther, 1985.
War Beneath The Sea. Submarine Conflict 1939–1945. John Murray, 1995.

Parker R.A.C., *Struggle For Survival*. OUP, 1989.

Parrish T., *Roosevelt And Marshall. Partners in Politics and War. The Personal Story*. William Morrow (New York), 1989.

Pawle G., *The War And Colonel Warden*. Harrap, 1963.

Plimmer C. and D., *A Matter Of Expediency. The Jettison of Admiral Sir Dudley North*. Quartet Books, 1978.

Potter J.D., *Fiasco. The Break-out of the German Battleships*. Stein & Day (New York), 1970.

Ranft B.McL. (Ed), *The Beatty Papers*, Vol I, *1902–1918*.
Vol II, *1916–1927*. Navy Records Society, 1989 and 1993.

Richardson C., *From Churchill's Secret Circle To The BBC. The Biography of Sir Ian Jacob*. Brassey's, 1991.

Roberts A., *Eminent Churchillians*. Weidenfeld & Nicolson, 1994.

Robertson T., *Channel Dash*. Evans Brothers, 1958.

Roskill S.W., *The War At Sea, 1939–1945*, Vol I, *The Defensive*,
Vol II, *The Period of Balance*,
Vol III pt 1, *The Offensive, June 1943–May 1944*. HMSO, 1954–1960.
The Secret Capture, Collins, 1959.
Hankey: Man of Secrets, Vol II, *1919–1931*. Collins, 1972.
Hankey: Man of Secrets, Vol III, *1931–1963*. Collins, 1974.
Naval Policy Between The Wars, Vol I, *1919–1929*. Collins, 1968.
Naval Policy Between The Wars, Vol II *1930–1939*. Collins, 1976.
Churchill And The Admirals, Collins, 1977.
HMS Warspite, US Naval Institute, 1997.

Saward D., *Bomber Harris*. Cassell, 1984.

Schofield B.B., *The Russian Convoys*. Pan, 1971.

Shakespeare G., *Let Candles Be Brought In*. Macdonald, 1949.

Shankland P. and Hunter A., *Malta Convoys*. Collins, 1961.

Simpson M. (Ed), *The Somerville Papers*, Naval Records Society, 1995.
    The Cunningham Papers, Vol I *1939–1942*, Naval Records Society, 1999.

Slessor J., *The Central Blue*. Cassell, 1956.

Spears E., *Assignment To Catastrophe*, Reprint Society, 1956.

Stephen M., *The Fighting Admirals. British Admirals of the Second World War*. Leo
    Cooper, 1991.

Syrett D. (Ed), *The Battle Of The Atlantic And Signals Intelligence: U-boat Situations
    and Trends, 1941–1945*. Naval Records Society, 1998.

Tarrant V.E., *Battleship Warspite*. Arms and Armour Press, 1990.

Temple Patterson A. (Ed), *The Jellicoe Papers*, Vol I, *1893–1916*.
    Vol II, *1916–1935*. Navy Records Society, 1967 & 1968.
    Tyrwhitt Of The Harwich Force. The Military Book Society, 1973.

Terraine J., *The Right Of The Line*. Hodder & Stoughton, 1985.
    Business In Great Waters. The U-boat Wars 1916–1945. Leo Cooper, 1989.

Thomas H., *The Spanish Civil War*. Penguin, 1977.

Till G., *Air Power And The Royal Navy 1914–1945. A Historical Survey*. Jane's,
    1979.

Tracy N., *The Collective Naval Defence Of The Empire, 1900–1940*. Naval Records
    Society, 1997.

Tute W., *The Deadly Stroke*. Collins, 1973.

Van der Vat D., *The Atlantic Campaign. The Great Struggle at Sea 1939–1945*.
    Hodder & Stoughton, 1988.

Villa B. Loring, *Unauthorised Action. Mountbatten and the Dieppe Raid*. OUP, 1989.

Warner O., *Cunningham of Hyndhope, Admiral of the Fleet*. John Murray, 1967.

Watt J., et al (Eds), *Starving Sailors*, National Maritime Museum, 1981.

Webster C. and Frankland N., *The Strategic Air Offensive Against Germany,
    1939–1945*. HMSO 1961.

Willmott H.P., *The Great Crusade*. Michael Joseph, 1989.

Winklareth R.J., *The Bismarck Chase. New Light on a Famous Engagement*.
    Chatham Publishing, 1998.

Winton J., *Carrier Glorious*. Leo Cooper, 1986.
    Ultra At Sea, Leo Cooper, 1988.
    Cunningham. John Murray, 1998.

Woodman R., *Arctic Convoys 1941–1945*. John Murray, 1994.

Woodward D., *Ramsay At War. The Fighting Life of Admiral Sir Bertram Ramsay*.
    William Kimber, 1957.

Zeigler P., *Mountbatten*, Collins, 1985.

3. UNPUBLISHED ARTICLES AND TALKS.

Admiral of the Fleet Sir Dudley Pound written by Geoffrey Blake, October 1943.

Admiral of the Fleet Sir Dudley Pound, by John Litchfield (undated).

Admiral of the Fleet Sir Dudley Pound, by Ronald Brockman, 1949.

Admiral of the Fleet Sir Dudley Pound, by Professor Peter Naylor at RUSI Military History Circle, 6 May 1987.

4. JOURNAL ARTICLES.

I. Cowman, Main Fleet to Singapore? Churchill, the Admiralty and Force Z. *The Journal of Strategic Studies*, 17(2), pp.79–93, (1994).

A. Danchev, Waltzing with Winston: Civil-Military Relations in Britain in the Second World War. *War in History* 2(2), pp.202–230, (1995).

J. Gardner, The Battle of the Atlantic, 1941. The First Turning Point? *The Journal of Strategic Studies*, 17(1), pp.109–123 (1994).

A. Gordon, The Admiralty and Imperial Overstretch, 1902–1941. *The Journal of Strategic Studies*, Vol. 17(1), pp.63–85 (1994).

D.G. Haglund, George C. Marshall and the Question of Military Aid to England, May–June 1940. *Journal of Contemporary History*, vol 15, pp.745–760, (1980).

A. Lambert, Seapower 1939–1940: Churchill and the Strategic Origins of the Battle of the Atlantic. *The Journal of Strategic Studies*, 17(1), pp.86–108 (1994).

J. Langdon, Too old or too bold? The removal of Sir Roger Keyes as Churchill's first Director of Combined Operations. *Imperial War Museum Review*, No 8, pp.72–84 1993.

P. Lowe, Great Britain and the Coming of the Pacific War, 1939–1941. *TRHS*, vol 24, pp.43–62 (1974).

D. Reynolds, Competitive Co-operation: Anglo-American relations in World War Two. *The Historical Journal*, 23(1), pp.233–245 (1980).

C.M. Scammell, The Royal Navy and the Strategic Origins of the Anglo-German Naval Agreement of 1935. *The Journal of Strategic Studies*, Vol 20(2), pp.92–118 (1997).

INDEX

Cadogan, Alexander, 157, 185
Cagliari, 173
Cairo, HMS, cruiser, 253
Callaghan, Admiral, 23
Campbell, Admiral, 48
Carter, Archibald, 118, 125, 170–1
Casablanca, 259–60
Cavendish-Bentinck, William, 251
Chamberlain, Austin, 79–82
Channel Dash, 208–11, 263
Chatfield, Admiral, Lord, 3, 6, 53,
    59, 62, 67, 73–4, 83, 86, 89–90,
    91, 95, 106–8, 115
Chelmsford, Lord, 51
Chetwode, Admiral, 74, 77–8, 79
Chilton, Admiral, 71–3
Churchill, Winston and *Altmark*,
    135–6; and Battle of Atlantic
    Committee, 177; and Bismarck,
    179–83; and Channel Dash,
    210–11; and convoys to Russia,
    237; and Cunningham AB, 162,
    189, 221–3; as First Lord,
    118–20; and Fisher J, 27–9, 119,
    120; and Force H, 174–5; and
    French fleet, 158–62; and French
    government, 152–5, 156; and
    Graf Spee, 133–4; and hunting
    U-boats, 125–9; and invasion of
    North Africa, 228; on Japanese
    threat, 193–7; on Jellicoe, 32;
    and Keyes, 141–7, 188; and
    Mountbatten, 213–15, 224; and
    Norway, 136–41; and Operation
    Catherine, 131–3; and Phillips,
    198; and Pound's resignation, 2;
    and PQ 17, 249; at Quebec,
    1943, 1; and sinking of *Prince of
    Wales* and *Repulse*, 199–200; and
    Somerville, 226; and Stark, 218;
    and strategy for 1943, 260–1,
    278–9; and Ten Year Rule, 44;
    on US entry to war, 204; attacks
    Royal Navy, 253–4; at
    Washington, 1941, 204–7; at

Washington, 1943, 2, 278–9;
    establishes Naval Staff College,
    21; proposes naval operations,
    37, 121–2, 135–6, 139–41; US
    ancestry, 8; visits Pound in
    hospital, 5
Ciano, Count, 165
Clayton, Captain, 231, 233, 243,
    245–7
Coastal Command, 176–7, 181, 187,
    209–10, 262–76
Colossus, HMS, battleship, 2, 29–35,
    47, 73
Colville, Jock, 5, 164
Colvin, Admiral, 81
Convoy, HG 76, 187; HX 228, 274;
    HX 229, 274; JW 51B, 249;
    JW 55B, 249; ON 166, 273;
    ONS 5, 275; PQ 12, 235–6;
    PQ 17, 239–49; PQ 18, 248–9,
    252; SC 118, 273; SC 121, 274;
    SC 122, 274
Convoying, 126–7
Cooper, Duff, 94, 108
Cork and Orrery, see Boyle
Cornwall, HMS, crusier, 226
Coronel, battle of, 25
Courageous, HMS, aircraft carrier, 128
Coventry, HMS, cruiser, 91
Cowan, Admiral, 47–9
Coward, Noel, 94
Creasy, Admiral, 59, 96, 125
Crete, battle of, 190–1
Cripps, Stafford, 254
Crutchley, Admiral, 90, 101
Cull, Paymaster Secretary, 95, 118
Cunningham, A.B. Admiral, 6, 7, 12,
    95–6, 197, 111–12, 116, 123,
    124, 160–2, 165, 172, 173, 175,
    183, 188, 189–92, 198, 202–3,
    218, 221, 223–4, 228, 253, 255,
    258, 269, 276–7, 285
Cunningham, J.H. Admiral, 111, 276
Curlew, HMS, cruiser, 92
Curzon, Lord, 51

314

Hamilton, Admiral, 238, 240–7
Hammond, Commander, US Navy, 123
Hankey, Maurice, 29, 44
Harmolov, Admiral, Russian Navy, 244
Harper, Admiral, 61–2
Harriman, Averill, 204
Harris, Air Marshal, 269–70
Harwood, Admiral, 50, 133, 174, 23, 276
Havock, HMS, destroyer, 97
Hemsted, Paymaster Secretary, 59–62, 70, 90, 95, 118
Henderson, Admiral, 104, 110, 115
Hermes, HMS, aircraft carrier, 194, 197, 226
Hewitt, Admiral, US Navy, 257
Hipper, German heavy cruiser, 176, 238
Hoare, Samuel, 94
Hodges, Admiral, 73, 80
Holland, Admiral, 178–9
Hood, HMS, battlecruiser, 47, 70, 81, 156, 178–9
Hopkins, Harry, 164, 184–5, 227–8
Horton, Admiral, 93, 96, 97, 176, 208, 256–7, 268–9, 273, 275, 286
Hotham, Captain, 95
Hudson, Captain, 117

Illustrious, HMS, aircraft carrier, 189, 197
Indomitable, HMS, aircraft carrier, 197, 253
Invergordon Mutiny, 79–83
Ironside, General, 120–1
Irving, David, 245
Ismay, General, 114, 123

Jacob, General, 114, 184–5, 206
James, Admiral, 54, 58, 109
Jellicoe, Admiral, 18, 22, 23, 30,
31–4, 35, 36, 37, 53, 56, 166, 286
Jerram, Admiral, 199
Joel, Commander, 2, 33–4
Joubert de la Ferté, Air Marshal, 265–6
Jutland, Battle of, 31–34

K, Force, 191, 220, 259
Kelly, Admiral, 81–2, 86
Kemp, Peter, 281
Kennedy-Purvis, Admiral, 107, 111, 250, 280
Keyes, Admiral, 6, 12, 15, 35, 39–40, 47–9, 50, 53–9, 73–4, 85, 104, 141–7, 187–8, 201, 251
King E., Admiral, US Navy, 186, 206, 216–17, 219, 220, 227–8, 237–8, 249, 255–6, 259–60, 273–4, 283
King, E.L.S, Admiral, 245
King George V, HMS, battleship, 178–81, 193, 225, 236, 254
Kirk, Admiral, US Navy, 231

Lambe, Admiral, 122, 204, 245–6
Layton, Admiral, 107, 111, 226
Leach, Captain, 180
League of Nations, 41, 42, 44, 51, 83
Lees, Admiral, 88–9
Lindemann, Professor, 185, 227
Litchfield-Speer, Captain, 91
Lithgow, Lord, 117
Little, Admiral, 6, 117, 218
Lutzow, German heavy cruiser, 238, 249
Lyster, Admiral, 175, 250

Madden, Admiral, 40, 47, 56–7, 62
Magnificent, HMS, battleship, 15
Maisky, Ivan, 249, 254
Malaya, HMS, battleship, 191, 193, 254
Manchester, HMS, cruiser, 178, 253
Marder, Arthur, 34, 115, 119, 136, 139–41

316

Markham, Henry, 171, 199
Marshall, General, US Army, 206, 216, 227–8, 260–1
Matapan, battle of, 189
May, Admiral, 16–17
Medhurst, Air Marshal, 251
Menzies, Stewart, 251
Miller, Surgeon Captain, 1–2, 280, 284
Melville, Colonel, 6
Montgomery, General, 276
Moore, Admiral, 111, 120, 202, 242, 245–6, 252, 273–4, 286
Mountbatten, Admiral, 1, 4, 47, 59, 119, 120, 213–15, 224, 281–2
Munich crisis, 108–9
Murray, Oswyn, 62, 80, 125

Naval Staff, divisions of, 117
Nelson, HMS, battleship, 81, 129, 193–5
Noble, Admiral, 176, 187, 221, 256, 273–4, 283
Norfolk, HMS, cruiser, 178–9
Norris, Admiral, 54, 75–7, 83, 89, 94, 103–4, 110, 114
North, Admiral, 85, 99, 125, 156, 167–71, 188
North Carolina, USS, battleship, 224–5
Norway, campaign, 136–41
Nyon, conference and patrols, 98, 111

OIC, 122, 187, 210, 231–2, 236, 242–7
Ohio, tanker, 253
Oppsoum, HMS, destroyer, 15
Onslow, Admiral, 103
Op. ANAKIM, 261; CATAPULT, 163–4, 169; CATHERINE, 120, 131–33; COLLAR, 173; DEMON, 189; DYNAMO, 149–51; GYMNAST/TORCH, 228, 255–8; HABBAKUK, 282–3; HUSKY, 261; JUPITER, 228; KNIGHT'S MOVE, 238, 241; MENACE, 168; PEDESTAL, 252–3; ROUNDUP, 227, 260–1; SLEDGEHAMMER, 227; TIGER, 190; WORKSHOP, 188
Oran, 98, 163–4

Pantelleria, 188
Parmoor, Lord, 51
Penelope, HMS, cruiser, 112
Phillips, Admiral, 58–9, 112, 123–5, 131, 132, 159, 179–83, 195–203, 233
Portal, Air Marshal, 1, 4, 6, 179, 204, 260–76, 283
Prinz Eugen, German heavy cruiser, 178–80, 249
Prince of Wales, HMS, battleship, 178–83, 183–7, 191, 193–203, 233
Pound, Barbara, 46, 90, 95, 224
Pound, Betty, 7, 17, 46, 65–6, 69, 84, 95, 223, 280
Pound, Dudley as ACQ, 67–79; and *Altmark*, 135–6; ancestry, British, 8; ancestry, US, 8–9; as ANCS, 59–66; appointed First Sea Lord, 111; and armistice terms, 1918, 40; awarded OM, 3, 284; and Bismarck, 178–83; birth, 10; chairman of CoS, change, 211–12; and Channel Dash, 208–11; and Chatfield, 62, 67, 88–9, 106–8, 109; as Chief of Staff, Med Fl., 53–9, 73, 88–90; on China station, 13; and choice as First Sea Lord, 112–16; and choice of chief of staff, 104–5; and Churchill, 38, 119–20, 146, 189, 193–8, 253–4, 260; and Coastal Command, 176–8, 209–10, 262–76; and Command of Main Fl., 108; and Command style, 59, 68–9, 104, 230–3; and

317

Pound, Dudley *(continued)*
    Command for TORCH, 180,
    222, 240; as C-in-C Med. Fleet,
    86–112; and Coronation review,
    99; and Cunningham, 95–6, 123,
    190–1, 255–6, 258, 285; and
    DFSL, 124–5, 249–51; and
    Darlan, 148–58; death, 5;
    declines peerage, 3, 284; and
    dentist, 84; as Director of Plans,
    50–2, 73, 232; and discusses
    French Fleet, 151–5, 158–62;
    and Dreyer, 250–1; and driving,
    94, 115, 123; and Dunkirk
    evacuation, 149–51; enters Royal
    Navy, 10; and entertainment, in
    Malta, 35, 94–5; and escort
    groups, 187; as Flag Lieutenant,
    15; funeral, 5–6; and Game
    Book, 11, 14; and Geneva
    Conferences, 63–4; Godfrey,
    service with, 50, 58, 96, 107,
    132–4, 159, 167, 230–1, 251–2;
    and *Graf Spee*, 133–4; health,
    112–15, 279–80, 284–5; and
    Horton, 256–7; and hospital,
    3–5, 284; and Intelligence,
    230–3, 235; and intervention in
    operations, 98, 134–5, 235–6;
    and Invergordon, 82–4; and
    Italian fleet, 94, 98–9, 108; and
    Japanese threat, 193–7, 205; and
    Jutland, 31–4; Keyes, serves with,
    15, 35, 39–40, 47–49, 50, 53–9;
    and Keyes as possible First Sea
    Lord, 56–7, 74, 141–7; and
    Keyes as DCO, 141–47, 187–8;
    and League of Nations, 51;
    marriage, 17; and Med. Fleet
    admirals, 96; departs Med. Fleet,
    112; and Med. Fleet staff, 90–1;
    and Mountbatten, 213–15, 224,
    281–2; and Munich mobilization,
    108–9; and Naval air policy, 65;
    as NA1SL, 27–9; and North,

    168–71; and Norway, 136–41;
    not made First Sea Lord,
    109–10; and Nyon patrols, 98,
    111; and Op. CATHERINE,
    131–3; in Operations Division,
    39, 47, 73, 232; and PQ 17,
    240–9; and Phillips, 58–9, 123–4,
    198–203; at Placentia Bay,
    Newfoundland, 183–7; in
    Planning Section, 36–9, 73, 232;
    and Quebec meeting, 1943, 1,
    281–2; and relaxation in wartime,
    123, 280; resigns, 2, 284; and
    Roskill, 102, 136, 139; and Royal
    Air Force, 266–76; Royal
    Humane Society medal, 20; and
    Russian convoys, 237–8; and
    Scapa Flow defences, 26,
    129–31; as Second Sea Lord, 13,
    83–6; Secretary, role of, 59–62;
    serves in *Colossus*, 29–40, 73;
    Grafton, 16; *King Edward VII*, 16;
    Magnificent, 15; *Opossum*, 14;
    Queen, 17; *Repulse*, 47–9; *Royal
    Sovereign*, 12; *St. Vincent*, 21–6;
    Superb, 19–21; and shooting, 55,
    59, 95, 110; and skiing, 65–6;
    and Somerville, 96, 102–3, 160,
    174–5, 226; and Spanish Civil
    War, 97–9; and Stark, 216–18;
    and strategy for 1943, 261,
    278–9; and stroke, 1, 283; and
    Taranto, 175; and temper, loss
    of, 101, 103–3; and threat of
    invasion, 166–8; and Tomkinson,
    3, 84–5; and torpedo course, 16;
    and Tovey, 180, 222, 240; and
    training, 75–7, 92–3, 97; and
    War College, 21, 83; and
    Warspite, 100–4; at Washington
    meeting, 1941, 204–7; at
    Washington meeting, 1943,
    278–9; and weakness in Med.
    Fleet, 111; and working routine,

Mediterranean, 94; and working routine as First Sea Lord, 121–3
Pound, George, 1, 37, 46, 95
Pound, Martin, 37, 46, 95
Power, Admiral, 199
Poynton, Lady, 123, 280

Queen, HMS, battleship, 17
Queen Elizabeth, HMS, battleship, 93–4, 99, 191, 193

Ramilles, HMS, battleship, 173, 176, 180, 193
Ramsay, A., Admiral, 117
Ramsay, B., Admiral, 105–6, 110, 115, 149, 150–1, 208–9, 257, 277
Reith, Lord, 94
Renown, HMS, battlecruiser, 2, 47, 70, 169, 173, 193–5, 236, 283
Repulse, HMS, battlecruiser, 47–9, 70, 78, 96, 178, 191, 193–203, 230
Resolution, HMS, battleship, 156, 193
Revenge, HMS, battleship, 180, 193
Rodney, HMS, battleship, 81, 180–3, 193–5
Roosevelt, President, 2, 164–5, 183–7, 204, 216, 237, 261, 286
Roskill, Stephen, 43, 54, 63, 102, 113–16, 120, 136, 139
Royal Oak, HMS, battleship, 26, 55–6, 129
Royal Sovereign, HMS, battleship, 12–13, 193
Royle, Admiral, 117, 174

St. Nazaire raid, 254
St. Vincent, HMS, battleship, 21, 22, 26
Scapa Flow, 22, 26, 30, 129–31
Scharnhorst, German battlecruiser, 139, 151, 176, 178, 208–10, 249
Schofield, Admiral, 114
Scott, Captain, 90, 104
Shakespeare, Geoffrey, 117

Singapore, 51, 193–203, 208
Singleton, Judge, 267
Slessor, Air Marshal, 4, 269, 273
Somerville, Admiral, 82, 91, 96, 97, 102–3, 110, 111, 115, 129, 131, 150–1, 156, 160–2, 163–4, 168–72, 173–5, 179–82, 188, 198, 203, 226, 250–1, 256, 281
Spanish Civil War, 93, 97–9
Stanhope, Earl, 116, 117
Stanning, Paymaster secretary, 123
Stark, Admiral, US Navy, 5, 6, 186, 197, 205–6, 216–18, 220, 224–5, 229, 249, 265–6, 280
Stresa Agreement, 87
Suffolk, HMS, cruiser, 178–83
Superb, HMS, battleship, 19–21, 58
Surcouf, French submarine, 162
Syfret, Admiral, 58, 226, 253, 286

Talbot, Admiral, 129
Taranto, battle of, 175
Tennant, Admiral, 125, 131, 150, 226
Ten Year Rule, 44
Tiger, HMS, battlecruiser, 78
Tirpitz, German battleship, 178, 193–4, 224, 234–5, 238, 240–9
Tomkinson, Admiral, 3, 47, 52, 59, 68, 78, 80–2, 84–5, 171
Tovey, Admiral, 82, 96, 111, 176, 178–83, 221–2, 234, 236–7, 240–9, 252, 269, 286
Trinidad, HMS, cruiser, 237
Tripoli, 189, 276
Turner, Admiral, US Navy, 186, 216
Tyrwhitt, Admiral, 6

Undaunted, HMS, submarine, 13

Valiant, HMS, battleship, 81, 93, 156, 191, 193
Vian, Admiral, 96, 180–1, 221

319